The Best
AMERICAN
ESSAYS
2004

GUEST EDITORS OF
THE BEST AMERICAN ESSAYS

The Best AMERICAN ESSAYS® 2004

Edited and with an Introduction
by LOUIS MENAND

Robert Atwan, Series Editor

HOUGHTON MIFFLIN COMPANY
BOSTON • NEW YORK 2004

ISSN 0888-3742
ISBN 0-618-35706-8
ISBN 0-618-35709-2 (pbk.)

Printed in the United States of America

VB 10 9 8 7 6 5 4 3 2

Contents

Foreword

AS THE NEW CENTURY anxiously arrived, I made a resolution to form an amiable discussion group that each year would read a few essay collections and nonfiction books published exactly one hundred years before. My group still consists of one person, myself, but I recommend the practice — each reading is like celebrating an anniversary. Last year I renewed acquaintance with three classics: W.E.B. Du Bois's *The Souls of Black Folk,* Jack London's *The People of the Abyss,* and Helen Keller's *The Story of My Life.* This year one of my favorites is *Compromises* by Agnes Repplier. I happen to own a hardcover copy of this volume of essays, published by Houghton Mifflin in 1904. Its advertised gilt top is still shiny and inviting, but until this year I had never poked around inside to sample the contents. The book originally cost $1.10, and I doubt I paid much more at the used-book store where I unearthed it.

A century has done little damage to this tight little book. Although its green cloth cover has faded to a shade as yet unnamed by Benjamin Moore, *Compromises* remains in remarkably healthy condition, a pleasure to handle and peruse: crisp thick paper, wide margins, a friendly and open typeface. You can cover all the print on the page with a standard three-by-five index card. As a deliberately slow reader, someone who silently voices a good sentence over several times just to admire its architecture and rhythm, I've grown fond of small, open pages that permit me the illusion of reading more rapidly than I actually do. My halting pace remains the same; the illusion of course comes from the action of turning pages more frequently, a satisfyingly tangible measure of progress we miss on a computer screen.

The book has survived splendidly. But can the same be said of its contents? Unlike those above-mentioned classics that deal head-on with race, poverty, and disability — all issues we confront today — *Compromises* instead is the sort of book that initially strikes one as having vanished from literary fashion. Du Bois, London, or Keller invites us to step into our collective future; Agnes Repplier's essays escort us backward into the past, usually to what she termed the "happy half-century" from 1775 to 1825. The style of essay she loved, the "light essay," was even then, at the turn of the twentieth century, rumored to have gone out of favor. In fact, when her first essays began appearing regularly in the 1880s, some critics attacked their antiquated style and dismissed them as a dead end. Yes, she admitted, she wrote about "the insignificant aspects of life," and it's true that she leaned closer to the manner of Jane Austen (whose books she appeared to know by heart) than to the growing realism of her time.

Agnes Repplier was once quite famous. A friend of many celebrated authors and public figures, she was — as was still possible in her time — renowned as an essayist and for nothing else. A self-educated, lifelong Philadelphian, she presided over the American essay for many decades. She lived a long, productive, and single life (*Compromises* contains her spirited defense of "The Spinster"), publishing numerous collections of essays, most of which first appeared in the *Atlantic Monthly,* a handful of biographies, a memoir, and several nonfiction studies. Born a few years before the Civil War, in 1857 (that's her date; I've seen others), she died in 1950, but by then fame had given way to obscurity. The early rumors she fought so hard to dispel about the death of the essay had been much exaggerated, but they nevertheless came true.

A devout Roman Catholic who had sporadically attended convent schools, she was by training and disposition conservative. But like many highly intelligent people of her era, her values and opinions were nuanced, refreshingly unpredictable, and not easily extrapolated from an allegiance to a political party. One would suppose, for instance, that given her polite literary manner, with its emphasis on cultivated judgment, she would prefer the poetry of James Russell Lowell to Walt Whitman, both of whom she knew personally. But here's the amusing way she recalled her meeting with Lowell, at the time one of Boston's leading literary figures and an arbiter of national taste. It is 1887 and she is thirty years old:

> His interest in me centered solely in the fact that I was a townswoman, or as good as a townswoman, of Walt Whitman, and fairly well acquainted with that unclassified genius. "Why," he asked, "do you Philadelphians call him the Good Gray Poet?"
>
> I explained that the name had been given to him by a fiery New York journalist, and that he, Mr. Whitman, liked it. He called himself the Good Gray Poet whenever he had the opportunity.
>
> "I dare say," grumbled Mr. Lowell. "But nobody calls me the Good Gray Poet, though I am as gray as Whitman, and quite as good — perhaps a trifle better."
>
> He paused, and for an instant I was on the point of saying, "Then there is only the poet to consider," but I forbore.

That little exchange — with its cutting irony and polite forbearance — goes to the heart of Repplier's writing style. She learned her Jane Austen well, and not in graduate seminars. It was life to her, not study. Beneath the decorous veneer of her essays, she hits hard and is invariably on target. By a "light essay" she hardly meant humorous, trivial, or slight. On the contrary, the essays are deeply rooted in research and reading, polished to her idea of perfection, literary without sounding academic, familiar without being confessional, discriminating without seeming dogmatic, civilized without sacrificing their edge. Early in her career, she eschewed opinions and issues, finding them destructive of companionable conversation. We get a sense of this from the Victorian-steeped titles of her first few collections: *Essays in Miniature, Essays in Idleness, In the Dozy Hours.* But as the First World War (she supported our entry) shed its darkness over Europe and the United States, she began to engage broader public issues, though not always in the spirit of the time. Later titles indicate her shift in attitude: *Counter-Currents, Points of Friction, Under Dispute, Times and Tendencies.*

Repplier's essays turn out to be not as obsolete as her critics — both early and late — judged them to be. She does connect with the contemporary essay, though not necessarily in tone or idiom. Many of her recurring subjects are still vital today and our essayists still confront them. A hundred years ago she addressed the differences between male and female novelists, and how they compete with each other; she wrote about the prevalent assumption that for women "there *are* no interests outside of marriage; no emotions, ambitions, nor obligations unconnected with the rearing of children"; she looked at American tourists crowding Europe: "noisy, self-assertive, and contemptuous"; she wondered to what extent it is permissible to "share our troubles" with others; she dissected conversational habits and was critical of specialists who can't speak without lecturing, or worse, storytellers who "usurp" the dinner table with their "potted" personal anecdotes, or perhaps worst of all, those who appear to be socially oblivious of the "unconvincing nature of argument." She enjoyed nothing more than unpedantic but thought-provoking discussion on any earthly topic — or beyond. I'm confident that she would have enjoyed this year's wide-ranging conversations. And cheerfully joined the discussion.

The Best American Essays features a selection of the year's outstanding essays, essays of literary achievement that show an awareness of craft and forcefulness of thought. Hundreds of essays are gathered annually from a wide variety of national and regional publications. These essays are then screened, and approximately one hundred are turned over to a distinguished guest editor, who may add a few personal discoveries and who makes the final selections. The list of notable essays appearing in the back of the book is drawn from a final comprehensive list that includes not only all of the essays submitted to the guest editor but also many that were not submitted.

To qualify for the volume, the essay must be a work of respectable literary quality, intended as a fully developed, independent essay on a subject of general interest (not specialized scholarship), originally written in English (or translated by the author) for publication in an American periodical during the calendar year. Today's essay is a highly flexible form, however, so these criteria are not carved in stone. As this year's volume demonstrates, contributors can also be long deceased. What matters is that their essays had never been previously published (James Agee and Tennessee Williams wrote the essays collected here in the early 1940s, but neither essay appeared in print until 2003).

Magazine editors who want to be sure their contributors will be considered each year should submit issues or subscriptions to: Robert Atwan, Series Editor, The Best American Essays, P.O. Box 220, Readville, MA 02137. Writers, editors, and readers can also contact me by writing to: Robert Atwan, Director, The Blue Hills Writing Institute, Curry College, 1071 Blue Hill Avenue, Milton, MA 02186-2395. You can also visit www.curry.edu and look for the writing institute under "Continuing Education." If you use the Curry College address, please be sure to put "Attention: Best American Essays" on the envelope. Writers and editors are welcome to submit published essays from any American periodical for consideration; unpublished work does not qualify for the series and cannot be reviewed or evaluated. Note that all submissions must be taken directly from the publication and not be in manuscript or printout format.

I'd like to dedicate this year's volume — the nineteenth in the series — to one of the contributors, Leonard Michaels ("My Yiddish"), a marvelous writer and gifted teacher, who died in May 2003. Although well known for his fiction, he also wrote and published numerous essays, two of which (also from *Threepenny Review*) had appeared in previous editions of *The Best American Essays:* "I'm Having Trouble with My Relationship," selected by Justin Kaplan for 1990, and "The Zipper," selected by Susan Sontag for 1992. I extend thanks to the Houghton Mifflin staff, especially Deanne Urmy, Melissa Grella, and Larry Cooper, for their always generous assistance. It was a pleasure this year to work with one of our most distinguished literary and cultural critics, Louis Menand. This year's wide-ranging collection vividly reflects his affection for the essay form and his appreciation of its dazzling variety.

R.A.

Introduction: Voices

YOU CANNOT TASTE a work of prose. It has no color and it makes no sound. Its shape is without significance. When people talk about writing, though, they often use adjectives borrowed from activities whose products make a more direct appeal to the senses — painting, sculpture, music, cuisine. People say, "The writing is colorful," or "pungent," or "shapeless," or "lyrical," and no one asks them where, exactly, they perceive those qualities. Discussions of "tone" and "texture" are carried on in the complete ontological absence of such things. (You could say that so are discussions of "meaning," but that's another philosophical problem.) Writing is a verbal artifact that, as it is being decoded, stimulates sensations that are unique to writing but that, for some reason, often have to be described in terms of nonverbal experiences.

One of the most mysterious of writing's immaterial properties is what people call its "voice." Editors sometimes refer to it, in a phrase that underscores the paradox at the heart of the idea, as the "voice on the page." Many editors think that a voice is what makes great writing great. Most writers do, too. Prose can show many virtues, including originality, without having a voice. It may be packed solid with intellectual nutrients; upon its import, much may seem to depend. It may avoid cliché, radiate conviction, be grammatically so clean that your grandmother could eat off it. But none of this has anything to do with this elusive entity, a "voice." There are probably all kinds of literary sins that prevent a piece of writing from having a voice, but there seems to be no guaranteed technique for creating one.

"Voice" is sometimes associated with "style," but they are not always the same. Writing can be stylish and still be voiceless, and this is as true of the plain, "just the facts" style as it is of the style of high figuration. Ingenuity, wit, sarcasm, euphony, frequent outbreaks of the first-person singular — any of these can enliven prose without giving it a voice. Of all the intangibles of good writing, voice is probably the most transcendental. You can set the stage as elaborately as you like, but either the phantom appears or it doesn't.

When it does make an appearance, the subject matter is often irrelevant. "I do not care for movies very much and I rarely see them," W. H. Auden wrote to the editors of *The Nation* in 1944; "further, I am suspicious of criticism as the literary genre which, more than any other, recruits epigones, pedants without insight, intellectuals without love. I am all the more surprised, therefore, to find myself not only reading Mr. Agee before I read anyone else in *The Nation* but also consciously looking forward all week to reading him again." A lot of the movies James Agee reviewed between 1942 and 1948, when he was *The Nation*'s film critic, were negligible then and are forgotten now. Auden was not merely being a curmudgeon. But you can still read those columns with pleasure. They continue to pass the ultimate test of good writing: it is more painful to stop reading them than it is to keep going. When you get to the end of Agee's sentences, you wish, like Auden, that there were more sentences.

Writing that has a voice is writing that has something like a personality. But whose personality is it? As with most things in art, there is no straight road from the product back to the person who made it. There are writers read and loved for their humor who are not especially funny people, and writers read and loved for their eloquence who, in conversation, swallow their words or can't seem to finish a sentence. Wisdom on the page correlates with wisdom in the writer about as frequently as a high batting average correlates with a high IQ: they just seem to have very little to do with one another. Charming people can produce prose of sneering sententiousness, and cranky neurotics can, to their readers, seem to be inexhaustibly delightful. Personal drabness, through some obscure neural kink, can deliver verbal blooms. Readers who meet writers whose voice they have fallen in love with usually need to make a small adjustment in order to hang on to their infatuation.

Some confusion about what it means for writing to have a voice arises from the metaphor itself. Many readers, and many writers, for that matter, think that effectiveness in writing has something to do with how close it is to speech. Writers often claim that they never write something that they would not say. It is hard to know how this could be literally true. Speech is somatic, a bodily function, and it is accompanied by physical inflections (tone of voice, winks, smiles, raised eyebrows, hand gestures) that are not reproducible in writing. Spoken language is repetitive, fragmentary, contradictory, ambiguous, loaded down with space holders (*like, um, you know what I'm saying*) — pretty much all the things writing teachers tell students not to do. But speakers are generally understood right away. You don't have to hear a sentence three times before you get it. On the other hand, you often have to read a sentence three times, occasionally even a well-written one. As a medium, writing is a million times weaker than speech. It's a hieroglyph competing with a symphony.

The other reason that speech is a bad metaphor for writing is that writing, for 99 percent of people who do it, is the opposite of spontaneous. Some writers write many drafts of a piece, and some write one draft, at the pace of a snail. But chattiness, slanginess, in-your-face-ness, and any other feature of writing that is conventionally characterized as "like speech" are all usually the results of intense experimentation, revision, calibrating, walks around the block, unnecessary phone calls, and recalibrating. Writers are people in whom *l'esprit de l'escalier* is a recurrent experience: they are always thinking of the perfect riposte when the moment for saying it has already passed. So they wait a few years and put it in print. Writers are not mere copyists of language; they are polishers, embellishers, perfecters. They are people who spend hours getting the timing exactly right — so that it sounds absolutely unrehearsed.

There's a wonderful story about the gap between speech and writing. It features the British critic Desmond McCarthy. McCarthy was a member of the Bloomsbury group, and, apparently, a legendary talker. His friends thought that his writing, which he produced reluctantly, gave a poor idea of his conversational gifts. So they hired a stenographer and invited McCarthy over. They hid the stenographer outside the door and had McCarthy hold forth. McCarthy obliged his friends by discoursing brilliantly for an hour or so, and then left. The friends waited impatiently for the transcription of his conversation to arrive. It did. They read it. The writing was completely banal.

Still, the claim that the written "voice" is an artificial construction of language, deliberate and self-conscious or impersonal and accidental but never spontaneous and natural, is not a claim most writers could accept. Writing is personal; it *feels* personal. The unfunny person who is a humorous writer does not think, of her work, "That's not me." Critics speak of a literary persona, which is a device for compelling a divorce between the author and the text. But no one, or almost no one, writes "as a persona." People write as people, and if there were nothing personal about the outcome, few would bother with it. Composition is a labor-intensive business. And what makes it especially so is that the rate of production is beyond the writer's control. The words don't just appear on a conveyor belt, and you package them up. You have to wait, and what you are waiting for is something inside you to come up with the words. That something, for writers, is the voice.

The real basis for the metaphor of voice in writing is not speaking. It is singing. You cannot know a singer from her speech, and although "natural phrasing" and "from the heart" are prized attributes of song, actually singing that way requires rehearsal, preparation, and getting in touch with whatever it is inside singers that, by a neural kink or the grace of God, enables them to turn themselves into vessels of musical sound. Right before he walked onstage at the opera house, Luciano Pavarotti is reported to have taken a big bite of an apple. That's how he helped his voice to sound fresh, spontaneous, and natural.

What writers hear, when they are trying to write, is something more like singing than like speaking. Inside your head, you're yakking away to yourself all the time. Getting *that* down on paper is a depressing, Desmond McCarthy–like experience. What you are trying to do when you write is to transpose the yakking into verbal music; and the voice inside, when you find it, which can take hours or days or weeks, is not your speaking voice. It is your singing voice — except that it comes out as writing. Writers labor under two anxieties. The first is that the voice that they found a hundred times in the past has gone forever, that they will never listen to it again. The other is that, having finally found it this time, they will lose it again before the piece is finished. Then, they know that, having sung its song, it will disappear again. This is the voice people are surprised not to encounter when they "meet the writer." The writer is not so surprised. One day, he or she will be back in front of the paper or the keyboard and have to find the voice all over again. Some writers, when they begin a new piece, spend hours frantically rereading their old stuff, trying to remember how they did it. Rereading rarely works, because nothing works reliably. Sooner or later, normally later than everyone involved would like, the voice shows up, takes a bite out of the apple, and walks onstage.

Most of the essays in this volume were picked by ear. I was searching for voices. Some are cool and some are anti-cool. I like both. There are many subjects here — for the subject, to a point, doesn't matter. Still, as a reader, my favorite kind of essay is the one that makes a lost time present — the essay that tells me how it was in New York City in the 1970s, or on a Manhattan bus in the 1940s, or at a midwestern high school, or during a summer on Cape Cod. Selfishly — and why shouldn't an editor be selfish? — I like to read stories about my own times. I never get tired of it. I feel as though I could do it forever, and I probably will.

Writing is a window. It opens onto vanished feelings and vanished worlds. Often it is the only window there is, the only access we will ever have to those things. It is more than a mere record, like a photograph, because it is also a sensibility, a point of view, a voice. It is the place where, fifty or a hundred years from now, people will go to see — or to hear — what it was like to be alive when we were alive. We were alive in 2003, and these pieces are part of what remains.

Louis Menand

The Best
AMERICAN
ESSAYS
2004

JAMES AGEE

America, Look at Your Shame!

FROM OXFORD AMERICAN

Editor's Note: "America, Look at Your Shame!" was written shortly after the Detroit race riots in June 1943. The essay was recently discovered among Agee's poetry manuscripts. As Michael A. Lofaro and Hugh Davis note in their introduction to the essay in the *Oxford American,* "The riot received front-page coverage in *PM,* a progressive, photo-oriented New York newspaper, and it was one of these *PM* photographs that prompted James Agee (1909–1955) to meditate, in this previously unpublished manuscript, on one of his own experiences with racism." (R.A.)

I KEEP REMEMBERING those photographs of the Detroit race riots which appeared in *PM.* Pages of them, and that typically *PM* headline, all over their front page.

AMERICA,
LOOK AT
YOUR
SHAME!

That disgusted me, as their headlines so often do, but as I looked at the photographs I got a good deal of respect for the paper in spite of everything. Then I realized that with a few exceptions *PM* had cornered the photographs. They were unavailable to any other paper. That was as perfect and typical a low as I had ever seen them touch. I wanted to write them. Or to do them as much damage as I possibly could. The liberals and the left. They had never shown themselves up better.

Look at your shame, indeed.

There was one in particular, that I couldn't get out of my head;

one of the less violent of them. It was the one which particularly showed that there were white people who were not only horrified by the riots but brave enough to do all they could for the Negroes. It showed two young men. They were holding up a terribly bleeding Negro man between them, and they looked at the camera as if they were at bay before a crowd of rioters, as perhaps they were not. The mixture of emotions on their faces was almost unbearable to keep looking at: almost a nausea of sympathy for the hurt man and for the whole situation; a kind of terror which all naturally unviolent people must feel in the middle of violence; absolute self-forgetfulness; a terrific, accidental look of bearing testimony — a sort of gruesome, over-realistic caricature; which was rather, really, the source of those attendant saints or angels who communicate with the world outside the picture in great paintings of crucifixions and exalted agonies.

The thing that made it so particularly powerful to me was that both these young men, one of them especially, so far as you could judge by study, were of a sort which is often somewhat sneered at, by most bad people and by many pretty good ones: rather humbly "artistic," four-effish people, of whom you might think that any emotion they felt would be tainted, at least, with fancy sentimentality.

It made me ashamed of every such reflex of easy classification and dismissal as I have ever felt — the more ashamed, because I had to wonder whether, in such a situation, I would have been capable of that self-forgetfulness and courage. It made me half-ashamed to keep looking at them, for that matter, as I had been doing again on that afternoon I am especially thinking of now. I care a great deal for such photographs; they do more, in certain ways, than any other art can. But there is also, in proportion to its best use, something criminal and indecent about the camera; and there is a great load of guilt on the eye that eats what it has predigested.

On this particular afternoon, which was the Sunday after the riots, I was up on East 92nd Street seeing a friend of mine, a photographer, and we spent quite a bit of the afternoon looking through things he had clipped and a few I had brought along. I had not seen my friend at leisure for a long time and we had a particularly good afternoon of it, in which the photograph I am speaking of turned up powerfully but casually, and moved off to become a sort of tinge in the back of the mind. By the end of the afternoon I had the unusual, gay sort of good opinion of myself, my friend, photography and what my senses could enjoy, which you are liable to get out of whiskey and easy pleasure if work causes the latter to turn up seldom enough. By the time I left to go downtown for supper, I was at the high point just short of where intoxication begins to droop into clumsiness or melancholy; and the minute I was outdoors the streets, in the very beautiful late of afternoon weather, improved, that if it can be improved, with the feeling of being alone for a little while, and with the sharp, tender enjoyment of a city I am ordinarily tired in.

At 91st Street, on York Avenue, I got on an 86th Street crosstown bus and sat far forward on the right. It started nearly empty, and filled up rather quickly; I did not much notice when, or with whom, because I was looking out a great deal through the front and side windows, especially as soon as the bus swung west onto 86th Street and the street and the bus were filled with the low, bright sunlight. It was a light so gay, generous and beautiful, it was almost as if it tasted of champagne and smelled of strawberries, hay and fresh butter. What it smelled of more, of course, was carbon monoxide, which can also be a festal sort of smell, when everything is right, and was now; and the edges of the hundreds of doors and windows, along the street, were cut in a blue-gold, clean compound of sunlight, monoxide and stone. I watched all the people, puddling and straggling along the walks, and as usual, wondered which were the Hitchcock agents and which were the harmless, and what might be going on in each mind as they thought, if they did, of what was happening to Hitler and his idea and his people, over where it was dark now, and they were counting their losses in the East, and giving out modified reports in the middle, and staggering under the bombers from the west. In an easy insensitive way, I began to be very sorry for all those people caught in the hopeless middle; even for Hitler and his damned idea, so monstrous except that they already seemed so hopeless.

Around me, I realized the bus was thicker and thicker with people, some standing, some packed on the seats, all swaying, pleasant and patient-seeming in the green and gold light which filled the bus. Across the aisle were some sailors, sitting, their faces very young and very red, in their very white uniforms. Halfway back in the bus were some young soldiers; the same quality of variegated physical perfection and of almost indecent cleanness, which so few civilians ever seem to have — like so many priests, or Sunday babies, or little girls in bride-of-heaven regalia, but even more likable; dumb, very likely, cruel, very possibly, developed and perfected for something I feel no trust in; yet about the best thing that ever turns up in human life. I liked them a great deal, and all my doubts of it cleared; I might not be perfectly sure what I wanted, but I was no longer personally sorry that within a week I was coming up for induction; I was almost glad; and if I were taken, many things could be worse. One of them, very possibly, would be to come out the other end of the war, still a virginal civilian.

I liked them still better as I watched them and began to hear them. I specially noticed one quite strong young sailor, just across from me; a big boy, bigger than I am, a little; and because his eyes and his face had a good deal in them which as a child I used to fear, and have always been shy of, I now liked him particularly well. It was the sort of face which only turns up, so far as I know, in the South — heavy jaw, a slightly thin yet ornate mouth, powerful nose, blue-white, reckless, brutal eyes. I knew the voice just as well, and the special, rather crazy kind of bravery; they made me feel at once as isolated and as matchlessly at home as if I were back in the South again. Nearly all these boys, it turned out, were Southerners, the soldiers as well as the sailors, and the loud large sailor and the loudest and littlest of the soldiers were just finding this out about each other. One was from Atlanta; the other knew Atlanta very well. They began testing each other out on street names and bars, then on people, which did not go quite so well, and now and then the others chimed in with a wisecrack or an exclamation more simpleminded. They were happy as hell to run into each other like this — not even Viennese refugees can lay it on so thick, and enjoy it so much, as Southerners when they meet by surprise in an alien atmosphere. They were drunk, about as drunk as I was, and that helped; but they would have leaned on their dialects like trimming ship in a yacht-race, even if they were sober. It is a very special speech, as unattractive to most Northerners as it is dear to natives, and I will not try to reproduce it here, beyond suggesting that its special broadenings, lifts, twangs and elisions, even if you didn't know the idiom by heart, which I do, were as charming and miraculous as if, in the same New York bus, a couple of Parsees had saluted each other according to their own language and ritual.

A part of it, of course, was that they were basically insecure; it was insecurity and the Southerner's incomparable, almost pathic pride, as well as love of country and loneliness, and the aching contempt for the North, which made them so spectacular, made so many Northerners on the bus look warm, cold or uneasy accordingly, and made the young sailors and soldiers begin to vocalize about the niggers on the bus and the God damned niggers in this f — ing town and the f — ing niggers all over the whole God damned f — in' Nawth. The word cut across my solar plexus like a cold knife, and the whole bus, except for those two voices and the comments of their friends, was suddenly almost exploded by an immensely thick quietness. I glanced very quickly back; one of the soldiers met my eyes with eyes like hot iron, and two seats behind him sat a Negro (it is a word I dislike, but most of the others are still worse); sat a colored man of perhaps fifty, in nickel-rimmed glasses, a carefully starched white shirt, and a serge suit, managing so to use his eyes that you could see only the nickel rims and the lenses.

The flailing voices went on and on, more and more fanciful, naked and cruel, and though I was listening with great care for every word, and heard every word, I was also so occupied that I heard very little, and remember almost nothing, now. It was all the old, ugly routines; what we wouldn't do to Boy son of a bitchin nigguh that tuck a seat by a white woman if we was in Atlanta; dey would; get a Nawthun nigguh down deah, you'd see what dey'd do; yaanh, reckin *dey'd* see thang a tyew. Three any ovem tried it, black rapin bastuhds; but there was very little of this I heard, because I was too sick to hear much, and too busy. I was trying to think what to do and what to say. I had, repeatedly, a very clear image of the moment I would get up, draw a standee aside, and hit the big young sailor who was, after all, very little bigger than me, as hard as I could on his bright, shaven jaw. I also had, repeatedly, the exact image of what would happen then. Singlehanded, that boy could tear me to pieces; what the crowd of them could do was a little beyond my imagination. I had the image of looking him in the eye; various ways, in fact, of looking him in the eye. One was the cold, controlled rage which is occasionally used to pick a fight and which my kind more occasionally uses to bring a sexual quarrel or an intellectual argument as near to nature as we are likely to go. One was the more-in-sorrow-than-in-anger look which is liable to compound some genuineness of feeling with plagiarisms from photographs of Lincoln and paintings of Veronica's veil; it is occasionally used, and effective, when somebody else's neurosis goes wild, but unless you are too good a human being to know you are using it, there is no uglier or more abject device of blackmail. One, worst of them all, was the blank eye which commits itself to nothing. But none of these, it was easy to see, were of any use unless I was ready to back them up physically, and I could hear, just as clearly as I could visualize, the phonograph-records of talk they would bring on; nigger-lover is the favorite word. I was also trying to think what to say; for I know from the past — and might have known by some of the Detroit photographs if I had thought of them just then — that their kind of talk and even action is sometimes completely quieted by the right kind of talking, and better quieted then into sullenness; quieted into deep abashment. I have a friend, a small and elderly man, who would have brought that effect almost instantly. But his size and his age would have been a part of it; still more, his perfect self-forgetfulness, his unquestioning intrepidity. I was neither small nor elderly, nor self-forgetful, nor intrepid, nor singlehearted in any one of my perceptions or emotions; I was simply fumbling at words and knowledges: Look here. What are you fighting this war about. I know how you feel, I know you're from the South, I'm from the South myself, I know (I may be, but the way I say it makes it a lie). Things are different there, and all this you see here goes against every way you believe is right. But you've got to get used to it. You've got to know it. This is one of the main things this war is about (is it? is it?). If it isn't about this we might as well not be fighting it at all (we might as well not, indeed). You'll ask me where I've got any right to tell you what you're fighting for. I'm not even in uniform. I'm not I know but I'll be in one soon — next week (will I? do I want to be?). But that's not the point anyhow (this is falling apart). Anyone on this bus has got a right to know the point and to tell it to you, white or black (I sound like a Tennessee senator; race, creed and *co*luh), we've got to make this a

free country where every human being can be well with every
other human being, regardless of race, creed or color, we've got to
make it a world like that. I don't believe you mean the harm you
say, honestly, but you've got to realize it, you might as well be fighting for Hitler as to fight for this country feeling the way you do.

It was all so much cotton-batting on my tongue. I couldn't
gather a phrase of it together and make it mean anything, even to
myself. Talking to them, talking for the corroboration of most of
the bus, unable to talk in my own language because my own language would mean nothing even if I could use it with enough belief to make it mean something to me. All the hopeless, bland, ad-
vertising-copy claims of the Four Freedoms was running in my
head; all the undersupplying of the Chinese; all the talk of the
"magnificent courage" of the Red Army, and all the Rice Krispies
which took the place of a second front; all the Bryn Mawr girls,
planning to police post-war Europe; all the *PM* articles and the
Wallace speeches and the slogans; I cannot know to this day with
how much justice they undermined me, and with how much cow-
ardice. I only know I could not believe a word I said; and had images of saying it and having the hell beaten out of me, and other
images of saying it with effect; and other images of a fight which
could be stopped by cops who are as much a phobia to me as rats;
and others of modest and of carefully worded and of modestly rhe-
torical statements by myself, repeated in the press; a small yet not
wholly undistinguished instant in the history of the world's long
Fight for Freedom; that hit me with self-disgust like a blow in the
belly; and I noticed that the big sailor was now standing, and an elderly Negro woman had his seat.

Whether he had stood rather than sit beside her, or out of an instant genuine courtesy, quickly repented, or out of mock courtesy,
I could not tell from anything he was saying; and this still further
perplexed me. If his motives were the first or the third, then it was
more than even I could bear, not to fight him; if he had felt one
moment of reflex courtesy, I felt friendliness towards him in spite
of all he was now saying. I listened hard, to learn, and could not
make out. One reason I could not make out was that I was also listening to the woman. She was talking very little, and crying a little,
and telling him, and the whole bus, that he ought to be ashamed,
talking that way. People never done him no harm. Ain't your skin

that make the difference, it's how you feel inside. Ought to be
ashamed. Just might bout's well be Hitluh, as a white man from
the South. Wearing a sailor's uniform. Fighting for your country.
Ought to be ashamed.

There was an immense relaxation in the quiet through the
whole bus; but not in me. I caught the eye, at that moment, of a
man about my age, in one of the longways seats across the aisle. He
was dressed in a brown, Sunday-looking suit. He may have been a
Jew, and more certainly would have described himself, without self-
consciousness or satire, as "an intellectual." We looked at each
other and a queer, sick smile took one corner of his face, and I felt
in my own cheeks that tickling, uncontrollable, nauseating smile
which is so liable to seize my face when I tell one close friend disastrous news of another.

I remembered the photograph in *PM,* and looked sternly at the
floor, with my cheek twitching.

That evening I told of the whole thing, as honestly as I could, to
several people who were down for drinks. They were quite shocked
by it, and seemed also rather favorably stirred by my honesty. That
embarrassed me a good deal, but not as painfully as I wish it might
have, and I found their agreement that they would have done the
same almost as revolting as my own performance in the doing of it,
and in the telling.

So now I am telling it to you.

KATHRYN CHETKOVICH

Envy

FROM GRANTA

THIS IS A STORY about two writers. A story, in other words, of
envy. I met the man at an artists' colony, and I liked him from the
first story I heard him tell, which was about how he'd once been
jilted by a blind date, after which he went right out and bought
himself some new clothes. He was working on his third book when
I met him, but he had no particular interest in talking shop. He
read the paper and watched sports on television. He was handsome in a shy, arrogant way, dressed safely but deliberately in his
white shirts and black jeans.

He was, I soon learned, struggling.

There may be women out there who do not love this beyond all
else in a man, but I'm not one of them.

He played pool after dinner in the barnlike common room of the
colony, and I would watch him through the window of the phone
booth door as I made my nightly call to my parents across the
country in California. My father, who was eighty-one and not in
good health, had recently fallen. He had damaged his back and
shoulder, but he was reluctant to go to the doctor, and my mother
was becoming frantic with worry and exhaustion. The anticipation
of those ten-minute phone calls — during which I did nothing but
listen, and even that not very well — dominated my days.

The booth itself was tiny, barely big enough for its folding chair,
shelf, and pay phone. The air felt pre-breathed and thick with the
molecules of other people's long-distance calls, of their quarrels
and appeasements. A small, squat window was positioned at eye

level if you were sitting down, and through it, while my parents'
distress poured into my ear, I could see a slice of the man, a helping from his waist to the middle of his thighs, as he played pool. I
watched him set his legs, wiggling them into place. As my mother
spoke in the tense, coded voice that signaled that my father was in
the room with her, I focused on the cue sliding forward and back
across his body like a bow. As long as I kept my eye trained on that
cue, I told myself, I would not get sucked through the tiny holes of
the receiver.

One afternoon, on the threshold of the building in which we
both had bedrooms, I ran into the man and, partly in a bid to keep
him talking, told him about my parents and my uncertainty about
what I should be doing to help them. His own father had died after
a long illness, he told me, so he had some idea what I was going
through.

Just then a staff member came by and complimented him on
one of his novels, neither of which I'd heard of — a fact that
helped to equalize the discrepancy between his two published
books and my none.

We both watched her walk away again, awkwardness rushing in
to fill the space she left behind. He looked back at me. "You have
to do your work," he said. "That's your first responsibility."

He meant, of course, my writing, and he spoke with a confidence I had never managed to feel about those hours of day-
dreaming at my desk, stringing together decorative little sentences
to describe small, made-up events. Work to me always meant a
job you were paid to do, necessary labor that someone else depended on.

He may have been struggling, but he knew what his work was.
That was the first thing I envied about him.

When my father, after at last agreeing to see the doctor, was immediately scheduled for major surgery, I made arrangements to fly
back to California. I left my computer and most of my belongings
behind to ensure my return to the colony, and I bought a copy of
the man's second novel to take with me. Over the next week I read
it in various locations — on the plane, in the hospital cafeteria, at
my parents' breakfast table. This life of waiting for what was going
to happen in my father's life now seemed like the only real one to

me, and the book like a token I had managed to smuggle out of a dream.

There were moments, reading, where the recognition was so strong, and the life on the page so vivid, I could feel my pulse speed up.

This book is good, I thought with joy — the way you can when it's the work of someone you don't really know and expect you never will. Because it's the very fact of not knowing the writer that gives you that proprietary thrill, that frees up the book to belong to you.

But I did know him, at least a little, so I also felt, intermittently, the stabs of dread familiar to all writers — that here were sentences, paragraphs, whole pages I not only admired but wished I had written.

And I suppose pride was also in the mix, because this man whose perception I envied had possibly liked me. I saw myself reflected, if in an incomplete and distorted way, in that possibility, the way you can see the ghost of yourself in a store window through which you can also see a real woman examining a shoe.

So from the start he was both man and writer, real and something more than real, to me. I had liked him as soon as I met him— a current rippled across my skin when he walked into a room — but something stronger kicked in once I met him on the page, naked and decked out in phrases I would never have thought of.

My father, having undergone a second, unanticipated operation, was still in the hospital when I returned to the colony. I spent four of the five-plus in-flight hours of the trip certain that the plane was going to crash, a conviction that every casual observation — the ominous silence from the cockpit, the flight attendants' huddled conversations in the galley — seemed only to confirm. Maybe this was just residual anxiety from having been on high alert for the previous few days, or maybe I was not at all sure at that point where I truly belonged and had simply found a colorful way to express that dilemma.

To fend off the guilty suspicion that I was abandoning my father, I reminded myself that I was returning to work, a choice that he, in all his years at the office, had taught me the value of making. But the moment I walked into the colony's dining room that night and my glance snagged on the man, his white shirt and Oscar Wilde hair, I knew it wasn't just my work I'd returned for.

I was falling for another writer, and I recognized my descent by its peculiar calling card: the fear of what I wanted. In my remaining week at the colony, confident that nothing would actually "happen" between us there, I engineered as many coincidental meetings with him as I could. Because we lived on opposite sides of the country and would probably never see each other again, I felt crestfallen, and safe.

My father remained in the hospital, not so much recovering as trading one complication for another, for the next two months. Once I got back home, I visited him every day and never got over the feeling, as I searched for a parking space and walked to the entrance and made my way down the wide squeaky hallway to his open door, that I was pulling myself along like a reluctant dog who might one day slip my collar and make a break for the car. I was afraid of finding some new test under way in my father's room or some new piece of equipment — evidence of more bad news. When a doctor would come in armed with nothing more ominous than a clipboard, I was afraid of that, too — afraid that my father would not be able to come up with the answers to basic questions like what hospital he was in or who the president was. Even though I routinely have trouble remembering what day of the week it is and can almost never name the date, it terrified me to see my father muddled by this kind of mild confusion. His had always been a sharp and certain mind, an accountant's mind; "sometimes wrong but never in doubt" was one of his favorite sayings.

One day as my brother and I were leaving my father's hospital room, I broke into tears — sudden, gulping sobs that overtook me and made it hard to breathe.

My brother put his arm around me and asked me what I was afraid of. Dad was not about to die, he assured me.

"I'm not afraid he's going to die," I found myself saying. "I'm afraid he's going to live."

I was afraid that my father was going to get what we all wanted: better enough to go home. And that once there, he was going to take the rest of us down with him, starting with my mother.

During that time, the fact that my husband and I had recently separated and I had neither a family of my own nor a full-time job behind which to hide left me exposed to my parents' needs, which were sizable. I tried to regard the time I was spending with one or the other of them as a job I would later be glad to have done, but this gladness was often undermined by my resentments and foul moods, by my running tally of the sacrifices I was making and the uncomfortable fact — hard to admit, even to myself — that I wasn't getting any writing done.

Then one day in my mailbox there was a letter from the man at the colony.

Of course I wrote him back right away, laboring for hours to strike an appropriately offhand tone. I drove my letter to the post office for faster pickup, and began waiting impatiently for a response. Before long we were corresponding, with a double-edged satisfaction that seemed destined to mark everything that happened between us. It was a simple thrill to see an envelope addressed in his hand in my mailbox — and then I would open the letter and begin answering it in my head, and the thrill would get complicated.

In the letters I wrote him, I was compelled to see my life as it must have looked from the outside: a lot of driving and errand-running, a lot of empty, necessary hours at the hospital. Meanwhile, his letters, chronicling his successes and failures at his desk, where he was at work on a novel about family troubles, reminded me of the writer's life I myself was failing to live.

I knew, from his descriptions of them, that his days were no easier than mine. He was still struggling, throwing away much of what he'd written, and I took a furtive solace in that. But occasionally he would report having had a good day, and I would feel, under my encouraging cheer, the shudder of panic you get when a friend deserts you by joining AA or leaving a bad marriage. It was one thing for him to be sitting down to it every day while I was not; but to hear that he might be getting somewhere made me feel abandoned and ashamed. He was pulling ahead in the great race of life, and he was throwing my own stasis into unbearable relief. Fortunately, over the next two months, such days were rare enough to discount.

Eventually my father came home to a house that had been fitted for his wheelchair-bound return: doors taken off their hinges, rugs

rolled up, and a hospital bed installed in the den, with a baby monitor so my mother could hear him call. My reluctance to visit him
got worse once he was home. At home bad things might be happening and no expert, no breezy young man with a stethoscope,
was there to take charge. There was only my mother, with her fraying nerves, and later a willing but underqualified aide and a nurse
who visited a couple of times a week. In the hospital there had at
least been the grim herd comfort of other ill people and other
worn-out families.

And of course the hospital was a place you could always leave. In
the hospital my father was someone else's responsibility. At home,
he was ours.

One night, encouraged by a recent letter and feeling at loose
ends at home, I called the man. I was anxious and uncomfortable
the whole time we talked, but as soon as we were off the phone I
couldn't wait to talk to him again. We talked periodically after that,
but it felt like the sort of dangerous pleasure you eventually have to
swear off, and I couldn't shake the feeling that each conversation
brought us closer to the inevitable one in which we would agree to
stop talking altogether, so I mostly tried to enjoy the idea of calling
him without actually doing it, all the while reminding myself that
there was a good chance that we would never speak again and that
even if we did, it certainly wasn't going to lead to anything.

As my father was ostensibly getting better, to the point where he
was able to drag himself around the house behind a walker, he was
also clearly getting worse. It was hard to get a firm sense of exactly
what was wrong, and for a while I was frustrated because he
seemed simply unwilling to make the necessary effort. But he
couldn't: he was too tired and discouraged; he was in too much
pain. Finally he agreed to go back to the hospital. As soon as he was
there, crammed into a corner of the busy emergency room, he
looked up at my mother with exhaustion and relief and said, "We
made the right decision to come back here." As if his body had just
been waiting for the signal, organ after organ began to shut down
over the next few days. Even so, he fought to stay alive. He elected
to go on a ventilator, after which he had to be heavily sedated and
eventually slipped into unconsciousness. His body by then was
wrecked.

Two weeks later we finally decided to disconnect the machine
that had been breathing for him. The doctor warned us that it

might take him as long as a week to die. The nurse we liked un-
hooked him from everything except the heart monitor and the
morphine drip before she left for the day, and another nurse took
over and wheeled him to a temporary room down the hall. My
brother and I took the first shift, sitting on opposite sides of the
bed and holding his hands. The television was on and we watched
it absent-mindedly. After the cramped busyness of the ICU, the
room we were in seemed peaceful, in a makeshift way, but my father did not. It seemed to me that he was no more resigned to dying than he had ever been, and I couldn't bring myself to say the
encouraging things that seemed called for, urging him to let go
and to trust that everything would be all right. But if he was waiting
to hear these, he didn't wait long; an hour later, he was gone.

I drove to the shopping center that afternoon under cover of
buying groceries and stopped to call the man from a pay phone. I
think he may have told me the story of the day his own father died,
but I don't remember for certain. What I remember is just my relief that he was home, that when the phone rang, he answered. I
remember standing outside a pizza parlor, watching the cars glide
in and out of their spaces, listening to his voice.

I had told my mother I would stay with her for a while, so I
moved my clothes and books and computer to her house, and began trying to write, without much success, in my father's study. In
the days immediately following his death, my sister and I had
sorted and cleared what looked like the most current piles. It felt
at the time as though we were working with the determined haste
of people trying to beat a storm or nightfall; now night had indeed
fallen, my father's death had become real, and I lacked the courage or energy to examine, much less remove, any of his things. In
the center of his otherwise cluttered desk I cleared a small space
for my work, and when I stepped into the room and saw it from a
distance, it looked not unlike one of those mysterious crop circles
— an emptiness created for no known reason.

I knew this was a strange time for me, living in my parents' house
again for the first time in twenty years, but it was probably even
stranger than I realized. I had a sense that my friends were listening in a particular way when we talked, forming opinions. I recognized that attitude of the concerned outsider; I have employed it
often enough myself.

The man, too, seemed worried about me and surprised me by

inviting me to come and visit him in New York. I still didn't know him well enough to feel comfortable with him, and I often felt nervous when I picked up the phone to call him. It was odd in one way and not odd at all in another to find myself sitting across the table from him in the apartment he had described to me in his letters. We talked for hours that first night, pushing the words back and forth while each of us tried to figure out what the other was saying underneath them. Finally I took my dishes to the sink and he came up behind me and, after all those months, put his hands on my shoulders.

Over the next two years, as we visited each other for weeks and then months at a stretch, the man and I settled into a routine that included a lot of satisfying time together and a number of anguished fights.

During the day, imagining him hard at work on his novel, I tried to work myself. My collection of short stories had finally been accepted and published by a university press the fall after my father died, and much as I thought I was prepared for the polite silence that greeted that publication, I must have been more disappointed than I realized, because I now found myself questioning my efforts more ruthlessly than ever. It sometimes took me a whole morning to get to my desk; once there, often I would turn on the computer and distract myself by opening a book or answering e-mail or fussing over a small editorial job. When I did manage to turn my attention to writing, I worried that the play I had begun working on was a mistake and that I should go back to writing fiction; on the other hand, I reasoned, if I really wanted to work on a play, a play was what I should work on — but then with every line I saw fresh evidence that I was going down the wrong road, and every step was taking me farther from the one thing I knew how to do: write stories. Except that by now I worried that I had already forgotten what I once knew about that, too. I hadn't written a story in what seemed a long time, and even though I remembered pretty much always feeling as if I didn't know what I was doing, even when I was doing it, I could see now that in fact I had known what I was doing before, and it was only now that I didn't.

I looked forward to evening, to the sight of the man, who still felt new and mysterious, walking through the door, and I also dreaded that moment because it meant either lying about what I had accomplished or, worse, telling the truth — and it meant having to hear about his day.

Because the man, who had been struggling so agreeably when I met him, had finally found his key, the way in. In the months it took me to produce a drifty fifteen-page story about the end of a marriage, a short play about a woman who sleeps with her best friend's husband, and seventy pages of a screenplay that had the desperate signs of "learning experience" written all over it, he piled up several hundred pages of his new novel.

It was, alas, good. My own reading told me this, but I had independent verification as well — because as sections were finished they flew almost immediately into print, and just as immediately the phone would begin to ring with congratulatory messages, comparisons to dead writers and to living writers whose reputations were so established they might as well be dead.

In the middle of this somewhat tense time the man came home one night, feeling frustrated after a couple of hard days, and asked if I would read some pages that were giving him trouble. I was immensely relieved to think that he, too, could produce bad work, and grateful that he was willing to show it to me.

I had the sudden wish to knock him to the floor and hike up my skirt, but I thought I would read the pages first.

He brought me olives and a glass of wine, and I sat down to read. Hoping for the worst and prepared to be encouraging.

"I don't understand," I said when I finished. "This is great."

"Do you really think so?" he asked hopefully. "You really think it's okay?"

"I think it's perfect. Funny, true, interesting." I managed to shove the words up my throat and out my mouth. I might have wished for it to be bad, but I couldn't tell him it was if it wasn't.

"Thank you. That's a huge relief. That really *really* helps. *Thank you.*"

You want to see bad work, *I'll* show you bad work, I thought, even as I was privately vowing never to show him another word I'd written.

I was forty, then forty-one, then forty-two years old. I had no children, the husband I had thought I would be with forever was gone, the father I had always assumed would one day really know me was dead, and I had no career to speak of. And now I was with a man who could do this.

The impulse to make love had passed.

When his novel was done, the man handed it in, and his editor called every hundred pages or so to say he was loving it, then called to say he was cutting the check, and finally called to say he wanted to take the man and me out for a celebratory dinner.

The day of that dinner, after putting in a few unhappy hours at my desk, I went out and bought myself a pair of black slacks and a silk blouse. The evening went well, I thought; the editor seemed to approve, and I felt, as always, gratified by that.

Halfway through the meal, when the editor said something polite about wanting to read some of my work, I did not know what to say, and the man intervened: "You did read it, actually. You passed on it."

In one of those bizarre coincidences that is proof of either the universe's intelligent plan or its gratuitous randomness, it happened that this editor was, in fact, the one person in New York who, two years earlier, had read and rejected my book before its publication by the university press. I might have thought, until that moment, that this unhappy fact belonged to the category of shameful secrets whose dark power is neutralized when someone actually speaks them aloud, but I saw immediately that it did not.

The editor, an urbane and gracious man, must have said something urbane and gracious then, but I couldn't hear him over the sound of my own voice in my head: Keep smiling, keep smiling!

Later that night, after the stony silence, the tears, the fury, I had to ask myself: What did I expect the man to do? I wanted it to be his fault, but it wasn't. I was angry about what he'd said, but I would have been angry about whatever he'd said, even if he'd said nothing — because what I was really angry about was having to go out to dinner with an editor on whom my work had made so little impression that he did not even remember reading it. An editor, it turned out, whom I *liked,* who I thought was not just funny and sweet but smart, and who was going to do everything in his power to make sure the man I was with got the notice he deserved.

Over the next several months, what had at first seemed like a pathologically extreme anticipation of the man's success on my part began to look like nothing more than a reasonable prediction. Advance copies of his book were released, and suddenly he was being interviewed, photographed, written and talked about by, it seemed, everyone. Clearly his book was on its way to becoming not *a* book but *the* book, and every day seemed to bring new evidence that he was on his way to becoming that rare thing, a writer whom people (not just other writers) have heard of.

On September 11, 2001, his book had been out about a week. In the shock of that day, he and I shuttled back and forth between the apartment and the television in the realtor's office down the hall. I felt the sensation of disaster, the weird chill of fear limned by exhilaration at the possibility that the world and all its fixed routines might have changed in a single day.

As we tried, along with everyone else, to think about what had happened and what would happen next, another question went unasked: What would it mean for the man's book? I was sure he was wondering this, and I was too, but I let the whole day go by without mentioning it. In those strange hours when anything seemed possible, it seemed not all that unlikely that the book on which the man I loved had spent ten years working might disappear before our eyes — and yet I said nothing.

I told myself that it would be unseemly, even in the privacy of our apartment, to focus on our petty concerns when thousands of people had lost their lives and the fate of the world itself was suddenly uncertain. But the truth is I didn't mention his book because I didn't want to. Because for one day, at least, for the first time in what felt like months, he and his work had been eclipsed — and I was relieved.

That was the place envy had delivered me to.

My friends, trying to be helpful, had this to say: "I could never do that, be involved with a writer who was that much more successful than I was."

But really, why not? Partly, I suppose, because a fellow writer's success makes it that much harder to console oneself with thoughts of what Virginia Woolf called "the world's notorious indifference." The world, Woolf said, "does not ask people to write poems and novels and histories; it does not need them. It does not care whether Flaubert finds the right word or whether Carlyle scrupulously verifies this or that fact." So when the man was merely gifted but not particularly rewarded, I was comfortable; we were in it together, comrades in a world that didn't care what we had to tell it. But now, what did his success prove, if not that when the gift is prodigious enough, the world *does* need us, it *will* pay?

When the subject of his success came up, often enough a friend would say, "The great thing is he really deserves it." Were they kidding? This was precisely what made it so hard. For once, the gods hadn't made the stupid mistake of smiling on another no-talent, well-connected charlatan. No, this was a genuinely excellent piece of work by a man who had dedicated his life to doing such work and was now being rewarded for it. Proof that the system was not essentially corrupt and misguided, incapable of recognizing true merit, after all.

Where was the comfort in that?

One morning, unable to focus on whatever I was working on, I suddenly thought of a passage of his. I got up and walked across the room to pull down from the shelf the magazine in which the passage appeared. This was the wrong thing to be doing, I knew. Still, I watched myself do it. Heart knocking like a lunatic on a door that will never open, I flipped through the pages. I found it. It wasn't as good as I'd remembered. It was better.

I refused to let myself form the question, but I knew it was in there, all the more powerful for going unasked: If I couldn't do that, what was the point of my doing it at all? With that peculiarly severe egotism of the insecure, I could not believe I would ever be the best, and I could not bear to be anything less.

But why, then, didn't I feel this when reading Wharton, or Faulkner (who crowed that a writer will not hesitate to rob his mother, "Ode on a Grecian Urn" being worth any number of old ladies)? Why aren't we all still eating our hearts out over Shakespeare? Why does it hurt only to read good work by the living? Why does the pain increase as the distance narrows between ourselves and those gifted others: those we know, those we know who are our age (or worse, younger), those we know who are our age and our friends? Worst of all, maybe, when the enviable other is someone we share our life with.

According to an appealingly commonsensical theory of human behavior known as Tesser's self-evaluation maintenance model, we all want to think well of ourselves, and one of the ways we enhance our own self-esteem is through our interactions with other people who are doing well. In what's known as the "reflective process," someone else's success can make us feel better about ourselves; this explains why, for example, we feel good when our favorite sports team — the individual members of which have never met us and probably have no desire to — wins. And it's probably part of what's behind the old model of marriage in which a striving, supportive woman was to be found behind every successful man. In addition to whatever material advantages they promised, the man's achievements were a feather in his wife's cap: a sign that she had succeeded in marrying well.

But this happy scenario holds only for those cases in which the other person is succeeding in an area outside one's own domain. When a rival succeeds, the "comparison process" begins: we measure ourselves against the successful other and feel diminished. Fortunately, this competitiveness is limited to a small number of areas. Unfortunately, those areas are extremely important; they're the ones on which our sense of self is based.

I came home one evening and the man asked about my day, which had been unremarkable. I asked about his and learned that the British rights to his now famous book had been sold for a whopping figure, higher than anyone had anticipated. It had been a big day, and he was proud and excited. It was the kind of news you want to call home with, and because his mother was no longer alive and he had no sisters, he had called his sister-in-law.

He hadn't known where to call me, he said, or he would have. But I could see it in his wary, eager face: he wanted to call someone whose enthusiasm he could trust.

The part that was his girlfriend put her arms around him and told him how happy she was, and the other part, the miserable writer within, kept her distance.

Not long after this, we broke up. At the end of a holiday trip to visit family in the West, I told the man I couldn't imagine going back to New York; it was too hard there. I told him there wasn't enough air for both of us in that apartment; I told him I was drowning. He asked me to be more specific, and I told him I just didn't think I was cut out for this life together.

"What life? What are you talking about?" It was late; we were arguing in the dark, on a sofa bed in his brother's house.

"This life. Where you're so . . . big, and I'm so little." It made me feel littler just saying it.

"I don't think of you as little."

The fact that I believed this helped not at all. I was drowning; what good did it do to hear that he thought I could swim?

But breaking up, it turned out, was not the answer, either. I still wanted him, and my pride, already inflamed, now fairly throbbed at the idea that it was my own weakness that kept me from having him. I was in pitched battle with myself, and the wrong side was winning.

A few months later, when I persuaded him to try again, I sensed this was our last good chance at being together. I also sensed, despite my recent conversion to the belief that problems are solved by talking, that this one, born of words, was one that words would never fix. The more I talked about it, the more secretive he would become, and the more guilty and resentful we would both feel.

It became, and remains, the thing we don't talk about.

When the man told me stories about his wife — his ex-wife, but she had a fearsome presence that made her more real to me than I sometimes felt to myself — I would feel a cool draft, as though someone had left the door to the future open a crack.

She had been a writer, too. During the happy, lean years of their marriage they would both write eight hours a day, fueled, in the starving-artist tradition, by a diet of rice and beans and jumbo packs of chicken thighs. They were going to publish together, the story went; their books would find their way to discerning, appreciative audiences. And when his first book made good on their bargain and hers did not, he tried to wait for her to catch up. She moved on to a second book and on to a second house, alone, where she hoped to work better without the distraction of his success. But the second book wouldn't come together; she couldn't finish it. It wasn't until they had finally separated, for good this time, that she gave herself the gift of putting that work away. As far as he knew, she had stopped writing altogether — except for an essay that had just been published in an anthology, which he learned about and bought one day.

In her essay, as I remember it now, his ex-wife wrote about what it felt like when she and her husband separated. I had a hard time reading this; I was simultaneously so curious to know what she thought of their life together and so afraid to find out that the sentences kept shorting out on me. But I got the gist: she not only stopped writing when her marriage to the man dissolved; for a time, she stopped *reading*.

Well, I was in much better shape than that! On the other hand, he and I were still together. Who knew what I would have given up by the time it was over?

What would have happened, I wondered, if the situation had been reversed, and she had published first? He would have kept on, I'm sure; her success might have been satisfying or frustrating to him — perhaps both — but he would never have given up.

I thought of Alice Munro's "Material," a story about women and men, writing and envy. In it, a woman comes across a published story written by her ex-husband and discovers in it an affecting, sympathetic portrait of another woman whom, in their real life together, he had mocked and treated callously. "How honest this is and how lovely, I had to say as I read . . . It is an act of magic, there is no getting around it; it is an act, you might say, of a special, unsparing, unsentimental love." But when she sits down later, to write him a letter of praise, the words that appear on the page are these: *"This is not enough, Hugo. You think it is, but it isn't."* And then she admits it to herself: she blames him, still; she envies and despises.

I've read this story half a dozen times over the years, and when I think of it, I always remember that woman envying her ex, the writer. But when I looked at it again recently, I was surprised to discover that it's not just him she envies but *them* — that is, not just her former husband but her current one. Different from each other as they seem, they have both "decided what to do about everything they run across in this world, what attitude to take, how to ignore or use things." What she envies is not something about being a writer, but something about being a man.

My father had been a managing partner — a phrase I had never stopped to consider before — of an accounting firm when I was growing up, and my mother was, therefore, the managing partner's wife. A corporate first lady whose job, in addition to running the house, was to entertain my father's business associates and accompany him on trips.

"Everywhere we went I was his wife," she told me recently. We were in what is now her house, standing next to a dresser on which was a smiling picture of my father that neither of us was looking at. "He was never my husband. I hated that."

"But you weren't in his field," I tried to explain. How could she possibly think that her situation was anywhere near as bad as mine was? "You weren't *trying* to compete with him."

"No, I didn't even have a field."

She had the purity, the self-righteousness, of unadulterated resentment. Here was the old-fashioned envy I envied — the clean, sweet fury of a woman who had a man to blame. Their life together had been dedicated to his job, and she had had only one choice: she could have left him. But how could she? She had no income of her own and four kids, the youngest of whom, that good-natured albatross, was me. Whereas I — I! — had had all the advantages, and I still felt resentful. Nothing righteous about *that*.

It's tempting to take comfort in generalizations, and I have. I see myself as belonging to a generation of women who were raised to believe that we could do and be whatever we wanted — by women who, by and large, had not enjoyed that freedom themselves (and who perhaps envied their daughters for it). I grew up still wanting all the old things — to be pretty, to be good, to be liked — and also wanting not to care about such things.

But old habits die hard. Maybe it was no coincidence that when I was feeling most outstripped by the man's success and talent, when I was reading those pages of his that I wished I had written, I responded by withholding from him the gift of myself. When he was being lauded and invited, the world praising his intelligence and imagination, my way of evening the score was to shy away from him.

As long as he wanted and didn't quite have *me*, the logic went, we would be even — and I could stop feeling so outdone by what he had that I wanted. But what did that really mean? That if I could not be happy I was ready to make us both miserable. And that my answer to his work was my *self*; he had his book to make the world love him, and I had my sex with which to take my revenge.

It reminded me of something that had happened not long before I met the man. I had written a short play, in which six women are doing what my characters always seem to be doing — sitting around talking. I had written it for a class, because at that point I was having trouble writing anything unless it was for a teacher who would tell me it was good. As it happened, the teacher didn't think this one was particularly good. She thought the stakes weren't high enough, and nothing much happened, and six people were too many for a play that was only ten minutes long.

Afterward, as I was leaving the room, discouraged but not quite convinced, a man from the class came up to me and told me he'd liked what I'd written.

All his plays were about rodeo men and the half-dressed women who were always crying at kitchen tables after they left. I now realized he had a much more subtle mind than I'd ever given him credit for.

"Thank you," I said.

He suggested that one thing the play might benefit from was the addition of a man, just at the very beginning, to pique the audience's interest.

I told him I'd consider that.

"You want to get a drink?" he asked me.

What are we here for, others or ourselves? Grandiose and overstated as it sounds, doesn't it come down to that? I always thought I would have at least a working answer to that question by this point in my life, but I don't; and in the absence of that certainty, everything feels provisional.

The last time I saw my mother, she and I talked, over a pleasant restaurant dinner that both of us were happy not to have cooked, about what will happen when she can no longer stay in her house. I love my mother. I want her to be happy and safe, free from worry.

And yet what do I find myself doing? Reassuring her that everything will be fine, leaving my nearby brother to look out for her, flying to the other side of the continent, and writing about the guilt I feel.

Another writer and I talk about some of this one night. Before I really knew her, I used to think of this woman as a relentlessly cheerful and optimistic person, so given to looking on the bright side that she wasn't even aware that's what she was doing. Tonight she reassures me, again, about the merits of a draft I've shown her, gushing in a way that makes me want simultaneously to embrace her and to run screaming from the room. But it's a good talk, full of confessed fear and desire, full of the agreement women love. We each order another glass of wine. I tell her, sounding less convinced to myself than I'd thought I was before I started talking, that I'm hopeful that my various crises of confidence may be opening the door to a new, more assured way of working.

When we get to her, she surprises me by revealing that she's been depressed lately. She feels as though all anyone wants to do these days is exercise furiously to stay in shape, and she wants . . . something else. She's losing track of the point of it all.

The next morning, my phone rings and it's her, telling me that she's just learned that her sister has inoperable cancer. I can hear the fear and grief in her voice, but I can also hear the mobilizing of forces, the list-making and dinner-cooking, the shoulder pressing gratefully to the wheel. She certainly wouldn't have wished for it, but she has a job again; it's clear what it is, it's clear it must be done, it's clear she knows how to do it and that she's good at it. She's suiting up to do what's been women's work since the beginning of time, and it would be hard to argue there's anything on earth more meaningful.

That's how I feel sitting here, anyway.

But then I think again of Munro's story "Material": "I envy and despise." Isn't the most important irony of that story the invisible one at its center — the fact that it was written by a woman, who gave to her gifted male doppelgänger the qualities and perceptions, the easy knowledge of how to ignore or use things, his ex-wife so envies?

Life, obviously, is about more than this. It's not as though anyone thinks that being a good writer makes you a good person. But it helps. (Isn't this perhaps one reason why women, as a whole, are more apt than men to see writing and reading as therapeutic acts? All that private time spent rendering and transforming personal experience on paper is easier to justify if the writer — and, ideally, reader — is healed in the process.) If you're truly talented, then your work becomes your way of doing good in the world; if you're not, it's a self-indulgence, even an embarrassment.

But how do you *know* you're good, if not by comparing yourself favorably to others (an essentially ungood activity)? And how many women are comfortable doing that?

Here's Edith Wharton: "If only my work were better, it would be all I need. But my kind of half-talent isn't much use as an escape."

Here's Joan Didion on the subject of her first novel: "It's got a lot of sloppy stuff. Extraneous stuff. Words that don't work. Awkwardness. Scenes that should have been brought up, scenes that should have been played down. But then *Play It As It Lays* has a lot of sloppy stuff. I haven't reread *Common Prayer,* but I'm sure that does too."

Or Dorothy Parker: "I want so much to write well, though I know I don't, and that I didn't make it. But during and at the end of my life, I will adore those who have." (Here is perhaps womanly envy in its purest form: one's own worthlessness worn as a hair-shirt reminder to love those who are better.)

It's hard to talk about the category of "women writers" or "women's writing" without feeling that you're picking at a scab that will never heal as long as you keep picking. On the other hand, vexed as they are, those categories continue to be meaningful, even if we can't always agree on just what the meaning is.

Most women I know are reluctant to say, "I am better than her, and her, and her — okay, I'll keep going," and most men I know rely, when necessary, on some formulation of exactly that. Plus women have not only each other to compete against (in devious and exhausting ways, requiring much track-covering and nice-making as they go) but men to envy; because it's still the case that women writers are compared to each other, and the big (as opposed to, say, lyrical) literary novel persists as an essentially male category. Women's books are still not talked about in the same way men's books are, and women are still sensitive to that.

As I was turning all this over in my mind, I thought again about meeting my boyfriend for the first time. How before I had known anything about him, I had known this would happen — that one day he would write his Big Book, and the world would roll a red carpet to his door. All those months when he was miserably, triumphantly cranking it out, page by artful page, I had known it — more certainly than I had ever known anything about my own life. (No wonder I had gotten so little of my own work done — I had been so preoccupied with monitoring his.)

Had I been clairvoyant, then? Or was it something more metaphysical: Had my fear acted like a cosmic magnet, drawing to itself the object of its obsession (forgetting for a moment that my boy-friend might have had anything to do with his own fate)?

Or had I, in some perverse way, got exactly what I wanted?

I had found a partner who, by being so good — and so success-ful — at what I wanted to do, had called my bluff. I didn't want to quit, it turned out. I wanted to find a way to keep writing, whether I could ever be good enough or not.

I did envy his talent — the way he could go off in the morning and come home at night with five smart pages, the way he could expertly tease out a metaphor, nail a character in a sentence, and tackle geopolitics or brain chemistry without breaking a sweat. I envied the fact that in airports and restaurants, strangers — read-ers! — would come up to him and rave about his book; I envied his easy acceptance at magazines that had been routinely rejecting my work for years.

For all that, though, I was startled to realize that I didn't wish I'd written his book, any more than I would have wished to wake up to-morrow looking like the beauty from a magazine cover. What I en-vied were what his talent and success had bestowed on him, a sense of the rightness of what he was doing. I wanted what women always want: permission. But he'd had that before this book was even writ-ten; it was, after all, the first thing I'd envied about him. It was ar-guably what enabled him to write the book in the first place.

I was raised to admire a life of service, and to this day, I do ad-mire it. When I see someone bend to the task of helping another, I think she is doing the work of all, the human job. But someone else's good deed never stabs my heart the way a good book does. I admire it, but I do not envy it. Whatever else it has done, my envy of the man has helped me see the difference between what I was raised to want, what I wish I could want, and what I do want.

I flatter myself that I'm doing better with it all, that I'm adjusting. The man and I are finally happy and at ease, for the most part, and his book and public stature are a fact of our life together.

But who am I kidding? At home sometimes I don't want to check the phone messages; when I step into a bookstore and see that stack on the new-book table, I can sometimes feel my heart rattling the bars of its cage. I read the reviews and the interviews, but not all of them; I want them to be good, and then I want to forget them. The book itself, which I've read twice, I don't even want to look at now.

That's how much better I'm doing.

And yet I am doing better, because something within me has sur-faced: another story. In this new story, every ugly impulse and selfish yearning, the whole insecure unlovable mess, has been given wing. There's no better self to protect anymore; the moral high ground has been ceded.

In this story, I don't do the work I was born to, perhaps not even the work I am best at, but the work I have chosen — incompletely, erratically, often unhappily and uncertainly.

In this new story, I write to refute the ex-wife, and to avenge her. She is my enemy and my friend.

I have met the circumstances that are larger than my capacity to be gracious, it turns out. I have come up against the limits of my goodness: someone I love has what I want, and he probably always will. What else is there to do for it? I might as well work.

JARED DIAMOND

The Last Americans

FROM HARPER'S MAGAZINE

I met a traveler from an antique land
Who said: Two vast and trunkless legs of stone
Stand in the desert . . . Near them, on the sand,
Half sunk, a shattered visage lies, whose frown,
And wrinkled lip, and sneer of cold command,
Tell that its sculptor well those passions read
Which yet survive, stamped on these lifeless things,
The hand that mocked them, and the heart that fed:
And on the pedestal these words appear:
"My name is Ozymandias, king of kings:
Look on my works, ye Mighty, and despair!"
Nothing beside remains. Round the decay
Of that colossal wreck, boundless and bare
The lone and level sands stretch far away.

— "Ozymandias," Percy Bysshe Shelley

ONE OF THE disturbing facts of history is that so many civilizations collapse. Few people, however, least of all our politicians, realize that a primary cause of the collapse of those societies has been the destruction of the environmental resources on which they depended. Fewer still appreciate that many of those civilizations share a sharp curve of decline. Indeed, a society's demise may begin only a decade or two after it reaches its peak population, wealth, and power.

Recent archaeological discoveries have revealed similar courses of collapse in such otherwise dissimilar ancient societies as the Maya in the Yucatán, the Anasazi in the American Southwest, the Cahokia mound builders outside St. Louis, the Greenland Norse, the statue builders of Easter Island, ancient Mesopotamia in the Fertile Crescent, Great Zimbabwe in Africa, and Angkor Wat in Cambodia. These civilizations, and many others, succumbed to various combinations of environmental degradation and climate change, aggression from enemies taking advantage of their resulting weakness, and declining trade with neighbors who faced their own environmental problems. Because peak population, wealth, resource consumption, and waste production are accompanied by peak environmental impact — approaching the limit at which impact outstrips resources — we can now understand why declines of societies tend to follow swiftly on their peaks.

These combinations of undermining factors were compounded by cultural attitudes preventing those in power from perceiving or resolving the crisis. That's a familiar problem today. Some of us are inclined to dismiss the importance of a healthy environment, or at least to suggest that it's just one of many problems facing us — an "issue." That dismissal is based on three dangerous misconceptions.

Foremost among these misconceptions is that we must balance the environment against human needs. That reasoning is exactly upside down. Human needs and a healthy environment are not opposing claims that must be balanced; instead, they are inexorably linked by chains of cause and effect. We need a healthy environment because we need clean water, clean air, wood, and food from the ocean, plus soil and sunlight to grow crops. We need functioning natural ecosystems, with their native species of earthworms, bees, plants, and microbes, to generate and aerate our soils, pollinate our crops, decompose our wastes, and produce our oxygen. We need to prevent toxic substances from accumulating in our water and air and soil. We need to prevent weeds, germs, and other pest species from becoming established in places where they aren't native and where they cause economic damage. Our strongest arguments for a healthy environment are selfish: we want it for ourselves, not for threatened species like snail darters, spotted owls, and Furbish louseworts.

Another popular misconception is that we can trust in technology to solve our problems. Whatever environmental problem you name, you can also name some hoped-for technological solution under discussion. Some of us have faith that we shall solve our dependence on fossil fuels by developing new technologies for hydrogen engines, wind energy, or solar energy. Some of us have faith that we shall solve our food problems with new or soon-to-be-developed genetically modified crops. Some of us have faith that new technologies will succeed in cleaning up the toxic materials in our air, water, soil, and foods without the horrendous cleanup expenses that we now incur.

Those with such faith assume that the new technologies will ultimately succeed, but in fact some of them may succeed and others may not. They assume that the new technologies will succeed quickly enough to make a big difference soon, but all of these major technological changes will actually take five to thirty years to develop and implement — if they catch on at all. Most of all, those with faith assume that new technology won't cause any new problems. In fact, technology merely constitutes increased power, which produces changes that can be either for the better or for the worse. All of our current environmental problems are unanticipated harmful consequences of our existing technology. There is no basis for believing that technology will miraculously stop causing new and unanticipated problems while it is solving the problems that it previously produced.

The final misconception holds that environmentalists are fearmongering, overreacting extremists whose predictions of impending disaster have been proved wrong before and will be proved wrong again. Behold, say the optimists: water still flows from our faucets, the grass is still green, and the supermarkets are full of food. We are more prosperous than ever before, and that's the final proof that our system works.

Well, for a few billion of the world's people who are causing us increasing trouble, there isn't any clean water, there is less and less green grass, and there are no supermarkets full of food. To appreciate what the environmental problems of those billions of people mean for us Americans, compare the following two lists of countries. First ask some ivory-tower academic ecologist who knows a lot about the environment but never reads a newspaper and has no interest in politics to list the overseas countries facing some of the worst problems of environmental stress, overpopulation, or both. The ecologist would answer, "That's a no-brainer, it's obvious. Your list of environmentally stressed or overpopulated countries should surely include Afghanistan, Bangladesh, Burundi, Haiti, Indonesia, Iraq, Nepal, Pakistan, the Philippines, Rwanda, the Solomon Islands, and Somalia, plus others." Then ask a First World politician who knows nothing, and cares less, about the environment and population problems to list the world's worst trouble spots: countries where state government has already been overwhelmed and has collapsed, or is now at risk of collapsing, or has been wracked by recent civil wars; and countries that, as a result of their problems, are also creating problems for us rich First World countries, which may be deluged by illegal immigrants, or have to provide foreign aid to those countries, or may decide to provide them with military assistance to deal with rebellions and terrorists, or may even (God forbid) have to send in our own troops. The politician would answer, "That's a no-brainer, it's obvious. Your list of political trouble spots should surely include Afghanistan, Bangladesh, Burundi, Haiti, Indonesia, Iraq, Nepal, Pakistan, the Philippines, Rwanda, the Solomon Islands, and Somalia, plus others."

The connection between the two lists is transparent. Today, just as in the past, countries that are environmentally stressed, overpopulated, or both are at risk of becoming politically stressed, and of seeing their governments collapse. When people are desperate and undernourished, they blame their government, which they see as responsible for failing to solve their problems. They try to emigrate at any cost. They start civil wars. They kill one another. They figure that they have nothing to lose, so they become terrorists, or they support or tolerate terrorism. The results are genocides such as the ones that already have exploded in Burundi, Indonesia, and Rwanda; civil wars, as in Afghanistan, Indonesia, Nepal, the Philippines, and the Solomon Islands; calls for the dispatch of First World troops, as to Afghanistan, Indonesia, Iraq, the Philippines, Rwanda, the Solomon Islands, and Somalia; the collapse of central government, as has already happened in Somalia; and overwhelming poverty, as in all of the countries on these lists.

But what about the United States? Some might argue that the environmental collapse of ancient societies is relevant to the modern decline of weak, far-off, overpopulated Rwanda and environmentally devastated Somalia, but isn't it ridiculous to suggest any possible relevance to the fate of our own society? After all, we might reason, those ancients didn't enjoy the wonders of modern, environment-friendly technologies. Those ancients had the misfortune to suffer from the effects of climate change. They behaved stupidly and ruined their own environment by doing obviously dumb things, like cutting down their forests, watching their topsoil erode, and building cities in dry areas likely to run short of water. They had foolish leaders who didn't have books and so couldn't learn from history, and who embroiled them in destabilizing wars and didn't pay attention to problems at home. They were overwhelmed by desperate immigrants, as one society after another collapsed, sending floods of economic refugees to tax the resources of the societies that weren't collapsing. In all those respects, we modern Americans are fundamentally different from those primitive ancients, and there is nothing that we could learn from them.

Or so the argument goes. It's an argument so ingrained both in our subconscious and in public discourse that it has assumed the status of objective reality. We think we are different. In fact, of course, all of those powerful societies of the past thought that they too were unique, right up to the moment of their collapse. It's sobering to consider the swift decline of the ancient Maya, who 1,200 years ago were themselves the most advanced society in the Western Hemisphere, and who, like us now, were then at the apex of their own power and numbers. Two excellent recent books, David Webster's *The Fall of the Ancient Maya* and Richardson Gill's *The Great Maya Droughts,* help bring the trajectory of Maya civilization back to life for us. Their studies illustrate how even sophisticated societies like that of the Maya (and ours) can be undermined by details of rainfall, farming methods, and motives of leaders.

By now, millions of modern Americans have visited Maya ruins. To do so, one need only take a direct flight from the United States to the Yucatán capital of Mérida, jump into a rental car or minibus, and drive an hour on a paved highway. Most Maya ruins, with their great temples and monuments, lie surrounded by jungles (seasonal tropical forests), far from current human settlement. They are "pure" archaeological sites. That is, their locations became depopulated, so they were not covered up by later buildings as were so many other ancient cities, like the Aztec capital of Tenochtitlán — now buried under modern Mexico City — and Rome.

One of the reasons few people live there now is that the Maya homeland poses serious environmental challenges to would-be farmers. Although it has a somewhat unpredictable rainy season from May to October, it also has a dry season from January through April. Indeed, if one focuses on the dry months, one could describe the Yucatán as a "seasonal desert."

Complicating things, from a farmer's perspective, is that the part of the Yucatán with the most rain, the south, is also the part at the highest elevation above the water table. Most of the Yucatán consists of karst — a porous, spongelike limestone terrain — and so rain runs straight into the ground, leaving little or no surface water. The Maya in the lower-elevation regions of the north were able to reach the water table by way of deep sinkholes called cenotes, and the Maya in low coastal areas without sinkholes could reach it by digging wells up to seventy-five feet deep. Most Maya, however, lived in the south. How did they deal with their resulting water problem?

Technology provided an answer. The Maya plugged up leaks on karst promontories by plastering the bottoms of depressions to create reservoirs, which collected rain and stored it for use in the dry season. The reservoirs at the Maya city of Tikal, for example, held enough water to meet the needs of about ten thousand people for eighteen months. If a drought lasted longer than that, though, the inhabitants of Tikal were in deep trouble.

Maya farmers grew mostly corn, which constituted the astonishingly high proportion of about 70 percent of their diet, as deduced from isotope analyses of ancient Maya skeletons. They grew corn by means of a modified version of swidden slash-and-burn agriculture, in which forest is cleared, crops are grown in the resulting clearing for a few years until the soil is exhausted, and then the field is abandoned for fifteen to twenty years until regrowth of wild vegetation restores the soil's fertility. Because most of the land under a swidden agricultural system is fallow at any given time, it can support only modest population densities. Thus it was a surprise for archaeologists to discover that ancient Maya population densities, judging from numbers of stone foundations of farmhouses, were often far higher than what unmodified swidden agriculture could support: often 250 to 750 people per square mile. The Maya probably achieved those high populations by such means as shortening the fallow period and tilling the soil to restore soil fertility, or omitting the fallow period entirely and growing crops every year, or, in especially moist areas, growing two crops per year.

Socially stratified societies, ours included, consist of farmers who produce food and nonfarmers such as bureaucrats and soldiers who do not produce food and are in effect parasites on farmers. The farmers must grow enough food to meet not only their own needs but also those of everybody else. The number of nonproducing consumers who can be supported depends on the society's agricultural productivity. In the United States today, with its highly efficient agriculture, farmers make up only 2 percent of our population, and each farmer can feed, on average, 129 other people. Ancient Egyptian agriculture was efficient enough for an Egyptian peasant to produce five times the food required for himself and his family. But a Maya peasant could produce only twice the needs of himself and his family.

Fully 80 percent of Maya society consisted of peasants. Their inability to support many nonfarmers resulted from several limitations of their agriculture. It produced little protein, because corn has a much lower protein content than wheat and because the few edible domestic animals kept by the Maya (turkeys, ducks, and dogs) included no large animals like our cows and sheep. There was little use of terracing or irrigation to increase production. In the Maya area's humid climate, stored corn would rot or become infested after a year, so the Maya couldn't get through a longer drought by eating surplus corn accumulated in good years. And unlike Old World peoples with their horses, oxen, donkeys, and camels, the Maya had no animal-powered transport. Indeed, the Maya lacked not only pack animals and animal-drawn plows but also metal tools, wheels, and boats with sails. All of those great Maya temples were built with stone and wooden tools and human muscle power alone, and all overland transport went on the backs of human porters.

Those limitations on food supply and food transport may in part explain why Maya society remained politically organized in small kingdoms that were perpetually at war with one another and that never became unified into large empires, like the Aztec empire of the Valley of Mexico (fed by highly productive agriculture) or the Inca empire of the Andes (fed by diverse crops carried on llamas). Maya armies were small and unable to mount lengthy campaigns over long distances. The typical Maya kingdom held a population of only up to fifty thousand people, within a radius of two or three days' walk from the king's palace. From the top of the temple of some Maya kingdoms, one could see the tops of the temples of other kingdoms.

Presiding over the temple was the king himself, who functioned both as head priest and as political leader. It was his responsibility to pray to the gods, to perform astronomical and calendrical rituals, to ensure the timely arrival of the rains on which agriculture depended, and thereby to bring prosperity. The king claimed to have the supernatural power to deliver those good things because of his asserted family relationship to the gods. Of course, that exposed him to the risk that his subjects would become disillusioned if he couldn't fulfill his boast of being able to deliver rains and prosperity.

Those are the basic outlines of Classic Maya society, which for all its limitations lasted more than five hundred years. Indeed, the Maya themselves believed that it had lasted for much longer. Their remarkable Long Count calendar had its starting date (analogous to January 1, A.D. 1 of our calendar) backdated into the remote preliterate past, at August 11, 3114 B.C. The first physical evidence of civilization within the Maya area, in the form of villagers and pottery, appeared around 1400 B.C., substantial buildings around 500 B.C., and writing around 400 B.C. The so-called Classic period of Maya history arose around A.D. 250, when evidence for the first kings and dynasties emerged. From then, the Maya population increased almost exponentially, to reach peak numbers in the eighth century A.D. The largest monuments were erected toward the end of that century. All the indicators of a complex society declined throughout the ninth century, until the last date on any monument was A.D. 909. This decline of Maya population and architecture constitutes what is known as the Classic Maya collapse.

What happened? Let's consider in more detail a city whose ruins now lie in western Honduras at the world-famous site of Copán. The most fertile ground in the Copán area consists of five pockets of flat land along a river valley with a total area of only one square mile; the largest of those five pockets, known as the Copán pocket, has an area of half a square mile. Much of the land around Copán consists of steep hills with poor soil. Today, corn yields from valley-bottom fields are two or three times those of fields on hill slopes, which suffer rapid erosion and lose most of their productivity within a decade of farming.

To judge by the number of house sites, population growth in the Copán valley rose steeply from the fifth century up to a peak estimated at around twenty-seven thousand people between A.D. 750 and 900. Construction of royal monuments glorifying kings became especially massive from A.D. 650 onward. After A.D. 700, nobles other than kings got into the act and began erecting their own palaces, increasing the burden that the king and his own court already imposed on the peasants. The last big buildings at Copán were put up around A.D. 800; the last date on an incomplete altar possibly bearing a king's name is A.D. 822.

Archaeological surveys of different types of habitats in the Copán valley show that they were occupied in a regular sequence. The first area farmed was the large Copán pocket of bottomland, followed by occupation of the other four bottomland pockets. During that time the human population was growing, but the hills remained uninhabited. Hence that increased population must have been accommodated by intensifying production in the bottomland pockets: probably some combination of shorter fallow periods and double-cropping. By A.D. 500, people had started to settle the hill slopes, but those sites were occupied only briefly. The percentage of Copán's total population that was in the hills, rather than in the valleys, peaked in the year 575 and then declined, as the population again became concentrated in the pockets.

What caused that pullback of population from the hills? From excavation of building foundations on the valley floor we know that they became covered with sediment during the eighth century, meaning that the hill slopes were becoming eroded and probably also leached of nutrients. The acidic hill soils being carried down into the valley would have reduced agricultural yields. The reason for that erosion of the hillsides is clear: the forests that formerly covered them and protected their soil were being cut down. Dated pollen samples show that the pine forests originally covering the hilltops were eventually all cleared, to be burned for fuel. Besides causing sediment accumulation in the valleys and depriving valley inhabitants of wood supplies, that deforestation may have begun to cause a "man-made drought" in the valley bottom, because forests play a major role in water cycling, such that massive deforestation tends to result in lowered rainfall.

Hundreds of skeletons recovered from Copán archaeological sites have been studied for signs of disease and poor nutrition, such as porous bones and stress lines in the teeth. Those skeletal signs show that the health of Copán's inhabitants deteriorated from A.D. 650 to 850, among both the elite and commoners, though the health of commoners was worse.

Recall that Copán's population was growing rapidly while the hills were being occupied. The subsequent abandonment of all of those hill fields meant that the burden of feeding the extra population formerly dependent on the hills now fell increasingly on the valley floor, and that more and more people were competing for the food grown on that one square mile of bottomland. That would have led to fighting among the farmers themselves for the best land, or for any land, just as in modern Rwanda. Because the king was failing to deliver on his promises of rain and prosperity, he would have been the scapegoat for this agricultural failure, which explains why the last that we hear of any king is A.D. 822, and why the royal palace was burned around A.D. 850.

Datable pieces of obsidian, the sharp rock from which the Maya made their stone tools, suggest that Copán's total population decreased more gradually than did its signs of kings and nobles. The estimated population in the year A.D. 950 was still around fifteen thousand, or 55 percent of the peak population of twenty-seven thousand. That population continued to dwindle, until there are few signs of anyone in the Copán valley after around A.D. 1235. The reappearance of pollen from forest trees thereafter provides independent evidence that the valley became virtually empty of people.

The Maya history that I have just related, and Copán's history in particular, illustrate why we talk about "the Maya collapse." But the story grows more complicated, for at least five reasons. There was not only that enormous Classic collapse but also at least two smaller pre-Classic collapses, around A.D. 150 and 600, as well as some post-Classic collapses. The Classic collapse was obviously not complete, because hundreds of thousands of Maya survived, in areas with stable water supplies, to meet and fight the Spaniards. The collapse of population (as gauged by numbers of house sites and of obsidian tools) was in some cases much slower than the decline in numbers of Long Count dates. Many apparent collapses of cities were nothing more than "power cycling"; i.e., particular cities becoming more powerful at the expense of neighboring cities, then declining or getting conquered by neighbors, without changes in the whole population. Finally, cities in different parts of the Maya area rose and fell on different trajectories.

Some archaeologists focus on these complications and don't want to recognize a Classic Maya collapse at all. But this overlooks the obvious fact that cries out for explanation: the disappearance of between 90 and 99 percent of the Maya population after A.D. 800, and of the institution of the kingship, Long Count calendars, and other complex political and cultural institutions. Before we can understand those disappearances, however, we need first to understand the roles of warfare and of drought.

Archaeologists for a long time believed the ancient Maya to be gentle and peaceful people. We now know that Maya warfare was intense, chronic, and unresolvable, because limitations of food supply and transportation made it impossible for any Maya principality to unite the whole region in an empire. The archaeological record shows that wars became more intense and frequent toward the time of the Classic collapse. That evidence comes from discoveries of several types since the Second World War: archaeological excavations of massive fortifications surrounding many Maya sites; vivid depictions of warfare and captives on stone monuments and on the famous painted murals discovered in 1946 at Bonampak; and the decipherment of Maya writing, much of which proved to consist of royal inscriptions boasting of conquests. Maya kings fought to capture and torture one another; an unfortunate loser was a Copán king with the to us unforgettable name of King 18 Rabbit.

Maya warfare involved well-documented types of violence: wars among separate kingdoms; attempts of cities within a kingdom to secede by revolting against the capital; and civil wars resulting from frequent violent attempts by would-be kings to usurp the throne. All of these events were described or depicted on monuments, because they involved kings and nobles. Not considered worthy of description, but probably even more frequent, were fights between commoners over land, as overpopulation became excessive and land became scarce.

The other phenomenon important to understanding all of these collapses is the repeated occurrence of droughts, as inferred by climatologists from evidence of lake evaporation preserved in lake sediments, and as summarized by Gill in *The Great Maya Droughts*. The rise of Maya civilization may have been facilitated by a rainy period beginning around 250 B.C. until a temporary drought after A.D. 125 was associated with a pre-Classic collapse at some sites. That collapse was followed by the resumption of rainy conditions and the buildup of Classic Maya cities, briefly interrupted by another drought around 600 corresponding to a decline at Tikal and some other sites. Finally, around A.D. 750 there began the worst drought in the past seven thousand years, peaking around the year A.D. 800, and suspiciously associated with the Classic collapse.

The area most affected by the Classic collapse was the southern highlands, probably for the two reasons already mentioned: it was the area with the densest population, and it also had the most severe water problems because it lay too high above the water table for cenotes or wells to provide water. The southern highlands lost more than 99 percent of its population in the course of the Classic collapse. When Cortés and his Spanish army marched in 1524 and 1525 through an area formerly inhabited by millions of Maya, he nearly starved because he encountered so few villagers from whom to acquire corn. The Spaniards passed within only a few miles of the abandoned ruins of the great Classic cities of Tikal and Palenque, but still they heard or saw nothing of them.

We can identify increasingly familiar strands in the Classic Maya collapse. One consisted of population growth outstripping available resources: the dilemma foreseen by Thomas Malthus in 1798. As Webster succinctly puts it in *The Fall of the Ancient Maya*, "Too many farmers grew too many crops on too much of the landscape." While population was increasing, the area of usable farmland paradoxically was decreasing from the effects of deforestation and hillside erosion.

The next strand consisted of increased fighting as more and more people fought over fewer resources. Maya warfare, already endemic, peaked just before the collapse. That is not surprising

when one reflects that at least five million people, most of them
farmers, were crammed into an area smaller than the state of Colo-
rado. That's a high population by the standards of ancient farming
societies, even if it wouldn't strike modern Manhattan dwellers as
crowded.

Bringing matters to a head was a drought that, although not the
first one the Maya had been through, was the most severe. At the
time of previous droughts, there were still uninhabited parts of the
Maya landscape, and people in a drought area or dust bowl could
save themselves by moving to another site. By the time of the Classic collapse, however, there was no useful unoccupied land in the
vicinity on which to begin anew, and the whole population could
not be accommodated in the few areas that continued to have reliable water supplies.

The final strand is political. Why did the kings and nobles not
recognize and solve these problems? A major reason was that their
attention was evidently focused on the short-term concerns of en-
riching themselves, waging wars, erecting monuments, competing
with one another, and extracting enough food from the peasants
to support all those activities. Like most leaders throughout human history, the Maya kings and nobles did not have the leisure to
focus on long-term problems, insofar as they perceived them.

What about those same strands today? The United States is also at
the peak of its power, and it is also suffering from many environmental problems. Most of us have become aware of more crowding
and stress. Most of us living in large American cities are encounter-
ing increased commuting delays, because the number of people
and hence of cars is increasing faster than the number of freeway
lanes. I know plenty of people who in the abstract doubt that the
world has a population problem, but almost all of those same people complain to me about crowding, space issues, and traffic experienced in their personal lives.

Many parts of the United States face locally severe problems
of water restriction (especially Southern California, Arizona, the
Everglades, and, increasingly, the Northeast); forest fires resulting from logging and forest-management practices throughout
the intermontane West; and losses of farmlands to salinization,
drought, and climate change in the northern Great Plains. Many
of us frequently experience problems of air quality, and some of

us also experience problems of water quality and taste. We are losing economically valuable natural resources. We have already lost American chestnut trees, the Grand Banks cod fishery, and the Monterey sardine fishery; we are in the process of losing swordfish and tuna and Chesapeake Bay oysters and elm trees; and we are losing topsoil.

The list goes on: All of us are experiencing personal consequences of our national dependence on imported energy, which affects us not only through higher gas prices but also through the current contraction of the national economy, itself the partial result of political problems associated with our oil dependence. We are saddled with expensive toxic cleanups at many locations, most notoriously near Montana mines, on the Hudson River, and in the Chesapeake Bay. We also face expensive eradication problems resulting from hundreds of introduced pest species — including zebra mussels, Mediterranean fruit flies, Asian longhorn beetles, water hyacinth, and spotted knapweed — that now affect our agriculture, forests, waterways, and pastures.

These particular environmental problems, and many others, are enormously expensive in terms of resources lost, cleanup and restoration costs, and the cost of finding substitutes for lost resources: a billion dollars here, ten billion there, in dozens and dozens of cases. Some of the problems, especially those of air quality and toxic substances, also exact health costs that are large, whether measured in dollars or in lost years or in quality of life. The cost of our homegrown environmental problems adds up to a large fraction of our gross national product, even without mentioning the costs that we incur from environmental problems overseas, such as the military operations that they inspire. Even the mildest of bad scenarios for our future includes a gradual economic decline, as happened to the Roman and British empires. Actually, in case you didn't notice it, our economic decline is already well under way. Just check the numbers for our national debt, yearly government budget deficit, unemployment statistics, and the value of your investment and pensions funds.

The environmental problems of the United States are still modest compared with those of the rest of the world. But the problems of environmentally devastated, overpopulated, distant countries are now our problems as well. We are accustomed to thinking of globalization in terms of us rich, advanced First Worlders sending our good things, such as the Internet and Coca-Cola, to those poor backward Third Worlders. Globalization, however, means nothing more than improved worldwide communication and transportation, which can convey many things in either direction; it is not restricted to good things carried only from the First to the Third World. They in the Third World can now, intentionally or unintentionally, send us their bad things: terrorists; diseases such as AIDS, SARS, cholera, and West Nile fever, carried inadvertently by passengers on transcontinental airplanes; unstoppable numbers of immigrants, both legal and illegal, arriving by boat, truck, train, plane, and on foot; and other consequences of their Third World problems. We in the United States are no longer the isolated Fortress America to which some of us aspired in the 1930s; instead, we are tightly and irreversibly connected to overseas countries. The United States is the world's leading importer, and it is also the world's leading exporter. Our own society opted long ago to become interlocked with the rest of the world.

That's why political stability anywhere in the world now affects us, our trade routes, and our overseas markets and suppliers. We are so dependent on the rest of the world that if a decade ago you had asked a politician to name the countries most geopolitically irrelevant to U.S. interests because of their being so remote, poor, and weak, the list would have begun with Afghanistan and Somalia, yet these countries were subsequently considered important enough to warrant our dispatching U.S. troops. The Maya were "globalized" only within the Yucatán: the southern Yucatán Maya affected the northern Yucatán Maya and may have had some effects on the Valley of Mexico, but they had no contact with Somalia. That's because Maya transportation was slow, short-distance, on foot or else in canoes, and had low cargo capacity. Our transport today is much more rapid and has much higher cargo capacity. The Maya lived in a globalized Yucatán; we live in a globalized world.

If all of this reasoning seems straightforward when expressed so bluntly, one has to wonder: Why don't those in power today get the message? Why didn't the leaders of the Maya, Anasazi, and those other societies also recognize and solve their problems? What were the Maya thinking while they watched loggers clearing the last pine forests on the hills above Copán? Here, the past really is a useful guide to the present. It turns out that there are at least a dozen reasons why past societies failed to anticipate some problems before they developed, or failed to perceive problems that had already developed, or failed even to try to solve problems that they did perceive. All of those dozen reasons still can be seen operating today. Let me mention just three of them.

First, it's difficult to recognize a slow trend in some quantity that fluctuates widely up and down anyway, such as seasonal temperature, annual rainfall, or economic indicators. That's surely why the Maya didn't recognize the oncoming drought until it was too late, given that rainfall in the Yucatán varies several-fold from year to year. Natural fluctuations also explain why it's only within the last few years that all climatologists have become convinced of the reality of climate change, and why our president still isn't convinced but thinks that we need more research to test for it.

Second, when a problem is recognized, those in power may not attempt to solve it because of a clash between their short-term interests and the interests of the rest of us. Pumping that oil, cutting down those trees, and catching those fish may benefit the elite by bringing them money or prestige and yet be bad for society as a whole (including the children of the elite) in the long run. Maya kings were consumed by immediate concerns for their prestige (requiring more and bigger temples) and their success in the next war (requiring more followers), rather than for the happiness of commoners or of the next generation. Those people with the greatest power to make decisions in our own society today regularly make money from activities that may be bad for society as a whole and for their own children; those decision-makers include Enron executives, many land developers, and advocates of tax cuts for the rich.

Finally, it's difficult for us to acknowledge the wisdom of policies that clash with strongly held values. For example, a belief in individual freedom and a distrust of big government are deeply ingrained in Americans, and they make sense under some circumstances and up to a certain point. But they also make it hard for us to accept big government's legitimate role in ensuring that each individual's freedom to maximize the value of his or her land holdings doesn't decrease the value of the collective land of all Americans.

Not all societies make fatal mistakes. There are parts of the world where societies have unfolded for thousands of years without any collapse, such as Java, Tonga, and (until 1945) Japan. Today, Germany and Japan are successfully managing their forests, which are even expanding in area rather than shrinking. The Alaskan salmon fishery and the Australian lobster fishery are being managed sustainably. The Dominican Republic, hardly a rich country, nevertheless has set aside a comprehensive system of protected areas encompassing most of the country's natural habitats.

Is there any secret to explain why some societies acquire good environmental sense while others don't? Naturally, part of the answer depends on accidents of individual leaders' wisdom (or lack thereof). But part also depends on whether a society is organized so as to minimize built-in clashes of interest between its decision-making elites and its masses. Given how our society is organized, the executives of Enron, Tyco, and Adelphia correctly calculated that their own interests would be best promoted by looting the company coffers, and that they would probably get away with most of their loot. A good example of a society that minimizes such clashes of interest is the Netherlands, whose citizens have perhaps the world's highest level of environmental awareness and of membership in environmental organizations. I never understood why, until on a recent trip to the Netherlands I posed the question to three of my Dutch friends while driving through their countryside.

Just look around you, they said. All of this farmland that you see lies below sea level. One fifth of the total area of the Netherlands is below sea level, as much as twenty-two feet below, because it used to be shallow bays, and we reclaimed it from the sea by surrounding the bays with dikes and then gradually pumping out the water. We call these reclaimed lands "polders." We began draining our polders nearly a thousand years ago. Today, we still have to keep pumping out the water that gradually seeps in. That's what our windmills used to be for, to drive the pumps to pump out the polders. Now we use steam, diesel, and electric pumps instead. In each polder there are lines of them, starting with those farthest from the sea, pumping the water in sequence until the last pump finally deposits it into a river or the ocean. And all of us, rich or poor, live down in the polders. It's not the case that rich people live safely up on top of the dikes while poor people live in the polder bottoms below sea level. If the dikes and pumps fail, we'll all drown together.

Throughout human history, all peoples have been connected to some other peoples, living together in virtual polders. For the ancient Maya, their polder consisted of most of the Yucatán and neighboring areas. When the Classic Maya cities collapsed in the southern Yucatán, refugees may have reached the northern Yucatán, but probably not the Valley of Mexico, and certainly not Florida. Today, our whole world has become one polder, such that events in even Afghanistan and Somalia affect Americans. We do indeed differ from the Maya, but not in ways we might like: we have a much larger population, we have more potent destructive technology, and we face the risk of a worldwide rather than a local decline. Fortunately, we also differ from the Maya in that we know their fate, and they did not. Perhaps we can learn.

ANNE FADIMAN

The Arctic Hedonist

FROM THE AMERICAN SCHOLAR

MY FATHER WAS AN INSOMNIAC. He used to while away the small hours of the night with mental games, of which his favorite was called I Shook Hands with Shakespeare. He had shaken hands with the actress Cornelia Otis Skinner, who had in turn presumably shaken hands with her father, Otis Skinner. He had shaken hands with Edwin Booth . . . and so on, down through Junius Brutus Booth, Edmund Kean, David Garrick, Thomas Betterton, Sir William D'Avenant, and Richard Burbage. Finally, as dawn crept through the blinds, William Shakespeare extended his hand. (My father admitted a shaky manual link between Kean, who was born in 1787, and Garrick, who died in 1779.)

I myself have shaken hands with the arctic explorer Vilhjalmur Stefansson. Our degrees of separation number only two. Aware of my febrile interest in the history of polar exploration, my father once mentioned that, many years earlier, he had been introduced to Stefansson.

"*Stefansson?*" I panted. "What was he like?"

"The only thing I recall," said my father, "is his unfortunate smell."

I didn't hold this against Stefansson; it was part and parcel of being an explorer. (One of his expeditionary companions once noted that "he considers any attention to cleanliness, hygiene and camp sanitation as 'military fads.'") In any case, through Stefansson (or, in some cases, through people *he* met), I have also clasped hands with Robert E. Peary, Matthew Henson, Fridtjof Nansen, Roald Amundsen, Robert Falcon Scott, and Ernest Shackleton —

the men who dominated the great period of arctic and antarctic exploration between 1880 and the First World War. I have spent many nights establishing these bonds (*Let's see . . . Stefansson must have met Amundsen in 1906, when they were both at Herschel Island; Amundsen visited Nansen in Norway in 1900 — or was it 1899?*), and, like my father, discovered that the handshaking game is far better at keeping one awake all night than at putting one to sleep.

The closest hand was the best; it still felt warm. For more than twenty years, I have therefore considered Vilhjalmur Stefansson "my explorer." During the course of three expeditions between 1906 and 1918, my explorer was the first white man to visit the Copper Inuit of Victoria Island; traveled twenty thousand miles by dogsled; discovered the world's last major landmasses, a series of islands in the Canadian archipelago; and set what a colleague called "the world's record for continuous Polar service" (five and a half years, an interval Stefansson considered nothing to boast about, since many of his Inuit friends had lived in the Arctic without apparent difficulty for more than eight decades).

What most endeared Stefansson to me was his conviction that the far north was not meant to be endured; it was meant to be enjoyed. If you knew what you were doing, you could have a "bully time" up there. His favorite temperature was −40°. (Temperatures below −50° were manageable but not quite so bully, since they required you to breathe through your mouth. "Your nose," he observed, "is less likely to freeze when there is cold air merely outside of it instead of both inside and out.") When he was above 66° north latitude, he insisted that his spirits were jollier, his appetite keener, and his wavy brown hair thicker. His most famous book, a 784-page account of his third expedition, was called *The Friendly Arctic.*

The Friendly Arctic? In 1921, when it was published, Macmillan might as well have brought out a book called *The Friendly Pit Viper.* The previous century had seen a series of arctic catastrophes, from Sir John Franklin's 1845 expedition in search of the Northwest Passage (130 dead of scurvy, starvation, and lead poisoning), to George Washington De Long's 1879 attempt to reach the North Pole from Siberia (20 dead of exposure, starvation, and drowning), to Adolphus Greely's 1881 expedition to Ellesmere Island (19 dead of exposure, starvation, and drowning). It was true that in 1909 Robert Peary claimed to have reached the North Pole, but he would have had a more comfortable journey had he not lost eight of his toes to frostbite on an earlier expedition.

The Friendly Arctic was an in-your-face title, and that's why Stefansson chose it. After all, he wrote, everyone knows what the Arctic is like:

> The land up there is all covered with eternal ice; there is everlasting winter with intense cold; and the corollary of the everlastingness of the winter is the absence of summer and the lack of vegetation. The country, whether land or sea, is a lifeless waste of eternal silence. The stars look down with a cruel glitter, and the depressing effect of the winter darkness upon the spirit of man is heavy beyond words. On the fringes of this desolation live the Eskimos, the filthiest and most benighted people on earth, pushed there by more powerful nations farther south, and eking out a miserable existence amidst hardship.

Wrong, wrong, wrong, wrong. Eternally icy? Montana, Stefansson explained, in the tone a parent might use to drum something obvious into an unusually dimwitted child, is far colder; arctic summers are hot; there are 762 species of arctic flowering plants. Silent? In the summer, the tundra resounds with the squawks of ducks, the cackles of geese, the cries of plovers, the screams of loons, and the howls of wolves (which, when heard on starlit nights, constitute "the most romantic sort of music"). Once the ice starts to freeze against the coast,

> there is a high-pitched screeching as one cake slides over the other, like the thousand-times magnified creaking of a rusty hinge. There is the crashing when cakes as big as a church wall, after being tilted on edge, finally pass beyond their equilibrium and topple down upon the ice; and when extensive floes, perhaps six or more feet in thickness, gradually bend under the resistless pressure of the pack until they buckle up and snap, there is a groaning as of supergiants in torment and a booming which at a distance of a mile or two sounds like a cannonade.

Depressing? According to Stefansson, "an Eskimo laughs as much in a month as the average white man does in a year." A benighted people? The Inuit are honest, considerate, courteous, hospitable, fun-loving, self-sufficient, and morally superior to any but the "rarest and best of our race."

In other words, the Arctic was not (as Peary had described it, using the sort of language to which readers had become accustomed) "a trackless, colorless, inhospitable desert"; it was a high-latitude Arcadia. Precipitation was light; gale-force winds were rare; water was abundant, even at sea, since salt leaches out of ice floes within a few seasons, rendering them deliciously fresh. Illness was infrequent; tuberculosis was seldom transmitted during the winter because "the spit is likely to freeze when it is voided." And the region flowed, if not with milk and honey, then with caribou, polar bear, walrus, and seals, all there for the taking (even if shooting seals beneath the polar ice "resembles hunting as we commonly think of it less than it does prospecting"). Why burden your sledges with heavy provisions, thereby limiting an expedition's duration and range, when, if you merely did what the Inuit had been doing for centuries, you could live off the land? "Do not let worry over to-morrow's breakfast interfere with your appetite at dinner," Stefansson liked to tell his men. "The friendly Arctic will provide."

If the Arctic was so friendly, it followed that you didn't need to be a masochist in order to explore it. Stefansson had nothing but contempt for "heroes who conquered the Frozen North," since he considered the Frozen North a myth and the metaphor of battle entirely wrongheaded (friends don't fight). He believed that this sort of bunkum had been invented to satisfy readers who, from the vantage of their overstuffed armchairs, found narratives of ease and pleasure less thrilling than hyperbolic accounts of "suffering, heroic perseverance against formidable odds, and tragedy either actual or narrowly averted." Stefansson's stance — partly a pose, but only partly — was that being an arctic explorer was no harder than any other job. He wrote to a friend that the prospect of returning to the far north was as pleasant as, and not much different from, the prospect of spending a winter in Heidelberg. Finding your way to a remote Inuit camp was "no more wonderful than knowing that a fifteen-minute walk will take you to the Flatiron Building from the Washington Arch." Why pretend you were bristling with machismo when living in the Arctic was a piece of cake?

*

I recognized the Stefansson shtick just last week when I was reading a German fairy tale to my seven-year-old son. Its plot revolved around a king who assigns progressively more impossible tasks to a cocksure young man — stealing a dragon's flying horse, stealing the dragon's coverlet, and finally stealing the dragon himself. The penalty for failure is death by dismemberment. Every time the king ups the ante, our hero says, "Is that all? That is easily done." In fairy tales, such characters are never punished for their bravado; they always perform their assigned tasks without breaking a sweat and end up marrying the king's daughter. In this case, the young man not only follows the prescribed formula for success but has the pleasure of seeing the dragon eat the king for dinner.

The voice of that young man is the same voice Tom Wolfe had so much fun with in *The Right Stuff*, that of the airline pilot who, as his plane seems about to crash, drawls into the intercom:

> "Now, folks, uh . . . this is the captain . . . ummmm . . . We've got a little ol' red light up here on the control panel that's tryin' to tell us that the *land*in' gears're not . . . uh . . . *lock*in' into position when we lower 'em . . . Now . . . I don't believe that little ol' red light knows what it's *talk*in' about — I believe it's that little ol' red *light* that iddn' workin' right" . . . faint chuckle, long pause, as if to say, *I'm not even sure all this is really worth going into — still, it may amuse you* . . . "But . . . I guess to play it by the rules, we oughta *hum*or that little ol' light . . ."

You know this pilot will never have an elevated pulse, never admit there's an emergency, and never crash the plane.

I first encountered this attitude of studied insouciance thirty years ago, when I took a wilderness course at the National Outdoor Leadership School in Wyoming, during an era of outdoorsman-ship considerably more primitive than the present one. Our catch-phrase was "No prob." Five weeks without tents or stoves? No prob. We slept under tarps suspended from trees and lit fires twice a day, forearming ourselves for rainy days by squirreling little bundles of dry sticks in our pockets — our six-foot-four-inch leader tenderly called them "twiggies," to underline how very cozy and unintimi-dating the whole venture was — just as Stefansson squirreled handfuls of dry *Cassiope tetragona* (arctic heather) in *his* pockets. No fancy freeze-dried food? No prob. We baked bread, pizzas, even birthday cakes by heaping hot coals on our frying pan lids, and cleaned the burnt pans with swags of limber pine, which we called Wind River Brillo. No food at all during the five-day "survival expedition" at the end of the course? No prob. We fished for trout and foraged for grouse whortleberries. Those five days were the hungriest of my life, but I wouldn't have dreamed of admitting it. (Stefansson: "Any traveler who complains about going three or four days without food will get scant sympathy from me.") That dragon was *easy* to steal.

A few years later, when I became an instructor at NOLS, the ratio of bluster to genuine *joie de vivre* declined precipitously. We poohpoohed Outward Bound, our competitor in the wilderness-skills field, as unnecessarily anhedonic. OB promised to build character by asking its disciples to face fear and hardship; NOLS asked, as Stefansson had, "What hardship?" One winter we took out a group of mountaineering students for a couple of weeks to climb Wind River Peak on skis. It was ten below zero, but we built both a small igloo and a gigantic snow cave, in whose toasty precincts we threw off most of our clothes and stretched as luxuriously as cats next to a radiator. At night, when we schussed the snowfields above Deep Creek Lakes, the hoarfrost reflected the full moon, and it was almost as bright as day.

This was small stuff, and very long ago. But, years later, it was enough to make me understand what Stefansson meant when he described hunting caribou on Banks Island on a cold, clear day: "In his exuberance of good health it is difficult for the arctic hunter to feel anything but pleasure in almost any kind of weather or almost any circumstance. I suppose what I am trying to explain is about what the Biblical writer had in mind when he spoke of a strong man rejoicing to run a race."

Stefansson had just the sort of upbringing you'd expect: pioneer-style, in a one-room cabin in the Dakota Territory, with scant food but plenty of Norse sagas recited in the evening by his Icelandic parents, who had emigrated first to Manitoba and then to the United States. When he was eighteen, he set himself up as a winter grazier, caring for the livestock of local farmers. The great blizzard of 1897 hit during his first season, and all his assistants quit, unwilling to work on skis or shovel their way into barns buried in snowdrifts. No prob. Stefansson carried on alone and, of course (because the young man in the fairy tale never labors in vain), didn't lose a single head of cattle.

At the University of North Dakota, Stefansson was thrown out of his boardinghouse for espousing Darwinism and then expelled from college for spotty attendance and "a spirit of insubordination." (His fellow students staged a mock funeral; his hearse was a wheelbarrow, his widow a black-clad classmate whose tears were facilitated by an onion wrapped in a handkerchief.) No prob. After finishing up at the University of Iowa and attending graduate school at Harvard, where he switched his field from divinity to anthropology, he was offered the post of ethnologist on the 1906 Anglo-American Polar Expedition to northwest Canada. He and his expedition never ended up intersecting, since he traveled overland to the Mackenzie Delta — solo, of course — and the ship that carried his colleagues failed to penetrate the ice beyond Point Barrow, two hundred miles to the west. No prob. He spent the winter living with the Inuit, collecting ethnographic artifacts, learning Inuktitut, and formulating his belief that the only way to get along in the Arctic was to dress and hunt and eat like a local. "I was gradually being broken in to native ways," he wrote.

> By the middle of October, I had thrown away my nearly outworn woollen suit and was fur clad from head to heel, an Eskimo to the skin. I never regretted the lack of a single item of such arctic clothing as money can buy in America or Europe . . . A reasonably healthy body is all the equipment a white man needs for a comfortable winter among the arctic Eskimos.

Two more expeditions followed, one primarily ethnographic, the other geographic and scientific. By the end of his tenth arctic winter, Stefansson was the uncontested master of what he called "polarcraft," a body of knowledge he later codified in a volume called the *Arctic Manual*. Although it was commissioned by the U.S. Army as a survival guide for Air Corps fliers who made emergency landings in the far north, its author couldn't resist transforming it into a how-to book on what *he* liked to do — live off the land, with minimal provisions, for years at a time. (For instance, a downed flier would be unlikely to make use of his suggestion that the best caribou-skin clothes are made by Inuit seamstresses with whom one has been acquainted for several seasons.)

The *Arctic Manual* is my favorite Stefansson book. The chances that I will ever need to apply its lessons may be slim. But just as devotees of Martha Stewart feel more secure knowing they could make a wedding centerpiece from belt buckles and gumdrops, even if they never actually have to, so I derive a certain degree of comfort from reading and rereading Stefansson's arctic tips. It reassures me to know that pussy willow fuzz can be used for the wick of a seal-oil lamp. That two lemon-sized chunks of iron pyrite, struck together, will start a fire faster than matches. That it is possible to cook with the hair and wool of a musk ox or grizzly bear, one hide being sufficient for two or three eight-quart pots. That if you are not ashore during the spring thaw, you should select a thick floe on which to spend the summer, and resume your travel in the fall. That a dead seal can be easily dragged, but a polar bear tends to flip upside down. That you should not rub decayed caribou brains on your clothes, since the hides will stiffen. That one advantage of skin boats is that they can be boiled and eaten. That the best way to approach a seal you wish to shoot is to look like a seal yourself: wear dark clothing, wriggle along the ice, and occasionally flex your legs from the knees as if scratching lice with your hind flippers.

It is important to understand that these pieces of advice are offered in a spirit not of grit-teethed stoicism — *I may be facing death, but, by God, at least I know enough not to rub decayed caribou brains on my clothes* — but of casual bonhomie, as if the author and the reader were in perfect agreement that this stuff is *fun*. Stefansson wasn't a survivor; he was a voluptuary. Why would anyone wish to wear wool when "nothing feels so good against the skin — not even silk — as underwear of the skin of a young caribou"? Why live in a house when an igloo, lit with a single candle, resembles "a hemisphere of diamonds"? Why employ Inuit or Indians to do one's hunting when one could have the thrill of doing it oneself? "I would as soon think of engaging a valet to play my golf," he observed, "or of going to the theatre by proxy."

Stefansson admitted that his hunting had not always been fruitful. In lean times he had eaten snowshoe lashings, sealskins intended for boot soles, and the remains of a bowhead whale that had been beached for four years. (It tasted like felt.) But when the Arctic chose to show its friendly aspect, its cuisine practically made him swoon. Frozen raw polar bear meat had the consistency of raw oysters; half frozen, it was more like ice cream. The soft, sweet ends of mammal, bird, and fish bones were scrumptious. Seal-blood soup, an especial favorite, warranted a recipe that might have intrigued Brillat-Savarin:

> When the meat has been sufficiently cooked it is removed from the pot which is still hanging over the fire. Blood is then poured slowly into the boiling broth with brisk stirring the while. In winter small chunks of frozen blood dropped in one after the other take the place of the liquid blood poured in summer . . . The consistency of the prepared dish should be about that of "English pea soup."

The pinnacle of northern fare was caribou flesh: in ascending order of "gustatory delight," the brisket, ribs, and vertebrae; the tongue; the head, especially the fat behind the eyes; the little lump of fat near the patella of the hind leg; and the marrow of the bones near the hoof, which was generally rolled into little balls and eaten raw. Stefansson maintained that a high-fat, all-meat diet not only pleased the palate but also cured depression, prevented scurvy, reduced tooth decay, and relieved constipation. (When he was in his late forties and living in New York City, he undertook to prove his nutritional theories by spending a year, under the supervision of Bellevue Hospital, on an exclusively carnivorous diet. Not only did he remain healthy, but he was proud to report that x-rays revealed an "unusual . . . absence of gas from the intestinal tract during the meat-eating period.")

Given the abundance of northern pleasures, it is not surprising that Stefansson envisioned a time when the Arctic would be viewed not as the end of the earth but as a vital crossroads. Musk oxen and reindeer would be domesticated for world consumption, "not for the exclusive delectation of wolves, wolverines, foxes and ravens." The skies would be filled with airplanes traveling the shortest routes between New York, London, Moscow, and Peking; the seas would be filled with submarines. In his book *The Northward Course of Empire,* he reproduced a graph conceived by an American sociologist named S. Columb GilFillan. The horizontal axis was chronological, from 3400 B.C. to 2200 A.D.; the vertical axis was meteorological. The great world centers were arrayed along this graph, with Upper Egypt (mean annual temperature 77°) succeeded by

Athens (63°), Rome (59°), Constantinople (57°), London (50°), and Moscow (39°), among others. The implication was clear: in a few hundred years the Arctic would be the nexus of civilization.

My Stefansson shelf grew over the years, augmented by birthday contributions from my husband. The books, all out of print, were beautiful old volumes with tissue-thin maps tucked in pockets at the back. They were all *by* Stefansson. It was only when I started work on this essay that I bought a half-dozen books *about* Stefansson. And that is where the probs began.

I learned that not everyone liked my explorer as much as I did. After Stefansson visited Australia on a lecture tour in 1925, a *Sydney Bulletin* reporter observed delicately that "our late visitor . . . is a many sided man. I would call him nothing less than an Hexagon, and he may even be an irregular crystal." Controversial during his lifetime (his peers thought him a publicity hound, his bosses thought him a troublesome maverick), Stefansson has attracted a new round of criticism in recent years — the same period of polar revisionism during which Peary was accused of fraud and Scott was exposed as a dangerous bumbler. The two most serious charges are that Stefansson abandoned his Inuit family and that he was responsible for the deaths of eleven men on his third expedition.

For two decades I had read Stefansson's laconic references to Fannie Pannigabluk, the widowed seamstress who accompanied him and his friend Natkusiak on much of his second expedition. It had never occurred to me that she was Stefansson's mistress; after all, he noted several times that every expedition required an Inuit seamstress to make and repair caribou-hide and sealskin clothing. Gísli Pálsson, an Icelandic anthropologist who has interviewed four of Stefansson's Inuit grandchildren, writes, "Pannigabluk was presented as primarily a domestic worker, with no formal recognition of her role as either spouse, partner, or key informant." Stefansson never publicly acknowledged either the relationship or the son it produced; nor, apparently, did he provide financial support. It is true that Robert Peary and Matthew Henson also had sons by Inuit women, and that both of them jettisoned their families in similar fashion. Peary went a step further and published a nude photograph of his mistress. But *Stefansson?* The man who wrote of the Inuit, "I cannot see how anyone who knows them can wish more for anything than that he was rich and could repay their kindness fully"?

The accusations that swirl around Stefansson's third expedition allege an even more serious abandonment. In July of 1913, the HMCS *Karluk* steamed out of Port Clarence, Alaska, en route to the Beaufort Sea, with Stefansson and half the members of the Canadian Arctic Expedition on board. (The rest were on two other ships, bound for scientific work in the Northwest Territories.) By mid-August, the *Karluk* was icebound. In mid-September, Stefansson, accompanied by three staff members and two Inuit, left the ship on a ten-day trip, ostensibly to provide fresh caribou for his men. Two days later, the sixty-mile-an-hour winds of the season's first blizzard dislodged the *Karluk*'s ice floe, and the ship drifted hundreds of miles to the west, far out of Stefansson's reach. The *Karluk* was eventually crushed in the ice, and most of its men made their way to Wrangel Island, north of Siberia. They suffered severe hardships there — starvation, snow blindness, frostbite, gangrene, and, in one case, the amputation of a toe with the tin shears used to make cooking pots from empty gasoline containers. Eleven died. Many years later, one of the survivors wrote: "Not all the horrors of the Western Front, not the rubble of Arras, nor the hell of Ypres, nor all the mud of Flanders leading to Passchendaele, could blot out the memories of that year in the Arctic."

It is indisputable that Stefansson left the ship; the question is whether he intended to return. In *The Ice Master: The Doomed 1913 Voyage of the* Karluk, Jennifer Niven argues that he did not: caribou were scarce in the area; he left his best hunters on board the *Karluk;* and — the most damning evidence — the ship's meteorologist believed that Stefansson, who had been observed reading the diaries from De Long's catastrophic 1879 expedition two days before he departed, left the ship "for fear of losing his life."

The Canadian historian Richard J. Diubaldo disagrees; in his scrupulously fair-minded biography *Stefansson and the Canadian Arctic,* he argues that "there is strong evidence to suggest that he wished he had never left." I share his view. If Stefansson had no intention of returning, why did he leave his chronometer and $1,300 on board? Why did he leave detailed instructions on the flags and beacons that were to guide his return over the ice? Why didn't he take the best sledges? After the blizzard, why did he hasten west along the coast to Cape Smythe, if not to overtake the *Karluk?*

I think Stefansson took off for a week because he couldn't bear to be on board a ship that wasn't moving, couldn't bear to sit around playing bridge or listening to his men give concerts on the mandolin and harmonica. Stasis was poison to him. But whether or not he abandoned ship, I am now convinced that he is responsible for the deaths of his men. He assembled the expedition hastily, recruiting an inexperienced crew that included a drug addict who carried his hypodermic needles around in a pocket-sized case. He insisted on using a ship that had been declared unsound by his captain. And though he was one of the greatest solo operators in history, he was a terrible leader. He had no idea how to organize large groups of men or large amounts of cargo, and he had so little regard for his staff and crew that, instead of welcoming them as soon as he arrived at the naval yard from which the *Karluk* would soon embark, he kept them waiting while he held a five-hour press conference.

Worst of all was his cavalier attitude toward the men he lost. His journal entry from August 11, 1915, when he heard the news, disposes of their fate in two sentences and then goes on to discuss possible ship charters. He blamed his men for being less competent than he would have been in their situation — in effect, for being so foolish as to succumb to the myth of the Frozen North. Did he fail to realize that *The Friendly Arctic* might not be the most tasteful title for a book about a botched venture on which eleven people died?

The frontispiece of *The Friendly Arctic* is a black-and-white photograph of Stefansson dragging a seal across the ice. He is wearing mukluks and a caribou-skin parka. Under his right arm he carries a rifle; under his left, a harpoon. His head is bare, and he is alone.

He selected the picture while he was living at the Harvard Club in New York City, beginning a feverish career of lecturing and writing that made him, in the words of one biographer, "the equivalent of a senior officer who has become too valuable to go out on combat patrols, and must sit at his headquarters surrounded by his staff." He shelved his plans to camp on an ice floe with one or two companions, moving with the polar drift for a couple of years. In-

stead, from his desk, he organized abortive schemes to colonize
Wrangel Island and breed reindeer on Baffin Island. He lived for
forty-four years after he returned from his third expedition, and —
because of illness, because his reputation in Canada declined, because he had kicked himself permanently upstairs — he never traveled in the Arctic again.

It is not as great a tragedy as the abandonment of one's family,
not as great as the loss of eleven lives, but it is nonetheless a tragedy that when *The Friendly Arctic* appeared, the Macmillan Company could not include the same note it had inserted before the title page of *My Life with the Eskimo* in 1913:

NOTE TO THE FIRST EDITION

The publishers regret that owing to Mr. Stefansson's departure on his
new expedition to the far North he was unable to read the final
proofs of this volume.

Caught

FROM THE NEW YORKER

KORTENHOF HAD HEARD of a high school where pranksters had put an automobile tire over the top of a thirty-foot flagpole, like a ring on a finger, and this seemed to him an impressive and elegant and beautiful feat that we at our high school ought to try to duplicate. Kortenhof was the son of a lawyer, and he had a lawyerly directness and a perpetual crocodile smile that made him fun company, if a little scary. Every day at lunch hour, he led us outside to gaze at the flagpole and to hear his latest thoughts about accessorizing it with steel-belted radial tires. (Steel-belted radials, he said, would be harder for administrators to remove.) Eventually we all agreed that this was an exciting technical challenge worthy of a heavy investment of our time and energy.

The flagpole, which was forty feet tall, stood on an apron of concrete near the high school's main entrance, on Selma Avenue. It was too thick at the base to be shinned up easily, and a fall from the top could be fatal. None of us had access to an extension ladder longer than twenty feet. We talked about building some sort of catapult, how spectacular a catapult would be, but airborne car tires were sure to do serious damage if they missed their mark, and cops patrolled Selma too frequently for us to risk getting caught with heavy equipment, assuming we could ever build it.

The school itself could be a ladder, though. The roof was only six feet lower than the ball at the flagpole's crown, and we knew how to get to the roof. My friend Davis and I volunteered to build a Device, consisting of ropes and a pulley and a long board, that would convey a tire from the roof to the pole and drop it over. If the Device didn't work, we could try lassoing the pole with a rope, standing on a stepladder for added elevation, and sliding a tire down the rope. If this failed as well, it still might be possible, with a lot of luck, to gang-Frisbee a tire up and out and over.

Six of us — Kortenhof, Davis, Manley, Schroer, Peppel, and me — met up near the high school on a Friday night in March. Davis came with a stepladder on top of his parents' Pinto station wagon. There had been some trouble at home when his father saw the ladder, but Davis, who was smarter and less kindhearted than his parent, had explained that the ladder belonged to Manley.

"Yes, but what are you doing with it?"

"Dad, it's Ben's ladder."

"I know, but what are you doing with it?"

"I just said! It's Ben's ladder!"

"Christopher, I heard you the first time. I want to know what you're doing with it."

"God! Dad! It's *Ben's ladder.* How many times do I have to tell you? It's *Ben's ladder!*"

To get to the main roof, you climbed a long, sturdy downspout near the music rooms, crossed a plain of tar and caramel-brown St. Louis gravel, and climbed a metal staircase and a sheer eight-foot wall. Unless you were me, you also had to stop and drag me up the eight-foot wall. The growth spurt I'd had the year before had made me taller and heavier and clumsier while leaving unaltered my pitiful arm and shoulder strength.

I was probably nobody's idea of an ideal fellow gang member, but I came with Manley and Davis, my best friends, who were good athletes and avid climbers of public buildings. In junior high, Manley had broken the school record for pull-ups, doing twenty-three of them. As for Davis, he'd been a football halfback and a starting basketball forward and was unbelievably tough. Once, on a January campout in a deserted Missouri state park, on a morning so cold we split frozen grapefruits with a hatchet and fried them over an open fire (we were in a phase of cook-it-yourself fruitarianism), we found an old car hood with a tow rope attached to it, irresistible, irresistible. We tied the rope to our friend Lunte's Travelall, and Lunte drove at ill-considered speeds along the unplowed park roads, towing Davis while I kept watch from the back seat. We were doing about forty when the road plunged unexpectedly down a hill. Lunte had to brake hard and steer into a skid to avoid rolling the Travelall, which cracked the tow rope like a whip and flung Davis at a sick-making velocity toward a line of heavy-duty picnic tables stacked up in falling-domino formation. It was the kind of collision that killed people. There was a sunlit explosion of sparkling powder and shattered lumber, and through the rear window, as the snow settled and Lunte slowed the vehicle, I saw Davis come trotting after us, limping a little and clutching a jagged shard of picnic table. He was shouting, he said later, "I'm alive! I'm alive!" He'd demolished one of the frozen tables — knocked it into a hundred pieces — with his ankle.

Also dragged to the roof, along with me, were the stepladder, lots of rope, two bald steel-belted radials, and the Device that Davis and I had built. Leaning out over the balustrade, we could sort of almost *touch* the flagpole. The object of our fixation wasn't more than twelve feet away from us, but its skin of aluminum paint matched the cloudy bright suburban sky behind it, and it was curiously hard to see. The six of us stood there wishing we could touch it, groaning and exclaiming with desire to touch it.

Although Davis was a better mechanic, I was more facile than he at arguing for doing things my way. As a result, little we built ever worked. Certainly our Device, as soon became apparent, had no chance. At the end of the board was a crude wooden bracket that could never have gripped the flagpole, especially under the added weight of a tire; there was also the more fundamental difficulty of leaning out over a balustrade and pulling hard on a heavy board to control it while also trying to push it against a flagpole that, when it was bumped, clanged and swung distressingly. We were lucky not to send the Device through a window on one of the floors below us. The group verdict was swift and harsh: *piece of shit.*

I laughed and said it, too: *piece of shit.* But I went off to one side, my throat thick with disappointment, and stood alone while everybody else tried the lasso. Peppel was swinging his hips like a rodeo man.

"Yee haw!"

"John-Boy, gimme that lasso."

"Yee haw!"

Over the balustrade I could see the dark trees of Webster Groves and the more distant TV-tower lights that marked the boundaries of my childhood. A night wind coming across the football practice field carried the smell of thawed winter earth, the great sorrowful world-smell of being alive beneath a sky. In my imagination, as in the pencil drawings I'd made, I'd seen the Device work brilliantly. The contrast between the brightness of my dreams and the utter botch of my executions, the despair into which this contrast plunged me, was a recipe for self-consciousness. I felt identified with the disgraced Device. I was tired and cold and I wanted to go home.

I'd grown up amid tools, with a father who could build anything, and I thought I could do anything myself. How difficult could it be to drill a straight hole through a piece of wood? I would bear down with the utmost concentration, and the drill bit would emerge in a totally wrong place on the underside of the wood, and I would be shocked. Always. Shocked. In tenth grade, I set out to build from scratch a refracting telescope with an equatorial mount and tripod, and my father, seeing the kind of work I was doing, took pity on me and built the entire thing himself. He cut threads in iron pipe for the mounting, poured concrete in a coffee can for the counterweight, hacksawed an old carbon-steel bedframe for the base of the tripod, and made a gorgeous lens mount out of galvanized sheet metal, machine screws, and pieces of a plastic ice cream carton. The only part of the telescope I built on my own was the eyepiece holder, which was the only part that didn't work right, which rendered the rest of it practically useless. And so I hated being young.

It was after one o'clock when Peppel finally threw the lasso high and far enough to capture the flagpole. I stopped sulking and joined in the general cheering. But new difficulties emerged right away. Kortenhof climbed the stepladder and tugged the lasso up to within a foot of the ball, but here it snagged on the pulley and flag cables. The only way to propel a tire over the top would be to snap the rope vigorously up and down:

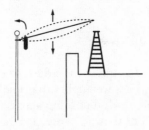

When we strung the tire out on the rope, however, it sagged out of reach of the top:

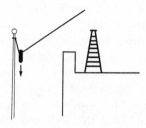

To raise the tire, Kortenhof had to pull hard on the rope, which, if you were standing on a ladder, was a good way to launch yourself over the balustrade. Four of us grabbed the ladder and applied counterforce. But this then wildly stressed the flagpole itself:

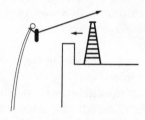

The flagpole, which was of a certain age, made ominous creaking and popping sounds as it leaned toward us. It also threatened, in the manner of a strained fishing rod, to recoil and cast Kortenhof out over Selma Avenue like a piece of bait. We were thwarted yet again. Our delight in seeing a tire rubbing up against the desired ball, nudging to within inches of the wished-for penetration, only heightened our anguish.

Two months earlier, around the time of her fifteenth birthday, my first-ever girlfriend, M —, had dumped me hard. She was a brainy girl with coltish corduroy legs and straight brown hair that reached to the wallet in her back pocket. (Purses, she believed, were girly and anti-feminist.) We'd come together on a church-membership retreat in a country house where I'd unrolled my sleeping bag in a carpeted closet into which M — and her own sleeping bag had then migrated by deliriously slow degrees. In the months that followed, M — had tactlessly corrected my most egregious mannerisms and my most annoying misconceptions about girls, and sometimes she'd let me kiss her. We held hands through the entirety of my first R-rated movie, Lina Wertmüller's *Swept Away,* which two feminist advisers from our church took a group of us to see for somewhat opaque political reasons. ("Sex but not explicit," I noted in my journal.) Then, in January, possibly in reaction to my obsessive tendencies, M — got busy with other friends and began to avoid me. She applied for transfer to a local private academy for the gifted and the well-to-do. Mystified, and badly hurt, I renounced what I called the "stagnation" of romantic attachments.

Although the flagpole situation was hopeless, Kortenhof and Schroer were yanking the rope more violently, causing the pole to lurch and shudder while the worriers among us — Manley and I — told them to stop. Finally, inevitably, somebody lost hold of the rope, and we all went home with a new problem: if the rope was still in place on Monday morning, the administration would guess what we'd been up to.

Returning the next night, Saturday, we smashed the padlock at the base of the pole, released the flag cables, and tried to jostle the rope free by tugging on the cables, with no success. The once stiff rope dangled flaccidly alongside the unconquered administrative mast, its frayed end twisting in the wind, twenty feet off the ground. We came back on Sunday night with a new padlock and took turns trying to shinny up the too thick pole, again with no success. Most of us gave up then — we may have had homework, and Schroer was heavily into *Monty Python,* which aired at eleven — but Manley and Davis returned to the school yet again and managed to release the rope by boosting each other and yanking on the cables. They put our padlock on the flagpole; and now it was our hostage.

Manley's parents were extremely permissive, and Kortenhof's house was big enough to exit and enter inconspicuously, but most of us had trouble getting away from our parents after midnight. One Sunday morning, after two hours of sleep, I came down to breakfast and found my parents ominously untalkative. My father was at the stove frying our weekly pre-church eggs. My mother was frowning with what I now realize was probably more fear than disapproval. There was fear in her voice as well. "Dad says he heard you coming in the front door this morning after it was light," she said. "It must have been six o'clock. Were you out?"

Caught! I'd been Caught!

"Yeah," I said. "Yeah, I was over at the park with Ben and Chris."

"You said you were going to bed early. Your light was off."

"Yeah," I said, looking at the floor. "But I couldn't sleep, and they'd said they'd be over at the park, you know, if I couldn't sleep."

"What on earth were you doing out there so long?"

"Irene," my father warned, from the stove. "Don't ask the question if you can't stand to hear the answer."

"Just talking," I said.

The sensation of being Caught: it was like the buzz I once got from some cans of Reddi-wip whose gas propellant I shared with Manley and Davis — a ballooning, dizzying sensation of being all surface, my inner self suddenly so flagrant and gigantic that it seemed to force the air from my lungs and the blood from my head.

I associate this sensation with the rushing heave of a car engine, the low whoosh of my mother's Buick as it surged with alarming, incredible speed up our driveway and into our garage. It was in the nature of this whoosh that I always heard it earlier than I wanted or expected to. I was Caught privately enjoying myself, usually in the living room, listening to music, and I had to scramble.

Our stereo was housed in a mahogany-stained console of the kind sold nowadays in thrift stores. Its brand name was Aeolian, and its speakers were hidden behind doors that my mother insisted on keeping closed when she played the local all-Muzak station, KCFM, for her dinner guests; orchestral arrangements of "Penny Lane" and "Cherish" fought through cabinetry in a muffled whisper, the ornate pendent door handles buzzing with voices during KCFM's half-hourly commercial announcements. When I was alone in the house, I opened the doors and played my own records, mostly hand-me-downs from my brothers. My two favorite bands in those pre-punk years were the Grateful Dead and the Moody Blues. (My enthusiasm for the latter survived until I read, in a *Rolling Stone* review, that their music was suited to "the kind of person who whispers 'I love you' to a one-night stand.") One afternoon, I was kneeling at the Aeolian altar and playing an especially syrupy Moodies effort at such soul-stirring volume that I failed to hear my mother's automotive whoosh. She burst into the house crying, "Turn that off! That awful rock music! I can't stand it! Turn it off!" Her complaint was unjust; the song, which had no rock beat whatsoever, offered KCFM-ish sentiments like "Isn't life strange? / A turn of the page . . . It makes me want to cry." But I nevertheless felt hugely Caught.

The car I preferred hearing was my father's car, the Cougar he commuted to work in, because it never showed up unexpectedly. My father understood privacy, and he was eager to accept the straight-A self that I presented to him. He was my rational and enlightened ally, the powerful engineer who helped me man the dikes against the ever-invading sea of my mother. And yet, by temperament, he was no less hostile to my adolescence than she was.

My father was plagued by the suspicion that adolescents were *getting away with something:* that their pleasures were insufficiently trammeled by conscience and responsibility. My older brothers had borne the brunt of his resentment, but even with me it would sometimes boil over in pronouncements on my character. He said, "You have demonstrated a taste for expensive things, but not for the work it takes to earn them." He said, "Friends are fine, but all evening every evening is too much." He had a phrase that he couldn't stop repeating whenever he came home from work and found me reading a novel or playing with my friends: "One continuous round of pleasure!"

At church, I knew a poetic girl named Fawn, who lived in a different school district. When I was fifteen, she and I struck up a poetic correspondence, and one Sunday in the summer she came home with us after church and spent the afternoon with me. We walked over to my old elementary school and played in the dirt: made little dirt roads, bark bridges, and twig cottages on the ground beneath a tree. Fawn's friends at her school were doing the ordinary cool things — drinking, experimenting with sex and drugs — that I wasn't. I was scared of Fawn's beauty and her savoir-faire and was relieved to discover that she and I shared romantic views of childhood. We were old enough not to be ashamed of playing like little kids, young enough to still become engrossed in it. By the end of our afternoon, I was about ready to whisper "I love you." I thought it was maybe four o'clock, but when we got back to my house we found Fawn's father waiting in his car. It was six-fifteen, and he'd been waiting for an hour. "Oops," Fawn said.

Inside the house, my dinner was cold on the table. My parents (this was unprecedented) had eaten without me. My mother flickered into sight and said, "Your father has something to say to you before you sit down."

I went to the den, where he had his briefcase open on his lap. Without looking up, he announced, "You are not to see Fawn again."

"What?"

"You and she were gone for five hours. Her father wanted to know where you were. I had to tell him I had no idea."

"We were just over at Clark School."

"You will not see her again."

"Why not?"

"Calpurnia is above suspicion," he said. "You are not."

Calpurnia? Suspicion?

Later that evening, my father, having cooled off, came to my room and told me that I could see Fawn again if I wanted to. But I'd already got the message. I began to send asinine and hurtful letters to Fawn, and I began to lie constantly to my father as well as to my mother. I'd seen what happened in the late sixties, when my brothers openly rebelled; I'd heard the shouting, and then, when my brothers were gone, I'd seen how sad and confused my parents were. For a while, at least, I could avoid open conflict by manufacturing two versions of myself: the official fifty-year-old boy and the unofficial adolescent. The unofficial adolescent never did anything particularly bad; what mattered was having something, anything, to conceal.

The misery of appearances was a main lesson of my childhood. There came a time in tenth grade when my mother asked me why all my undershirts were developing holes at navel level. The official version of me had no answer, but the unofficial adolescent did. In 1974, at my high school, crew-neck white undershirts were fashion death, but my mother came from an old-fashioned world in which colored T-shirts were evidently on a moral par with waterbeds and roach clips, and she refused to let me wear them. Every morning, therefore, after I left the house, I pulled down my undershirt until it didn't show at the collar, and I safety-pinned it to my underpants. (More than once, pins opened and stuck me in the belly.) When I could get away with it, I also went to the boys' bathroom and changed out of certain grievously bad shirts. My mother, in her thrift, favored inexpensive tab-collared knits, usually of polyester, which advertised me equally as an obedient little boy and a middle-aged golfer, and which chafed my neck as if to keep me ever mindful of the shame of wearing them.

For four years, from seventh through tenth grade, my social failure was grossly overdetermined — I had a large vocabulary, a giddily squeaking voice, horn-rimmed glasses, poor arm strength, too obvious approval from my teachers, irresistible urges to shout unfunny puns, a near-eidetic acquaintance with J.R.R. Tolkien, a big chemistry lab in my basement, a penchant for intimately insulting any girl unwise enough to speak to me, and so on — but the real cause of my failure, as I saw it, was my mother's refusal to let me wear jeans or sneakers to school. Manley, my old friend, remained cordial to me in the classes we shared, but he wore jeans and painter's coveralls and played drums and could do twenty-three pull-ups, and after he was elected class president he would have needed Christlike charity not to shun me socially.

Help, when it finally came, was the result of two lucky compromises. In tenth grade, I discovered straight-legged Levi's corduroys, which cleared the radar on all fronts, and I became more active in the youth fellowship at the Congregational church. I'd joined the fellowship in seventh grade, because I hated Boy Scouts and my parents insisted that I belong to something. By the mid-seventies, the senior-high fellowship was a vortex of cigarette smoke, acoustic guitars, faded denim, social activism, and pretty girls. At its peak, under the leadership of the charismatic Reverend Bob Mutton, it had 150 members, most of them from other churches. Kortenhof defected to us from the Episcopalians, Manley from the Unitarians. The fellowship crowd was suddenly an in-crowd, and I, through sheer dumb luck, was in. I grew six inches in six months. After years of marginal lunching in school cafeterias, I found a home at one of the crowded fellowship tables, presided over by Peppel, Kortenhof, and Schroer.

*

At lunch on Monday, Kortenhof gleefully reported that our pad-lock was still on the flagpole and that the Stars and Stripes had not been raised. (It was 1976, and the high school was lax in its pa-triotic duties.) The obvious next step, Kortenhof said, was to form a proper group and demand official recognition. So we wrote a note —

Dear Sir,
We have kidnapped your flagpole. Further details later.

— made a quick decision to sign it "U.N.C.L.E.," and delivered it to the mail slot of the high school principal, Mr. Knight.

Mr. Knight was a red-haired, red-bearded, Nordic-looking giant. He had a sideways, slightly shambling way of walking, with fre-quent pauses to hitch up his pants, and he stood with the stooped posture of a man who spent his days listening to smaller peo-ple. We knew his voice from his all-school intercom announce-ments. His first words — "Teachers, excuse the interruption" — often sounded strained, as if he'd been nervously hesitating at his microphone, but after that his cadences were gentle and off-handed.

What the six of us wanted, more than anything else, was to be recognized by Mr. Knight as kindred spirits, as players outside the ordinary sphere of student misbehavior and administrative force. And for a week our frustration steadily mounted, because Mr. Knight remained aloof from us, as impervious as the flagpole (which, in our correspondence, we liked to represent as personally his).

After school on Monday, we cut and pasted words and letters from magazines:

WE rEspect*FULL*y dEmanD that YOU offIcIallY ReCOgnize *our* OR-ganization AT 2:30 PM tuESday. BEGIN with "tEACHers, EXcUse the interRuption . . ." if properLY dONE, we will re*TURN* fLAgpole some-TIME wED.

U.n.C.L.E.

The phrase "Teachers, excuse the interruption" was Manley's idea, a poke at Mr. Knight. But Manley was also worried, as was I, that the administration would crack down hard on our little group if we got a reputation for vandalism, and so we returned to school that night with a can of aluminum paint and repaired the damage we'd done to the flagpole in hammering the old lock off. In the morning, we delivered the ransom note, and two-thirty found the six of us, in our respective classrooms, unreasonably hoping that Mr. Knight would make an announcement.

Our third note was typed on a sheet of notepaper headed with a giant avocado-green HELLO:

> Being as we are a brotherhood of kindly fellows, we are giving you one last chance. And observing that you have not complied with our earlier request, we are hereby reiterating it. To wit: your official recognition of our organization over the public address system at 2:59, Wednesday, March 17. If you comply, your flagpole will be returned by Thursday morning.
>
> U.N.C.L.E.

We also made an U.N.C.L.E. flag out of a pillowcase and black electrician's tape and ran it up the flagpole under cover of night. But Mr. Knight's office didn't even notice the flag until we pointed it out to teachers — two maintenance workers were then sent outside to cut our lock with a hacksaw and lower the pirate flag — and he ignored the note. He ignored a fourth note, which offered him two dollars in compensation for the broken school padlock. He ignored a fifth note, in which we reiterated our offer and dispelled any notion that our flag had been raised in celebration of St. Patrick's Day.

By the end of the week, the only interest we'd succeeded in attracting was that of other students. There had been too much huddling and conspiring in hallways, too much blabbing on Kortenhof's part. We added a seventh member simply to buy his silence. A couple of girls from the fellowship grilled me closely: Flagpole? Uncle? Can we join?

As the whispering grew louder, and as Kortenhof developed a new plan for a much more ambitious and outstanding prank, we decided to rename ourselves. Manley, who had a half-insolent, half-genuine fondness for really stupid humor, proposed the name DIOTI. He wrote it down and showed it to me.

"An anagram for 'idiot'?"

Manley giggled and shook his head. "It's also 'tio,' which is 'uncle' in Spanish, and 'di,' which means 'two.' U.N.C.L.E. Two. Get it?"

"Di-tio."

"Except it's scrambled. DIOTI sounds better."

"God, that is stupid."

He nodded eagerly, delightedly. "I know! It's so stupid! Isn't it great?"

Nine of us were piling out of two cars very late on the last Saturday of the school year, wearing dark clothes and dark stocking caps, carrying coils of rope, and zipping up knapsacks that contained hammers, wrenches, pliers, screwdrivers, and customized floor plans of the high school — in my knapsack there was also Easter candy and green plastic Easter hay, five rhymed quatrains that I'd typed on slips of bond paper, and other special equipment — when a police car rounded the corner of Selma Avenue and turned on its searchlight.

My instinct in police situations, honed by years of shooting off fireworks in a community where they were banned, was to take off running into the dark of the nearest lawn. Half of DIOTI came loping and scattering after me. It was a long time since I'd run through dark lawns uninvited. There was dew on everything, and you could encounter a dog, you could hook your foot in a croquet wicket. I stopped and hid in a clump of rhododendrons in which Schroer, the *Monty Python* disciple, was also hiding.

"Franzen? Is that you? You're making an incredible amount of noise."

As my breathing moderated, I could hear the breathing of the squad car's engine in the distance, the murmur of discussion. Then, more distinctly, a shouted whisper: "Ally-ally-out-'n'-free! Ally-ally-out-'n'-free!" The voice belonged to Holyoke, one of our new recruits, and at first I didn't understand what he was saying. The equivalent call on my own street was Ally-ally-in-come-free.

"The story," Holyoke whispered as we returned to the patrol car, "is we're tying a door shut. Gerri Chopin's front door. We're going to the Chopins' house to tie her door shut. We're using the ropes to tie the door. And the tools are for taking off the hinges."

"Michael, that doesn't make any —"

"Why take off the hinges if we're tying —"

"Hello!"

"Hello, officer!"

The patrolman was standing in his headlight beams, examining knapsacks. "What are you doing with such a big rope?" he said.

"That's not a big rope," Peppel said. "That's several small ropes tied together."

There was a brief silence.

The officer asked us if we knew that it was after one o'clock.

"Yes, we do know that," Manley said, stepping forward and squaring his shoulders. He had a forthright manner whose ironic hollowness no adult, only peers, seemed able to detect. Teachers and mothers found Manley irresistible. Certainly, in spite of his shoulder-length hair, my own mother did.

"So what are you doing out so late?"

Manley hung his head and confessed that we'd intended to tie the Chopins' screen door shut. His tone suggested that he could see now, as he couldn't five minutes ago, what a childish and negative idea this was. Standing behind him, three or four of us pointed at the Chopins' house. That's the Chopins' house right there, we said.

The officer looked at the door. We would seem to have been a rather large crew, with a lot of ropes and tools, for the task of tying one screen door shut, and we were less than a hundred yards from the high school in prime pranking season. But it was 1976 and we were white and not drunk. "Go home to bed," he said.

The squad car followed Kortenhof's station wagon back to his house, where, in his bedroom, we decided not to make a second attempt that night; the situation was too dangerous now. If we waited until Tuesday, we could get a better cover story in place. We could say, I said, that we were observing an unusual stellar occultation by the planet Mars, and that we needed tools to assemble a telescope. I insisted that everyone memorize the bogus name of the bogus star: NGC 6346.

Luckily, the sky was clear on Tuesday night. Davis escaped his house by jumping out a window. Schroer spent the night at Peppel's and helped him push the family car out of earshot before starting it. Manley, as usual, simply got into his father's Opel and drove it to my house, where I'd climbed from my bedroom window and retrieved pieces of my hitherto useless telescope from the bushes where I'd hidden them.

"We're going to watch Mars occult NGC 6346," Manley recited.

A long-standing misery of appearances was the shallowness of my supposed love of science. I liked reading about science, but my practice of it was strictly magical. I longed to get my hands on a bit of pure selenium or rubidium, because who else had pure selenium or rubidium in their home? But if a chemical wasn't rare, colorful, flammable, or explosively reactive, there was no point in stealing it from school. My father, my rational ally, who by his own testimony had married my mother because "she was a good writer and I thought a good writer could do anything," and who'd chafed against her romantic nature ever since, encouraged me to be a scientist and discouraged me from fancy writing. One Christmas, as a present, he built me a serious lab bench, and for a while I enjoyed imagining myself keeping a more rigorous notebook. My first and last experiment was to isolate "pure nylon" by melting a scrap of pantyhose in a crucible. Turning to astronomy, I again was happy as long as I was reading books, but these books reprinted pages from amateur stargazing logs whose orderly example I couldn't follow even for one minute. I just wanted to look at pretty things.

Riding with Manley through the ghostly streets of Webster Groves, I was moved for the same reason that snow had moved me as a child, for its transformative enchantment of ordinary surfaces. The long rows of dark houses, their windows dimly reflecting the streetlights, were as still as armored knights asleep under a spell. It was just as Tolkien had promised: there really was another world. The road, devoid of cars and fading into distant haze, really did go ever on and on. Unusual things could happen when nobody was looking.

On the roof of the high school, Manley and Davis gathered ropes to rappel down exterior walls while Kortenhof and Schroer set off for the gym, intending to enter through a high window and climb down on one of the folded-up trampolines. The rest of DIOTI went in through a trapdoor, past a crawl space, and out through a biology-department storage room.

Our floor plans showed the location of the thirty-odd bells that we'd identified while canvassing the school. Most of the bells were the size of half-coconuts and were mounted in hallways. During a lunch hour, we'd given a boost to Kortenhof, who had unscrewed the dish from one of these bells and silenced it by removing the clapper — a pencil-thick cylinder of graphite-blackened metal —

from its electromagnetic housing. Two teams of two now headed off to disable the other bells like this and collect the clappers.

I had my slips of paper and worked alone. In a second-floor hallway, at knee level between two lockers, was an intriguing little hole with a hinged metal cap. The hole led back into obscure scholastic recesses. Manley and I had often passed idle minutes speaking into it and listening for answers.

In my laboratory at home, I'd rolled one of my slips of paper up tightly, sealed it inside a segment of glass tubing with a Bunsen flame, and tied and taped a piece of string around the tube. This ampule I now lowered through the little rabbit hole until it dropped out of sight. Then I tied the string to the hinge and shut the metal cap. On the slip of paper was a quatrain of doggerel:

> The base of a venetian blind
> Contains another clue.
> Look in the conference room that's off
> The library. (What's new?)

In the venetian blind was other doggerel, which I'd planted during school hours:

> There is a clue behind the plate
> That's on the western side
> Of those large wooden fire doors
> Near room three sixty-five.

I went now and unscrewed the push plate from the fire door and taped another slip to the wood underneath:

> And last, another bookish clue
> Before the glorious find.
> *The Little Book of Bells'* the one;
> Its code is seven eight nine.

There were further quatrains hidden on an emergency-lighting fixture, rolled up inside a projection screen, and stuck in a library book called *Your School Clubs*. Some of the quatrains could have used a rewrite, but nobody thought they were a piece of shit. My idea was to enchant the school for Mr. Knight, to render the building momentarily strange and full of possibility, as a gift to him; and I was in the midst of discovering that writing was a way to do this.

During the previous two months, students from the five high

school physics classes had written and produced a farce about Isaac Newton, *The Fig Connection*. I had cochaired the writing committee with a pretty senior girl, Siebert, toward whom I'd quickly developed strong feelings of stagnation. Siebert was a tomboy who wore bib overalls and knew how to camp, but she was also an artist who drew and wrote effortlessly and had charcoal stains and acrylic smudges on her hands, and she was also a fetching Catholic girly-girl who every so often let her hair down and wore high-waisted skirts. I wanted all of her and resented other boys for wanting any part of her. Our play was so warmly received that one of the English teachers suggested that Siebert and I try to publish it. As everything had gone wrong for me in junior high, suddenly everything was going right.

Toward three o'clock, DIOTI reconvened on the roof with booty: twenty-five clappers and five metal dishes, the latter daringly unbolted from the bigger bells that were mounted on high walls. We tied the clappers together with pink ribbon, filled the largest dish with plastic hay and Easter candy, nestled the clappers and the smaller dishes in the hay, and stashed the whole thing in the crawl space. Returning home then, Peppel and Schroer had the worst of it, pushing Peppel's car back up a hill and into his driveway. I crept into my house less cautiously than usual. I hardly cared if I was Caught; for once, I had something they couldn't take away from me.

And to go back to school four hours later and see the place so peopled after seeing it so empty: here was a foretaste of seeing clothed in the daylight the first person you'd spent a night with naked.

And the silence then, at eight-fifteen, when the bells should have rung but didn't: this quiet transformation of the ordinary, this sound of one hand clapping, this beautiful absence, was like the poetry I wanted to learn to write.

At the end of first period, a teacher's voice came over the classroom speakers to announce that the bells were out of order. Later in the morning, the teacher began to announce not only the time but also, oddly, the temperature. Summer heat poured through the open windows, and without the usual prison-yard clanging the crowds in hallways seemed de-regimented, the boundaries of the hours blurred.

Manley at lunchtime brought happy news: the reason Mr. Knight wasn't making the announcements himself was that he was following the clues. Manley had spied him on the second floor, peering down into the rabbit hole. Despite the familiar tone we took with him, few members of DIOTI, certainly not I, had ever exchanged two words with Mr. Knight. He was the ideal, distant, benign, ridiculous Authority, and until now the notion that he might come out to play with us had been purely hypothetical.

The only shadow on the day was that a Device of mine again failed to work. Davis called me after school to report that Mr. Knight had lost the glass ampule down the rabbit hole. A canny English teacher, the same one who thought our play should be published, had promised Davis anonymity in exchange for the lost clue. I recited it over the phone, and the next morning the bells were working again. Kortenhof, who had had two hundred DIOTI bumper stickers printed up, went outside with Schroer in broad daylight and applied them to every rear bumper in the faculty parking lot.

That summer, my cousin Gail, my aunt and uncle's only child, was killed at the wheel of her car in West Virginia. My mother's mother was dying of liver disease in Minneapolis, and I became morbidly aware that there were fifty thousand nuclear warheads on the planet, several dozen of them targeting St. Louis. My wet dreams felt apocalyptic, like a ripping of vital organs. One night I was awakened by a violent clap of thunder and was convinced that the world was over.

It was the sweetest summer of my life. "One continuous round of pleasure," my father kept saying. I fell under the spell of Robert Pirsig and Wallace Stevens and began to write poetry. During the day, Siebert and I shot and edited a Super-8 costume drama with Davis and Lunte, and at night we painted a Rousseauian jungle mural on a wall at the high school. We were still just friends, but every evening that I spent with her was an evening that she didn't spend with other boys. On her birthday, in July, as she was leaving her house, three of us jumped her from behind, blindfolded her, tied her wrists, and put her in the back of Lunte's car. We had a surprise party waiting on a riverbank beneath an interstate overpass, and to Siebert's increasingly plaintive questions — "Jon? Chris?

Guys? Is that you?" — we said nothing until Lunte did forty-three in a thirty zone. The cop who pulled us over made us unblind her. When he asked her if she knew us, you could see her considering her options before she said yes.

In August, Siebert went away to college, which allowed me to idealize her from a distance, communicate mainly in writing, put energy into new theatrical projects, and casually date someone else. Late in the fall, a publisher bought *The Fig Connection* for a hundred dollars, and I told my parents that I was going to be a writer. They weren't happy to hear it.

DIOTI's first prank of the new year was to batik a queen-size bedsheet and unfurl it over the school's main entrance on the morning that an accrediting committee from the North Central Association arrived to inspect the school. I built a Device involving two sheet-metal levers, a pulley, and a rope that ran across the roof and dangled by a third-floor courtyard window. When we pulled the rope on Monday morning, nothing happened. Davis had to go outside, climb to the roof in plain view, and unfurl the banner by hand. It said DIOTI WELCOMES YOU, NCA.

Through the winter, subgroups of DIOTI staged smaller side-pranks. I had a taste for scenes involving costumes and toy guns. Davis and Manley kept climbing buildings, proceeding on a typical Saturday night from the gargoyled bell tower of Eden Seminary to the roofs of Washington University and finally to the kitchen of the Presbyterian church, where freshly baked Sunday cookies were available to intruders.

For the main spring prank, we chose as a victim one of my favorite teachers, Ms. Wojak, because her room was in the middle of the second floor and had a very high ceiling, and because she was rumored to have disparaged DIOTI. Our membership was back up to nine, including a girl named Swift, and it took us four hours on a Wednesday night to empty thirty rooms of their desks, herd the desks down stairs and through hallways, and pack them, floor to ceiling, into Ms. Wojak's room. There was good wee-hour bonhomie in turning a corner in a lonely hallway and seeing two or three colleagues assiduously portaging furniture. Some of the rooms had transoms that Manley or Davis could climb through. To get into the others, we took the hinges off the door of the main office and made use of the keys that teachers habitually left in their mail slots.

Since I was fifty as well as seventeen, I'd insisted that we bring masking tape and markers and label the desks with their room numbers before moving them, to simplify the job of putting them back. Even so, I was sorry when I saw what a violent snarl we'd made of Ms. Wojak's room. I thought she might feel singled out for persecution, and so I wrote the words CENTRALLY LOCATED on her blackboard. It was the only writing I did for DIOTI that spring. I didn't care about Mr. Knight anymore; the work was all that mattered.

During our graduation ceremonies, at the football field, the superintendent of schools told the story of the desks and cited their masking-tape labels as evidence of "a new spirit of responsibility" among young people today. DIOTI had secreted a farewell banner, batiked in school colors, in the base of the football scoreboard, but the Device I'd built to release it hadn't worked well in trials the night before, and, in any case, vigilant administrators had snipped the release line before Holyoke, disguised in a fisherman's outfit and dark glasses, arrived to pull it. After the ceremony, I wanted to tell my parents that it was now official: I was the author of a new spirit of responsibility among young people today. But of course I couldn't, and didn't.

That summer, I expected to start drinking and having sex. Siebert had returned from college by herself (her family had moved to Texas), and we had already done some heavy stagnating on her grandmother's living room sofa. Now Lunte and his family were about to embark on a two-month camping trip, leaving Siebert to house-sit for them. She would be in the house by herself, every night, for two months.

She and I both took jobs downtown, and on our first Friday she failed to show up for a lunch date with me. I spent the afternoon wondering whether, as with M —, I might be coming on too strong. But that evening, while I was eating dinner with my parents, Davis came to our house and delivered the news: Siebert was in St. Joseph's Hospital with a broken back. She'd asked Davis to take her to the top of the Eden Seminary bell tower the night before, and she'd fallen from a thirty-foot downspout.

The news was sickening. Even as I tried to absorb it, though, my immediate concern was that my parents were getting it directly, before I could tailor it. I felt as if I and all my friends had been Caught in a new, large, and irrevocable way. My mother, as she listened to Davis, was wearing her darkest scowl. She'd always preferred the well-spoken Manley to the more lumpy Davis, and she'd never had much use for Siebert, either. Her disapproval now was radiant and total. My father, who liked Siebert, was upset nearly to the point of tears. "I don't understand what you were doing on the roof," he said.

"Yeah, well, so anyway," Davis said miserably, "so she wasn't on the roof yet. I was on the roof trying to reach down and, you know, help her."

"But, Chris, my God," my father cried. "*Why were the two of you climbing on the roof at Eden Seminary?*"

Davis looked a little pissed off. He'd done the right thing by giving me the news in person, and now, as a reward, my parents were beating him up. "Yeah, well, so anyway," he said, "she like called me last night and she wanted me to take her up to the top of the tower. I wanted to use rope, but she's a really good climber. She didn't want the rope."

"There's a nice view from the tower," I explained. "You can see all around."

My mother turned to me severely. "Have you been up there?"

"No," I said, which was accidentally the truth.

"I don't understand this at all," my father said.

In Davis's Pinto, as the two of us drove to Eden, he said that he'd gone up the downspout ahead of Siebert. The downspout was solid and well anchored to the wall, and Siebert had followed him easily until she reached the gutter. If she'd just extended her hand, Davis said, he could have reached down from the roof and pulled her up. But she seemed to panic, and before he could help her the focus went out of her eyes, her hands flew back behind her head, and she went straight down, twenty-five feet, landing flat on her back on the seminary lawn. The thud, Davis said, was horrible. Without thinking, without even lowering himself off the gutter, he jumped down thirty feet and broke his fall with the roll he'd practiced after lesser jumps. Siebert was moaning. He ran and banged on the nearest lighted windows and shouted for an ambulance.

The grass at the base of the downspout was not as trampled as I'd expected. Davis pointed to the spot where the EMTs had

put Siebert on a rigid pallet. I forced myself to look up at the gutter. The evening air at Eden, incoherently, was mild and delicious. There was twilight birdsong in the freshly foliated oak trees,
Protestant lights coming on in Gothic windows.

"You jumped down from there?" I said.

"Yeah, it was really dumb."

Siebert, it turned out, had been fortunate in landing flat. Two of
her vertebrae were shattered, but her nerves were intact. She was
in the hospital for six weeks, and I went to see her every evening,
sometimes with Davis, more often alone. A guitarist friend and I
wrote inspirational songs and sang them for her during thunder-
storms. It was dark all summer. I lay on the Luntes' pool table with
rum, Löwenbräu, Seagram's, and blackberry wine in my stomach
and watched the ceiling spin. I didn't hate myself, but I hated adolescence, hated the very word. In August, after Siebert's parents
had taken her home to Texas with a cumbersome back brace and a
lot of painkillers, I went on a date with a different girl and had, according to my journal, an excellent time making out.

Adolescence is best enjoyed without self-consciousness, but self-
consciousness, unfortunately, is its leading symptom. Even when
something important happens to you, even when your heart's getting crushed or exalted, even when you're absorbed in building
the foundations of a personality, there come these moments when
you're aware that what's happening is not the real story. Unless you
actually die, the real story is still ahead of you. This alone, this
cruel mixture of consciousness and irrelevance, this built-in hollowness, is enough to account for how pissed off you are. You're
miserable and ashamed if you don't believe your adolescent troubles matter, but you're stupid if you do. This was the double bind
from which our playing with Mr. Knight, our taking something so
very useless so very seriously, had given us a fifteen-month re-
prieve.

But when does the real story start? At forty-three, I feel grateful
almost daily to be the adult I wished I could be when I was seventeen. I work on my arm strength at the gym; I've become pretty
good with tools. At the same time, almost daily, I lose battles with
the seventeen-year-old who's still inside me. I eat half a box of
Oreos for lunch, I binge on TV, I make sweeping moral judgments,

I run around town in torn jeans, I drink martinis on a Tuesday night, I stare at beer-commercial cleavage, I define as uncool any group to which I can't belong, I sneak cigarettes on the roof, I feel the urge to key Range Rovers and slash their tires; I pretend I'm never going to die.

The double bind, the problem of consciousness mixed with nothingness, never goes away. You never stop waiting for the real story to start, because the only real story, in the end, is that you die. Along the way, however, Mr. Knight keeps reappearing: Mr. Knight as God, Mr. Knight as history, Mr. Knight as government or fate or nature. And the game of art, which begins as a bid for Mr. Knight's attention, eventually invites you to pursue it for its own sake, with a seriousness that redeems and is redeemed by its fundamental use-lessness.

For an inexperienced midwesterner in the fast-living East, college turned out to be a reprise of junior high. I managed to befriend a few fellow lonelyhearts, but the only pranks I was involved in were openly sadistic — pelting a popular girl with cubes of Jell-O, haul-ing an eight-foot length of rail into the dorm room of a bearded in-ternational-studies major. Manley and Davis sounded no happier at their respective schools; they were smoking a lot of pot. Lunte had moved to Moscow, Idaho. Holyoke, still with DIOTI, orga-nized a final prank involving a classroom waist-deep in crumpled newspaper.

Siebert came back to St. Louis the next summer, walking without pain, wearing clothes in the style of Annie Hall, and working with me on a farce about a police inspector in colonial India. My feel-ings toward her were an adolescent stew of love-and-reconsider, of commit-and-keep-your-options-open. We spent our last night of the summer in the house of a friend whose parents were away. In the morning, Manley and Davis came to the door with a white cane, Davis's dimwitted spaniel, Goldie, and a pair of swimming goggles that they'd dipped in black paint. It was my birthday, and they invited me to put the goggles on. Thus blinded, I was given the cane and Goldie's leash. I amused my friends by trying to eat pancakes, blind, at a pancake house. Siebert went home then, and I sat in the back seat of the car while Goldie was dropped off and the three of us traveled on arterials in a baking August sun.

I guessed that we were going to the Arch, on the riverfront, and we were. I gamely went tap-tapping through the Arch's underground lobby, my sense of hearing growing sharper by the minute. Davis bought tickets to the top of the Arch while Manley incited me to touch a Remington bronze, a rearing horse. Behind us a man spoke sharply: "Please don't touch the — Oh. Oh. I'm sorry."

I took my hands away.

"No, no, please, go ahead. It's an original Remington, but please touch it."

I put my hands back on the bronze. Manley, the little jerk, went off to giggle someplace with Davis. The park ranger's hands led mine. "Feel the muscles in the horse's chest," he urged.

I was wearing mutilated swimming goggles. My cane was a quarter-inch dowel rod with one coat of white paint. I turned to leave.

"Wait," the ranger said. "There are some really neat things I want to show you."

"Um."

He took my arm and led me deeper into the Museum of Westward Expansion. His voice grew even gentler. "How long have you been — without your sight?"

"Not long," I said.

"Feel this tepee." He directed my hand. "These are buffalo skins with the hair scraped off. Here, I'll take your cane."

We went inside the tepee, and for a daylong five minutes I dutifully stroked furs, fingered utensils, smelled woven baskets. I hadn't slept at all the night before, and the crime of deceiving the ranger felt more grievous with each passing minute. When I escaped from the tepee and thanked him, I was dripping with sweat.

At the top of the Arch, I was finally unblinded and saw: haze, glare, coal barges, Busch Stadium, a diarrheic river. Manley shrugged and looked at the metal floor. "We were hoping you'd be able to see more up here," he said.

It often happened on my birthday that the first fall cold front of summer came blowing through. The next afternoon, when my parents and I drove east to a wedding in Fort Wayne, the sky was scrubbed clean. Giant Illinois cornfields, nearly ripe, rippled in the golden light from behind us. You could taste, in air fresh from crossing Lake Superior, almost everything there was to know about life around here. And how devoid of interiors the farmhouses looked in light so perfect! How impatient to be harvested the cornfields seemed in their wind-driven tossing! And how platonically green the official signs for Effingham! (Its unofficial name, I surmised, was Fuckingham.) The season had changed overnight, and I was reading better books and trying to write every day, starting over from scratch now, by myself.

My father was exceeding the speed limit by an unvarying four miles per hour. My mother spoke from the back seat. "What did you and Chris and Ben do yesterday?"

"Nothing," I said. "We had breakfast."

ADAM GOPNIK

The Unreal Thing

FROM THE NEW YORKER

FOR THE PAST four years, a lot of people have been obsessed with the movie *The Matrix*. As the sequel, *The Matrix Reloaded,* arrived in theaters this week, it was obvious that the strange, violent science-fiction film, by the previously more or less unknown Wachowski brothers, had already inspired both a cult and a craze. (And had made a lot of money into the bargain, enough to fuel two sequels; *Matrix Revolutions* is supposed to be out in November.) There hasn't been anything quite like it since *2001: A Space Odyssey*, which had a similar mix of mysticism, solemnity, and mega-effects. Shortly after its mostly unheralded release, in 1999, *The Matrix* became an egghead *extase*. The Slovenian philosopher Slavoj Zizek's latest work, *Welcome to the Desert of the Real*, took its title from a bit of dialogue in the film; college courses on epistemology have used *The Matrix* as a chief point of reference; and there are at least three books devoted to teasing out its meanings. (*Taking the Red Pill: Science, Philosophy and Religion in The Matrix* is a typical title.) If the French philosopher Jean Baudrillard, whose books — *The Gulf War Did Not Take Place* is one — popularized the view that reality itself has become a simulation, has not yet embraced the film, it may be because he is thinking of suing for a screen credit. (The "desert of the real" line came from him.) The movie, it seemed, dramatized a host of doubts and fears and fascinations, some half as old as time, some with a decent claim to be postmodern. To a lot of people, it looked like a fable: *our* fable.

The first *Matrix* — for anyone who has been living in Antarctica for the past four years — depended on a neatly knotted marriage between a spectacle and a speculation. The spectacle has by now become part of the common language of action movies: the amazing "balletic" fight scenes and the slow-motion aerial display of destruction. The speculation, more peculiar, and even, in its way, esoteric, is that reality is a fiction, programmed into the heads of sleeping millions by evil computers. When we meet the hero of the *Matrix* saga, he's a computer programmer — online name Neo — who works in a generic office building in a present-day, Chicagolike metropolis. Revelation arrives when he's recruited by a mysterious guerrilla figure named Morpheus, played by Laurence Fishburne with a baritone aplomb worthy of Orson Welles. Morpheus offers Neo a choice between two pills, one blue and one red: "You take the blue pill, the story ends, you wake up in your bed and believe whatever you want to believe. You take the red pill . . . and I show you how deep the rabbit hole goes." Neo takes the red pill and wakes up as he really is: a comatose body in a cocoon, his brain penetrated by a cable that inserts the Matrix, an interactive virtual-reality program, directly into his consciousness. All the people he has ever known, he realizes, are recumbent in incubators, stacks of identical clear pods, piled in high towers; the cocooned sleepers have the simulation piped into their heads by the machines as music is piped into headphones. What they take to be experiences is simply the effect of brain impulses interacting with the virtual-reality program. Guerrilla warriors who have been unplugged from the Matrix survive in an underground city called Zion, and travel in hovercraft to unplug promising humans. Morpheus has chosen to unplug Neo, it turns out, because he believes Neo is the One — the Messiah figure who will see through the Matrix and help free mankind. The first film, which told of Neo's education by Morpheus and his pursuit of the awesomely cute and Matrix-defying Trinity (the rubber-suited Carrie-Anne Moss), ends with Neo seeing the Matrix for what it is: a row of green digits, which he has learned to alter as easily as a skilled player can alter the levels of a video game.

What made the spectacle work was the ingenuity and the attention to detail with which it was rendered. The faintly greenish cast and the curious sterility of life within the Matrix; the reddish grungy reality of Morpheus's ship; the bizarre and convincing interlude with the elderly Oracle; and, of course, those action se-

quences, the weightless midair battles — few movies have had so
much faith in their own mythology. And the actors rose to it,
Laurence Fishburne managing to anchor the whole thing in a
grandiloquent theatricality. Even Keanu Reeves, bless him, played
his part with a stolidity that made him the only possible hero of the
film, so slow in his reactions that he seemed perfect for virtual reality, his expressions changing with the finger-drumming time lag of
a digital image loading online.

If it was the spectacle that made the movie work, though, it was
the speculations that made it last in people's heads. It spoke to an
old nightmare. The basic conceit of *The Matrix* — the notion that
the material world is a malevolent delusion, designed by the forces
of evil with the purpose of keeping people in a state of slavery —
has a history. It is most famous as the belief for which the medieval
Christian sect known as the Cathars fought and died, and in great
numbers, too. The Cathars were sure that the material world was a
phantasm created by Satan, and that Jesus of Nazareth — their
Neo — had shown mankind a way beyond that matrix by standing
outside it and seeing through it. The Cathars were fighting a losing
battle, but the interesting thing was that they were fighting at all. It
is not unusual to take up a sword and die for a belief. It is unusual
to take up a sword to die for the belief that swords do not exist.

The Cathars, like the heroes of *The Matrix*, had an especially
handy rationale for violence: if it ain't real, it can't really bleed.
One reason that the violence in *The Matrix* — those floating fistfights, the annihilation of entire squads of soldiers by cartwheeling
guerrillas — can fairly be called balletic is that, according to the
rules of the movie, what is being destroyed is not real in the first
place: the action has the safety of play and the excitement of the
apocalyptic. Of course, the destruction of a blank, featureless, mir-
rored skyscraper by a helicopter, and the massacre of the soldiers
who protect it, has a different resonance now than it did in 1999.
The notion that some human beings are not really human but,
rather, mere slaves, nonhuman ciphers, and therefore expendable,
is exactly the vision of the revolutionary hero — and also of the
mass terrorist. The Matrix is where all violent fanatics insist that
they are living, even when they are not.

It would have been nice if some of that complexity, or any complexity, had made its way into the sequel. But — to get to the bad

news — *Matrix Reloaded* is, unlike the first film, a conventional comic-book movie, in places a campy conventional comic-book movie, and in places a ludicrously campy conventional comic-book movie. It feels not so much like *Matrix II* as like *Matrix XIV* — a franchise film made after a decade of increasing grosses and thinning material. The thing that made the Matrix so creepy — the idea of a sleeping human population with a secondary life in a simulated world — is barely referred to in the new movie; in fact, if you hadn't seen the first film, not just the action but the basic premise would be pretty much unintelligible. The first forty-five minutes — set mainly in Zion, that human city buried deep in the earth — are particularly excruciating. Zion seems to be modeled on the parking garage of a giant indoor mall, with nested levels clustered around an atrium. Like every good-guy citadel in every science-fiction movie ever made, Zion is peopled by stern-jawed uniformed men who say things like "And what if you're wrong, God damn it, what then?" and "Are you doubting my command, Captain?" and by short-haired and surprisingly powerful women whose eyes moisten but don't overflow as they watch the men prepare to go off to war. Everybody wears earth tones and burlap and silk, and there are craggy perches from which speeches can be made while the courageous citizens hold torches. (The stuccoed, soft-contour interiors of Zion look like the most interesting fusion restaurant in Santa Fe.)

The only thing setting Zion apart from the good-guy planets in *The Phantom Menace* or *Star Trek* is that it seems to have been redlined at some moment in the mythic past and is heavily populated by people of color. They are all, like Morpheus, grave, orotund, and articulate to the point of prosiness, so that official exchanges in Zion put one in mind of what it must have been like at a meeting at the Afro-American Studies department at Harvard before Larry Summers got to it. (And no sooner has this thought crossed one's mind when — lo! there is Professor Cornel West himself, playing one of the councilors.) Morpheus, winningly laconic in the first film, here tends to speechify, and, in a sequence that passes so far into the mystically absurd that it is almost witty, leads the inhabitants of Zion in a torch-lit orgy, presumably meant to show the machines what humans can do that they can't; the humans heave and slam well-toned bodies in a giant rave — Plato's Retreat to the last leaping shadow. Neo and Trinity make love while this is going on, and we can see the cable holes up and down Neo's back, like a fashion-forward appliqué. (Soon, everyone will want them.) No cliché goes unresisted; there is an annoying street kid who wants Neo's attention, and a wise councilor with swept-back silver hair (he is played by Anthony Zerbe, Hal Holbrook presumably having been unavailable) who twinkles benignly and creases up his eyes as he wanders the city at night by Neo's side. Smiles gather at the corner of his mouth. He's that kind of wise.

More damagingly, once Zion has been realized and mundanely inhabited, most of the magic disappears from the fable; it becomes a cartoon battle between more or less equally opposed forces, and the sense of a desperately uneven contest between man and machine is gone. The Matrix, far from being a rigorously imposed program, turns out to be as porous as good old-fashioned reality, letting in all kinds of James Bond villains. (They are explained as defunct programs that refused to die, but they seem more like character ideas that refused to be edited.) Lambert Wilson appears as a sort of digital Dominique de Villepin — even virtual French-men are now amoral, the mark of Cain imprinted on their fore-heads, so to speak, like a spot of chocolate mousse. He is called the Merovingian (*Holy Blood, Holy Grail* having apparently been added to the reading list) and announces that "choice is an illusion cre-ated between zose wis power and zose wisout" as he constructs a virtual dessert with which he inflames the passion of a virtual woman. The stunning Monica Bellucci appears as his wife, who sells out his secrets in exchange for a remarkably chaste kiss from Neo, while Trinity looks on, smoldering like Betty in an *Archie* comic. (But then Monica is Italian, a member of the coalition of the willing.) Then there are his twin dreadlocked henchmen, dressed entirely in white, who have all the smirking conviction of Siegfried and Roy. Even the action sequences, which must have been quite hard to make, remind one of those in the later Bond films; interesting to describe, they are so unbound by any rules ex-cept the rule of Now He'll Jump Off That Fast-Moving Thing Onto the Next Fast-Moving Thing that they are tedious to watch. A long freeway sequence has the buzzing predictability of the video game it will doubtless become. In the first film, the rules of reality were bendable, and that was what gave the action its surprises; in the new one there are hardly any rules at all. The idea of a fight between Neo and a hundred identical evil "agents" sounds cool but is unintentionally comic. Dressed in identical black suits and ties, like the staff of MCA in the Lew Wasserman era (is that why they're called agents?), they simultaneously rush Neo and leap on him in a giant scrum; it's like watching a football team made up of ten-year-olds attempt to tackle Bronko Nagurski — you know he's going to rise up and shake them off. Neo has become a superhuman power within the Matrix and nothing threatens him. He fights the identical agents for fifteen minutes, practically yawning while he does, and then flies away, and you wonder — why didn't he fly away to start with? As he chops and jabs at his enemies, there isn't the slightest doubt about the outcome, and Keanu Reeves seems merely preoccupied, as though ready to get on his cell phone for a few sage words with Slavoj Zizek. There are a few arresting moments at the conclusion when Neo meets the architect of the Matrix. But by then the spectacle has swept right over the speculation, leaving a lot of vinyl and rubber shreds on the incoming tide.

For anyone who was transfixed by the first movie, watching the new one is a little like being unplugged from the Matrix: What was I experiencing all that time? Could it have been . . . *all a dream?* A reassuring viewing of the old movie suggests that its appeal had less to do with its accessories than with its premise. Could it be that what you took to be your life was merely piped into your brain like experiential Muzak? The question casts a spell even when the spell casters turn out to be more merchandisers than magi.

Long before the first *Matrix* was released, of course, there was a lot of fictional life in the idea that life is a fiction. The finest of American speculators, Philip K. Dick, whose writing has served as the basis of some of the more ambitious science-fiction movies of the past couple of decades (*Blade Runner, Total Recall, Minority Report*), was preoccupied with two questions: How do we know that a robot doesn't have consciousness, and how do we know that we can trust our own memories and perceptions? *Blade Runner* dramatized the first of these two problems, and *The Matrix* was an extremely and probably self-consciously Dickian dramatization of the second. In one of Dick's most famous novels, for instance, *The Three Stigmata of Palmer Erdrich,* a colony of earthmen on Mars, trapped in a miserable life, take an illegal drug that transports them into "Perky

Pat Layouts" — miniature Ken and Barbie dollhouses, where they live out their lives in an idealized Southern California. Like Poe, Dick took the science of his time, gave it a paranoid twist, and then became truly paranoid himself. In a long, half-crazy book called *Valis*, he proposed that the world we live in is a weird scramble of information, that a wicked empire has produced thousands of years of fake history, and that the fabric of reality is being ripped by a battle between good and evil. The Dick scholar Erik Davis points out that, in a sequel to *Valis*, Dick even used the term "matrix" in something like a Wachowskian context.

In the academy, too, the age-old topic of radical doubt has acquired renewed life in recent years. In fact, what's often called the "brain-in-the-vat problem" has practically become its own academic discipline. The philosopher Daniel Dennett invoked it to probe the paradoxes of identity. Robert Nozick, famous as a theorist of the minimal state, used it to ask whether you would agree to plug into an "experience machine" that would give you any experience you desired — writing a great book, making a friend — even though you'd really just be floating in a vat with electrodes attached to your brain. Nozick's perhaps too hasty assumption was that you wouldn't want to plug in. His point was that usually something has to happen in the world, not just in our heads, for our desires to be satisfied. The guerrilla warriors in *The Matrix*, confirming the point, are persuaded that the Matrix is wrong because it isn't "real," and we intuitively side with them. Yet, unlike Nozick, we also recognize that it might be a lot more comfortable to remain within the virtual universe. That's the decision made by a turncoat among the guerrillas, Cypher. (Agents of the "machine world" seal the pact with him over dinner at a posh restaurant: "I know this steak doesn't exist," Cypher tells them, enjoying every calorie-free bite. "I know that when I put it in my mouth the Matrix is telling my brain that it is juicy and delicious. After nine years, you know what I realize? Ignorance is bliss.")

A key feature of *The Matrix* is that all those brains are wired together — that they really can interact with one another. And it was, improbably, the Harvard philosopher and mathematician Hilary Putnam who, a couple of decades back, proposed the essential Matrixian setup: a bunch of brains in a vat hooked up to a machine that was "programmed to give [them] all a *collective* hallucina-

tion, rather than a number of separate unrelated hallucinations."
Putnam used his Matrix to make a tricky argument about meaning:
since words mean what they normally refer to within a community,
a member of the vatted-brain community might be telling the
truth if it said it was looking at a tree, or, for that matter, at Monica
Bellucci. That's because the brains in that vat aren't really speaking
our language. What they are speaking, he said, is "vat-English," because by "a tree" they don't mean a tree; they mean, roughly, a tree
image. Presumably, by "Monica Bellucci" they mean "the image of
Monica Bellucci in *Malèna,*" rather than the image of Monica
Bellucci in *Matrix Reloaded,* brains-in-vats having taste and large
DVD collections.

Like most thought experiments, the brain-in-the-vat scenario
was intended to sharpen our intuitions. But recurrent philosophical examples tend to have a little symbolic halo around them, a
touch of their time — those angels dancing on the head of a pin
were dancing to a thirteenth-century rhythm. The fact that the
brain-in-a-vat literature has grown so abundant, the vat so vast, suggests that it has a grip on our imagination as a story in itself.

And there, in retrospect, might lie the secret of the first *Matrix:*
beyond the balletic violence, beyond the cool stunts, the idea that
the world we live in isn't real is one that speaks right now to a general condition. For the curious thing about the movie was that
everybody could grasp the basic setup instantly. Whether it occurs
in cult science fiction or academic philosophy, we seem to be fascinated by the possibility that our world might not exist. We're not
strangers to the feeling that, for much of our lives, we might just
as well *be* brains-in-vats, floating in an amniotic fluid of simulations.
It doesn't just strike us as plausibly weird. It strikes us as weirdly
plausible.

When, in the first film, Neo sees the Matrix for what it is, a
stream of green glowing digits, and thus is able to stop bullets by
looking at them, the moment of vision is not simply liberating. It is
also spooky and, in a Dickian way, chilling. This moment is the opposite of the equivalent scene in *Star Wars,* a quarter century ago,
when Luke Skywalker refuses to wear the helmet that will put him
in contact with his targeting machinery, and decides instead to
bliss out and trust the Force, the benevolent vital energy of the universe. Neo's epiphany is the reverse: the world around him is a cas-

cade of cold digital algorithms, unfeeling and lifeless. His charge is not to turn on and tune in but to turn off and tune out.

This moment of discovery — that the world is not merely evil but fake — has become a familiar turn in American entertainment. (*The Truman Show* does it with stage sets, but the virtual-reality versions are played out in *Dark City* and *eXistenZ* and, especially, the fine, frightening film noir *The Thirteenth Floor,* in which the hero drives to the edge of Los Angeles and discovers that the landscape beyond is made of the glowing green lines and honeycombs of a computer graphic — that he has been living his life within someone else's program.) Even if we don't remotely buy the notion that reality has been drowned by its simulations, we accept it as the melodramatic expression of a kind of truth. The Grand Guignol is possible only because the Petit Guignol exists.

There are so many brains in vats around, in fact, that we need to remind ourselves why we don't want to be one. In a long article on the first *Matrix* film, the Princeton philosopher James Pryor posed the question "What's so bad about living in the Matrix?," and, after sorting through some possible answers, he concluded that the real problem probably has to do with freedom, or the lack of it. "If your ambitions in the Matrix are relatively small-scale, like opening a restaurant or becoming a famous actor, then you may very well be able to achieve them," Pryor says. "But if your ambitions are larger — e.g., introducing some long-term social change — then whatever progress you make toward that goal will be wiped out when the simulation gets reset . . . One thing we place a lot of value on is being in charge of our own lives, not being someone else's slave or plaything. We want to be *politically free.*"

Here's where the first *Matrix* pushed beyond the fun of seeing a richly painted dystopia. Although the movie was made in 1999, its strength as a metaphor has only increased in the years since. The monopolization of information by vast corporations; the substitution of an agreed-on fiction, imposed from above, for anything that corresponds to our own reality; the sense that we have lost control not only of our fate but of our small sense of what's real — all these things can seem part of ordinary life now. ("More Like *The Matrix* Every Day" was the title of a recent political column by Farai Chideya.) In a mood of Dickian paranoia, one can even start to wonder whether the language we hear constantly on television and talk radio ("the war on terror," "homeland security," etc.) is a sort of vat-English — a language from which all earthly reference has been bled away. This isn't to say that any of us yet exist within an entirely fictive universe created by the forces of evil for the purpose of deluding a benumbed population — not unless you work for Fox News, anyway. But we know what it's like to be captive to representations of the world that have, well, a faintly greenish cast.

Especially in view of the conventionality of the second film, it's clear that the first film struck so deep not because it showed us a new world but because it reminded us of this one, and dramatized a simple, memorable choice between the plugged and the unplugged life. It reminded us that the idea of free lives is inseparable from the idea of the real thing. Apparently, we needed the reminder. "Free your mind!," the sixties-ish slogan of the new film, is too ambitious to be convincing, and betrays the darkness that made the first film so unusual. "Unplug thy neighbor!," though, still sounds *just* possible.

A Sudden Illness

FROM THE NEW YORKER

WE WERE IN Linc's car, an aging yellow Mercedes sedan, big and steady, with slippery blond seats and a deep, strumming idle. Lincoln called it Dr. Diesel. It was a Sunday night, March 22, 1987, nine-thirty. Rural Ohio was a smooth continuity of silence and darkness, except for a faintly golden seam where land met sky ahead, promising light and people and sound just beyond the tree line.

We were on our way back to Kenyon College after spring break. Linc, my best friend, was driving, his arm easy over the wheel. My boyfriend, Borden, sat behind him. I rode shotgun, a rose from Borden on my lap. Slung over my arm was a 1940s taffeta ball gown I had bought for $20 at a thrift shop. I was nineteen.

The conversation had dropped off. I was making plans for the dress and for my coming junior year abroad at the University of Edinburgh. My eyes strayed along the right shoulder of the road: a white mailbox, the timid glint of an abandoned pickup's taillight. The pavement racing under the car was gunmetal gray. We were doing fifty miles an hour or so. A balled-up bag from a drive-through burger joint bumped against my ankle.

A *deer.*

At first, he was only a suggestion of an animal, emerging from the darkness by degrees: a muzzle, a sharp left eye. Then the headlights grasped him.

He was massive — a web of antlers over his head, a heavy barrel, round haunches lifting him from the downward slope of the highway apron. Briefly, his forehooves rested on the line between the shoulder and the highway. I saw his knee bending, the hoof lifting: he was stepping into the car's path.

In the instant that I spent waiting for the deer to roll up over the car's hood and crash through the windshield I was aware of my body warm in the seat, Linc's face lit by the dash, Borden breathing in the back, the cool sulfur glow of the car's interior, the salty smell of the burger bag. I watched the deer's knee and waited for it to straighten. I drew a sharp breath.

The bumper missed the deer's chest by an inch, maybe two. The animal's muzzle passed so close that I could see the swirl of hair around his nostrils. Then he was gone behind us.

I blinked at the road. My eyes caught something else. A brilliant light appeared through the top of the windshield and arced straight ahead of the car at terrific speed. It was a meteor. It burned through the rising light of the horizon and vanished in the black place above the road and below the sky.

My breath escaped in a rush. I turned toward Linc to share my amazement. He was as loose as he had been, his eyes slowly panning the road, his long body unfolding over the seat. I looked back at Borden and could just make out his face. They had seen nothing.

I was about to speak when an intense wave of nausea surged through me. The smell from the bag on the floor was suddenly sickening. I wrapped my arms over my stomach and slid down in my seat. By the time we reached campus, half an hour later, I was doubled over, burning hot, and racked with chills. Borden called the campus paramedics. They hovered in the doorway, pronounced it food poisoning, and left.

I fell asleep sitting up on my bed, leaning against Borden's shoulder. In the morning, my stomach seethed. I walked to the dining hall and sat with Linc, unable to eat. In my history seminar, I drank from a water bottle and tried to concentrate. After class, I walked to my apartment and heated some oatmeal. I swallowed a spoonful; nausea rose in my throat and I pushed the bowl away.

In the next few days, everything I ate made my abdomen balloon. I radiated heat, and my joints and muscles felt bruised. Every day on the way to classes, I struggled a little harder to make it up the hill behind my apartment. Eventually, I began stopping halfway to rest against the trunk of a tree.

One morning, I woke to find my limbs leaden. I tried to sit up but couldn't. I lay in bed, listening to my apartment-mates move through their morning routines. It was two hours before I could stand. On the walk to the bathroom, I had to drag my shoulder along the wall to stay upright. Linc drove me to the campus physician, who ran test after test but couldn't find the cause of my illness. After three weeks of being stranded in my room, I had no choice but to drop out of college. I called my sister and asked if she could drive me home to Maryland.

I sat in the doorway of the apartment while Borden and Linc packed my sister's car. As they pushed the last of my belongings into the back seat, a downpour broke over them. We pulled out, and Kenyon was lost in a falling grayness. I turned to wave to Borden and Linc, but I couldn't see them anymore.

My mother's house was a dignified Colonial that sat back from the road, behind a pine tree that had been mostly denuded by Hurricane Agnes and an anemic cherry tree that would soon collapse onto the den. In the back yard stood a hemlock that had been missing its upper third since my brother and I accidentally set it on fire. Inside, the house was a warren of small rooms that had suited our two-parent, four-kid, two-collie family when my parents bought it, in 1971. My father had walked out in 1977, the elder collie had died three days later, and the house had gradually emptied until my departure for Kenyon, which had left only my mother and my cat, Fangfoss.

The sun was setting as we pulled up to the back door. I walked upstairs and lay down in my childhood bedroom, which overlooked the back yard and the charred tree. The next morning, I stepped on a scale. I had lost twenty pounds. The lymph nodes on my neck and under my arms and collarbones were painfully swollen. During the day, I rattled with chills, but at night I soaked my clothes in sweat. I felt unsteady, as if the ground were swaying. My throat was inflamed and raw. A walk to the mailbox on the corner left me so tired that I had to lie down.

Sometimes I'd look at words or pictures but see only meaningless shapes. I'd stare at clocks and not understand what the positions of the hands meant. Words from different parts of a page appeared to be grouped together in bizarre sentences: "Endangered Condors Charged in Shotgun Killing." In conversation, I'd think of one word but say something completely unrelated: "hotel" became "plankton"; "cup" came out "elastic." I couldn't hang on to a thought long enough to carry it through a sentence. When I tried to cross the street, the motion of the cars became so disorienting that I couldn't move. I was at a sensory distance from the world, as if I were wrapped in clear plastic.

I had never been in poor health and didn't have an internist, so I went to my old pediatrician. I sat in a child's chair in a waiting room wallpapered with jungle scenes, watching a boy dismember an action figure. When my doctor drew the thermometer from my mouth, he asked me if I knew that my temperature was 101. He swabbed my throat, left for a few minutes, and returned with the news that I had strep throat. Puzzled by the other symptoms, he prescribed antibiotics and suggested that I see an internist.

The doctor I found waved me into a chair and began asking questions and making notes, pausing to rake his fingers through a hedge of dark hair that drifted onto his brow. He ran some tests and found nothing amiss. He told me to take antacids. A few weeks later, when I returned and told him that I was getting worse, he sat me down. My problem, he said gravely, was not in my body but in my mind; the test results proved it. He told me to see a psychiatrist.

I went to Dr. Charles Troshinsky, a respected psychiatrist whom I had seen when I was fifteen, after my high school boyfriend had died suddenly. He was shocked at how thin I was. I was just under five feet five, but my weight had dropped to a hundred pounds. Dr. Troshinsky said that he had seen several people with the same constellation of symptoms, all referred by physicians who dismissed them as mentally ill. He wrote my internist a letter stating that he would stake his reputation on his conclusion that I was mentally healthy but suffering from a serious physical illness.

"Find another psychiatrist," my internist said over the phone, a smile in his voice. How did he explain the fevers, chills, exhaustion, swollen lymph nodes, dizziness? What I was going through, he suggested, was puberty. I had just turned twenty. "Laura, everyone goes through this," he said with the drizzly slowness one uses with a toddler. "It's a normal adjustment to adulthood. You'll grow out of it in a few years." He told me to come back in six months.

"But I'm not happy with my treatment," I said.

He laughed. "Well, I am."

I called his secretary and asked for my medical records. I sat on my bedroom floor and flipped through the doctor's notes. *Couldn't handle school,* he had written. *Dropped out.*

My next doctor was a plump, pink man with the indiscriminate gaiety of a golden retriever. He was halfway through a hair transplant, and clumps of hair were lined up in neat rows on his scalp, like spring seedlings.

I again tested positive for strep, and he renewed the antibiotics. He ran a blood test for a virus called Epstein-Barr and found a soaring titer, a measurement of the antibody in my system. I had, he said with pep-rally enthusiasm, something called Epstein-Barr virus syndrome. He had it, too, he said, but he had discovered nutritional-supplement pills that cured it. "Whenever I feel it coming on," he said, "I just take these." He talked about how much skiing he could do.

I took the supplements. They had no effect. Nor did the antibiotics; the strep raged on. The doctor changed my prescription repeatedly, to no avail.

At the end of one of my appointments, the doctor followed me into the waiting room and asked my mother to make an appointment so that he could test her for strep. She said she felt fine, but he insisted that she might be infected but asymptomatic.

Our appointments fell on the same day. I went in first and sat while a nurse swabbed my throat. A few minutes later, the doctor bounded in, waving the positive-test swab, and bent over to look at my throat. I'd had strep for nearly three months. I dropped my face into my hands. He straightened abruptly and backed out of the room, repeating that the pills would cure the Epstein-Barr. "I go skiing a lot!" he hollered from down the hall.

I was still crying as I paid the bill. The receptionist gave me a sympathetic smile. She understood how I felt, she said, because she had Epstein-Barr, too. "It's amazing," she said. "The doctor has found that everyone working here has it."

I sat down. Several other patients were sitting near me, and I asked if the doctor had given any of them a diagnosis of Epstein-

Barr. Each one said yes. While we were talking, my mother emerged from the doctor's office. He had told her that she, too, had Epstein-Barr.

That year, millions of cicadas boiled up from the ground, teemed over tree limbs, and carpeted lawns and roads. The TV news showed people eating them on skewers. Cicadas burrowed into the house, scaled the curtains, swung from our clothes. I sat in bed, watching them bounce off the windowpane and nosedive into the grass, where they flapped and floundered as if they were drowning. Newton, the Dalmatian puppy my mother had adopted, zigzagged around the yard and snapped them out of the air. We called them flying dog snacks.

My world narrowed down to my bed and my window. I could no longer walk the length of my street. My hair was starting to fall out. I hadn't had a period in four months. My mouth and throat were pocked with dozens of bleeding sores and my temperature was spiking to 101 every twelve hours, attended by a ferocious sweat; in addition to the strep, I now had trench mouth, a rare infection of the gums. Sleeping on my side was uncomfortable because I had little body fat left and my bones pressed into the skin on my hips, knees, and shoulders.

In sleep, I dreamed of vigorous motion. I had swum competitively for ten years, from age seven to seventeen. I had been riding horses since childhood. Smitten with thoroughbred racing, I had spent my mid-teens learning to ride short-stirrup at a gallop, and praying that I wouldn't grow too tall to become a jockey. At Kenyon, I had been a tennis junkie. Now, as I lost the capacity to move, sports took over my dream world. I won at swimming in the Olympics, out-pedaled the *peloton* in the Tour de France, skimmed over a racetrack on a Kentucky Derby winner. When I woke, I felt the weight of illness on me before I opened my eyes.

Most of the people around me stepped backward. Linc said my friends asked him how I was, but after one or two get-well cards I stopped hearing from them. Now and then, I called people I had known in high school. The conversations were awkward and halting, and I felt foolish. No one knew what to say. Everyone had heard rumors that I was sick. Someone had heard I had AIDS. Another heard I was pregnant.

I missed Borden. At Kenyon, I had often studied in a deli run by a groovy guy named Craig, who cruised around the place in fluorescent-yellow sunglasses. It was there, in September of 1986, that Borden had first smiled at me. He was a senior, with a gentle, handsome face and wavy black hair. He had torn up his knee running track, and to avoid walking he used a battered bike to get around campus. The bike had no chain, so he could really ride it only downhill, wiggling it to keep it going when the ground leveled out. On the uphills, he stabbed at the ground with his good leg, Fred Flintstone style. Eventually, some frat brothers kidnapped the bike and hung it from a tree over the Scrotum Pole, a stone marker that had earned its nickname during a legendary fraternity vaulting incident.

From the day we met in the deli, Borden and I had been inseparable. Since I left Kenyon, he had sent me off-color postcards and silly drawings, mailed between papers and finals and graduation. I wrote dirty limericks and mailed them back to him.

That summer, he showed up at my door. He got a job as an assistant editor at a foreign-policy quarterly, moved in with me and my mother, and took care of me, making plans for the things we'd do when I got better.

Of my friends, only Linc visited. Home for the summer in Chicago, he drove Dr. Diesel fifteen hours to my house, where he would sit in a dilapidated denim armchair at the foot of my bed. The seat on the chair had collapsed, but he sat there anyway, his long thighs pointing up at the ceiling. Each time he saw me after a long absence, a wide startled look would pass over his face. He once said that he could sense the disease on me. I knew what he meant. I was disappearing inside it.

I saw my next physician only once. My jeans slid down my hips as I walked into the exam room, and he watched me tug them up. He asked how often I weighed myself. Often, I replied.

You shouldn't weigh yourself, he said, and you have to eat. I'm not dieting, I replied. Girls shouldn't be so thin, he said. I know, I don't want to be this thin. Yes, yes, but girls *shouldn't* be so thin.

After the appointment, I went to the bathroom, and as I opened the door to leave the doctor nearly fell into me. I was halfway home when I realized that he had been trying to hear if I was vomiting.

The next doctor was a pretty, compact woman with a squirrelly brightness. She found that I still had strep and changed the antibiotics. She ran the same tests that everyone else had run, and, again, the results were normal. I fought off the strep, but the other symptoms remained. I kept returning to see this doctor, hoping she could find some way to make me feel better. She couldn't, and I could see that it was wearing on her.

In September, I was so weak that on a ride over to her office I had to drop my head to my knees to avoid passing out. When the nurse entered, I was lying down, holding my head, the room swimming around me. She took my blood pressure: 70/50. The doctor came in. She wouldn't look at me.

"I don't know why you keep coming here," she said, her lips tight.

I told her that I felt faint and asked about my blood pressure. She said that it was normal and left, saying nothing else. She then went to see my mother, who was in the waiting room. "When is she going to realize that her problems are all in her head?" the doctor said.

I returned home, lay down, and tried to figure out what to do. My psychiatrist had found me to be mentally healthy, but my physicians had concluded that if my symptoms and the results of a few conventional tests didn't fit a disease they knew of, my problem had to be psychological. Rather than admit that they didn't know what I had, they made a diagnosis they weren't qualified to make.

Without my physicians' support, it was almost impossible to find support from others. People told me I was lazy and selfish. Someone lamented how unfortunate Borden was to have a girlfriend who demanded coddling. Some of Borden's friends suggested that he was foolish and weak to stand by me. "The best thing my parents ever did for my deadbeat brother," a former professor of his told him, "was to throw him out." I was ashamed and angry and indescribably lonely.

For seven months I had remained hopeful that I would find a way out of my illness, but the relentless decline of my body, my isolation, and the dismissal and derision I was experiencing took their toll. In the fall of 1987, I sank into a profound depression. I stopped seeing my physician and didn't try to find a new one. One afternoon, I dug through my mother's drawer and found a bottle of Valium that had been prescribed for back spasms. I poured the pills onto the bed and fingered them for an hour, pushing them into lines along the patterns on the quilt. I thought about Borden and couldn't put the pills in my mouth.

I went back to Dr. Troshinsky. He told me to make an appointment with Dr. John G. Bartlett, the chief of the Division of Infectious Diseases at Johns Hopkins University School of Medicine. Bartlett was the foremost authority in his field, Dr. Troshinsky said. If there was an answer, he would have it.

At Johns Hopkins, after a lengthy exam and review of my records, Dr. Bartlett sat down with Borden and me. My internists, he said, were wrong. My disease was real.

"You have chronic fatigue syndrome," he said. He explained that it was one of the most frustrating illnesses he had encountered in his practice; presented with severely incapacitated patients, he could do very little to help them. He suspected that it was viral in origin, although he believed that the Epstein-Barr virus was not involved; early lab tests had linked the virus to CFS, but subsequent research had demonstrated that some patients had had no exposure to the virus. He could offer no treatment. Eventually, he said, some patients recovered on their own.

"Some don't?"

"Some don't."

That night, for the first time since March, I didn't dream of being an athlete. I dreamed of being ill. In my dreams, I was never healthy again.

In the ensuing months, I began to improve. I hitched Newton to a leash and she tugged me through the neighborhood, first one block, then two, then three. My feet, soft from months in bed, blistered. The fever remained, but I was less prone to chills.

In the fall of 1988, Borden began graduate studies in political philosophy at the University of Chicago, and I felt well enough to move there with him. From the airport, we took a cab to Hyde Park, where Borden had rented a one-room apartment. The front door appeared to have been crowbarred for criminal purposes at least once. Inside, there was a mattress splayed across plastic milk crates and a three-legged dresser propped up on a brick. Roaches skittered over the walls and across the floor. The bathtub was heaped with used kitty litter. A weeks-old hamburger sat on the stove, shrunken into a shape that resembled the head of a mummy. The roaches were in various attitudes of repose around it.

We gave the mummy head a proper burial, roachproofed our toothbrushes by storing them in the refrigerator, and tried to make ends meet on Borden's $9,000-a-year stipend and our savings. The apartment was four flights up, with no elevator, so most days I spent my time inside, reading about the French Revolution and listening to our neighbor throw things at her husband.

I wanted to be useful but I wasn't strong enough for a conventional job. The one thing I could still do, however, was write. Shortly after arriving in Chicago, while watching a video of the 1988 Kentucky Derby, I had an idea for an article on the impact of overcrowded fields on the race. I researched and wrote the piece, then mailed it to an obscure racing magazine. I got a job offer: $50 per story, no benefits. I took only assignments that I could do from home and wrote them in bed. The magazine never paid me, but my bylines drew assignments at better publications, ultimately earning me regular work covering equine medicine and horse industry issues at *Equus*.

I was growing much stronger, but whenever I overextended myself my health disintegrated. One mistake could land me in bed for weeks, so the potential cost of even the most trivial activities, from showering to walking to the mailbox, had to be painstakingly considered. Sometimes I relapsed for no reason at all. Living in perpetual fear of collapse was stressful, but on my good days I was functioning much better. By 1990, I could walk all over Hyde Park, navigate the stairs of the apartment with ease, and, for half an hour on one blissful afternoon, ride a horse. Three years after becoming ill, I wrote to Linc about the curious sensation of growing younger.

In the summer of 1991, while visiting my mother during Borden's summer break, he and I decided to drive to New York to see the racetrack at Saratoga. A ten-hour road trip was risky, but I had grown tired of living so confined a life.

As we set out, the skies darkened. By the time we reached the interstate, a ferocious thunderstorm was crashing around us. Rain and hail hammered the roof of the car and gusts of wind buffeted us across the lane. We were caught in speeding traffic, but because the sheets of rain sweeping down the windshield limited visibility to a blurry tinge of lights ahead and behind, we couldn't slow down or pull over. It was more than an hour before we were able to escape into a rest stop. I sat on the floor of the bathroom, looking out a high window and watching the trees sway. The rain tapered off. My hands were shaking.

We had planned to stop at the New Jersey farmhouse where our friends Bill and Sarah were staying, but we were very late. Borden called them on a pay phone while I waited in the car, watching him through the beads of rain on the windshield. He climbed back in, and we sat with the engine idling. I was frightened by the draining sensation in my body.

Should we turn around? I asked. Borden's brow furrowed. Sometimes you've gotten a second wind, he said gently, as if asking a question. I wanted to believe him, so I agreed. He put the car in gear and we drove in silence. I felt worse and worse. I think we should turn around, I said, struggling to push the words out. We're closer to Bill's than we are to home, he said. If we keep going, you can rest sooner. He was scared now, leaning forward, driving fast. We entered New Jersey. We have to turn around, I said. Please. My head was pressed against the window, and I was crying. We're almost there, he said. We turned into the farmhouse driveway. There were rows of melons in the field.

Bill took us to a guest room. Borden turned on the TV and left me to rest. By the time he returned to check on me, I was sweating profusely and chills were running over me in waves. He took my hand and was horrified: it was gray and cold, and the veins had vanished.

He spread blankets over me and tried to help me drink a glass of milk. I couldn't sit up, so he cupped my head in his hand and tipped the milk into my mouth sideways. It ran down my cheek and pooled on the pillow. My teeth chattered so much that I couldn't speak. Borden called an emergency room. The nurse thought that I was in shock and urged him to rush me in. But we were far from the hospital, and doctors had never been able to help. I was sure that being moved would kill me.

Borden lay down and held me. Wide awake, I slid into delirium. I was in a vast desert, looking down at a dead Indian. His body was desiccated and hardened, his skin shiny and black and taut over his sinews, his arms bent upward, hands grasping, clawlike. His shriveled tongue was thrust into an empty eye socket. I lay there and trembled, whispering *I love you, I love you, I love you* to Borden through clenched teeth. *I'm sorry,* he said.

Hours passed. The sun rose over the melon field.

Borden drove me back to my mother's house. I lay exhausted for three days. When I opened my eyes on the morning of the fourth day, I had a black feeling. I couldn't get up.

For as long as two months at a time, I couldn't get down the stairs. Bathing became nearly impossible. Once a week or so, I sat on the edge of the tub and rubbed a washcloth over myself. The smallest exertion plunged me into a "crash." First, my legs would weaken and I'd lose the strength to stand. Then I wouldn't be able to sit up. My arms would go next, and I'd be unable to lift them. I couldn't roll over. Soon I would lose the strength to speak. Only my eyes were capable of movement. At the bottom of each breath, I would wonder if I'd be able to draw the next one.

The corpse of the Indian hung in my mind. Borden and I never spoke of it, or of the events of that night, and we never spoke of the future. To corral my thoughts, he made lists with me: candy bars from A to Z, Kentucky Derby winners, vice presidents in backward order, NFL quarterbacks, Union Army commanders. Over and over, I asked him if I was going to survive. He always answered yes.

Late one night, as I walked down the hall, I heard a soft, low sound and looked down the stairway. I saw Borden, pacing the foyer and sobbing. I started to call to him, then stopped myself, realizing that he wished to be alone. The next morning, he was as cheerful and steady as ever. But sometimes when I looked out the window I'd see him walking around the yard in endless revolutions, head down, hands on his temples.

One afternoon in September, he came in, sat on my bed, and told me that classes were starting and he had to return to Chicago. Before he left, he gave me a silver ring engraved with the words *"Vous et nul autre."* You and no other. I slid it on my finger and pressed my face to his chest.

With Borden in Chicago and my mother at work, I needed assistance to get through the day. I went through several helpers hired from nanny services. The first one clattered in with stacks of crimson-beaded Moroccan shoes and harem pants. She dumped them on my bed. "Twenty for the shoes, thirty for the pants," she said. She prowled through the house, appraising the furniture. "How much do you want for your refrigerator?" she asked.

When I asked the woman who followed to take Newton into the back yard, she opened the front door and shooed the dog onto the street. Lying in bed upstairs, I heard the dog barking gleefully as she galloped westward. I called to the woman but got no response. I sat up and looked out the window. The woman was standing high in our apple tree, mouth open, gaping at the vacant sky. The dog returned; the woman did not.

The third helper sympathized and commiserated, then bustled around downstairs while I lay upstairs in bed. It wasn't until she abruptly vanished that I discovered she had been packing armloads of my belongings into her car each evening. I went to the closet and found only a hanger where my taffeta ball gown had been.

On a rainy afternoon in January of 1993, I was sitting on the bed reading a magazine when the room began whirling violently. I dropped the magazine and grabbed on to the dresser. I felt as though I were rolling and lurching, a ship on the high seas. I clung to the dresser and waited for the feeling to pass, but it didn't. At five the next morning, I woke with a screeching, metal-on-metal sound in my ears. My eyes were jerking to the left, and I couldn't stop them. My eyes, upper lip, and cheeks were markedly swollen.

I went to a neurologist for tests. A technician asked me to lie down on a table. He produced something that looked like a blowtorch and pushed it into my ear. A jet of hot air roared out, spinning the vestibular fluid in my inner ear. It triggered such a forceful sensation of spinning that I gripped the table with all my strength, certain that I was about to fly off and slam into the wall. The tests determined that my vertigo was neurological in origin and virtually untreatable. The doctor prescribed diuretics and an extremely low-sodium diet to control the facial edema, which seemed to be linked to the vertigo. He could do little else.

The vertigo wouldn't stop. I didn't lie on my bed so much as ride it as it swung and spun. There was a constant shrieking sound in my ears. The furniture flexed and skidded around the room, and the walls folded and unfolded. Every few days there was a sudden plunging sensation, and I would throw my arms out to catch myself. The leftward eye-rolling came and went. Sleep brought no respite; every dream took place on the deck of a tossing ship, a runaway rollercoaster, a plane caught in violent turbulence, a falling elevator. Looking at anything close-up left me reeling. I couldn't read or write. I rented audiobooks, but I couldn't follow the narratives.

Borden called several times a day. He told me about Xenophon and Thucydides, the wind off Lake Michigan, the athletic feats of the roaches. When I asked him about himself, he changed the subject.

On Valentine's Day, a package from Borden arrived in the mail. Inside was a gold pocket watch. I hung it from my window frame and stared at it as the room bent and arced around it. Weeks passed, and then months. The watch dial meted out each day, the light sliding across it: reddish in the morning, hard and colorless at midday, red again at dusk. In the dark, I could hear it ticking.

Outside, the world went on. Linc got married, my siblings had children, my friends got graduate degrees and jobs and mortgages. None of it had any relation to me. The realm of possibility began and ended in that room, on that bed. I no longer imagined anything else. If I was asked what month it was, I had to think a while before I could answer.

While I was lying there, I began to believe that we had struck the deer back in 1987, that he had come through the windshield and killed me, and that this was Hell.

Two years passed. In late 1994, Borden took his qualifying exams, and left Chicago. When I first saw him, lugging his green backpack, he was so thin that I gasped.

In 1995, by tiny increments, the vertigo began to abate. Eventually I could read the back of a corn flakes box. My strength began to return. Instead of sitting on the edge of the tub with a washcloth, I could sit on the shower floor while the water ran over me. The first time I showered, dead skin peeled off in sheets. A hair stylist came and cut off eight inches of my hair, which had been growing like kudzu for several years and was now nearing my waist. In time, I could walk down the stairs almost every day. I sat on the patio looking at the trees.

Since my visit to Johns Hopkins, I had searched for an internist I could trust. In 1988, CFS had been officially recognized and described by the Centers for Disease Control and Prevention. Subsequent research suggested endocrinologic, immunologic, and neurologic abnormalities in many CFS patients, though the cause remained elusive. Physicians were becoming aware of the disease, but many of them knew less about it than I did. Others hawked dubious treatments. For a while, I tried almost anything. A few treatments caused disastrous side effects. The rest did nothing.

Then a friend referred me to Dr. Fred Gill, a renowned infectious-disease specialist. He was an angular, elegant man with a neat, Amish-style beard rimming a sharp jawline. As Borden and I told him my story, I found my stomach tightening in anticipation of a dismissive verdict. But Dr. Gill listened for the better part of an hour. When he had finished, he nodded. He couldn't cure me, he said, but he would do everything he could to help me cope with the illness. In the following years, Dr. Gill managed my symptoms and coordinated my care with other specialists.

Eager to be productive, I called my *Equus* editor, Laurie Prinz, and asked if I could write something. She assigned a story on equine surgery and told me not to worry about a deadline. I did the interviews on the phone from bed. Because looking at the page made the room shimmy crazily around me, I could write only a paragraph or two a day. When I could no longer stand the spinning, I'd take a pillow into the yard and lie in the grass with Newton, fixing my eyes on the treetops while she dissected a bone. It took me six weeks to write 1,500 words, but, four years after the abortive trip to Saratoga, I was coming back.

In 1996, with Borden and Fangfoss the cat, I moved into a small apartment in northwest Washington, D.C. One block away stood a fire station, and if Washington has an arson district we were in the heart of it. At the Taiwanese consulate, which was next door, a group of protesters soon set up camp, hauled in a loudspeaker, and blasted a Chinese rallying song, sung by shrieky children. They apparently had a loop tape, so the song never ended. It was like listening to a bone saw. After a few weeks, I started dreaming to it.

I turned up my radio and wrote as much as I could, mostly equine veterinary medical articles for *Equus*. On breaks, I took brief walks. I bought new shoes — I'd been lying around in socks for years — and discovered that my feet had shrunk two sizes. I had lived for so long in silence and isolation that the world was a sensory explosion. At the grocery store, I dragged my hands along the shelves, touching boxes and bags, smelling oranges and pears and apples. At the hardware store, I'd plunge my arm into the seed bins to feel the pleasing weight of the grain against my skin. I was a toddler again.

After years of seeing people almost exclusively on television, I found their three-dimensionality startling: the light playing off their faces, the complexity of their hands, the strange electric feel of their nearness. One afternoon, I spent fifteen minutes watching a shirtless man clip a hedge, enthralled by the glide of the muscles under his skin.

On a cool fall day in 1996, I was sifting through some documents on the great racehorse Seabiscuit when I discovered Red Pollard, the horse's jockey. I saw him first in a photograph, curled over Seabiscuit's neck. Looking out at me from the summer of 1938, he had wistful eyes and a face as rough as walnut bark.

I began looking into his life and found a story to go with the face. Born in 1909, Red was an exceptionally intelligent, bookish child with a shock of orange hair. At fifteen, he was abandoned by his guardian at a makeshift racetrack cut through a Montana hayfield. He wanted to be a jockey, but he was too tall and too powerfully built. That didn't stop him, though. He began race riding in the bush leagues and fared so badly that he took to part-time prizefighting in order to survive. He lived in horse stalls for twelve years, studying Emerson and the *Rubáiyát*, piloting neurotic horses at "leaky roof" tracks, getting punched bloody in cow-town clubs, keeping painfully thin with near-starvation diets, and probably pills containing the eggs of tapeworms.

He was appallingly accident-prone. Racehorses blinded his right eye, somersaulted onto his chest at forty miles per hour, trampled him, and rammed him into the corner of a barn, virtually severing his lower leg. He shattered his teeth and fractured his back, hip, legs, collarbone, shoulder, ribs. He was once so badly mauled that the newspapers announced his death. But he came back every time, struggling through pain and fear and the limitations of his body to do the only thing he had ever wanted to do. And in the one lucky moment of his unlucky life he found Seabiscuit, a horse as damaged and persistent as he was. I hung Red's picture above my desk and began to write.

What began as an article for *American Heritage* became an obsession, and in the next two years the obsession became a book. Borden and I moved to a cheap rental house farther downtown, and I arranged my life around the project. At the local library, I pored over documents and microfilm I requisitioned from the Library of Congress. If I looked down at my work, the room spun, so I perched my laptop on a stack of books in my office, and Borden jerry-rigged a device that held documents vertically. When I was too tired to sit at my desk, I set the laptop up on my bed. When I was too dizzy to read, I lay down and wrote with my eyes closed. Living in my subjects' bodies, I forgot about my own.

I mailed the manuscript off to Random House in September 2000, then fell into bed. I was lying there the following day when the room began to gyrate. Reviewing the galleys brought me close to vomiting several times a day. Most of the gains I had made since 1995 were lost. I spent each afternoon sitting with Fangfoss on my back steps, watching the world undulate and sliding into despair.

In March 2001, Random House released *Seabiscuit: An American Legend*. Five days later, I was lying down when the phone rang. "You are a best-selling writer," my editor said. I screamed. Two weeks later, I picked up the phone to hear him and my agent shout in tandem, "You're number one!" Borden threw a window open and yelled it to the neighborhood.

That spring, as I tried to cope with the dreamy unreality of success and the continuing failure of my health, something began to change in Borden. At meals, he sat in silence, his gaze disconnected, his jaw muscles working. His sentences trailed off in the middle. He couldn't sleep or eat. He was falling away from me, and I didn't know why.

He came into my office one night in June, sat down, and slid his chair up to me, touching his knees to mine. I looked at his face. He was still young and handsome, his hair black, his skin seamless. But the color was gone from his lips, the quickness from his eyes. He tried to smile, but the corners of his mouth wavered. He dropped his chin to his chest. He began to speak, and fourteen years of unvoiced emotions spilled out: the torment of watching the woman he loved suffer; his feelings of responsibility and help-

lessness and anger; his longing for children we probably couldn't
have; the endless strain of living in obedience to an extraordinarily
volatile disease.

We talked for much of the night. I found myself revealing all the
grief that I had hidden from him. When I asked him why he hadn't
said anything before, he said he thought I would shatter. I recognized that I had feared the same of him. In protecting each other
from the awful repercussions of our misfortune, we had become
strangers.

When we were too tired to talk anymore, I went into the bedroom and sat down alone. I slid his ring from my finger and
dropped it into a drawer.

We spent a long, painful summer talking, and for both of us
there were surprises. I didn't shatter, and neither did he. I prepared myself for him to leave, but he didn't. We became, for the
first time since our days at Kenyon, alive with each other.

One night that fall, I walked to the back of the yard. As Fangfoss
hunted imaginary mice in the grass, I looked out at the hill behind
the house. Beyond it, downtown Washington hummed like an
idling engine, the city lights radiating over the ridge. I looked west,
where a line of row-house chimneys filed down the hill until they
became indistinguishable from the trunks of the walnut trees at
the road's end. Borden came out and joined me briefly, draping
his arms over my shoulders, then he went inside. I watched the
screen door slap behind him.

As I turned back, I saw a slit of light arc over the houses and van-
ish behind the trees. It was the first meteor I had seen since that
night in Linc's car. I thought, for the first time in a long time, of
the deer.

In the depths of illness, I believed that the deer had crashed
through the windshield and ushered me into an existence in which
the only possibility was suffering. I was haunted by his form in
front of the car, his bent knee, the seeming inevitability of catastro-
phe, and the ruin my life became.

I had forgotten the critical moment. The deer's knee didn't
straighten. He didn't step into our path, we didn't strike him, and I
didn't die. As sure as I was that he had taken everything from me, I
was wrong.

The car passed him and moved on.

TIM JUDAH

Passover in Baghdad

FROM GRANTA

BAGHDAD WAS NOT the most obvious place to celebrate Passover. Saddam had fallen barely a week before it began, looters were
rampaging through the city, dozens of buildings were on fire, and
Islamic hard-liners were arming militias. What's more, in a city of
almost five million people there were only a handful of Jews left.

Until the Second World War roughly a quarter of Baghdad's
population was Jewish. In June 1941, following a Nazi-inspired
coup, 179 Jews died and almost 1,000 were wounded in a pogrom
while the police and army stood by. Until 1948 there were still
150,000 Jews in Iraq, but by 1951, after the Israeli government had
organized airlifts, the vast majority of them had left. The government placed severe restrictions on those who stayed. Even so, a
community of some 6,000 lingered on. But now, according to
those that remain, their numbers add up to the grand total of 34
people.

While most Iraqi Jews left for Israel after its creation in 1948, significant numbers also made their way to Britain and the United
States, especially those from the middle classes — the Saatchi family, for example. Some wealthy Iraqi Jews did remain in the country
after 1951, knowing that to leave was to lose everything: Jews who
emigrated were stripped, not just of their citizenship, but also of all
their property and other assets. In the end, however, their wealth
could not protect them and indeed often made them targets for
murder and blackmail. So they left too, for Israel, Britain, Holland,
and Canada.

Today it is hard to imagine that so many Jews once lived here.

But if you look carefully in parts of town that used to be Jewish, like Bataween, on the east bank of the Tigris, or around Rashid Street, a bustling commercial area, you can still see brickwork patterned into Stars of David. You can also see places where molded stars have been hacked away. What you can't see are the stories.

Although the majority of Iraqi Jews left in 1950 and 1951, in fact they had been emigrating for a lot longer than this. In the eighteenth century Baghdadi Jews began to make their way to India and beyond, which is the beginning of my story. My father was born in 1924 in Calcutta and this was his background. He came to Britain when he was four and, except for a single holiday a few years ago, he never went back. When he returned from the holiday he told us a surprising anecdote. Several times he had wanted to ask for something, and on each occasion a Hindi word he had no idea that he knew popped out of his mouth. The words had lain dormant, lodged somewhere deep in his mind, for seventy years or so.

When he died in November 2002 he was buried in strict accordance with Sephardi tradition. At the Hoop Lane cemetery in Golders Green in London all the tombstones on one side stand upright, that is, in the Ashkenazi or European way, and all the Sephardi tombs are flat, in the Oriental and Middle Eastern Jewish way. The night before we buried him we wrote some notes for the rabbi to help him in his oration, and in them we described how proud my father had been of his Baghdadi Jewish heritage.

My father's family left Baghdad or Aleppo or all the other Middle Eastern cities they traced their roots to during the late nineteenth century. They left behind the rotting corners of the Ottoman Empire and headed for the great commercial hubs of the British Empire and beyond: Bombay, Calcutta, Singapore, Hong Kong, and Shanghai. Some left even earlier than this. On my grandmother's side, David Sassoon, founder of a prodigious commercial dynasty, fled Baghdad in about 1829 before eventually settling in Bombay.

When I was growing up, "Baghdad" was a place that lurked like those Hindi words deep in family memory, but it was no more present than this. After all, no one in my family had actually been there. My grandmother herself had been born in Calcutta.

And yet from my childhood I remember what I now realize were echoes, faint ripples of Baghdad, which still survived. My father and grandmother played backgammon and would laugh *Inshallah* — "God willing" — when something was to be wished for. When we break the fast at Yom Kippur we still eat pomegranates. In Baghdad during the war I found myself eating the same food we used to eat, and sometimes still do on High Holy Days in London, such as chicken with okra or ladyfingers. Iraqis would say, "Do you know what that is?" and I would tell them I did — but never why.

I had gone to Baghdad to report the war for the *Economist* and the *New York Review of Books*. But of course I also had my own personal reasons for wanting to be there. Before I left, I joked that I was going to be the first Judah — of my family anyway — back in Baghdad for more than a century. But being Jewish, especially in Saddam's Iraq, was hardly something you wanted to advertise, and from the visa application onward — which demanded the applicant's religion — I said nothing about the subject. When my government translator, discussing her views on foreigners, said, "Of course, we hate the Jews," then added generously, "You know, I think that even among the Jews there might be some good people," I just nodded and kept my mouth shut. It had taken me ten months to get a visa, and now, with war about to break out, I had no intention of being expelled.

As a foreign correspondent I spent more than a decade covering the Balkan wars and their aftermath. But after September 11 no one was interested in the Balkans anymore. I realized I would have to start working in Arab and Muslim Middle Eastern countries, something I had always shied away from previously. Being Jewish and with an obviously Jewish name meant I was nervous both personally and professionally. Of course there are many Jewish correspondents who cover the Middle East, but how you feel about covering this story and whether your own feelings might somehow cloud your objectivity can only be an individual decision.

But when I got to Afghanistan in October 2001, I was surprised to find I felt quite relaxed. Sometimes I was asked if I was an infidel, and once if I was "thinking of Jesus." To this I replied with a cautious "Sometimes," and the man who asked me the question seemed happy to leave it there.

Then I went to Iran and no one asked me anything. When I got back, though, I had lunch with the press attaché at the Iranian embassy, who spent the meal complaining about the pieces I'd written. As we finished eating he said, "And anyway, what does 'Judah' mean?"

"Nothing, it's just a name," I said.

Looking straight at me, he said, "Because in Farsi it means 'Jewish.'"

Just before going to Baghdad, I went to Jordan and people began to ask questions. "Judah? Judah? What sort of a name is that?" they asked. But every time, before I had a chance to reply, they said, "So you must be from here and have Arab family?" I was startled — "Judah" is, after all, just an anglicization of the Hebrew "Yehuda." But now it turned out that there was a prominent Jordanian-Palestinian family whose name was pronounced, if not transliterated, in exactly the same way as mine. It made me feel less nervous.

On the night of March 11, I crossed the border into Iraq, the country where my ancestors lived for 2,500 years. Here I was — the first Judah back. I felt absolutely nothing. Perhaps the feeling will come, I told myself.

This was not, anyway, the right moment for personal reflection or for hunting down my roots or, in fact, for mentioning anything Jewish in any context at all. Every few days foreign journalists were being expelled. Some were arrested and jailed. I needed to be careful. I limited myself to sending a few e-mails to friends and relatives asking them if they had any relevant information that I could use once things were safe.

The bombing campaign began on March 20. The Americans reached Firdos Square, just by the Palestine Hotel (where the foreign press were based), on the afternoon of April 9. For the next few days I was busy with work, but then I realized that if I wanted to do Passover in Baghdad I had better get organized. Before the bombing had ended I had received an e-mail from a friend of a friend of a friend in London asking me if I could try to find their elderly mother and aunt. They were desperate for news. All the telephone exchanges had just been bombed, but I had a satellite phone.

I asked my driver to take me to the address they'd given me, but he refused. It was too late in the day, and besides, he said, Bataween market was full of "Ali Babas," or robbers, and he did not want to risk his life or his car. The next day I got another car. The house turned out to be only a few minutes' drive from the Palestine Hotel. To avert attention I told him to park farther away, down the street. The house stood alone in a street covered, like much of the rest of the city, in rubbish. The people on the balcony of the low-rise block opposite watched me, an obvious foreigner, with interest.

After I banged on the door it opened a crack and an old lady peeped out. "My name is Tim Judah," I explained. "I am from London and I have a message from your family." She stared at me. I said in a whisper, "My name is Judah — *Yehuda! Yehuda!* — Let me in!" Cautiously she opened the door.

The old ladies, Um Daoud ("Mother of Daoud") and her sister Mariam, were still suspicious. I explained that I had come with a message from Um Daoud's daughter, who had asked me to find out if they were alive and, if so, how they were. Did they have enough food and money? I sat awkwardly on a sofa in the front room, which was a jumble of furniture and bags. Mariam paced about; Um Daoud, sitting in a chair with a rug over her knees, looked thin and drawn. She reminded me of my grandmother, who used to sit in just the same way, with the same sort of rug tucked over her lap. "You are Jewish?" one of them asked suspiciously. "Yes, yes," I said, I hoped not too impatiently. I could feel the tension in the room subside.

"We are frightened," said Um Daoud. "Thank you for coming, but we are Jews and they will come and ask who you are and we will have trouble. Please tell the family we are okay." I explained that the war was over, that there was no more Mukhabarat (secret police), and no government. Saddam was finished. Um Daoud shot back instantly, "There are thousands of Saddams in this country. Did anyone see you come? You had better go."

The eve of Passover, the Seder night, when Jews recount the story of the coming out of Egypt, was the very next day. I wondered if Um Daoud and her sister, or the Baghdadi Jewish community, had any plans. "It is the eve of Passover tomorrow," I said hopefully. "Are you doing something? Have you got matzo?"

They looked at me as if I were mad. "No! We are frightened. We are not doing anything."

Two days later it was the first day of Passover. I went to the Meir Tweg synagogue, the only synagogue left in Baghdad. It was hidden behind a high wall, close to where the old ladies lived. Unless you knew what you were looking for you would never find it. There is nothing on the outside to identify the building or the compound as a synagogue.

I banged on the steel door. Eventually a young man, whom I later learned was the Muslim caretaker, peered out and gestured to me that the synagogue was closed and that I should go away. When I insisted that I wanted to come in, he popped his head out of the door, checked to see if anyone was looking, and then pointed at his watch and told me to come back later.

By now the friend of the friend of the friend was passing on more messages from families in Britain and elsewhere, desperate for news of their relatives in Baghdad. I got a new driver and set out to hunt for them. "You," said the driver suspiciously. "What religion?" "Christian," I replied, as matter-of-factly as I could, and on we drove.

After I'd banged for several minutes at the gates of one house in a predominantly middle-class and Christian part of the city, an old lady, Victoria, finally appeared on its flat roof. "Who are you?" she quavered. I tried to explain, but even though she spoke English I didn't think it was a good idea to be shouting my business in front of the whole street. "Please come down," I pleaded. "But I don't know you," she remonstrated. Eventually Victoria tottered to the gate. Her Alsatian was working himself into a frenzy. "Neither my son nor my daughter are here, come back tomorrow," she said.

That evening a surprising new e-mail arrived from the friend of the friend of the friend.

> plans for airlift r underway for those who r ready to move immediately. no need for passports. if you have the chance please explain that this is a chance which cannot be repeated for a while. our estimates that only 15 people r ready to move out with no hesitation. the children of the two old ladies are begging them to just leave if the chance presents itself.

No more explanations were forthcoming. Exactly who was organizing this airlift? Where would the plane take these people to? When would they leave? How much warning would people be given? I was not told. All I was asked to do (by whom exactly? — even this was unclear, and I decided not to inquire too deeply) was to find the city's Jews and ask them a simple question: If you have the chance to go in a week or two — leaving everything behind — will you go?

Suddenly my job had changed. Passover was taking an unexpected turn. As my colleagues started to look around for new angles and stories, I began to hide. I did not want anyone to ask me what I was doing, and I particularly didn't want anyone to ask me if I knew anything about the remnant of the Jewish community in Baghdad.

The next day, I found Ishak and Yusef and their mother, Sara. Ishak was forty-three and Yusef thirty-six; during the bombing I turned forty-one. I felt a kind of instant familiarity with them; after all, it was only a twist of fate which made me the visitor and them the visited and not the other way around. Ishak was a businessman and Yusef worked as a jeweler while also studying for a doctorate in linguistics. They both spoke English, and while they had been keeping a low profile during the bombing, they were not as frightened as the old people I'd met.

Yusef told me that he was not surprised to see me. "The other day I dreamt that someone, like an angel, or from the Red Cross, would come to visit us soon and ask us whether we wanted to leave." I asked them if they *did* want to leave, because the people organizing the airlift needed to know. They began to shower me with questions. "If we leave now, can we come back later to sell our property? Can we leave without passports?"

I went back to my hotel to give them time to think. When I returned to the house the next day, Sara began to cry. She had had a dream that her husband, who had died the previous year, had implored her "not to leave him." But the brothers argued that there was little point in staying, as, apart from anything else, there were no Jewish girls to marry. What future was there for them in Iraq? Surely the future was grandchildren?

With Ishak acting as my guide, driving a 1960 Ford Zodiac that his father had imported, we managed to hunt down more of the Jewish community. We got past the steel door of the synagogue and found two old men who lived in rooms beside it. They seemed quite happy. One of them, unshaven, sunning himself in his pajamas, looked exactly like my father just before he died. They told me they did not want to go anywhere and asked me to send their love to their families and to tell them they were fine. We sent a message to the head of the community asking him to come and meet us, but when we went back to the synagogue the next day, the guardian informed Ishak, in Arabic, "He doesn't want to see him. Tell him he is out of Baghdad." Ishak said, "He is frightened."

I went to ask Um Daoud and Mariam what they wanted to do. "After you were here last time they came and broke down the door," they told me. I was alarmed: perhaps the Mukhabarat was not finished after all. I saw that the door had been barricaded to keep it upright. But it wasn't the Mukhabarat, as it turned out. Someone, acting through malice or confusion, had told the Americans that there were two armed men holed up in the women's house. So seven American soldiers carried out a raid. Um Daoud said, "They were looking for two men with swords, but I told them, 'I will tell you the truth. We are just two Jewish girls here!'" The Americans had returned the next day with a military ration pack as a gift, to say sorry.

When I asked the women if they wanted to leave, they said that they did. But then they told Ishak in Arabic that they did not.

Over the next few days I ferried news back and forth between families in Iraq and abroad explaining what was — or what was not — happening. I exchanged many e-mails with the friend of the friend of the friend. I found two women in their thirties and their elderly uncle. Unlike the other people I'd met, they had no close family abroad, spoke only Arabic, and were not the remnant of an educated and wealthy class. Chickens ran through their smoke-blackened house. With no close family in Britain or Holland or anywhere else, their only option was Israel. One woman wanted to go, the other two did not. The old man gave me the address of a cousin in New York whom he had last heard from in 1985. He clung to this, evidently believing that if only the man could be found, he would send for them and everything would be all right.

As they dithered I asked them what they wanted me to tell the organizers of the airlift. They told me they wanted to stay. Ishak was outraged. "You will be corrupted or they will make you convert," he told them. Then he said to me, "Once a man in a desert found people who were dying of thirst. They said, 'Give us water,' so he did. Then they said, 'This is warm. We want cold water!' So the man could do nothing and left them. So let's go. They are crazy."

Ishak told me people's stories as we searched. "There," said Ishak, passing one house, "lived a family of two girls and two boys and their parents. There was also a sister, in Lebanon. It was 1972. At eight o'clock in the morning one of the girls went to school, but when she came back in the afternoon she found men from the Mukhabarat there, including Khairallah Tulfah. You know who he was? Saddam's uncle. There was blood on the floor. 'What happened? What happened?' shouted the girl. They told her, 'Your family left for Iran.' She said, 'Without me? Look, here are their passports.' She was about seventeen years old. Then she said, 'Please give me some money,' because the police had stolen everything in the house, jewelry, everything precious. 'I want to live,' she told them, but they told her they had nothing. She became half crazy. Our community and our parents gave her money and made contact with her sister, and she left."

As we passed another house Ishak said, "Here was another family who were very wealthy and killed for their money. There was a man aged sixty or sixty-five. He married a young girl, Jewish, very beautiful. He owned three factories. He bought her a car, but the Mukhabarat would come after her and stop her. 'Give us a kiss,' they'd say. Once she went to stay with her sister, and the Mukhabarat went to the husband and cut off his ears and the tip of his nose. When the wife heard, she came back. This was in 1973. Then, four or five days later, the Mukhabarat came back and took them. Later, a friend of my father who worked in the Mukhabarat told him that they dissolved his body in acid. I don't know what happened to the girl. No one ever heard of her again."

All the time I kept thinking how fortunate I had been that my ancestors had decided that there was not much of a future to be had in Baghdad. But why were these people, even if they were only a handful, still here in 2003? Everyone I asked came up with something, but most of their reasons were unclear. It was a painful question to answer. Why had they decided to stay when their parents, brothers, sisters, and almost everyone else they knew had left, either by the end of 1951 or whenever there had been other opportunities to leave since then?

Victoria's daughter, Rahel, a thirty-eight-year-old doctor who lived with her mother, told me, as we drove to find her elderly aunt, "I blame my parents. They lost every chance to go." Her colleagues at the office had put up a calendar on the wall to taunt her, with a slogan from Saddam: "Damn, damn the dirty Jews!"

When I asked Victoria about her story, she told me that her father had died, before the Second World War, when she was very young. Her sister didn't work and had never married. She was therefore responsible for looking after both her mother and her sister. In 1951, when she was still a medical student, she had wanted to leave. "I wanted to go and arranged everything for us to go to Israel. But my mother refused and so did my sister. I was angry, but I loved my mother and did not want her to know that I was angry." After she married there had been opportunities to leave in the early 1960s and then in the early 1970s, but her mother refused again, as did her husband. Property had been a problem. Those who left before 1951 had been allowed to take the equivalent of twenty U.S. dollars with them. They lost their property and were stripped of their citizenship. The same thing happened to those who left after them.

After this, periods of repression came and went. There were periods when Jews were arrested and they disappeared, and certain jobs were barred for Jews. Among the worst of times was that which followed the 1967 Six Day War, when Ahmed Hassan al-Bakr, who became president in 1968, used the issue of Israel to distract Iraqis from domestic concerns. During this period in particular, being Jewish was dangerous and there was both official and unofficial harassment. Saddam was al-Bakr's deputy and increasingly the real power broker. He finally assumed the presidency himself in July 1979. There were so few Jews left in Iraq by this point that the president could play a more subtle game. Saddam needed Western support for his war against Iran, and presented himself as a protector of minorities, mostly Christian. But at the same time he played the Palestinian card to garner support in the Arab world, and also borrowed increasingly from the rhetoric of the Islamists. His official media frequently spewed out virulent anti-Semitism.

Back in 1969, at the height of al-Bakr's rule, fourteen men, nine of them Jewish, were hanged in Tahrir Square after show trials in which they were accused of spying for Israel. Iraqi radio called on people to come out to celebrate, and up to half a million did. "Come and enjoy the feast!" it said. "Death to Israel! Death to all traitors!" chanted the people. That evening Victoria talked her husband into taking her to the square. "Their necks were as long as this," she said, indicating her forearm. She wrote down some of the men's names for me. She crooked her body and said, "They were hanging like this." I asked her what happened next. "I cried," she said.

"And your husband?"

"He said nothing."

Victoria told me several times, "I pray to God that when the Messiah comes he will not revive him [Bakr]. *I always pray to God about this.*"

I asked Victoria if, if she could turn the clock back to 1951, she would have left, whatever her mother and sister had said. She just smiled and said, "I don't know. I can't imagine this."

Victoria's house, like the other houses I had visited, was ramshackle. It contained several large old refrigerators, and there were piles of clothing and bric-a-brac in various rooms. I had the impression, in all of these houses, that the reason for the mess, the reason these houses were in need of paint and work, wasn't just lack of money. It was as though an argument had raged on and off for sixty years among the people who had lived in these rooms about whether they should stay or go. Why bother to invest in your house if you might one day leave and the law stated that Jews who left Iraq could not sell their property?

I asked Um Daoud why she had stayed. I knew from the e-mails she was getting and I was reading to her that she had almost a dozen grandchildren abroad — but she had never seen them. She pointed at her sister with a quick, low, stabbing movement.

Sara, the mother of Ishak and Yusef, told me her story. She was born in 1938 in Al Kifl, a little town about an hour and a half's drive south of Baghdad. There had been a community of 250 Jews there. When Israel was created, she told me, the Jews were happy, and behind closed doors at least, they celebrated. But then the atmosphere began to change. There were anti-Jewish demonstrations, Jews began to be arrested, restrictions were placed on them by the government, and they no longer felt safe. Also they believed Israel was the Promised Land. In 1950 and 1951 most of the community left. They went by bus from Al Kifl to Baghdad, from where they flew to Cyprus, and from there to Israel. In 1951 Sara was thir-

teen years old. I asked her what she remembered of people leaving. "They were crying," she said. "They were remembering the
good times with their neighbors."

At home there were fights. Her mother would ask her father,
"Why do you want to leave us with the Muslims? Aren't you afraid
of our destiny?" He maintained that he was successful in Iraq, that
he made good money. He sold clothes and silks. "We were afraid,"
said Sara, "but we used to take our mother's side. I would cry, but
my father was stubborn and despotic." In the end, she said, "he did
not want to hear anything about going. I loved him as a father, but
he was a dictator."

Suddenly all the Jews had left Al Kifl, and Sara's family were the
only ones left. They moved to Baghdad. In 1959 Sara married and
the story began again. Her husband was Jewish and had been a
Communist. After 1951 he left the party and pursued his career as
a lawyer, although with difficulty after new anti-Jewish restrictions
were enforced in the early 1960s. For the whole of the marriage
the question hung in the air, but Sara's husband always refused to
go. He loved his country and wanted to die there. Sara explained,
"The same problem that we had had with my father reappeared
again with my husband. I would say, 'What about our sons? They
will need to get married,' and he would say, just as a Muslim Iraqi
would have done, 'It is the will of God.'"

Sara told me that in Al Kifl her family had lived next to the
shrine of Ezekiel the prophet. Every year thousands of Jews would
come to make a pilgrimage there. A couple of days before I talked
to Sara, I had visited the nearby town of Karbala. Here I had seen
tens of thousands of Shiite Muslims beating their breasts and
heads and converging on the golden-domed mosques of the city to
mourn the imam Hussein, who had died there in 680. At the
height of the pilgrimage there may have been up to a million pilgrims in Karbala at any one time.

I asked Sara when the Jews would make their pilgrimage, and
she said that it used to take place in the week after Passover. In fact,
she said — scrabbling through a Jewish calendar — it would have
to be done by, well, tomorrow.

We began to debate. Would the road be safe? What about the
Shiites? A day or two before, one of the Shia leaders had been arrested by the Americans, and his followers had been protesting,

writing slogans in blood on the road outside the Palestine Hotel.
But we decided to try to go anyway.

We set off the next morning. The road was open and there were no
checkpoints. American military convoys jostled for space with the
rest of the traffic. When we got to Al Kifl we made our way to the
shrine, behind the old covered market. Because it was Friday, the
Muslim day of prayer, the shops were shut, and just as we got there
a Shiite imam was leading his flock into the tomb to pray. He politely told Sara to put on a headscarf. We went to have lunch while
the prayers took place. Ishak was nervous and did not feel safe.
Men ambled around with Kalashnikovs. There had been fighting
with the Americans here and the main street was pockmarked with
bullet holes. Outside the little restaurant were three minivans with
coffins strapped to their roofs. They were Shiites being taken for
burial at their nearby holy city of Najaf.

When we went back, prayers had not yet finished. We sat outside
a teahouse in the covered market while inside a group of men
watched a DVD chronicling the crimes of Saddam. Sara told me
that until 1951 about five thousand Jews used to come to Al Kifl
during Passover week. And people still came after 1951, at least until 1967, after which it grew too dangerous. Then in 1984 a group
of twenty Jews had come from Baghdad, and in 1989 Sara, her family, and another family had come, but no Jews to her knowledge
had made the pilgrimage since then.

We wandered back to the gate of the shrine and met a young
man who was waiting there for his father. He told us, without being
asked, that the market used to belong to Jews and added that now
Indians and Iranians came to pray at the shrine. I asked if Jews
came too, and he said, "I don't know, because I don't know what
they look like."

Before the Jews left Al Kifl, the Jews and the Shiites had shared
the shrine. They would come at different times of day and steer
clear of it on one another's holy days.

Inside the shrine was the tomb of the prophet Ezekiel. There
were still Hebrew inscriptions on the walls. The tomb was surrounded by a large wooden covering, like a sarcophagus. We lit
candles and the guardian, who realized from the way we talked and
acted that we were Jewish, opened a tiny door at the bottom of the
covering. By crouching down we could see the actual, concrete-

covered tomb. It had Hebrew script on one end. The guardian told us he would welcome the Jews to come back to pray here. Sara walked around and kissed the corners of the tomb.

Later Sara told me she was both exhilarated and saddened by what we had done. The past, she said, her childhood in Al Kifl, had seemed "like yesterday." But now perhaps this would be her last visit.

On the way back to Baghdad we stopped at the ruins of Babylon. Much of the ancient city was reconstructed under Saddam; the rest is crumbling walls in dips and mounds, and the whole site is dominated by one of his nearby palaces. A few American soldiers were mooching about, some guarding the site, some tourists.

This was where this story began, and this was where it was ending. In 606 B.C. the Babylonians brought the first group of Jews from Judah into exile here. In 597 B.C. King Nebuchadnezzar brought several thousand more, including Ezekiel. Ezekiel told his people that, following the destruction of Jerusalem, the exiles were the hope of Israel's redemption. When the time was right, God would lead them back to the Promised Land.

I left Iraq on May 1. The planned airlift still hadn't happened, and the people who were supposed to be organizing it — exactly who they were was still unclear — had started to argue that airlifting a handful of people was not only unnecessary but might even be "bad for the Jews." Bad for those who would be left behind, and bad politics in a region — and world, even — that already believes that one of the main reasons for the war was to help Israel. Those who wanted to go would be helped to do so individually.

As Sara and Ishak and I drove back to Baghdad, I tried to imagine my ancestors here. At home my father had always told me that we came to Iraq with the exiles of 597 B.C. (How did he know this, I always wondered.) I tried to picture my forebears, in the fields or perhaps in the shops or the market, but I couldn't. A cold gray dust filled the air. Wrecked cars and burnt-out tanks littered the road back to Baghdad. On either side were dried-out, churned-up fields and the remains of unfinished concrete buildings. So my ancestors lived here for 2,500 years? So what? My pilgrimage was over. I will never need to do it again.

(To protect those who remain in Baghdad, I have changed their names.)

WAYNE KOESTENBAUM

My '80s

FROM ARTFORUM

Les Fleuves m'ont laissé descendre où je voulais.
　　— Arthur Rimbaud

I MET TAMA JANOWITZ once in the 1980s. (Was it 1987?) She probably doesn't remember our encounter. She was a visiting fellow at Princeton, where I was a graduate student in English. At a university gathering, Joyce Carol Oates complimented the ostentatious way that Tama and I were dressed. Seeking system, I replied, "Tama is East Village. I'm West Village."

I had little to do with art in the '80s. I saw Caravaggio in Rome and Carpaccio in Venice. I neglected the contemporary. For half the decade I lived in New York City and yet I didn't go to a single Warhol opening. Missed opportunities? My mind was elsewhere.

My mind was on *écriture feminine* as applied to homosexuals. I was big on the word "homosexual." I read *Homosexualities and French Literature* (edited by George Stambolian and Elaine Marks). I read Hélène Cixous. On a train I read *Roland Barthes by Roland Barthes* (translated by Richard Howard): I looked out dirty windows onto dirty New Jersey fields. I began to take autobiography seriously as a historical practice with intellectual integrity. On an airplane I read Michel Leiris's *Manhood* (translated by Richard Howard) and grooved to Leiris's mention of a "bitten buttock"; I decided to become, like Leiris, a self-ethnographer. I read Gide's *The Immoralist* (translated by Richard Howard) in Hollywood, Florida, while lying on a pool deck. I read many books translated by Richard Howard. In the '8os I read *The Fantastic* by Tzvetan Todorov (translated by Richard Howard) and meditated on the relation between fantasy and autobiography. I brought Richard Howard flowers the first time I met him (1985), in his book-lined apartment. He assured me that I was a poet.

I discovered the word "essentialism" in the late '8os. I should have discovered it earlier. Sex-and-gender essentialism was a dread fate. I feared that it was my condition. In the early '9os, after I stopped worrying about my essentialism, I realized that I'd never been an essentialist after all.

Too many of these sentences begin with the first-person singular pronoun. Later I may jazz up the syntax, falsify it.

I am typing this essay on the IBM Correcting Selectric III type-writer I bought in 1981 for $1,000. I borrowed the money from my older brother, a cellist. It took me several years to pay him back.

In the '8os I worked as a legal secretary, a paralegal, and a legal proofreader. I freelanced as a typist, $1.50 per page. I temped for Kelly Girl; one pleasurable assignment was a stint at the Girl Scouts headquarters. I taught seventh- through twelfth-grade English at a yeshiva. I tutored a man from Japan in English conversation. I didn't turn a single trick.

This morning I asked my boyfriend, an architect, about the 1980s. I said, "Let's make a list of salient features of our '8os." We came up with just two items: cocaine, AIDS.

In 1980, after Reagan was elected, I began, in repulsed reaction, to read the *New York Times*. Before then, I'd never read the news-paper.

I remember a specific homeless woman on the Upper West Side in the '8os. She smelled predictably of pee or shit and hung out in an ATM parlor near the Seventy-second Street subway stop. She seemed to rule the space. Large, she epitomized. Did I ever give her money? I blamed Reagan.

A stranger smooched me during a "Read My Lips" kiss-in near the Jefferson Market Public Library: festive politics. I had stumbled onto the ceremony. Traffic stopped.

A cute short blond guy named Mason used to brag about sex parties; I was jealous. I didn't go to sex parties. He ended up dying of AIDS. I'm not pushing a cause-effect argument.

In 1985 I read Mario Mieli's *Homosexuality and Liberation*. I bought, but did not read, an Italian periodical, hefty and intellectually substantial, called *Sodoma: Rivista omosessuale di cultura*. That year, I turned to Bataille for bulletins on the solar anus, for lessons on smart, principled obscenity.

A handsome brunet poet came to my apartment, and I dyed his hair blond. I had a crush on him. He talked a lot about Foucault. The poet and I had bought the dye on Sixth Avenue in the Village. In my kitchen he stripped to his undershorts, which had holes. His nipples were large and erect: impressive! I'd never seen such ready-to-go nipples. He leaned over the kitchen sink; I washed his hair and applied the dye. I kept my undershirt on during the session; I wasn't proud of my body (though in retrospect I respect its scrawniness). I continued to read Foucault throughout the '80s. Foucault never deeply moved me. I switched to Blanchot in the late '90s.

My boyfriend worked out downstairs. We lived above a gay gym: the Body Center, corner of Sixth and Fifteenth, now the David Barton Gym. After midnight we could hear loud music coming through our radiators: the Body Center's cleanup crew had turned up the sound system.

Geographical facts: during the '80s, I lived in Cambridge, Baltimore, New York, New Haven. The important city was New York: 1984–88. There, I worked out at the McBurney Y. I swam in its skanky, dank, tiny, cloudy, overwarm pool. I recall a not handsome

guy shaving off his body hair at the sink. Careful, I didn't once enter the Y's cramped sauna.

I read all of Proust in summer 1986. Proust and summer passed
quickly. That same summer I reread James Schuyler's *The Morning
of the Poem* and experienced an AIDS-panic-related sense of life's
brevity; houseguest, I sat on an Adirondack chair in Southold,
Long Island. My host, hardy in the garden, was ill with AIDS. I recall wild blueberries I picked with him, and his reticence, and
mine.

In 1986 or '87 I heard Eve Kosofsky Sedgwick give a lecture on
"unknowing" in Diderot's *The Nun*. I had just read her *Between Men*.
Her difficult lucidity gave my stumbling concepts one warm, fruitful context.

In 1984 I took a course in feminist theory with Elaine Showalter at
Princeton and decided to be a male feminist. I decided not to write
a dissertation about John Ashbery and W. H. Auden. Instead, I
wanted to write a flaming treatise. In a seminar on the Victorian
novel, Showalter showed slides of Charcot's hysterics in *arcs-en-cercle*
and of fin-de-siècle faces disfigured by syphilis. I flipped out with
intellectual glee. Hysteria would be my open sesame.

In the '8os I was happiest when writing "syllabic" poems. Supersti-
tiously I discovered my existence's modicum of dignity and value
by counting duration in syllables on my fingers, while I typed, on
the same Selectric I am using now.

I saw *Taxi zum Klo* and *Diva:* two films that made a dent. I went to
all the gay movies. *L'Homme blessé.* On TV I saw *Brideshead Revisited*
and the Patrice Chéreau production of Wagner's *Ring.* I went to
Charlie Chan movies (guilty pleasure) at Theater 8o St. Marks;
there, my treat was buying a blue mint from the transparent vessel on the dim-lit lobby's counter. I saw *Shoah:* only the first part.
I heard Leonie Rysanek sing Elisabeth in *Tannhäuser* and Ortrud
in *Lohengrin* and Kundry in *Parsifal* at the Met, and Sieglinde in
Die Walküre in San Francisco. I heard Christa Ludwig's twenty-fifth-

anniversary performance at the Met: Klytämnestra in Strauss's *Elektra,* December 20, 1984.

I wore a bright red Kikit baseball jacket and red espadrilles. I decided that bright blue and red — Day-Glo, neon, opalescent — were passports to private revolution. I wore a paisley tux jacket and black patent-leather cowboy boots. I didn't mind looking vulgar, slutty, off-base.

I spent a lot of the '80s thinking about Anna Moffo, soprano — her career's ups and downs, her timbre's uncanny compromise between vulnerability and voluptuousness. I regret not buying her Debussy song album, used, at Academy Records on West Eighteenth Street: on the soft-focus cover, she wore a summer hat. The LP era ended.

I focused on my sadness as if it were an object in the room, a discrete, dense entity, impervious to alteration. I never used the word "subjectivity" in the '80s, though I was fond of "gap," "blank page," "masculine," and "feminine." I planned to call my first book of poems *Queer Street,* nineteenth-century British slang for shady circumstances, debt, bankruptcy, blackmail. I had come across the phrase in Robert Louis Stevenson's *Dr. Jekyll and Mr. Hyde.*

In 1980 my new boyfriend gave me a 45 rpm single (blue-labeled Chrysalis) of Blondie's "Call Me" (from *American Gigolo*). We considered it our theme song. Then I stopped listening to "popular" music. Not consciously. Not programmatically. The defection happened naturally.

In 1981 I made an onion-bacon-apple casserole from *Joy of Cooking.* I served it, as a main dish, to a schizophrenic friend. A few years later she sent me a letter, dated 1975. This significant confusion of chronology meant that she had cracked up. I began methodically to cook from Marcella Hazan. I tirelessly stirred risotto in a cheap aluminum saucepan with high sides. I made a *bombe aux trois chocolats* from Julia Child: a molded dessert, for which I used a beige Tupperware bowl.

*

In 1983 I served a friend a veal roast stuffed with pancetta. We agreed that the roast tasted like human baby. We blamed the pancetta.

Sometime in the mid-'80s I stopped swallowing cum. I don't miss its taste.

The first guy I knew with AIDS died at age thirty-five. His name was Metro. I've written about this death before, and I hesitate to repeat myself. I have almost no visual memory of Metro, though I recall his precision and hypercapability; we lay on a stony beach, Long Island Sound, more rock than sand. What sand there was he dusted off his body with decisive, practiced gestures.

I went to Paris for the first time in the '80s: I wore blue leather gloves purchased on Christopher Street. In a rue Jacob hotel bedroom I woke up sweat-drenched, feverish; I observed the wallpaper's mesmerizing, dull pattern, its refusal to serve as reliable augury. On the flight back from Paris I read Marianne Moore's prose and picked up pointers from its ornery mannerism.

Despite my best efforts, I existed in history, not as agent but as frightened, introspective observer. I began to fine-tune my sentences — a fastidiousness I learned from Moore's prose. Precise sentences were my ideals, though in practice I was slipshod and sentimental. I began to seek a balance between improvisation and revision. I revised by endlessly retyping.

I read Freud in the '80s. He was always describing me, my likenesses, my forebears. Anna O. became my touchstone. I decided that psychoanalysis was the hysterical child born from Freud's anus.

In 1981 I read Susan Sontag's *On Photography.* In 1982 I read her *Under the Sign of Saturn.* I swore allegiance to the aphorism. But I didn't read Walter Benjamin until the '90s.

In 1981 I published for the first time: a story, "In the White Forest," in a small periodical, *Pale Fire Review.* In 1982 I stopped writing fiction. The last story I wrote, "Liberty Baths," autobiographically reported my San Francisco bathhouse experiences of summer 1979. A guy I met at the baths took me to his loft. A commercial photographer, he shot a whole roll of me nude, from the rear. I was insulted that he didn't photograph me frontally. I should have been grateful that he found one angle comely.

I spent the summer of 1983 writing fifty sonnets. My stylistic model was Auden's sequence "In Time of War": I loved his phrase "Anxiety / Received them like a grand hotel." I put together a manuscript called, unadventurously, *Fifty Sonnets*. It never got published as a book. In one of the sonnets, I rhymed "Callas" and "callous."

The world was doing its best to ignore the fact that I was a writer. In search of fragile legitimacy, I obsessively submitted work to periodicals. Rejection slips arrived, sometimes with a beckoning "Thanks!" or "Sorry!" or "Send more?" I always sent more, immediately, with a treacly letter, informing the hapless editor how much the invitation to send more had meant to me.

I was not thinking about the world. I was not thinking about history. I was thinking about my body's small, precise, limited, hungry movement forward into a future that seemed at every instant on the verge of being shut down.

I didn't take the HIV test until the '90s. I spent most of the '80s worried about being HIV-positive, only discovering, in the '90s, that I was negative. My attitude in the '80s was: Wait and see. Wait for symptoms. When a friend suggested I get tested, I broke off the friendship. It wasn't much of a friendship. She wanted us to write a collaborative book on Verdi's Oedipus complex. A semi-invalid, she sent me on errands to buy dollhouse furniture — her hobby.

I heard Leontyne Price sing a recital at the Met on March 24, 1985. I still remember the sensation of her voice in my body. I think she gave *"Chi il bel sogno di Doretta"* from *La Rondine* as an encore.

*

I read Derrida's *Spurs* (translated by Barbara Harlow). I wondered why he didn't use testicles — instead of vaginas and veils — as metaphors. Invaginate, indeed! In the 1980s I made snap judgments.

Poems I published in the '8os, in small periodicals, but never collected into a book: "Where I Lived, and What I Lived For," "*Carmen in Digital for a Deaf Woman*," "Teachers of Obscure Subjects," "The Babysitter in the Ham Radio." I published my first full-length essay in 1987: its polite subtitle was "Oblique Confession in the Early Work of John Ashbery."

In the '8os I wrote book reviews for the *New York Native,* a now defunct gay newspaper. Among my subjects: James Schuyler's *A Few Days,* John Ashbery's *April Galleons,* Sylvère Lotringer's *Overexposed: Treating Sexual Perversion in America.*

Does any of this information matter? I am not responsible for what matters and what doesn't matter. Offbeat definition of materialism: a worldview in which every detail matters, in which every factual statement is material.

I bought soft-core porn magazines — *Mandate, Honcho,* others — from a newsstand on Fourteenth Street. I felt guilty about my insatiably scopophilic core; culpable, it could never get its fill of images. Over the years I began to notice changes in porn bodies: the men were growing younger. Now, when I look back at those magazines (I've saved many), the men seem like old friends, guys I went to school with. Max Archer. Chad Douglas. Jesus.

I have always had a rather limited circle of friends; although I am superficially gregarious, most human contact makes me, eventually, uncomfortable. I didn't realize this fact in the '8os. During those years, I was intensely ill at ease.

I stopped using drugs (pot, cocaine) when I began to take AIDS seriously. Health suddenly mattered: I wanted always to feel tiptop, without chemical enhancement.

*

If my '80s don't match yours, chalk up the mismatch to the fact that I am profoundly out of touch with my time. I never chose to nominate myself as historical witness.

Notice, please, my absence of nostalgia.

I started dyeing my hair in 1984: reddish highlights. I stopped in 1988. I returned to nature.

My mission in the '80s was to develop my aestheticism. My mission in the '90s was to justify my aestheticism.

In 1988 I started teaching at Yale. I decided to wear bow ties. I had several: red polka dot, blue polka dot, amber with black triangles, neon yellow. The first semester, I taught a required core course on Chaucer, Spenser, and Donne. I also taught my first elective: a seminar decorously titled "Literature and Sexuality: Counter-traditions." I was hyperconscious of authorities. In 1989 I published my first book, *Double Talk: The Erotics of Male Literary Collaboration*. When the published book first arrived in my apartment, I admired its cover — George Platt Lynes's photograph *The Birth of Dionysus* — but wished the book were a novel instead: same cover, different contents.

In New Haven, outside my apartment, 1989, I was mugged. A guy said, "Give me your wallet or I'll blow your brains out."

In 1989 I developed a sustaining, mood-brightening crush on the UPS man. Hundreds — thousands — of men and women in New Haven must have had a crush on that same UPS man. The first time he appeared at my doorstep with a package, I thought that a *Candid Camera* porn movie had just begun. If you want me to describe him, I will.

When I look back at the '80s I see myself as a small boat. It is not an important, attractive, or likable boat, but it has a prow, a sail, and a modest personality. It has no consciousness of the water it moves through. Some days it resembles Rimbaud's inebriated vessel. Other, clearer days, it is sober and undemonstrative. There are few images or adjectives we could affix to the boat; there are virtually no ways to classify it. Its only business is staying afloat. Thus the boat is amoral. It has been manufactured in a certain style. Any style contains a history. The boat is not conscious of the history shaping its movements. The boat, undramatic, passive, at best pleasant, at worst slapdash, persistently attends to the work of flotation, which takes precedence over responsible navigation. As far as the boat is concerned, it is the only vessel on the body of water. How many times must I repeat the word "boat" to convince you that in the '80s I was a small boat with a minor mission and a fear of sinking? The boat did not sink.

LEONARD MICHAELS

My Yiddish

FROM THE THREEPENNY REVIEW

IN PARIS one morning in the seventies, walking along rue Mahler,
I saw a group of old men in an argument, shouting and gesticulat-
ing. I wanted to know what it was about, but my graduate school
French was good enough only to read great writers, not good
enough for an impassioned argument or even conversation with
the local grocer. But then, as I walked by the old men, I felt a shock
and a surge of exhilaration. I did understand them. My God, I possessed the thing — spoken French! Just as suddenly, I crashed. The
old men, I realized, were shouting in Yiddish.

Like a half-remembered dream, the incident lingered. It seemed
intensely personal, yet impersonal. Meaning had come alive in me.
I hadn't translated what the old men said. I hadn't done anything.
A light turned on. Where nothing had been, there was something.

Philosophers used to talk about The Understanding as if it were
a distinct mental function. Today they talk about epistemology or
cognitive science. As for The Understanding, it's acknowledged in
IQ tests, the value of which is subject to debate. It's also acknowledged in daily life in countless informal ways. You're on the same
wavelength with others or you are not. The Paris incident, where I
rediscovered The Understanding, made me wonder if Descartes's
remark, "I think, therefore I am," might be true in his case, but not
mine. I prefer to say, "I am, therefore I think." And also, therefore,
I speak.

Until I was five, I spoke only Yiddish. It did much to permanently qualify my thinking. Eventually I learned to speak English,
then to imitate thinking as it transpires among English speakers.

To some extent, my intuitions and my expression of thoughts remain basically Yiddish. I can say only approximately how this is true. For example this joke:

> The rabbi says, "What's green, hangs on the wall, and whistles?"
> The student says, "I don't know."
> The rabbi says, "A herring."
> The student says, "Maybe a herring could be green and hang on the wall, but it absolutely doesn't whistle."
> The rabbi says, "So it doesn't whistle."

The joke is inherent in Yiddish, not any other language. It's funny and, like a story by Kafka, it isn't funny. I confess that I don't know every other language. Maybe there are such jokes in Russian or Chinese, but no other language has a history like Yiddish, which for ten centuries has survived the dispersion and murder of its speakers.

As the excellent scholar and critic Benjamin Harshav points out, in *The Meaning of Yiddish,* the language contains many words that don't mean anything — *nu, epes, tokeh, shoyn.* These are fleeting interjections, rather like sighs. They suggest, without meaning anything, "so," "really," "well," "already." Other Yiddish words and phrases, noticed by Harshav, are meaningful but defeat translation. Transparent and easy to understand, however, is the way Yiddish serves speech — between you and me — rather than the requirements of consecutive logical discourse; that is, between the being who goes by your name and who speaks to others objectively and impersonally. For example, five times five is twenty-five, and it doesn't whistle.

Yiddish is probably at work in my written English. This moment, writing in English, I wonder about the Yiddish undercurrent. If I listen, I can almost hear it: "This moment" — a stress followed by two neutral syllables — introduces a thought which hangs like a herring in the weary droop of "writing in English," and then comes the announcement, "I wonder about the Yiddish undercurrent." The sentence ends in a shrug. Maybe I hear the Yiddish undercurrent, maybe I don't. The sentence could have been written by anyone who knows English, but it probably would not have been written by a well-bred Gentile. It has too much drama, and might even be disturbing, like music in a restaurant or an elevator. The sentence obliges you to abide in its staggered flow, as if what I mean were inextricable from my feelings and required a lyrical note. There is a kind of enforced intimacy with the reader. A Jewish kind, I suppose. In Sean O'Casey's lovelier prose you hear an Irish kind.

Wittgenstein says in his *Philosophical Investigations,* "Aren't there games we play in which we make up the rules as we go along, including this one." *Nu.* Any Yiddish speaker knows that. A good example of playing with the rules might be Montaigne's essays, the form that people say he invented. *Shoyn,* a big inventor. Jews have always spoken essays. The scandal of Montaigne's essays is that they have only an incidental relation to a consecutive logical argument but they are cogent nonetheless. Their shape is their sense. It is determined by motions of his mind and feelings, not by a pretension to rigorously logical procedure. Montaigne literally claims his essays are himself. Between you and him nothing intervenes. A Gentile friend used to say, in regard to writing she didn't like, "There's nobody home." You don't have to have Jewish ancestors, like those of Montaigne and Wittgenstein, to understand what she means.

I didn't speak English until I was five because my mother didn't speak English. My father had gone back to Poland to find a wife. He returned with an attractive seventeen-year-old who wore her hair in a long black braid. Men would hit on her, so my father wouldn't let her go take English classes. She learned English by doing my elementary school homework with me. As for me, before and after the age of five, I was susceptible to lung diseases and spent a lot of time in a feverish bed, in a small apartment on the Lower East Side of Manhattan, where nobody spoke anything but Yiddish. Years passed before I could ride a bike or catch a ball. In a playground fight, a girl could have wiped me out. I was badly coordinated and had no strength or speed, only a Yiddish mouth.

For a long time, Yiddish was my whole world. In this world family didn't gather before dinner for cocktails and conversation. There were no cocktails, but conversation was daylong and it included criticism, teasing, opinionating, gossiping, joking. It could also be very gloomy. To gather before dinner for conversation would have seemed unnatural. I experienced the pleasure of such conversation for the first time at the University of Michigan, around 1956.

It was my habit to join a friend at his apartment after classes. He made old-fashioneds and put music on the phonograph, usually chamber music. By the time we left for dinner, I felt uplifted by conversation and splendid music. Mainly, I was drunk, also a new experience. Among my Jews, conversation had no ritual character, no aesthetic qualities. I never learned to cultivate the sort of detachment that allows for the always potentially offensive personal note. Where I came from, everything was personal.

From family conversation I gathered that, outside my Yiddish child-world, there were savages who didn't have much to say but could fix the plumbing. They were fond of animals, liked to go swimming, loved to drink and fight. All their problems were solved when they *hut geharget yiddin.* Killed Jews. Only the last has been impossible for me to dismiss. Like many other people I have fixed my own plumbing, owned a dog and a cat, gotten drunk, etc., but everything in my life, beginning with English, has been an uncertain movement away from my *hut geharget* Yiddish childhood. When a BBC poet said he wanted to shoot Jews on the West Bank, I thought, "*Epes.* What else is new?" His righteousness, his freedom to say it, suggests that he believes he is merely speaking English, and antisemitism is a kind of syntax, or what Wittgenstein calls "a form of life." But in fact there is something new, or anyhow more evident lately. The *geharget yiddin* disposition now operates at a remove. You see it in people who become hysterical when they feel that their ancient right to hate Jews is brought into question. To give an example would open a boxcar of worms.

It's possible to talk about French without schlepping the historical, cultural, or national character of a people into consideration. You cannot talk that way about Yiddish unless you adopt a narrow scholarly focus, or restrict yourself to minutiae of usage. The language has flourished in a number of countries. Theoretically, it has no territorial boundary. The meaning of Yiddish, in one respect, is No Boundaries. In another respect, for "a people without a land," the invisible boundaries couldn't be more clear. There is mutual contempt between what are called "universalist Jews" and Jewish Jews. It's an old situation. During the centuries of the Spanish Inquisition, Jews turned on Jews. In Shakespeare's *The Merchant of Venice* — assuming the merchant Antonio is a gay *converso,* or new Christian, and Shylock is an Old Testament moralistic Jewish Jew

— the pound of flesh, a grotesquely exaggerated circumcision, is to remind Antonio (who says "I know not why I am so sad") of his origins.

The first time I went to a baseball game, the great slugger Hank Greenberg, during warm-up, casually tossed a ball into the stands, a gift to the crowd of preadolescent kids among whom I sat. My hand, thrusting up in a blossom of hands, closed on that baseball. I carried it home, the only palpable treasure I'd ever owned. I never had toys. On Christmas nights I sometimes dreamed of waking and finding toys in the living room. *Tokeh?* Yes, really. If there is a support group for Christmas depressives, I will be your leader. The baseball made me feel like a real American. It happened to me long before I had a romance with the mythical blonde who grants citizenship to Jews. By then I was already fifteen. I had tasted *traif* and long ago stopped speaking Yiddish except when I worked as a waiter in Catskills hotels. What Yiddish remained was enough to understand jokes, complaints, insults, and questions. As guests entered the dining room, a waiter might say, "Here come the *vildeh chayes,*" or wild animals. One evening in the Catskills I went to hear a political talk, given in Yiddish. I understood little except that Yiddish could be a language of analysis, spoken by intellectuals. I felt alienated and rather ashamed of myself for not being like them.

Family members could speak Polish as well as Yiddish, and some Hebrew and Russian. My father worked for a short while in Paris and could manage French. My mother had gone to high school in Poland and was fluent in Polish, but refused to speak the language even when I asked her to. Her memory of pogroms made it unspeakable. In Yiddish and English I heard about her father, my grandfather, a tailor who made uniforms for Polish army officers. Once, after he'd worked all night to finish a uniform, the officer wouldn't pay. My grandfather, waving a pair of scissors, threatened to cut the uniform to pieces. The officer paid. The Germans later murdered my grandfather, his wife, and one daughter. Polish officers imprisoned in Katyn forest and elsewhere were massacred by Stalin. This paragraph, beginning with the first sentence and concluding with a moral, is in the form of a *geshichte,* or Yiddish story, except that it's in English and merely true.

At the center of my Yiddish, lest I have yet failed to make myself clear, remains *hut geharget yiddin,* from which, like the disgorged

contents of a black hole in the universe, come the jokes, the thinking, the meanings, and the meaninglessness. In 1979, American
writers were sent to Europe by the State Department. I went to Poland and gave talks in Warsaw, Poznan, and Cracow. I was surprised
by how much seemed familiar, and exceedingly surprised by the intelligence and decency of the Poles, a few of whom became friends
and visited me later in America. One of the Poles whom I didn't
see again was a woman in Cracow with beautiful blue eyes and
other features very like my mother's. I was certain that she was a
Jew though she wore a cross. I didn't ask her questions. I didn't
want to know her story. I could barely look at her. I detest the word
"shiksa," which I've heard used more often by friendly antisemites
than Jews, but in my personal depths it applies to her.

As suggested earlier, in Yiddish there is respect for meaninglessness. If the woman in Cracow was passing as a Catholic, was she
therefore a specter of meaninglessness who haunted me, the child
of Polish Jews, passing as an American writer? A familiar saying
comes to mind, "If you forget you are a Jew, a Gentile will remind
you," but, in the way of forgetting, things have gone much further.
Lately, it might take a Jew to remind a Jew that he or she is a Jew.
Then there is a risk of ruining the friendship. For an extreme example, I have had depressing arguments with Jewish Stalinists who,
despite evidence from numerous and unimpeachable sources that
Stalin murdered Jews because they were Jews, remain Stalinists.
It's as if they would rather die than let personal identity spoil their
illusions. Thus, the Jewish face of insanity says to me, "Stalin was
a good guy. He just got a bad rap." A demonic parallel to this mentality is in the way Nazis used material resources, critical to their
military effort, to murder Jews even as the Russian army was at
the gates. They would rather die, etc. In the second century,
Tertullian, a father of the Christian church, insisted that absurdity
is critical to belief. His political sophistication seems to me breath-
taking, and also frightening in its implications. As the believers
multiply everywhere, it becomes harder to believe — rationally —
in almost anything.

Paradox as a cognitive mode is everywhere in Yiddish. It's probably in the genes and may explain the Jewish love of jokes. The
flight from sense to brilliance effects an instant connection with listeners. Hobbes calls laughter "sudden glory," which is a superb

phrase, but I've seen the Jewish comics Lenny Bruce and Myron Cohen reduce a nightclub audience to convulsive and inglorious agonies of laughter. When I worked in the Catskills hotels I noticed that it was often the *tumler,* or the hotel comic and hell-raiser, to whom women abandoned themselves. Jerry Lewis, formerly a *tumler,* said in a televised interview that at the height of his fame he "had four broads a day." As opposed to Jerry Lewis, Hannah Arendt preferred disconnection. She used the snobbish word "banal" to describe the murderer of millions of Jews, and later said in a letter that despite the abuse she had received for using that word, she remained "lighthearted."

Family was uncles and aunts who escaped from Poland and immigrated to the United States. They stayed with us until they found their own apartments. I'd wake in the morning and see small Jews sleeping on the living room floor. My aunt Molly, long after she had a place of her own, often stayed overnight and slept on the floor. She was very lonely. Her husband was dead, her children had families of their own. A couch with a sheet, blanket, and pillow was available, but she refused such comforts. She wanted to be less than no trouble. She wore two or three dresses at once, almost her entire wardrobe. She slept on the floor in her winter coat and dresses. To see Molly first thing in the morning, curled against a wall, didn't make us feel good. She was the same height as my mother, around five feet, and had a beautiful intelligent melancholy face. I never saw her laugh, though she might chuckle softly, and she smiled when she teased me. She used to *krotz* (scratch) my back as I went to sleep, and she liked to speak to me in rhymes. First they were entirely Yiddish. Then English entered the rhymes.

> *Label, gay fressen.*
> *A fish shtayt on de tish.*
>
> Lenny, go eat.
> A fish is on the table.

Shtayt doesn't exactly mean "is." "Stands on the table" or "stays on the table" or "exists on the table" would be somewhat imprecise, though I think "A fish exists on the table" is wonderful. I once brought a girlfriend home, and Aunt Molly said, very politely, "You are looking very fit." Her "fit" sounded like "fet," which suggested "fat." My girlfriend squealed in protest. It took several minutes to calm her down. The pronunciation of "fet" for "fit" is typical of Yiddishified English, which is almost a third language. I speak it like a native when telling jokes. The audience for such jokes has diminished over the years because most Jews now are politically liberal and have college degrees and consider such jokes undignified or racist. A joke that touches on this development tells of Jewish parents who worry about a son who studies English literature at Harvard. They go to see Kittredge, the great Shakespeare scholar, and ask if he thinks their son's Yiddish accent is a disadvantage. Kittredge booms, "Vot ekcent?"

As a child I knew only one Jew who was concerned to make a *bella figura.* He was a highly respected doctor, very handsome, always dressed in a fine suit, and, despite his appearance, fluent in Yiddish. His office was in the neighborhood. He came every morning to my father's barber shop for a shave. A comparable miracle was the chicken-flicker down the block, a boisterous man who yelled at customers in vulgar funny Yiddish. This man's son was a star at MIT. In regard to such miracles, an expression I often heard was "He is up from pushcarts." It means he went from the Yiddish immigrant poverty to money or, say, a classy professorship. The day of such expressions is past. In the sixties there were Jewish kids who, as opposed to the spirit of Irving Howe's *The World of Our Fathers,* yelled, "Kill the parents." The suicidal implication is consistent with the paradoxical Yiddish they no longer spoke.

If I dressed nicely to go out, my mother would ask why I was *fapitzed,* which suggests "tarted up." Yiddish is critical of pretensions to being better than a Jew, and also critical of everything else. A man wants to have sex or wants to pee — what a scream. A woman appears naked before her husband and says, "I haven't got a thing to wear." He says, "Take a shave. You look like a bum." Henry Adams speaks of "derisive Jew laughter." It is easy to find derision produced by Jews, but Adams's word, aside from its stupid viciousness, betrays the self-hate and fear that inspires antisemitism among the educated, not excluding Jews. Ezra Pound called his own antisemitic ravings "stupid." The relation of stupidity and evil has long been noted.

Jewish laughter has a liberal purview and its numerous forms,

some very silly, seem to me built into Yiddish. Sometime around
puberty, I decided to use shampoo rather than hand soap to wash
my hair. I bought a bottle of Breck. My father noticed and said in
Yiddish, "Nothing but the best." I still carry his lesson in my heart,
though I have never resumed using hand soap instead of shampoo.
What has this to do with Yiddish? In my case, plenty, since it raises
the question, albeit faintly, "Who do you think you are?"

What I have retained of Yiddish, I'm sorry to say, isn't much
above the level of Aunt Molly's poems. But what good to me is Yiddish? Recently, in Rome, during the High Holidays, a cordon was
established around the synagogue in the ghetto, guarded by the
police and local Jews. As I tried to pass I was stopped by a Jew. I was
amazed. Couldn't he tell? I said, "*Ich bin a yid. Los mir gayen arein.*"
He said, "Let me see your passport." *La mia madrelingua* wasn't his.
This happened to me before with Moroccan Jews in France. I've
wondered about Spinoza. His Latin teacher was German, and the
first Yiddish newspaper was published in Amsterdam around the
time of his death. Did he know Yiddish?

I'm sure of very little about what I know except that the Yiddish I
can't speak is more natural to my being than English, and partly
for that reason I've studied English poets. There is a line in T. S.
Eliot where he says words slip, slide, crack, or something. Come off
it, Tom, I think, with words you never had no problem. Who would
suspect from his hateful remark about a Jew in furs that Eliot's family, like my mother's ancestors in Vienna, was up from the fur business? Eliot liked Groucho Marx, a Jew, but did he wonder when
writing *Four Quartets,* with its striking allusions to Saint John of
the Cross, that the small dark brilliant mystical monk might have
been a Jew?

"Let there be light" are the first spoken words in the Old Testament. This light is understanding, not merely seeing. The Yiddish
saying "To kill a person is to kill a world" means the person is no
longer the embodiment or a mode of the glorious nothing that is
the light, or illuminated world. This idea, I believe, is elaborated in
Spinoza's *Ethics.* Existence — or being — entails ethics. Maybe the
idea is also in Wittgenstein, who opens the *Tractatus* this way: "The
world is everything that is the case." So what is the case? If it's the
case that facts are bound up with values, it seems Yiddish or

Spinozist. Possibly for this reason Jewish writers in English don't write about murder as well as Christians. Even Primo Levi, whose great subject is murder, doesn't offer the lacerating specificity one might expect.

In regard to my own writing, its subterranean Yiddish keeps me from being good at killing characters. The closest I've come is a story called "Trotsky's Garden," where I adopt a sort of Yiddish intonation to talk about his life. I'd read a psychological study that claimed Trotsky was responsible for murders only to please Lenin, his father figure. If so, his behavior was even worse than I'd thought. I wrote my story out of disappointment. I had wanted to admire Trotsky for his brilliant mind, courage, and extraordinary literary gifts. His description of mowing wheat in his diaries, for example, almost compares with Tolstoy's description of the same thing in *Anna Karenina*. Yiddish can be brutal, as, for example, *Gay koken aff yam*, which means "Go shit in the ocean," but in regard to murder, what Jew compares with Shakespeare, Webster, Mark Twain, Flannery O'Connor, Cormac McCarthy, or Elmore Leonard? The Old Testament story of Abraham and Isaac, which is of profound importance to three faiths, stops short of murder, but it is relevant to the children in contemporary religious terrorism.

A story by Bernard Malamud begins with the death of a father whose name is Ganz. In Yiddish, *ganz* means "all" or "the whole thing" or "everything." Metaphorically, with the death of Ganz, the whole world dies. Everything is killed. Malamud couldn't have named the father Ganz if he had written the story in Yiddish. It would be too funny and undermine all seriousness. The death of a father, or a world-killed-in-a-person, is the reason for Hamlet's excessive grief, a condition feared among Jews for a reason given in the play: "All the uses of this world seem to me weary, stale, flat, and unprofitable." Because Hamlet Senior is dead, Hamlet Junior is as good as dead. Early in the play he jokes about walking into his grave, and the fifth act opens, for no reason, with Hamlet in a graveyard, and then he actually jumps into a grave. On the subject of grief, in "Mourning and Melancholia," Freud follows Shakespeare. Like Hamlet, who demands that his mother look at the picture of his father, Freud makes a great deal of the residual, or cathectic, force of an image. Again, regarding my Yiddish, when I once wrote about my father's death, I restricted my grief to a few images and a simple lamentation: "He gave. I took." My short sentences are self-critical, and have no relation to the work of writers known for short sentences. They are only Yiddish terseness seizing an English equivalent.

Shakespeare's short sentences — like "Let it come down," "Ripeness is all," "Can Fulvia die?" — seem to me amazing. I couldn't write one of those. This confession brings a joke instantly to mind. The synagogue's janitor is beating his breast and saying, "O Lord, I am nothing." He is overheard by the rabbi, who says, "Look who is nothing." Both men are ridiculed. A Jewish writer has to be careful. Between schmaltz and irony there is just an itty bitty step.

My mother sometimes switches in midsentence, when talking to me, from English to Yiddish. If meaning can leave English and reappear in Yiddish, does it have an absolutely necessary relation to either language? Linguists say, "No. Anything you can say in German you can say in Swahili, which is increasingly Arabic." But no poet could accept the idea of linguistic equivalence, and a religious fanatic might want to kill you for proposing it. Ultimately, I believe, meaning has less to do with language than with music, a sensuous flow that becomes language only by default, so to speak, and by degrees. In great fiction and poetry, meaning is obviously close to music. Writing about a story by Gogol, Nabokov says it goes la, la, do, la la la, etc. The story's meaning is radically musical. I've often had to rewrite a paragraph because the sound was wrong. When at last it seemed right, I discovered — incredibly — the sense was right. Sense follows sound. Otherwise we couldn't speak so easily or quickly. If someone speaks slowly, and sense unnaturally precedes sound, the person can seem too deliberative; emotionally false, boring. I can tell stories all day, but to write one that sounds right entails labors of indefinable innerness until I hear the thing I must hear before it is heard by anyone else. A standard of rightness probably exists for me in my residual subliminal Yiddish. Its effect is to inhibit as well as to liberate. An expression, popular not long ago, "I hear you," was intended to assure you of being understood personally, as if there were a difference in comprehension between hearing and really hearing. In regard to being *really* heard, there are things in Yiddish that can't be heard in English. *Hazar fisl kosher.* "A pig has clean feet." It is an expression of contempt for hypocrisy. The force is in Yiddish concision. A pig is not clean. With clean feet it is even less clean. Another example: I was talking to a friend about a famous, recently deceased writer. The friend said, "He's *ausgespielt*." Beyond dead. He's played out. So forget it. Too much has been said about him.

Cultural intuitions, or forms or qualities of meaning, dancing about in language, derive from the unique historical experience of peoples. The intuitions are not in dictionaries but carried by tones, gestures, nuances affected by word order, etc. When I understood the old men in Paris, I didn't do or intend anything. It wasn't a moment of romantic introspection. I didn't know what language I heard. I didn't understand that I understood. What comes to mind is the assertion that begins the Book of John: "In the beginning was the word." A sound, a physical thing, the word is also mental. So this monism can be understood as the nature of everything. Like music that is the meaning of stories, physical and mental are aspects of each other. Yiddish, with its elements of German, Hebrew, Aramaic, Latin, Spanish, Polish, Russian, Romanian, is metaphorically everything. A people driven hither and yon, and obliged to assimilate so much, returned immensely more to the world. How they can become necessary to murder is the hideous paradox of evil.

When I was five years old, I started school in a huge gloomy Victorian building where nobody spoke Yiddish. It was across the street from Knickerbocker Village, the project in which I lived. To cross that street meant going from love to hell. I said nothing in the classroom and sat apart and alone, and tried to avoid the teacher's evil eye. Eventually she decided that I was a moron, and wrote a letter to my parents saying I would be transferred to the "ungraded class," where I would be happier and could play ping-pong all day. My mother couldn't read the letter so she showed it to our neighbor, a woman from Texas named Lynn Nations. A real American, she boasted of Indian blood, though she was blond and had the cheekbones, figure, and fragility of a fashion model. She would ask us to look at the insides of her teeth, to see how they were cupped. To Lynn this proved descent from original Americans. She was very fond of me, though we had no conversation, and I spent hours in her apartment looking at her art books and eating forbidden foods. I could speak to her husband, Arthur Kleinman, yet another furrier, and a lefty union activist, who knew Yiddish.

Lynn believed I was brighter than a moron and went to the

school principal, which my mother would never have dared to do, and demanded an intelligence test for me. Impressed by her Katharine Hepburn looks, the principal arranged for a school psychologist to test me. Afterward, I was advanced to a grade beyond my age with several other kids, among them a boy named Bonfiglio and a girl named Estervez. I remember their names because we were seated according to our IQ scores. Behind Bonfiglio and Estervez was me, a kid who couldn't even ask permission to go to the bathroom. In the higher grade I had to read and write and speak English. It happened virtually overnight, so I must have known more than I knew. When I asked my mother about this she said, "Sure you knew English. You learned from trucks." She meant: while lying in my sickbed I would look out the window at trucks passing in the street; studying the words written on their sides, I taught myself English. Unfortunately, high fevers burned away most of my brain, so I now find it impossible to learn a language from trucks. A child learns any language at incredible speed. Again, in a metaphorical sense, Yiddish is the language of children wandering for a thousand years in a nightmare, assimilating languages to no avail.

I remember the black shining print of my first textbook, and my fearful uncertainty as the meanings came with all their exotic Englishness and devoured what had previously inhered in my Yiddish. Something remained indigestible. What it is can be suggested, in a Yiddish style, by contrast with English. A line from a poem by Wallace Stevens, which I have discussed elsewhere, seems to me quintessentially goyish, or antithetical to Yiddish:

It is the word *pejorative* that hurts.

Stevens effects detachment from his subject, which is the poet's romantic heart, by playing on a French construction: "word *pejorative*," like *mot juste*, makes the adjective follow the noun. Detachment is further evidenced in the rhyme of "word" and "hurts." The delicate resonance gives the faint touch of hurtful impact without obliging the reader to suffer the experience. The line is ironically detached even from detachment. In Yiddish there is plenty of irony, but not so nicely mannered or sensitive to a reader's experience of words. Stevens's line would seem too self-regarding; and the luxurious subtlety of his sensibility would seem unintelligible, if not ridiculous. He flaunts sublimities here, but it must be said that elsewhere he is as visceral and concrete as any Yiddish speaker.

I've lost too much of my Yiddish to know exactly how much remains. Something remains. A little of its genius might be at work in my sentences, but this has nothing to do with me personally. The pleasures of complexity and the hilarity of idiocy, as well as an idea of what's good or isn't good, are in Yiddish. If it speaks in my sentences, it isn't I, let alone me, who speaks.

When asked what he would have liked to be if he hadn't been born an Englishman, Lord Palmerston said, "An Englishman." The answer reminds me of a joke. A Jew sees himself in a mirror after being draped in a suit by a high-class London tailor. The tailor asks what's wrong. The Jew says, crying, "Vee lost de empire." The joke assimilates the insane fury that influenced the nature of Yiddish and makes it apparent that identity for a Jew is not, as for Palmerston, a witty preference.

BEN MILLER

Bix and Flannery

FROM RARITAN

1

THERE WAS an elderly woman in Davenport who had encountered Flannery O'Connor at the Iowa Writers' Workshop in the
late 1940s. I heard Blanche's side of the story many times but
never tired of it, partly because she did not take any relish in the
telling, always pushing her water glass aside so the liquid would not
be infected by the dirty details. Blanche lived in the Mississippi Hotel with her twin sister, Sadie. In the winter, when sidewalks were
icy, the tiny duo clung to the brick buildings, shuffle-stepping sideways like paisley-scarved mountain climbers with a disdain for the
vertical. Neither had married. Both smoked like chimneys and
sported a fine coat of facial down that appeared blond or brown,
depending on whether the shades were drawn. From a distance
of twenty feet, one might have thought they were identical. But
to get up close was to note only differences. Sadie's blue eyes,
Blanche's green ones. Sadie's wide smile, Blanche's thin frown.
Sadie's lilting voice, Blanche's teacherly drone. After graduating
from the University of Iowa with an M.A. in English, Blanche immediately enrolled in business school and, a few years later, received an accounting degree — a smart move, given her attach-
ment to formal verse. And that kind of writing she never gave up,
continually testing herself against the great poetic forms (sonnet,
sestina, villanelle . . .) and reading the results at a succession of local writing groups — Wordsmiths, Mississippi Valley Literary Society, the Penfeather League, and, finally, Writers' Studio. That's

where we met in 1978. I was in ninth grade, decades younger than any other member. This did not seem so strange to me, however, as I'd never had friends my own age: an overweight kid who found acceptance only in the most unconventional social circles, befriending school janitors, parking lot guards, teachers' aides. In addition to a surfeit of widows and homemakers, regular Writers' Studio attendees included a flashy poet who worked for the federal government (by flashy I mean lime suits and matching cologne), a middle-aged fry cook who arrived on a Harley, a retired Sante Fe lineman, a Vietnam vet with long dry hair, a balding gymnastics coach with a whispery voice, a lanky fifty-four-year-old haiku writer who lived with his mother, and a mysterious blond woman with a slight Southern accent who'd married young, divorced too late, and could be found weekdays in the hosiery department of Younker's department store, standing as still as the mannequins. Meetings were every Thursday night at seven-thirty. The initial sessions I attended were held on the second floor of a clapboard building just off the deserted pedestrian mall in downtown Rock Island, Illinois. The room was impossibly hot and dim. One slender window stuck in the down position. A ceiling fan that moved only when the haiku writer stood on his folding chair and gave it a spin. An old Kelvinator that buzzed to little effect. For a quarter, members could purchase a warm bottle of cola from the treasurer, but no one ever did, and when better digs were found across the river in Davenport, those drinks were left behind for the next unfortunate tenant to refuse. Our new home was the gym of a defunct Catholic school that had been halfheartedly converted into a community center. A folding table of banquet length stood in the middle of a floor crisscrossed with faint skid marks made decades earlier by the children of Irish and German immigrants. The voice of each reader echoed, and when I closed my eyes to listen, the sensation was of hearing rhymed shouts at a great, muting distance. Poets predominated and nature was the topic of choice — flowers, trees, birds. Most who wrote fiction targeted the juvenile audience and dreamed of publishing in *Boys' Life*, *Reader's Digest*, and *Guideposts*. Such wholesome magazines weren't my preferred reading, but still, it was thrilling to hear a member report a sale. Imagine that: money for words! One woman had sold the same story more than a dozen times — so much success she dared not write another sentence, for fear it would tarnish her reputation as the club's most successful author. When it came time to read, she would simply lift her big gray head and report the current earnings of "Mallie and the Snail," which climbed over the years to a total in excess of $200. Most members, however, were serious about craft and none more so than Blanche. She rewrote constantly — on the way to the club in the back of the lineman's Datsun, during the meeting while sitting at the folding table — erasing and replacing words right up until the last moment. And then, shaking her head, she would lift the yellow legal pad and apologize profusely for the inept result of her endless labor. Which wasn't to say she was humble. Far from it. If she could do no right, then neither could we. Each week she brutally took us to task for our linguistic and grammatical inadequacies, quoting *Elements of Style* while waving an ember-tipped Pall Mall. As little as one hanging clause or misplaced noun could set her off, and special ire was reserved for the incorrect use of "lay." Rather than be subjected to a ten-minute lecture on that subject, the rest of us kept all derivations of that word out of our stories and poems. (And even now, more than twenty years later, I'm still reluctant to have a character take a nap — much better he or she drink a cup of coffee.) At the conclusion of the meeting there would be a caravan to Riefe's, a diner famous for crunchy onion rings and home to more shades of brown than a fungus farm. And it was there, in a drab booth studded with greasy silver nubs, that I'd get up my courage and plead with Blanche to tell me about her famous classmate, until at last the water glass was pushed aside and her not-so-delicate features cleaved toward an invisible center point. First of all, what I must understand was that Flannery spoke with such an ugly accent that Paul Engle, founder of the Workshop, was forced to read her stories to the class. Second of all, Flannery did not keep appointments, promising to meet Blanche at the Odeon movie theater one winter afternoon and never showing up, preferring to stay home with "that typewriter and hot pot."

2

The block I grew up on was terraced, each house occupying a cramped plane all its own. Below lived the driver of a Budweiser truck and his phlegmatic wife, a bartender at a levee dive called

Aunt Sarah's Carousel. Above, in a small but stately white house, lived a retired realtor with a bad heart, worse vision, and a little pug. Every noon John appeared on the glassed-in back porch like a svelte apparition. Black jacket and pants. White shirt and polka-dot bow tie. Brown fedora on his bald head and Mikey's chain-link leash in his right hand. After John hooked the leash to the back-yard clothesline, the dog would commence running back and forth, an activity that would not stop until John reappeared six or seven hours later, the pearly skin of his neck glowing in the fading light. He was a proud, pristine man. In better days, an award-win-ning gardener. His rose bushes were wild by this time but still pro-duced large blooms that on windy days bobbed up and down like the heads of flushed supplicants inspired to prayer by the molting boxes of files that my father, in despair at the state of his law prac-tice, had put out to rot in the side yard. Every Saturday John's sister Alice and her husband Eddy, a retired tugboat captain, drove down from LeClaire, Iowa, and did John's weekly grocery shopping at Eagle's Supermarket on Kimberly Road. My mother replenished what perishables ran out during the week and often I was asked to run up the hill to deliver the carton of milk or eggs, the bunch of bananas, the box of Tiparillo cigars. This I did not mind. Being trusted to deliver cigars after dark seemed a task akin to smuggling contraband over the Mexican border. I'd stuff the brown bag un-der my arm and zigzag up the hill toward the back steps, which were illuminated by a spotlight affixed under the eaves. John would be waiting on the back porch to make the pickup, cued by the phone call I'd made a few minutes before — no hat or jacket after dark, just the polka-dot bow tie and a red sweater-vest hang-ing loosely on his thin shoulders. After the transfer of the bag came the invitation to step inside for a 7-Up. I never refused. In fact, had he ever forgotten to invite me in, I would have reminded him to do so, as I was enchanted with his orderly, air-conditioned house. The door leading from the porch to the kitchen had a five-dollar bill taped to it. This was for a burglar. If John ever came back after chaining up Mikey and found the money gone, he would know it was not safe to enter — that someone had sneaked into the house during the five minutes he was outside. I thought the ploy incredibly clever, as I did his use of old undershirts as rags, sand-filled Pabst cans as paperweights, and flattened soapboxes as coasters. He had cable TV and if it was summer, a baseball game would be on. If no game was on, we'd sit in the kitchen and he'd tell stories in the same terse, tantalizing fashion that Blanche did — leaving out everything but one or two details. Between us on the yellow table would be his tea mug emblazoned with the Cincinnati Reds logo, my green mottled bottle of 7-Up, a box of vanilla Archway cookies, numerous pill bottles, a plastic pill counter, a five-band radio, and a pistol with a long black barrel. My eyes rarely left the last item. The grain of the handle gleamed and the trigger too was shiny, as if it had been pulled many times. John claimed Alice had badgered him into buying the gun after his first heart attack, worried he wouldn't have the strength to fend off an intruder. This may have been true but I noted John was not uncomfortable around the weapon. He carried it from room to room like a water glass, an impressive nonchalance that spoke of his life before becoming a real estate agent. In the 1940s there had been Coast Guard service in New Orleans. And before that: shoe shining, door-to-door hawking of insurance and encyclopedias, a stint on the Midwest boxing circuit, and a job running numbers for a cigar shop in the lobby of the Kahl Building. This may sound like the makings of a robust life narrative but John did not indulge in romance. Each time I scooted to the edge of my seat to ask for the glorious details, he'd press the plastic tip of the cigar to his lips and exhale a wall of creamy smoke that was replenished until I shut up and the whining became internal. *Why did old people with zilch to talk about grab your shoulder and yak for what seemed like hours while Blanche and John, who had real stories to tell, say next to nothing — reduce juicy subject matter to a few dry drops?* The torture was most extreme when John would relax a little and tell of his two encounters with celebrity. The first had occurred at a hotel in Keokuk, Iowa, in the mid-1930s. The elevator opened and out stepped Primo Carnera, heavyweight champion of the world. John approached the Italian giant. They shook hands. And then? And then John reached for the cigar in the ashtray and built a wall of smoke around the memory. Whatever words he and Carnera exchanged, I would not be privy to. And neither would I ever get a clear picture of Davenport's most famous native, jazz cornetist Bix Beiderbecke, whom John had often seen rushing through the lobby of the Kahl, toward the stairs that led to the musicians' union. Was that face as little and pale as it looked in the photographs? Was the hair slicked back? What kind of coat, hat, shirt? Carrying a horn? If so, was the case leather or wood? On one occasion I kept on until I drove him to the old stove, where he put on a pot of tea water and stared at the chipped enamel between the burners until the whistle blew. Stubbornness, I thought it was. A fierce modesty. But now I know better — why the stories never flew, compounded into the soothing myth that I so needed. It wasn't the glitter of the years John carried with him but the littleness of experience. The startling, scraping feel of the calluses on Carnera's battered right hand. The wan, hopeful faces of the men sitting at the cigar store counter, putting down the family money.

3

At times Blanche and John could not hide their disgust at my illusions regarding the power of celebrity. Blanche's lips would protrude, forming a chapped pink platter under her sniffing nose. John's bald head would sink and weave back and forth, as if ducking punches in slow motion. In me they saw the future and it flickered like a cheap television set. Your life wasn't your own until someone famous led you to it. What they could not know, however, was that I did not represent my generation. Yes, other kids coveted facts about idols, but those boys and girls, unlike me, spent much of the day outside, playing in streets and yards. They gave each other nicknames. They chased and punched and kissed and more than kissed. The passion for Shawn Cassidy and Reggie Jackson *supplemented* life, that gush of air into lungs, the heat of sun on skin. They came to their gods out of power, as budding equals. You could see the confidence in the focusing eyes of the batter on the playground and the girl brushing her hair in the shadow of the school wall — yes, they clearly believed themselves to be blessed, unimaginably talented and beautiful. But my family was different. We were discouraged — to steal a statistical term from the Bureau of Labor — struggling to elude the aura of ineptness that surrounded our lives. Each week Father saw three or four "flicks," as he called them, exchanging a lonely law office for the crowded matinee at the Capital Theater. Mother traded her woes for the misery of those in worse trouble, listening to radio talk shows and reading true crime books late into the night, accounts of the Clutter murders and the Manson massacre, biographies of the Boston Strangler, Richard Speck, Dr. Sheppard. My five younger siblings escaped through drugs, sports, dating, or, in the case of one sister, playing the flute, Bolling's *Suite for Flute,* hour after hour. I wrote in an automatic manner. No stopping. College-ruled notebooks filling with tiny script. Each paragraph a raft carrying me farther away from the chaos of the household. One tale concerned Flannery O'Connor's love affair with Bix Beiderbecke. Could never have happened. Flannery was only seven when Bix died of pneumonia in Jackson Heights, Queens. But the details fell neatly into place and still adhere twenty-six years later. A narrative with no beginning or middle. A story that is all happy ending, a temporary antidote to the confounding complexity of reality. *Flannery's stern kisses curing Bix of alcoholism. Bix's tender hugs curing Flannery of lupus. The two moving to New York and renting the smallest possible apartment so as to constantly be on top of each other. Bix getting a steady job at the Cotton Club with Duke Ellington and then quitting to start his own band at the dawn of the Swing Era. Flannery's Southern brogue quickly thinning as a result of long stoop conversation with a Hell's Kitchen landlady by the name of Gigi. Flannery practicing newly learned Northern words on the manager of Alp's drugstore and the members of Bix's band, including Jack Teagarden. Bix completing his first classical composition since "In a Mist." Flannery finishing a story set at the Cotton Club. The two sitting in the Rainbow Room, sipping each other's eyes. The two holding hands in Central Park. The two at the Polo Grounds, spitting out peanut shells, munching popcorn. The two exchanging corny Christmas gifts:* To Flannery, my bird of paradise. To Bix, my horn of plenty. *The two dining at the Park Avenue home of Flannery's publisher and being toasted as "the couple of the century!" Count Basie kissing Flannery's ruby wedding ring. Katherine Anne Porter hugging Bix. Flannery's mother coming to visit and lifting the rag rugs, trying to find where Flannery's accent has gone. Mother only too happy to get back to Georgia and Bix laughing when her plane lifts off from Idlewild. Flannery volunteering at the Bronx Zoo and bringing Bix with her one afternoon and introducing him to all the exotic fowl:* Teelie, meet someone who blows even louder than you do. *Bix warning Chet Baker about his drinking and Chet Baker listening, cleaning up for good at the age of twenty-five. Bix and Flannery hosting a party at which Louis Armstrong and Robert Penn Warren are introduced. Bix and*

Flannery starting a family late, after fifteen years of fearful discussion. The birth of a little boy named Frank, in honor of the late saxophone player Frankie Trumbauer. The birth of a little girl named Maple, in honor of the Iowa City street on which the two met. Bix with one child on each knee. Flannery singing "Froggie Went A-Courtin'." Bix sliding in the mute and playing "Stardust" after the children have gone to bed. Flannery getting up early the next morning and writing her first love story, typing until the end of this sentence: The darkness wasn't in him, it was around him, little black wings nesting in the creases of an ill-fitting dinner jacket.

RICK MOODY

Against Cool

FROM GINGKO TREE REVIEW

DISCLAIMERS FIRST! Whatever *cool* is or was — that term bandied about relentlessly from the 1950s to the present (by teens, by hipsters, by cultural critics, by baby boomers), that term which lately concludes all arrangements made between young people ("So I'll see you on St. Marks Place at seven? Cool.") — I, your narrator, *do not now consider myself cool and never have been cool.* As a teenager, when questions about cool are at their most rigorous, when a lack of cool implies the possibility of lifelong psychotherapy, I wore Levi's corduroys in the rainbow shades — yellow cords, red cords, powder-blue cords; I wore flannel slacks, Oxford button-downs, tweed jackets; my hair was not long enough to be beatnik nor short enough to be clean-cut, and it *poofed* in ways that best recall Michael Landon during the *Little House on the Prairie* years; I liked to mix plaids; I loved my parents and was all broken up about their divorce; I preferred, where music was concerned, Cat Stevens, Yes, Jethro Tull, and other bands even more embarrassing to enumerate, when all around me was Grateful Dead and Rolling Stones; I went to boarding school; I came from the suburbs; I read science fiction — for example, Frank Herbert's *Dune* trilogy (more volumes added later), Isaac Asimov's *Foundation* books, everything Kurt Vonnegut ever published; I cried easily, was sentimental, loved New England autumns, made elaborate protestations of love from my high school radio show, fell in love as swiftly as I contracted head colds. In an area of inquiry where *credibility is everything*, where credentials are essential, where any deviation from this orthodoxy of the unstated and recondite is actionable, I was and am an interloper. I am, in fact, uncool.

This fact suggests an initial axiom on the subject: *If you have to talk about cool, you are not it.*

Second disclaimer: there is no Platonic category of *coolness.* As with what movies endure (your *Forrest Gump* is my *One Flew Over the Cuckoo's Nest,* or vice versa), as with what novels define an era, what is cool is often in dispute, quickly outmoded, neglected soon thereafter. The very proposition that we might say what *cool* exactly denotes is risky, inadvisable from the outset, since cool, in a sort of pop culture version of Heisenberg's uncertainty principle, alters what it pleasing finds. This book or record or movie or trend, hitherto cool, becomes precipitously irrelevant in the inexorable march of time. Cool, therefore, is not a moral question (like what is virtuous or what is beautiful), although its slipperiness may be of interest. Cool, in fact, is probably more easily reckoned by its absences than its presences (Del Close and John Brent make the same point on their 1961 Mercury album, *How to Speak Hip:* "It's easier to say what *isn't* cool"). Would we not all agree that if a school of thought or a trend becomes the subject of a feature in *Sixteen* or *People* or in like purveyors of mass trends, it is clearly *no longer cool?* Would we not agree that whatever *cool* is, it is not what the Sears catalogue once said was fashionable (foul weather gear, camouflage pants), nor is cool apparent, in even the most infinitesimal degree, in the complete output of Michael Bolton, Barry Manilow, or Barbra Streisand, unless, and this is surely a disagreeable possibility, irony is cool?

Yet, as was once noted of the pornographic, *don't we know it when we see it?* We do. We do know *cool* when we see it. Or we can get pretty close. And therefore a discussion of its history is potentially useful. Because, in an absence of clearly delineated American ethics, in a period of cultural relativism, in a political environment in which both American parties have amplified their rhetoric to such a degree that the other side is *beneath contempt,* in which religion seems no longer able to rationally or effectively deploy its messages except through moral intimidation or force, in which families are no longer the ethical bulwarks they felt themselves to be in the past, in such a millennial instant cool has become *the* system of ethics for the young in America. Cool, it seems, is one thing that kids believe in. Cool is what they talk about,[1] cool is what motivates them, cool is what they occasionally live and die for, at least in some precincts. So what are they saying, these kids, when they say something is *cool?*

Well, the *OED* gives us early Teutonic and Anglo-Saxon derivations for the word: *c–lian, cole* (as in *Merlin, or the early history of King Arthur,* circa 1450: "As they that wolde ride in the cole of the mornynge"), *colen, kole, koole, cule, cuill, coole* (Coverdale, 1535: "Like as the wynter coole in the haruest"), prior to our first modern usages (as in Addison, 1713: "But see where Lucia, Amid the cool of yon high marble arch, Enjoys the noon-day breeze"). The word was in play throughout the nineteenth century, first as a description of temperature and then figuratively as a term (noun or verb) that might connote *mood* as well, as in Lord Macaulay's *History of England:* "The lapse of time which cools the ardour of friends whom he has left behind"; it also turned up as a synonym for impudence, in, e.g., Durivage and Burnham's *Stray Subjects* (1846): "You are the coolest specimen of a genuine scamp that it has ever been my ill luck to meet with." There were any number of slang idioms making use of *cool: cooling one's coppers,* in which we treat the dehydration from a prior night's drinking; *cooling the heels,* or waiting, dating back to the mid-eighteenth century; *cool as a cucumber,* from 1700 on; a *cool* sum of money (*a cool million,* e.g.), from the 1720s; *cool pleasure,* from the 1820s on, as in *Death Comes for the Archbishop* — "He took a cool pleasure in stripping the Indians of their horses" — and *cool crape,* which has connoted a funeral shroud since the early nineteenth century. Perhaps it's not *church* or *door* in the pantheon of often-employed Anglo-Saxon words; nonetheless *cool* has had a real popularity since the dawn of our tongue.

The contemporary usage, the one with which we're concerned here, seems to date from the end of World War II (only eighty years or so after Lord Macaulay) and, like so many twentieth-century English-language phenomena, to find its initial articulation on this side of the Atlantic in popular culture. In particular, what was *cool,* after the globe had finished its convulsions, was a moment in the history of jazz. In the late 1940s, Miles Davis, who was until then most prominently known as a sideman in Charlie Parker's band, convened an ensemble, with Gil Evans and Gerry Mulligan as arrangers (Davis and Evans would later go on to work on seminal orchestral jazz albums like *Porgy and Bess* and *Sketches of Spain*), designed to address some problems with the form in which they were working. The Miles Davis Nonet, as it came to be known, featured six horns (trumpet, trombone, French horn, tuba, alto and baritone sax), piano, bass, and drums, and was conceived as a reaction against bebop. This bebop style, which was preeminently influential at the same time, and which is credited mainly to Davis's boss, Charlie Parker, and to Dizzy Gillespie, was fast and technically virtuosic, as Davis himself points out in his autobiography, *Miles*: "Bird and Diz played this hip, real fast thing, and if you weren't a fast listener, you couldn't catch the humor or the feeling in their music . . . Bird and Diz were great, fantastic, challenging — but they weren't sweet."

Davis's nonet, and the sessions that came out of it, had a different intent. Sweetness and melody were their ambition, a less fiery tone. The results, dubbed *Birth of the Cool* by Pete Rugolo, an A&R man at Davis's record company, were, according to no less an authority than Count Basie, "slow and strange but good, really good." Davis himself says, "We shook people's ears a little softer than Bird or Diz did, took the music more mainstream. That's all it was." Davis sees this softness in the *Birth of the Cool* sessions as a gambit to ensure the safety of *white* listeners in an idiom that was primarily African American, but this seems now to understate unnecessarily the accomplishments of *Birth of the Cool*. The jazz of Miles Davis's nonet is evocative in its restraint, is supple and sure-footed, both in the composed passages and in the way Davis's solos eschew vibrato and begin to articulate the vulnerability and the ferocity that came to characterize his playing later. This jazz is *cool*, then, in Davis's devotion to expression first, to the emotional center of jazz, rather than to athleticism, rather than to mastery of an instrument.

Would Rugolo's offhand title for the nonet sessions be the first reference to this ubiquitous term as we hear it so much these days? There are a lot of opinions on the subject. Eric Partridge's *Dictionary of Slang and Unconventional English* gives the sense of *cool* as "good and modern" as a term in jazz circles since 1945, but can give no source but an article from the *Observer* of 1956. Partridge also offers *cool* as "(of a singer) slow and husky," since 1948, or coeval with the Miles Davis sessions. *Harper's Magazine* itself, in an article of 1950, is meanwhile *hip to the craze,* noting, "the Bop musician's use of 'cool' instead of 'hot' as a word of highest praise." But Garry Giddins, the eminent jazz critic, believes that the actual usage may predate the Davis sessions by years, as in Charlie Parker's 1947 recording of "Cool Blues," or in Doris Day's 1941 recording of J. P. Johnson's "Keep Cool, Fool." Giddins says, "Black musicians in the 1930s used *cool* in the literal sense, to contain feeling, to play with restraint." Still, there is a sense, toward midcentury, of jazz and popular music affecting the meaning of the word *cool* finally and permanently, so that Macaulay or Addison would have been surprised by its connotation *à la mode.* Partridge makes this transition abundantly clear, quoting F.E.L. Priestley: " '*Cool* became a word of praise when *hot* ceased to be one; that is, when hot jazz went out of fashion to be displaced by bop or bebop, a later — a 'progressive' or 'modern jazz.'"

There's an implicit cultural fusion in this way of speaking. That is, a white arranger and A&R man (Rugolo) coins the term to describe sessions by a black musician (Davis), who is himself attempting a music that fuses both elements of a black idiom (jazz, and especially the style and form of bebop) with a white style — a jazz slower and more given to melody than to loose improvisation. This is the way words are generated in America, I'm trying to say, by use and reuse, by experiment and malapropism, across a great spectrum of cultures and subcultures and communities ("hot" jazz originated in France, and "cool" jazz was reactively American), and so in this usage jazz serves not only as the locus for the meaning of the word *cool,* but also as a laboratory for the way in which the term gets disseminated: spontaneously, loosely, in an improvisatory way, as a delineator of passions and moods and styles. Which is to say that if *cool* is an example, our American popular argot is now finally multiethnic and vigorous across boundaries of class and religion. We chatter and chatter is good and in the groove of chatter words become flexible and porous and intoxicating and they perform a breathy *ars nova.*

Given this kind of energy coming out of the jazz world (there wasn't rock-and-roll yet), it's not surprising that the next group to champion the term *cool* and to make it a part of daily language, at least according to myth, was a mostly white group of writers and thinkers who brought to the term a long-lasting value and meaning in the margins of postwar America. I mean the Beats. Those coiners and harvesters of new locutions, of "hip" and "gone cat," etc. Their appearance in American culture had quite a bit to do with *cool*.

Oddly, though, Jack Kerouac, who in 1948 articulated the term "beat" to describe his generation (borrowing it from Herbert Huncke), infrequently employed the word *cool* himself. Using up-to-the-minute and very *cool* technology — a recent CD-ROM publication on Kerouac and the Beats entitled *A Jack Kerouac ROMnibus* — I have been able to do a full-scale search on the appearance of the term in a large sampling of Kerouac works. While I can find few appearances in selections of his poems, or in selections from *The Subterraneans* or *The Town and the City*, his later work, *The Dharma Bums*, does have eight incidental appearances of the word *cool*, seven of which are used in connection with weather descriptions ("The trail would suddenly come into a *cool* shady part," or "Then as it got *cool* in the late afternoon" [italics mine]). Only one passage seems tangentially to address the issue of contemporary cool, yet is far from conclusive: "Whenever people dropped in to visit us at the cottage, I'd always put my red bandana over the little wall lamp and put out the ceiling light to make a nice *cool* red dim scene to sit and drink wine and talk in." (By way of a control sample, I also checked for the word *hip*, in *Dharma Bums* — three mentions, of which two had to do with an anatomical part — and the word *beat*, in which all eight mentions had to do with drumming or fistfights.) I did find, however, that the Viking Press advertisement for *Dharma Bums* used the word *cool* in its plot summary, in the contemporary fashion: "They come swinging down to San Francisco — to hot girls and cool jazz, to wild parties and wild poets . . ."

Meanwhile, in a passage toward the end of *On the Road* — Kerouac's sloppy, joyous, and fabulously passionate rant about youth in the late forties — the author does begin to articulate what *cool* might mean in a broader nonmusical context, apart from the idiom of jazz. The passage in question takes place in chapter four in the third section of the book, which begins with encomiums about the jazz written and played then by African Americans. Black jazz. The scene is San Francisco (to which city "cool" jazz migrated later in its existence), and features Dean Moriarty (a.k.a. Neal Cassady, who in any true account of *cool* must be said to carry the torch from the Beat years to the "hippie" enclave of Ken Kesey, the Merry Pranksters, and the Grateful Dead) and Sal Paradise, a.k.a. Kerouac. Here they are visiting a jazz club on the Barbary Coast:

> Out we jumped in the warm, mad night, hearing a wild tenorman bawl-ing horn across the way . . . The behatted tenorman was blowing at the peak of a wonderfully satisfactory free idea, a rising and falling riff that went from "EE-yah!" to a crazier "EE-de-lee-yah!" . . . Uproars of music and the tenorman *had it* and everybody knew he had it.

What is the celebrated *it* of this formulation? Kerouac doesn't take up the question right away, because he is busy with further descriptions of jazz soloing: "The tenorman hauled back and stamped his foot and blew down a hoarse, baughing blast, and drew breath, and raised the horn and blew high, wide, and scream-ing in the air . . . Dean was in a trance." And later, during a ballad: "Here we were dealing with the pit and prune-juice of poor beat life itself in the god-awful streets of man, so the tenorman said it and sang it, 'Close — your —' and blew it way up to the ceiling and through to the stars and on out — 'Ey-y-y-y-y-y-es.'" The values of jazz, the intangible values of the music, abstractions about spon-taneity and feeling, are in the process of being transferred by Kerouac from the music onto the players of the music. What's cool about jazz has become a characteristic of jazzmen. This becomes clearer as the scene begins to involve carousing around town with the aforementioned tenorman ("'Yes! Ain't nothin I like better than good kicks!'") rather than listening to him play. Here, as in Kerouac's fanciful prose, jazz becomes a way of life, rather than a musical idiom; jazz is a process, jazz is a series of intentions, jazz is a style.

Thus, in the next scene, *cool* does turn up — in a nascent stage — and it's during a rather homophobic passage (though "Carlo Marx," the Ginsberg character, "Old Bull Lee," who stands in for William Burroughs, as well as Neal Cassady and perhaps even Kerouac himself, were practicing homosexuals with varying fre-quency, Kerouac was certainly not *gone* enough yet to find gay life *cool*): "We saw a horrible sight in the bar: a white hipster fairy had come in wearing a Hawaiian shirt and was asking the big drummer if he could sit in . . . The fairy sat down at the tubs and they started the beat of a jump number and he began stroking the snares with soft goofy bop brushes, swaying his neck with that complacent Reichi-analyzed ecstasy that doesn't mean anything except too much tea and soft foods and goofy kicks on the *cool* order. But he didn't care. He smiled joyously into space and kept the beat." A similar and less troubling usage appears in a 1950 letter from Kerouac to Cassady: "A raw mind and a cool mind are two different minds. The raw mind is usually associated with the physical life, whether athletic, work, or just beat . . . ; the cool mind is the intellectual emphasis and the physical counterpart of it is a kind of gracefulness . . . a gracefulness that is almost effeminate."

Cool, here, mirrors the difficulties of the "cool" jazz style after Miles Davis's *Birth of the Cool.* What is cool, after Miles moved on to his Gil Evans collaborations and then on to his terrific quintet (with John Coltrane et al.), is what's white, what's deracinated, what's goofy, perverse, cerebral. The jazz of Chet Baker, with (as Gary Giddins puts it) "his movie-star good looks"; Dave Brubeck's academic, intellectual jazz: odd time signatures and Middle Eastern modalities. And yet, despite these judgments, directly after Kerouac's brief invocation of the term *cool* in chapter four of *On the Road,* he takes on, at last, the task of defining the "it" his tenorman "had" at the opening of the passage, for the simple reason that these values — *cool,* and the ineffable IT — are related, are harmonious, are consonant:

> I wanted to know what "IT" meant. "Ah well" — Dean laughed — "now you're asking me impon-der-ables — ahem! Here's a guy and everybody's there, right? . . . All of a sudden somewhere in the middle of the chorus he *gets it* — everybody looks up and knows; they listen; he picks it up and carries. Time stops. He's filling empty space with the substance of our lives, confessions of his bellybottom strain, remembrance of ideas, rehashes of old blowing. He has to blow across bridges and come back and do it with such infinite feeling soul-exploratory for the tune of the moment that everybody knows it's not the tune that counts but IT."

"Then," Kerouac says, "I began talking; I never talked so much in my life."

This is *cool,* finally, in its transitional moment, in which it is em-

bodied in Kerouac; he is cool, IT is cool; and cool crests, perhaps
not yet in the explicitly modern usage of the word, but rather as a
way of carrying oneself, a way of marking an attitude that extends
beyond language and the capacity of language to denote, that pre-
empts the civilizing and hypocritical layers *of straight culture*, that focuses instead on a deportment, an ephemeral and unstated aspect,
a perfume of the infinite, a wisp of the spiritual, in which improvisation and spontaneity enable numinous predisposition, access to
the ether. IT's not a product or an extract or a medication. IT is
cool and cool is an approach characterized by feeling, by passions,
and you find it in the riotous voice of Kerouac's narratives, as well
as in the riffing of Ginsberg's poems in the later fifties, who among
his catalogue of great minds *destroyed by madness* includes the following characters:

> angelheaded hipsters burning for the ancient heavenly connection
>   to the starry dynamo in the machinery of night,
> who poverty and tatters and hollow-eyed and high sat up smoking
>   in the supernatural darkness of cold-water flats floating across
>   the tops of cities contemplating jazz,
> who bared their brains to Heaven under the El and saw
>   Mohammedan angels staggering on tenement roofs illuminated,
> who passed through universities with radiant *cool* eyes
>   hallucinating . . .

As you also find *cool* in the withering comedy of William Burroughs, in his *lapsed idealism* (as Mary McCarthy put it); even the
opening of *Naked Lunch* (1957), in its recoiling from warmth,
seems to prefigure the rising of cool as a reptilian cultural impera-
tive: "I can feel the heat closing in, feel them out there making
their moves, setting up their devil doll stool pigeons, crooning over
my spoon and dropper I throw away at Washington Square Station,
vault a turnstile and two flights down the iron stairs, catch an up-
town A train." *Heat* is slang for the authorities (dating to about
1936, according to Partridge, or only slightly ahead of the whole
"hot" and "cool" jazz issue), but here it's *heat* that is opposed by the
narrator, and thus the narrator is *cool* — as any reader would agree
who has drifted through the icy nightmare of *Naked Lunch*, one of
the century's great examples of sang-froid. Yet it is also a novel
beautiful and irate in its melancholy:

America is not a young land: it is old and dirty and evil before the settlers, before the Indians. The evil is there waiting. And always cops: smooth college-trained state cops, practiced, apologetic patter, electronic eyes weigh your car and luggage, clothes and face; snarling big city dicks, soft-spoken country sheriffs with something black and menacing in old eyes color of a faded gray flannel shirt.

Burroughs, that "gone cat" in *On the Road,* opposes the power of the state with the renegade but slightly detached passions of individuals. Cool individuals. The state usually wins, but the logic, as in Kerouac and Ginsberg, is passionately individualistic. Thus, in Burroughs, we get an implied articulation of *cool* as (again according to Partridge) "retaining complete control — or so the addict believes — while 'turned on' (drug exhilarated)," and, by extension, staying *cool* when the cops come for the bust.

I loved this Beat writing as a young reader. The velocity and spirit, the opposition to the stuffiness of academic writing (to the monolithic sobriety of New Criticism), the sheer, dizzy glee. What the great Beat writers did for American letters was appropriate America's one truly indigenous music form, jazz, and fuse the lessons of that music with the transcendentalism that had been irrigating American literature for a century. The Beats yoked Miles and Bird to Whitman and Emerson. And by the late fifties and sixties, the cool Beat idiom had become as frankly spiritual as its transcendentalist models. The theme becomes explicit in their work, as in Kerouac's 1960 journal entry: "Anybody can become a 'hipster' O Mailer . . . Broyard, . . . et al., but even the dumbest college kid who believes in God is beat, beatific and blessed." Unfortunately, the ambition concealed in this "transcendentalist" message was ultimately lost on Kerouac: the later journal entries, from the mid- to late sixties, by which time he was *drinking around the clock,* are grueling to read. Kerouac squandered his talent fantastically. Perhaps the process ("First thought, best thought," as Ginsberg said), and the freedom of Beat activity, the blissful singularity of it, couldn't be sustained for long. Both Burroughs and Kerouac (and Cassady later) resorted to considerable amounts of drugs to catalyze their work, and the cost was the highest of all costs. They left their best work behind while young.

Meanwhile, *cool,* through its relationship to the movement of the Beats, began to assume its new shape in other efforts. For example, in the person of Gwendolyn Brooks, an African-American poet writing in 1960: "We real cool. We / Left school. We / Lurk late. We / Strike straight. We / Sing sin. We / Thin gin. We / Jazz June. We / Die soon." Or in Lawrence Ferlinghetti's *Coney Island of the Mind,* adapting (in 1958) the narrative of Christ's passion to a Beat vocabulary: "You're hot / they tell him / And they cool him / They stretch him on a tree to cool / And everybody after that / is always making models / of this Tree . . . Only he don't come down / from His Tree / Him just hang there / on His Tree / looking real Petered out / and real cool." In Ferlinghetti's poem (which, in earlier stanzas, also makes use of "hip" and "cat" in the retelling of the Galilean odyssey), all the possible *cools* intersect, the cooling-down cool, the cool of jazz, the cool of "self-possession," as Partridge gives it. The Lamb of God *unites meanings,* makes contemporary slang stick, as in Kerouac's beatification of the Beat. *Jesus Christ, one cool, hep cat.*

By 1960, though, the Beats with their jazz and their tea and their smack and their cross-country driving escapades were coexisting like Neanderthals in the era of the Cro-Magnon. Something had happened in the intervening years, something had diverted the fickle attentions of young people, and I mean, of course, *the idiot bastard cousin* of "cool" jazz or bebop — *the dread menace of rock-and-roll.* Anti-music. Devil's spawn. Music of hellions. If jazz was a fertile crescent for American colloquial language, rock-and-roll, its very name a slang term for *getting it on,* would prove to be a hothouse, a factory, a furious industry for neologism, right from its initial *a wop bop a loo bop a lop bam boom.* From rock-and-roll and its culture came terminology like *boogie, boogaloo, doo wop, shang-a-lang, mojo, punk, bump and grind, hardcore, hip-hop,* and *grunge,* and many other manic turns of phrase, sacred and profane. Therefore, rock-and-roll has much to say about *cool.*

Jerry Lieber and Mike Stoller, who (in the period before artists wrote their own material) were the preeminent mythicists and fabulators of rock-and-roll, invoked the sociology of cool occasionally. *Cool* is in one of their hits for Elvis Presley, "Fools Fall in Love": "Fools fall in love in such a hurry . . . Oh! They got their love torches burning / when they should be playing it cool"; and it's in one of their finer tunes for the black vocal group the Coasters,

"Three Cool Cats" (a prominent early cover for the Beatles):
"Three cool cats / Are coming up the corner in a beat-up car . . .
Three cool chicks are walking down the corner." Danny and the Ju-
niors, in their 1958 number one, "Let's Go to the Hop," had a little
to say about *cool* — "You can swing it, you can groove it / You can
really start to move it at the hop / Where the jockey is the smooth-
est / And the music is the coolest" — as did Del Viking in his 1957
hit, "Cool Shake." And if you'll pardon a few anachronistic examples, I can finish the catalogue: the Beatles lifted the "playing it
cool" formulation from "Fools Fall in Love" for their hit "Hey
Jude," the number one single for the entire decade from 1960 to
1969 ("Don't you know that it's the fool who plays it cool / By making his world a little colder"). There's "Cool Jerk," that infinitely
covered classic. And, on the margins, the Stooges with "Real Cool
Time," composed in 1970 and consisting mainly of repetitions of
the line "We're gonna have a real cool time tonight." There's the
Hollies with their "long cool woman in a red dress"; there's Kool
and the Gang; there's the Little River Band with "Cool Change"
and Pablo Cruise (in 1981) with "Cool Love." There's Squeeze
with "Cool for Cats." Rickie Lee Jones, "Coolsville." There's the
Blues Brothers gorging themselves on a "cool watermelon sandwich." There's John Gale's "Indistinct Notion of Cool." Queen
punned on rockabilly cool on the 1980 hit "Crazy Little Thing
Called Love": "She gives me hot and cold fever / Then she leaves
me in a cool, cool sweat." Bruce Springsteen raised the issue in his
account of Vietnam vets coming home, "Born in the U.S.A.": "I'm
a long gone daddy in the U.S.A. . . . I'm a cool rocking daddy in the
U.S.A." David Bowie used it in "Diamond Dogs"; Sparks used it in
"Cool Places"; Devo used it in their awesome satire "Through Being Cool." And so forth.

But though rock-and-roll, since the fifties, had and has a lot to
say *about* cool, it doesn't *embody* the tricky concept. Not in the way
Miles Davis or John Coltrane or Jack Kerouac embodied cool.
Here we have to venture forth with a number of discernments.
Notwithstanding the Sun sessions version of "Mystery Train," or
the spontaneous portions of the 1968 "comeback" special in which
he jammed with Scotty Moore and Bill Black, *Elvis, it turns out, was
not entirely cool.* He was alluring, erotic, intense, but for the purposes of this argument he didn't have IT. I make this judgment, in

part, after having spent an afternoon reading Elvis's lyrics in their entirety (A to Z), and after having ruminated over the vexing fact of Elvis *after* the 1968 special, the Elvis who sang "America the Beautiful" and "When the Saints Go Marching In," the Las Vegas Elvis, the Elvis who accepted a special citation from President Nixon, the Elvis of the later movies, the Elvis who presided, in his last tours, over the very kind of hack musicianship that rock-and-roll was designed to slay. *Elvis was not cool.* Elvis was an entertainer with a grand sentimental streak. An entertainer capable of mesmerizing and delighting. But he wasn't cool. And you know what? The Beatles, except for a few fleeting moments ("Strawberry Fields Forever," "Dear Prudence," "Twist and Shout," side three of *The White Album,* most of *Revolver*), even when they got *beyond fab,* were not really cool either. Anything having to do with Paul McCartney, it should be clear at this late date, is not and cannot be *cool,* no matter how hummable the melodies. John struggled valiantly to forge a credibility for his fellow Liverpudlians, but even he ("Just Like Starting Over") ultimately succumbed to professionalism. The Rolling Stones are not now cool (although they may have been in one song: "Gimme Shelter"), and the Who are not now cool (Broadway!), and the Clash were not terribly cool and the Talking Heads were not cool, though David Byrne in his 1985 book version of *True Stories* used the word *cool* often enough that his editor, Nan Graham, had to suggest alternatives. In fact, rock-and-roll (and by extension most popular music), by virtue of its relation to the promotion and business of large multinational entertainment providers, has, since the sixties, when the British first trammeled our shores, traded in the possibility of *cool* for a longevity associated with paychecks. Rock-and-roll has become a job opportunity for younger people not otherwise gifted with business acumen. Thus we arrive at that captioned American postcard, from the eighties, of the kid with the green mohawk: "Too cool for school, too dumb for the real world . . . Guess I'll start a band."

Myself, I lived by rock-and-roll, I learned as much from it as I did from *Moby-Dick* and *The Scarlet Letter,* I wept over certain songs and albums, I waited breathlessly for new releases, I quoted song lyrics when asked to quote poetry in English class, I learned about community at rock-and-roll shows, I learned about the passions through the passions of forty-fives. But lately the ecstasy of three minutes and fifteen seconds of guitar racket is elusive. Where did the promise go? Where is the deliverance, the goofy, cool intoxication rock-and-roll once accomplished? Where is a rock-and-roll about which might be said, as Richard Meltzer opined in his (1970) *Aesthetics of Rock,* "For an experience to be artistically viable, it must be 'cool,' that is, it must be serious enough to attract reflective interest and primary emotional response and yet contain a tinge of the comic or benign just great enough to prevent overindulgence in this seriousness."

Well, there are a few examples left. There is some vestigial *cool* in the old battered idiom. These exceptions have to do, mainly, with the conjunction of Beat process with aspects of jazz and American transcendentalism, with the beatified emphasis on the spontaneous and the ephemeral and the excitable and the spiritual, and the way in which these things stew with the counterculture of the late sixties. Bob Dylan, Jerry Garcia, Joni Mitchell, Neil Young, Patti Smith, the Velvet Underground, Marvin Gaye, Nina Simone were *cool* in the rock era. The Bob Dylan of "Subterranean Homesick Blues": "Don't follow leaders / Watch your parking meters." The Bob Dylan who said, "To live outside the law you must be honest," who said, "I came out of the wilderness and just naturally fell in with the Beat Scene." The Marvin Gaye of "What's Going On?" The Patti Smith of *Horses.* The Velvets of "Sister Ray." The Jerry Garcia of *Live Dead.*

That these rock-and-roll artists became very popular, that *cool* became with them pandemic among the American young — these facts demonstrate the *metastasis* that took place in the realm of youth culture during the sixties. In my history of cool, the sixties are when the word *cool* goes from being meaningful to becoming hackneyed. As Thomas Frank notes in his fascinating (if uncool by virtue of excessive theorizing) *Conquest of Cool,* this has everything to do with the attention of straight society, with articles in *Time, Life,* and *Mademoiselle* ("Flaming Cool Youth of San Francisco Poetry"), with Leonard Bernstein's *West Side Story* (and its theme entitled "Cool"), with Maynard G. Krebs (the televised beatnik of *The Many Loves of Dobie Gillis*), with the mass attention that signified the creative exhaustion of the Beat revolution, and with it the ability of merchandisers and advertisers to define cool culture as a demographic and to begin to attempt to sell things to this group, as well as *to make of it a commodity in itself,* a category of status that America might find a way *to purchase:*

> Before the 1960s, young people had always been an established part of marketing and a staple image in advertising art, largely because of their still unformed tastes and their position as trend leaders. This was especially true in the 1920s. But during the 1960s, this standard approach changed. No longer was youth merely a "natural" demographic to which appeals could be pitched: suddenly youth became a consuming position to which all could aspire.

Frank's account — for example, of Pepsi's shift toward an image of "Pepsi hip" in the late sixties — captures an essential aspect of the way youth culture is deployed in business. There is, in Frank's view, an inextricable link between "straight" culture and the hip margins: "Now the copy [in 1966] is smart-alec in tone rather than inviting, and the overt explanations of 'Pepsi-ness' are replaced with hip phrases and anti-establishment wit. An ad depicting surfers describes them as 'Board members / of the Pepsi Generation.'"

But, while effectively accounting for the way merchandising concepts get reproduced in our civilization of signs, Frank fails to deal exhaustively with the *meaning* of a word like *cool* (which, beyond the title, doesn't get much treatment in *Conquest of Cool* anyhow, not like *hip,* which gets *charts:* "Hip Appliance Advertising, *Life* Magazine, as a Percentage of All Appliance Advertising, 1958–1972.") Frank's book avoids describing what was being marketed in the sixties and seventies so that it may instead concentrate on *how:* "Apart from certain obvious exceptions at either end of the spectrum of commodification (represented, say, by the MC5 at one end and the Monkees at the other), it was and remains difficult to distinguish precisely between authentic counterculture and fake."

It remains difficult to say what counterculture *means.* It remains difficult to define *cool.* It remains difficult to think of a tribe of underemployed hitchhikers, drug dealers, and poets, to take the square view, as *meaning much of anything at all.* Advertising, according to the scheme Thomas Frank describes, simply puts *cool* in play and then, through a large-scale distribution, makes it accessible to a horde of Americans, in this way *moving some product.* Yet this process shouldn't imply that the condition of *cool* doesn't or couldn't, in some fertile way, *exist*. Just because a word is used to market a product shouldn't disqualify the word, shouldn't reduce it to mere signifier. If cool gets used, pragmatically speaking, it must get used to connote something. And maybe this is best demonstrated in an example, in the case of the American product most frequently associated with the word *cool* in the last three decades: the mentholated cigarette brand Kool, manufactured by Brown & Williamson.[2]

Kool is B&W's flagship brand and has been marketed nationally in this country since the mid-thirties — or not long before the first appearance of the word *cool* in jazz subculture. At the dawn of this robust life, the Kool advertising campaign made no mention of *cool* in the contemporary sense (the name Kool probably referred to the taste of menthol). In fact, the original Kool advertising copy merely reflected the fact that Kool carried coupons: "Free coupons bring handsome gifts." But in 1962, the advertising strategy for Kool cigarettes shifted suddenly toward — as an official B&W brand history terms it — a "problem/solution" approach. The problem addressed in the 1962 advertisements, according to these official communications, was a *lack of cool*, and the solution, obtainable through lighting up one of the Kool cigarettes (which in 1962 had a 2.9 percent market share of total cigarette consumption), was "extra coolness." As B&W says, "Kool was the only U.S. domestic cigarette to make so specific and proven a claim."

If Kool cigarettes, by virtue of their title, somehow affected the word choice, the *cool*, of jazz cats in the late thirties and early forties (in "Keep Cool, Fool," et al.) through the conjunction of their mentholated brand and the dawn of bebop, and if Kool influenced the renovation of the old Anglo-Saxon word *cool* and from there seeped into the values and the subconscious of jazz culture, by the late fifties the brand was nonetheless playing catch-up. Suddenly it was the Beats and the kids who were deploying the slang. In the late fifties and early sixties, Kool was symbiotically pitching itself back to these very wordsmiths it had first influenced. By 1969, for example, the linkage between *cool* and Kool was entirely explicit in the brand's courting of women smokers with the "Lady Be Cool" line (rekindled in the 1997 hip-hop-oriented "B Kool" billboard campaign). Kool cigarettes, it was now clear, provide *cool*. That's how they were sold. Meanwhile, in 1975, in a gesture of unmitigated postmodernism, Kool sponsored its first jazz festival, yoking the music to the cigarette once and for all. The festival has existed ever since.

The proof of all this adroit word choice has been in the bottom line: the Kool "problem/solution" campaign of 1962 resulted in an additional percentage point of market share, as well as an additional 4.5 billion units sold. At their peak, in the late seventies, after two decades of sales increases, total Kool sales were on the order of 59.4 billion units per annum.

All of which is to say that in the sixties, *cool* continued to be a major site for linguistic play. As in the postwar years, when a jazzy spontaneity was evident in the way the word was used, by the mid-sixties any number of *cool* idioms had become abundantly popular in the argot of kids. *Keep cool, cool it, cool out, cool in, cool hand, cool cat, cool as a virgin, cool beans, coolcock, in the cooler, cool off, cool one,* were all part of the hip dictionary. From a term that mainly described a certain kind of music in 1945, *cool* had multiplied and subdivided, like the various constituencies using it, geometrically, exponentially. Corporations tried to co-opt the tongue of the kids, as above, by making use of *cool,* but the kids were acting simultaneously to co-opt the language of business for their own comic revolutionary ends. As is most often the case when there is real enthusiasm and real love of language, meaning proved more powerful than the merchandise. Street language, street impulses, the vigorous solecisms of folks, won. You also see this kind of revenger's energy in the case of Kool-Aid (of which more below), which, in the sixties, became important to American cool culture in a very novel way.

Tom Wolfe's *Electric Kool-Aid Acid Test* (1968) is a good primary text for tracking the motility of *cool* in the sixties, not only because Wolfe himself deploys the term — in frank imitation of the lingo he heard at the time — but also because he quotes it frequently among interview subjects: writer Ken Kesey and his band of mid-sixties LSD-dropping Day-Glo Merry Pranksters, who, for a brief couple of years, wrought a very cool havoc on the west side of the American continent and stirred up, in the process, a bona fide *alternative lifestyle.* Wolfe, for all his arch bravado, is attuned to the movement of ideas and to their tectonic shiftings. And perhaps for these reasons, he opens *Electric Kool-Aid* with a witty pun: "That's good thinking there, Cool Breeze. Cool Breeze is a kid with three or four days' beard sitting next to me on the stamped metal bottom of the open back part of a pickup truck." Cool Breeze, who turns up but once more in *Electric Kool-Aid,* is here not only a signifier for the slightly awkward but ambitious *cool* of the Pranksters, but, as a hippie primitive, he is also faintly comic amid the run-down technology of a good old American pickup truck.

And that's just at the outset. Wolfe uses the word *cool* a lot: "The Chief; out on bail. I expect the whole random carnival to well up into a fluorescent yahoo of incalculably insane proportions. In fact, everybody is quiet. It is all cool." Or: "Some of the old Perry Lane luminaries' *cool* was tested and they were found wanting"; "Chuck is one of the nicest people in the world and Sandy can trust him. If only he can remain cool." Etc.

In addition to using the word, Wolfe does a fine job of getting at the cool of Kesey's ideas, at their Beat origins. Here he is certainly amplifying Kerouac's notion of the unstated IT of cool as it was expressed in the California of the mid-sixties:

> The Life — that *feeling*— The Life — the late 1940s early 1950s American Teenage Drive-In Life was *precisely* what it was all about — but how could you tell anyone about it? But of course! — the *feeling*— out here at night, free, with motor running and the adrenaline flowing, cruising in the neon glories of the new American night — it was very Heaven to be the first wave of the most extraordinary kids in the history of the world — only 15, 16, 17 years old, dressed in the haute couture of pink Oxford shirts, sharp pants, snaky half-inch belts, fast shoes — with all this Straight-6 and V-8 power underneath and all this neon glamour overhead, which somehow tied in with the technological superheroics of the jet, TV, atomic subs, ultrasonics — Postwar American suburbs — glorious world!

Wolfe is rendering a late-night drug-induced rant of Kesey's. It's a spirited and funny monologue (which goes on for about three pages), and it's clearly indebted to Kerouac's high style, with a Kerouacian emphasis on the evanescent, uncanny aspect of life ("It couldn't be put into words anyway"). But there are a few telling alterations to the Beat construct of cool as it is recycled in Kesey's posse. Though Neal Cassady, the Dean Moriarty of *On the Road,* was

present in this band of Merry Pranksters — he was the driver of
the famous Prankster bus (and otherwise seemed to stand mainly
on the fringes of the action) — though Ginsberg turned up periodically at Kesey's house, though even Kerouac made an appearance in the Pranksters' "movie" (when the Pranksters were in
NYC) — "Here was Kerouac and here was Kesey and here was
Cassady in between them, once the mercury for Kerouac and the
whole Beat Generation and now the mercury for Kesey and the
whole — what? — something wilder and weirder out on the road"
— in spite of a perfect Beat pedigree, there was an optimism and
an enthusiasm missing from the Pranksters' activity. The Beat process was somewhat intact ("Kesey's explicit teachings were cryptic,
metaphorical; parables, aphorisms"), but not the *meaning*. Wolfe
says of the hippie kids of the period, "They had no particular philosophy, just a little leftover Buddhism and Hinduism from the *beat*
period." The message got a little incoherent, a little malevolent, a
little *white*. But that's the least of it.

With a movement among the Pranksters toward vagueness and
inactivity and, on occasion, even *pathology* (Sandy Lehmann-Haupt's
psychotic break on the bus that no one quite bothered about), the
notion of cool also slid sideways, so that some activities that would
not have been *cool* earlier, in the fifties, were now routinized, made
tolerable. The meaning of cool shifted slightly, away from the *spiri-
tus mundi*. There are two passages in *Electric Kool-Aid* that depict this
transition. The first has to do with the meeting between Kesey's
Pranksters and the motorcycle gang called the Hell's Angels.

Kesey met the Angels through Hunter S. Thompson, Wolfe tells
us, and took to them right away. Kesey's lumberjack charm apparently didn't put off the Angels either — "Kesey was a stud who was
just as tough as they were" — and they agreed to an invitation to
party with Kesey's group immediately. The Angels, as they arrived
at Kesey's domain, were a little reticent at first, but soon they fused
with the loose, unpredictable flow of things, so much so that even
Wolfe seems remarkably unjudgmental about the ensuing carnival:
"The Hell's Angels party went on for two days and the cops never
moved in. Everybody, Angels and Pranksters, had a righteous time
and no heads were broken." While the democratic principles of
this meeting seem honorable according to a Beat sort of cool —
even an Angel was an *Angel* if he was *on the bus* — the passive accep-

tance of, for example, a gang rape scene that took place at the Pow Wow chilled my readerly affections for Prankster activity considerably:

> The girl had her red and white dress pushed up around her chest, and two or three would be on her at once, between her legs, sitting on her face in the sick ochre light of the shack with much lapping and leering and bubbling and gulping through furzes of pubic hair while sweat and semen glistened on the highlights of her belly and thighs and she twitched and moaned, not in protest, however, in a kind of drunken bout of God knew what and men with no pants on were standing around, cheering, chiding, waiting for their turn, or their second turn, or the third until she had been fenestrated in various places at least fifty times.

Given that the woman in question was drunk or drugged or both, not at the peak of her decision-making skills, young and vulnerable, one wonders if she still, to this day, views this particular *afternoon delight* as consensual, or if *gang bang* (as Wolfe terms it) is really the correct terminology. Whatever the scene was, it sure wasn't *cool*. Nonetheless, in concluding the passage, Wolfe uses the word again, as if out of an anxiety about the whole violent Angels scene: "The Angels respected [Kesey] and they weren't about to screw around with him. He was one of the coolest guys they had ever come across."

As a footnote, it's worth noting that Ginsberg, too, whom the Angels tolerated (according to Wolfe) as a sort of wise freak, an imponderable, wrote about this cultural event in "First Party at Ken Kesey's with Hell's Angels":

> Cool black night thru the redwoods . . .
> at 3 A.M. the blast of loudspeakers
> hi-fi Rolling Stones Ray Charles Beatles . . . ,
> a little weed in the bathroom, girls in scarlet
> tights, one muscular smooth skinned man
> sweating dancing for hours, beer cans
> bent littering the yard, a hanged man
> sculpture dangling from a high creek branch,
> children sleeping softly in their bedroom bunks.
> And 4 police cars parked outside the painted
> gate, red lights revolving in the leaves.

I'd suggest that the tights here, with their inflamed hue, are a tacit admission of the sexual coercion taking place on the premises, while the revolving squad car lights at the poem's close anticipate the encircling force arrayed against a *cool* that had begun to veer a little too close to felony, a felonious cool, a *cool* that was no longer so inviting.

Not long after the Angels party, Kesey went on the lam, fleeing drug-related charges, and the Pranksters began to fray, though they remained coherent enough to begin a string of large-scale, organized LSD raves, in Los Angeles and elsewhere, in a subterranean effort to disseminate further their mad charm. It's here that the word *cool,* the cool of the Pranksters, collided with another squeaky-clean American food product, *a soft drink and its history,* with truly strange results.

Like many great American beverages, Kool-Aid began its life making somewhat spurious medicinal claims. According to Kraft Foods, owners of Kool-Aid's Perkins Product Company since 1953, the initial inventor of Kool-Aid was one "E. E. (Edwin) Perkins of Hendley, Nebraska," who, in 1914, "established a printing office and mail-order business, offering household remedies." Perkins's company later moved to Hastings, Nebraska (the Hastings Museum, "home of Kool-Aid," is now located there), and "expanded to include the manufacture and distribution of about 125 flavorings, spices and household products." In 1927, Kool-Aid became a powder, instead of a syrup, and assumed its present name. The name, I should point out, is roughly coeval with Kool cigarettes, and, again, not too far ahead of the great blossoming of *cool lingo,* in the late thirties and forties. In 1931, Kool-Aid became the sole product of the Perkins Product Company, after which Perkins sold out, in the fifties. Since then, Kraft has "innovated the Kool-Aid business with pre-sweetened Kool-Aid (1964)" and such catchy new styles as "Kool-Aid Bursts (1991), Kool-Aid Island Twists (1995), and Mega Mountain Twists (1997)."

(I love these excessive names of American products! I love all derangement of language in merchandising! I love all hype and bluster and exaggerated language! And I'm especially taken with the very Beat names of some of the recent Kool-Aid varieties, with their "wild, twisted-up flavors": Oh Yeah Orange-Pineapple, Man-O

Mango Berry, Soarin' Strawberry Lemonade, Kickin' Kiwi Lime, etc.)

The *very, incredibly cool* Kool-Aid Frequently Asked Questions site on the World Wide Web corrects some misconceptions about the beverage that are important to catalogue at this juncture: (1) Kool-Aid has been used effectively as a hair dye for children. (2) Unofficial taste tests by soft drink–obsessed Internet consumers indicate that Kool-Aid's "super fruity" designation of recent vintage is identical to the so-called "regular" Kool-Aid of old. (3) However, it is *not* true, as previously supposed, that James Jones and the People's Temple members committed mass suicide (in Jonestown) by dissolving cyanide in grape Kool-Aid. "The followers of Jones," according to the Kool-Aid FAQ, "drank cyanide-laced Flavor-Aid, a cheap imitation of Kool-Aid." (4) Kool-Aid in Great Britain is sometimes sold on the black market, at seventy-five cents a packet — a significant markup. (5) And, *irrefutably true, though subject to total suppression by all Kraft Foods materials that I was able to gather,* is that in 1966 the Merry Pranksters, under the de facto leadership of Kenneth Babbs (while Kesey was a fugitive), held their famous "Electric Kool-Aid Acid Test" in Compton, Los Angeles (not far from where, less than six months earlier, the Watts riots had raged) — at which the catalytic drug of the evening was tendered in a solution made with the famous medicinal beverage of E. E. (Edwin) Perkins, *Kool-Aid.*

A product made *cool* by virtue of its name.

Tom Wolfe thus describes the *love potion,* quoting an acid-test participant called Claire Brush:

> The [Pranksters' home movie] continued, some slides were shown of flowers and patterns, this and that . . . then a large trash can, plastic, was carried to the middle of the room, and all were invited to help themselves to the Kool-Aid it contained . . . Since Kool-Aid is a staple in the homes of Del Close and Hugh Romney and other friends of mine, I thought it was a natural thing to serve.

The Compton acid test continued in the usual fashion, with a fair amount of mayhem and mystery and boredom and carnage, with police ceaselessly monitoring the activity (LSD wasn't yet illegal and thus the Pranksters couldn't be busted on a lysergic rap). But soon Wolfe's description takes a sinister turn. A particularly

bad trip by one female attendee was recorded *over a loudspeaker*, recorded by Babbs and other Pranksters, and broadcast in a seminal
moment at the L.A. test:

> Babbs is getting it all over the microphone to make it *part of the test* —
> not an isolated event — but All-one, anorechtic freakout — *Who cares!*
> Romney looks at Babbs and Who Cares! — well, Babbs cares, with one
> part of him, but with another his devotion is to the Test, to the Archives,
> Who Cares in the Prankster Archives, and the cry wails over the hall,
> into every brain . . . Romney can't get this insane cry out of his head,
> *Who cares . . .* and he is back at the microphone, with his mission now, his
> voice furrowing into the microphone: "Listen, this girl's brains are com-
> ing out! And who cares?"

Few attended to the woman's cries, or perhaps her panic sub-
sided (as bad trips often do), but the ennui of the acid tests had begun, at which point one kid asked the police for a cigarette and,
amazingly, the cop slipped out for smokes and came back with *a
pack of Kools,* but the fun had gone out of the expedition, the passion of Kesey had gone out of it, a passion itself deracinated when
compared to the joy advocated by Kerouac, *no one particularly cared
any longer,* though caring, and the passions in general, had once (in
an elegant way) been integral to the mission of cool. There was division among the Pranksters about the leadership of Kenneth
Babbs; there was division about being in L.A. instead of San Francisco; there was division about the nature and purpose of the
Pranksters. By the end of the Electric Kool-Aid Acid Test, the
Pranksters as a community were threatened, perhaps terminally so.
They may have lingered, persisted, but the mantle of cool had
passed beyond them. When Kesey returned from Mexico he began
talking about going "beyond acid," and his new caution and his retrospection about the Bus and its inhabitants was palpable (in
Wolfe's account). Cool, as a social experiment, was wearing out its
time.

Thus, with the end of the Pranksters, cool became a term primarily and mostly related to drug chatter — is he *cool* (does he
smoke)? Was it *cool* (was the location free of cops)? — in the precise sense that Del Close and John Brent discussed the word *cool* in
How to Speak Hip (1961): "[To be cool is to] protect yourself from
police intervention." The energy around *cool* had shifted away

from jazz, away from black Americans (as Wolfe says: "The big thing with spades on the hip scene has always been the quality known as *cool.* And LSD freaking well blows that whole lead shield known as cool, like it brings you right out front, hang-ups and all"), away from writers, away even from Kerouac and Kesey. Cool, instead, had become something that was possessed by drug users and free-love espousers and rock-and-roll musicians. In fact, among the standard-bearers for several years would be the house band from the Prankster acid tests at Kesey's house, viz., the Grateful Dead. For example, Jerry Garcia, of the Dead, in a posthumous collection of interviews (*Garcia,* by the editors of *Rolling Stone*), uses the word *cool* a couple of times, first in connection with his album *Workingman's Dead:* "After we got busted [in New Orleans in 1971], we went home to make our record. And while we were making our record, we had a big, bad scene with our manager. Actually, making the record was the only *cool* thing happening — everything else was just sheer weirdness" (italics mine). And, later, in discussing the legacy of the beatniks in San Francisco, as perceived by Garcia's generation: "They liked . . . *jazz.* You know: 'Jazz, man. Dig it.' Rock & roll wasn't *cool,* but I *loved* rock & roll. I used to have these fantasies about 'I want rock & roll to be, like, respectable music.' I wanted it to be like art."

These instances of the word presage entirely the meaning that we associate with *cool* now. Cool, once it had passed into the early seventies, meant not much more than *modern and good.* And potentially much less. This was the *cool* of the Dead, and it had a vestigial spontaneity, a jazz and Beat spontaneity, it had *space,* it had throw-weight, at least until the mid-seventies when the Dead's sets began to achieve morbid predictability (short songs, break, drum solo, space, longer songs), when the Dead went "disco," when they fossilized, and as went the Dead, so went the word, at least for a time.

And this is when I come into the story as an observer. This is the beginning of the *cool* of my growing-up years. A cool America in which we were taught that LSD would enable you to change the traffic light from red to green *at will,* that you should not take LSD, therefore, because *it would cause traffic accidents,* an America that learned to accept as routine that a man holding highest office might use skullduggery or tape recordings to discredit his enemies, an America in which the coolest thing, the free concert, carried the possibility of murder (Altamont, 1970), in which military incursion into neutral countries was considered explicable, in which the free expression of youth culture was circumscribed, in which youth culture had conspicuous traces of *hard luck* upon it, a cool America in which *Billy Jack* was cool, or *Walking Tall* was cool. My America. I personally thought that Elton John was *the man,* or Al Pacino in *Serpico,* or Gene Hackman in *The French Connection,* or just about anybody in *The Poseidon Adventure.* (I thought that the end of *The Poseidon Adventure* — in which the Gene Hackman character *asks God to take him so that others might live,* as he lets go of the steam valve in the belly of the cruise liner and drops to his death — was *really cool.*)

Yet, by the mid-seventies, when the singer-songwriter school was wearing thin and with it the whole flaccid enterprise of California rock-and-roll, people were nonetheless realizing that literature had once again become cool, suddenly, with the words "a screaming comes across the sky," in the mad, cabalistic invention of *Gravity's Rainbow,* in the fury of Donald Barthelme's unequaled experiments in short prose, in John Ashbery's poems, or in the tremendous innovative assault of the Living Theater (a pride of New York artists walks into a theatrical space, takes off its clothes, and *just starts talking* — without script or theme or character), or in the violent electric period of Miles Davis (who probably comes closer, in his life's work, to *embodying cool* than any other single American artist). About the time I came into the story, cool was poised to make one last effort at a comeback.

I didn't know about any of this at the time. I was trying to get comfortable among my contemporaries. My time was spent, hours of it, attempting to make myself presentable, shucking layers of clothing, donning new ones, trying to mat my absurd hair, committing acts of home surgical intervention upon skin blemishes. I amounted to a desperate series of premeditated strategies for fitting in, none of them successful. However, when I went away to school, in New Hampshire, I suddenly began to learn, intuitively, that there was such a thing as *cool,* and that it was a quality I might ape, or aspire to. It was around me in the upperclassmen and -women, and, oddly enough, *it was completely synthesized and represented in the person of one of my coevals there,* a guy from the Philadelphia area named Jamie Neilson.

From ninth through twelfth grade, Neilson was a one-man side-show of creativity, comedy, malice, and charm. He was blond and attractive (later it seemed that every woman I knew had been in-volved with him); he wrote great poetry — according to my stan-dards at the time; he was no slouch as an athlete. According to ru-mor, he consumed legendary amounts of drugs and alcohol; he flouted all "major school rules"; he swam naked at the dam; he broke curfew; he swiped my copy of *Freak Out* by the Mothers of In-vention; he did ribald skits in chapel; he acted; he sang; he was everywhere at once, tormenting people, praising them, visiting them in their dreams; he was, by the standards of my school, a cool work of art.

There's one of these guys at every high school.

So I decided, in completing this investigation of *cool*, to see what Benjamin R. Neilson, Jr., himself now an instructor in English at a boarding school, as well as a dean of the senior class, a husband and father, a regular citizen, thought of *cool* now. I asked Jamie first about Kerouac and that ancient Beat model of cool, and then about whether he thought about the term now. So here's the one-time urchin of cool, as he would describe himself now:

> Whatever we thought was cool was miles from anything Kerouac had in mind. What he thought of as cool was a lot more *difficult* than what we did. By the time we got to cool it had lost all of its earnestness and it had an almost complete lack of self-awareness.
>
> And the unfortunate thing about cool in our era was that it wasn't very nice. Being cool was about distance. Sparring, in that verbal kind of way, conferred cool. If possible, frighten all fuckers away from ever *thinking* about judging you.
>
> I didn't perceive until I had been away from school for years that try-ing to be cool was about selling out in the worst way. We were trying des-perately to be distant, to have a critical detachment that would allow us to sit in judgment. And as anti-establishment as we styled ourselves, that wish to be the one doing the judging was strictly generic arrogance.
>
> As you may have inferred from the foregoing, my career as a Cool Guy is somewhat painful for me to contemplate.

Neilson's cultural analysis mirrors the difficult realities of the *last gasp of cool* in America, as he and I both experienced it, which is to say the punk rock upheavals of the late seventies. Out of a few stray particles of Beat and jazz and hippie energy (Richard Hell and the Voidoids swiping a line from a 1959 song called "The Beat

Generation" and coming up with their version, "Blank Generation"; Patti Smith updating the Burroughs style for her monumen-
tal album *Horses;* Ginsberg recording with the Clash), a rock-and-
roll style was formulated in London and New York that seemed, for
a moment, to change everything. What was degraded and unattractive, perverse and inept, was celebrated and accorded the highest respect of all. Guys and women (finally) who could scarcely play
their instruments called attention to all the scabs and sores of contemporary society, in a style that featured wit, energy, and inven-
tiveness. Punk *included anyone.* There was no in-crowd or out-
crowd. The more marginal you were, the better. (At a Devo concert
I went to, on New Year's Eve of 1978, the area where the disabled
people were clustered in their wheelchairs seemed to be the most
important section of the theater. The disabled were *more* Devo,
more plugged into the sinister contradictions of the straight life,
the tyranny of beauty.) Almost overnight, many at my boarding
school went from the groovy tie-dyed threads of the Grateful Dead
to the giddy vindictiveness of the Sex Pistols ("We're vacant! We
don't care!").

Never was a cultural movement so quick to extinguish itself. As a
dramatic evocation of the transition, I think most often of Exene
Cervenka's commentary about the punk scene in Los Angeles, as
depicted in part six of the Time/Life *History of Rock 'n' Roll.*
Cervenka describes the initial community spirit of punk and the
way that community quickly became permeated by a sinister edge:
"Everything went along just great until at some point the audiences went from being relatively intelligent and understanding
people to being kinda young scary kids who liked to spit at the
bands a lot . . . We kept begging them to stop spitting at us." There
were earlier signs of trouble, too, for example in one of the
Stooges' last shows, in the mid-seventies, in their hometown of Detroit (as described by Iggy Pop in *Please Kill Me*):

> This guy kept whipping eggs at me. I had on this little ballerina costume
> and a G-string and everything and I just got sick of it. It was a biker
> hangout, you know? So I finally just stopped everything and I said,
> "Okay, I'm calling the fucker down!" Everybody clears out and here's
> this guy, about six foot three . . . You know, I had little ballet shoes on,
> and it was just like seeing a train coming . . . He just got me. But he
> didn't deck me, he could knock me down, it was real weird. Finally, the

blood got to be too much for him so he just stopped and said, "Okay, you're cool."

Some of this — performers assaulting the audience, audience assaulting performers — was play, was innovation, but some of it was no cooler than the gang rape at Kesey's house or the "who cares" desolation of the late acid tests. Some of this was contempt for fellow men. By the end of the seventies, there was already developing an *us and them* of cool, divisions within divisions, bickering, lack of ambition, careerism, heroin addiction, death. By the time punk burned itself out, cool was a way to constitute community, but mostly this was a community *that kept others out* — as in the sequence in Woody Allen's 1980 film *Stardust Memories,* in which the filmmaker, whom Allen portrays, imagines himself on a train (one of those broken-hearted locals that run to the end of the line) full of sad, destitute, homely, *beat* Americans, the elderly, the obese, the disabled, a train running exactly parallel to another train, this other full of happy, beautiful, charming, cool people. Allen looks from his car, the train of the bereaved, into the next, the cool car, desperate for a way to effect passage from here to there.

If the seventies were bad, the eighties were worse, and I refuse on principle to admit that the eighties contributed anything at all to the history of *cool.* Or to much else, excepting the national debt. The connotation of the word *cool* in that dark period didn't change (one friend of mine, a writer well known in the eighties, protested, when I asked about it, "I used 'cool' to describe the weather!") — *good and modern,* in the Partridge sense; *satisfactory and acceptable,* according to the *Random House Historical Dictionary of American Slang* (which cites, for example, a 1980 University of Tennessee freshman theme: "There are a couple of cool guys on my floor. The rest are a bunch of shitheads"). Otherwise, in the eighties, there is little viable youth culture that is not being wholly and entirely controlled by *multinational entertainment providers.* The most conservative president of the postwar era occupies the Oval Office. *Crack cocaine* contributes a compelling new example of alliteration to the national vocabulary. *Cool* is isolated in pockets like indie rock (Hüsker Dü, the Replacements), advanced semiotics and cultural criticism (Slavo Zizek, Jane Gallup, Greil Marcus), independent cinema (Jim Jarmusch, Steven Soderbergh). Meanwhile, the culturally accepted notion of cool, ever more powerful over the margins, adheres in *Slaves of New York, Less Than Zero,* and *Bright Lights, Big City.* Jill Eisenstadt uses *cool* in one of the period's finer coming-of-age novels, *From Rockaway:* "You can say anything to Seaver; he's cool," or "'I's cool, ma'am,' says Sloane. 'You ain't gotta worry, we're his friends.'" But elsewhere there is an unbelievable paucity of self-knowledge masquerading as *cool.* The second-person narrator of Jay McInerney's *Bright Lights, Big City,* for example, says of himself, in a moment of high introspection,

> [In college] you succeeded in faking everyone out, and never lost the fear that you would eventually be discovered a fraud, an impostor in the social circle. Which is just about how you feel these days. Even now, as you puff yourself up with tales of high adventure in magazine publishing, you can see Elaine's eyes wandering out over the room, leaving you behind.

When the Ironman Nightlife Decathlons lurch to a close, the architects of eighties cool begin to wonder what lay beneath. It is clear, in these moments of candor, how far we have fallen from the cool of the forties and fifties. This cool, *in the most dramatic shift in the whole history of the word,* has again become *literally cool.* Devoid of feeling, or noteworthy only for its nostalgia about the time — way back — when human emotions mattered. You see it preeminently in the work of Bret Easton Ellis, in the deliberately flattened affect of his *chef d'oeuvre:*

> I don't like driving down Wilshire during lunch hour. There always seem to be too many cars and old people and maids waiting for buses and I end up looking away and smoking too much and turning the radio up to full volume. Right now, nothing is moving even though the lights are green. As I wait in the car, I look at the people in the cars next to mine.

Literally cool. From a cool that was meant to be evocative and emotionally dextrous (Miles Davis's cool jazz), to a cool that was cerebral and goofy (Burroughs and Ginsberg), to a cool that was rigorously opposed to state power and straight culture (Kesey, the Pranksters, the hippies), to the all-inclusive insurrection of the seventies, we have, in the eighties, a cool that means *dead inside.*

Chilled-out cool, to use nineties locution. Flat, lifeless, dim, empty, dead cool.

And that's about where things remain. Here's cool as described in some recent catalogue copy *for a lava lamp:* "The key to being cool: Wear clothes as black as the base of this pop icon. Watch the primordial goo rise up through the illuminated blue liquid . . . Note how this is just like life. Order another espresso and decide you are deep and should go back to writing beat poetry. Cool, Daddy-O!" Here's cool from a *New York Times* article about smokeless cigarettes: "But smokers must lift the device to their lips for each puff, as if smoking a kazoo. This is not exactly the *cool* image of Humphrey Bogart." Here's *Times Book Review* editor Charles McGrath describing the state of American publishing: "It was pretty *cool* for Farrar, Straus to take a run at [Stephen] King." A recent General Foods International Coffees coupon extols "Cool Ways to Unplug: Lusciously flavorful delightfully easy recipe ideas." At the close of the Tommy Lee Jones vehicle *Volcano* ("The Coast is Toast!"), Jones asks his screen daughter how she liked watching L.A.'s Beverly Center being detonated by a bomb squad. Her reply: "It was cool, Dad."

Are any of these examples legitimately cool? Even one?

A last-chance cottage industry of *cool* has sprung up in the world of hip-hop, in the jive of inner-city and faux-inner-city entertainers, the cool of Kool Herc, Kool Moe Dee, Kool Nutz, Kool Keith, Kool G. Rap, L L Cool J, and, most recently, of Coolio. Since this represents the dialectical weight of cool swinging back toward black Americans, I find it temporarily exciting and interesting. When a slang term gets neglected by one mob of citizens, it is often elsewhere the site of rehabilitation. As an example of this, I find Coolio's *Gangster's Paradise* album, like the really terrific hip-hop albums of old (*Fear of a Black Planet, Straight Outta Compton*) — and despite a fair amount of tough-guy posturing — a genuinely moving evocation of the difficulties of urban life, featuring "gangsters and thugs," like "young n — fighting the case with public defenders," as well as "this little girl just now taking training wheels off her bike, while her daddy gets twenty-five to life," in addition to a grand cast of innocent bystanders, of which Coolio observes, "Be it wrong or right, these are the Geto Highlites [sic]." His line of cool is also the cool of the detached observer, the distant relation of the low-affect Bret Easton Ellis cool, and perhaps not unlike the cool of blues musicians of the thirties who played with elegiac restraint, amid burdens of racism and poverty, where cool is all survival, where cool is *beating the rap,* living to tell.

Cool is a "grunt of assent," as my former classmate Jamie Neilson put it. It's ubiquitous. It's meaningless. It's no better than "neat" or "keen" or "sweet" or any of the other shifters in the pantheon of Anglo-Saxon single-syllable grunts of assent whose only reason to be is phatic, to ensure the continuity of communication, the insistence on noise, the bluster of a Young America that is no longer certain what it means or what it wants to mean or if it is capable of meaning at all. "Like . . . cool," Beavis says to his cartoon sidekick, Butt-head, as they gaze at some meager television fare, at some forgettable output from the *medium cool* ("Some like it cold," as Marshall McLuhan says), and his rap is funny and devastating and sad, all at the same time. What does *he* think he means?[3]

Sisters and brethren, kids all grown up now, adults of America (kids with kids of your own), remember those chambers where we once kicked back, avoiding homework or the first years of our nine-to-fives — in sudden, comical embraces, hoisting early-morning beers, drinks stolen from our parents, or later, the convenience apartments in which we worried about income and outflow, worried about our futures, what were we going to do, about the ineffable thing that we all wanted to have, that quality that seemed to slip away from us, out of reach, like a mooring line fraying and slipping, briefer than the neutrinos, briefer than the subatomics, this thing that others seemed to have, this *unknown tongue* (as Richard Meltzer calls it), the unknown tongue of a cool that made the opening of *Lolita* perfect, or the moment when James Dean says, "You're tearing me apart!" in *Rebel Without a Cause,* or the gumsnapping cool of Grace Paley's voice in *Enormous Changes at the Last Minute,* or the cool of Aretha Franklin shouting the word "respect," the cool of Neil Young's "Cortez the Killer," the cool of the Ramones. Where is the cool hidden in all these moments of bliss that are past now, moments when we felt suddenly vitally *here* and *good* and *modern* and *happy* and ready to go, to drive, like roadrunners, like continental explorers, across the impediments of a continent? Where is the cool we once thought we had or

thought we wanted? Shimmering interstate mirage, never to mate-
rialize? Cultural spook of a credulous age?

Gone, gone, long gone. Cool is spent. Cool is empty. Cool is ex post
facto. When advertisers and pundits hoard a word, you know it's
time to retire from it. To move on. I want to suggest, therefore, that
we begin to avoid *cool* now. Cool is a trick to get you to buy garments made by sweatshop laborers in Third World countries. Cool
is the Triumph of the Will. Cool enables you to step over bodies.
Cool enables you to look the other way. Cool makes you functional,
eager for routine distraction, passive, doped, stupid. I would like
now to suggest some alternatives. For the young people, *young
learning knights and maidens* who want something of their own, lest
the words they know are words that refer only to *adjustable rate
mortgages* and *price-earnings ratios* and the like. My initial thought
was *lucid,* but too many syllables, too hard to say; so then I worked
with *sublime* for a while: still too many syllables, but it has the right
drift. *Sublime* points at the beyond, the way *cool* once did, the way
Miles did, the way Coltrane did. Similar problems with *humble.*
Humble gets at the disappearance that was at the heart of cool, the
selflessness, but doesn't sound active enough. What about *meek*
or *warm* or *cooked* or *brum* (it used to refer to prostitutes) or *raw*
or *spared* or *fraught.* I like the sound of *the Fraught Generation. We belong to the Fraught Generation!* The records I like are *fraught!* Kurt
Cobain, though not cool, was certainly *fraught!* Or how about *goss,*
the nineteenth-century slang word short for "gossamer"? These
times are *goss.* Or how about *guff?* Or *crass?* Or how about *dorf,
euchred, flint, prim, sleek, tranced, scrag,* or *relinquent?* How about
pipient?

But this job is best left to you, users of the American tongue.
Seize control of your splendid language. Work your alchemical
mumbo-jumbo. Mix up your slang. Blow your innumerable horns.
Play well. Play with feeling.

Notes

1. For example, here's a list of cool people compiled by representative tenth- and
eleventh-graders from a private high school in the Philadelphia area: Joseph Stalin,
the Blues Brothers, Rosie O'Donnell, Dave Matthews (rock-and-roll personality),

Charles Bukowski, Mahatma Gandhi, Martin Luther King, Jr., Miles Davis, Bob
Marley, Jack Kerouac, "Dad" (for a grand total of three citations), Will Smith (of
Men in Black, for a grand total of five citations, or more than any other personality
in the survey), Eric Cartman (of the animated television show *South Park*, three
mentions), the Spice Girls ("except the corny one"), "Mom" (three citations), "because she always helps; she always knows the right answer, because her values and
morals are (in my view) perfect," or, in another case, "because she puts up with me
on a daily basis and yet still she loves me. She makes my lunch every day and is always trying to impress me and show me that she cares. I think she's the coolest person on earth." Everybody is listed in the survey once: "I think everyone is cool at
some point in time. It is hard to come up with just one definition of 'cool.' Cool is
being bold and independent, but within reason. Everybody is cool." James Dean;
Harrison Ford; Sean Connery; Robert Plant of Led Zeppelin (two citations); Bugs
Bunny; Louis Armstrong, "the great music maker"; Leonardo da Vinci; "my dog,"
twice over, " 'cause she is"; Leonardo di Caprio; Homer Simpson (for a grand total
of five citations), "he just has it"; Kramer (from *Seinfeld*), Matthew Broderick; John
Belushi; William H. Macy (actor, star of *Fargo*); Bruce Willis; Jim Carrey; Jon
Fishman (drummer); Drew Carey (comedian); David Gilmour (of Pink Floyd);
Hurricane Schwartz (weatherman); Bart Simpson; "my brother," because "he is
definitely an individual. He does not classify under any adolescent group. He is fun
and realistic. He always knows what to do or say to make anybody feel better, or to
see any kind of point"; Jerry Garcia (two citations); George Carlin; Lee Iaccoca;
Frank Lloyd Wright; Bob Dylan; Homer (I hoped this was the Greek epic poet, but
I'm afraid it is simply another Homer Simpson reference); Carlos Santana; Eryka
Badu (soul singer); Busta Rhymes (hip-hop personality); Puff Daddy (hip-hop personality), of whom it is said that he has "money, friends, and fame. He does what he
does because his friend, Biggie, was killed in a drive-by shooting"; Michael Jordan
(three citations), who "makes the most money in history"; Neil Young; "my friends:
they are cool because they are relaxed"; Prince William, who "dresses exceptionally
well"; Mrs. O'Keefe, "my tutor and she makes me laugh and helps to take the pressure off of school"; Liz Eldred, who "has been going out with my brother Jeff for
five years, which makes her cool"; Jim Morrison; "the Fonze"; Mao Tse-tung, "because he had a neat haircut and good taste in clothes"; God, the almighty: "he created everything, thus he must be at least a little cool. Also, it isn't smart to say that
an all-seeing, omnipotent being is uncool."

2. Marcel Danesi, in his book *Cool: The Signs and Meanings of Adolescence,* avers that
smoking is one of the essential signs of coolness among adolescents. He also includes the following (apparently in decreasing order of importance): "quantity of
alcohol consumption, 'doing' drugs, music preference within the clique, dance-re-
lated activities, strategic use of physical aggression, dress, sexual promiscuity and
prowess, individuality or 'weirdness,' academic achievement, automobile owner-
ship, and physical appearance." Smoking, in Danesi's semiotics, also occasions a
number of possible cool subrituals, such as "the initial procedure employed to insert the cigarette into the mouth," "the inhaling procedures used," and the "butt-
ing-out procedure used."

3. The high school students quoted had a few ideas about the meaning of the
word: "Cool is being friends with everybody (not just the popular people) or at least
not being rude to them"; "Although there is no exact definition, there is a less obvi-

ous definition: what a person thinks is cool is something that they like"; or cool is "when you have lots of money and great clothes"; "In school being cool is dressing well and even being mean to people. Tantalizing and tormenting kids is considered funny and cool. To be cool you go to parties and hang all over guys, you have to be an airhead or dress from J. Crew." One respondent commented that to be cool "you have to take the hand you are dealt and make the best out of every situation." A cool person might also be known as "nice, intelligent, in the New Age, good looking, loveable, caring, and da bomb"; or, in another formulation, "The so-called 'cool people' treat anybody who isn't part of their group like crap. They are obnoxious and are just rude in general. They make fun of people constantly and are way too interested in drinking and drugs." Cool is "whatever you think it is," or it is "to be liked by everyone," or it is "different for everybody because no two people are the same," or "cool is an opinion," but, on the other hand, "what is not cool is a social state of being. By this I mean that someone is not cool for their image, but for who they really are, or what they do." You can see, moreover, that "within different groups of people, different people are cool" (a sentence I really admire). Another respondent feels that "humility is a good characterization of coolness." One last young writer believes that to be cool is to be "vegetarian."

KYOKO MORI

Yarn

FROM HARVARD REVIEW

1

THE YELLOW MITTENS I made in seventh-grade home econom-
ics proved that I dreamed in color. For the unit on knitting, we
were supposed to turn in a pair of mittens. The two hands had to
be precisely the same size so that when we held them together,
palm to palm, no extra stitches would stick out from the thumb,
the tips of the fingers, or the cuff. Somewhere between making the
fourth and the fifth mitten to fulfill this requirement, I dreamed
that the ball of yellow yarn in my bag had turned green. Char-
treuse, leaf, Granny Smith, lime, neon, acid green. The brightness
was electric. I woke up knowing that I was, once again, doomed for
a D in home ec.

I don't remember what possessed me to choose yellow yarn for
that assignment. Yellow was a color I never liked; perhaps I was
conceding defeat before I started. Mittens, as it turns out, are just
about the worst project possible for a beginner. Each hand has to
be knitted as a very small tube, with the stitches divided among
four pointed needles that twist and slip unless you are holding
them with practiced confidence. The pair won't be the same size
if you drop or pick up extra stitches along the way, skip a couple
of decreases in shaping the top, or knit too tightly in your nervous-
ness and then let up in relief as you approach the end. You might
inadvertently make two right mittens or two lefts because you
forgot that the thumb has to be started in a different position for
each hand. I ended up with two right hands of roughly the same

size and three left hands that could have been illustrations for a fairy tale. *Once upon a time there lived three brothers, each with only one hand — large, medium, and very small — and, even though the villagers laughed at them and called them unkind names, the brothers could do anything when they put their three left hands together . . .*

I didn't knit again until graduate school when I met a woman from Germany with a closetful of beautiful sweaters. Sabina came to our seminar wearing a soft angora cardigan one week, a sturdy fisherman's pullover the next.

"I make all my sweaters," she said. "I can teach you."

I told her about my mitten fiasco.

"Knitting is easy," Sabina insisted. "A sweater's bigger than a mitten but much simpler."

"The patterns will confuse me."

"You don't need patterns. You can make things up as you go."

Sabina took me to a local yarn store, where I bought skeins of red cotton yarn. Following her instructions, I first knit the body of the sweater: two flat pieces, front and back, with a few simple decreases to shape the shoulders and the neck. The pieces were surprisingly easy to sew together. Sabina showed me how to pick up the stitches along the arm opening, connect the new yarn, and knit the sleeves, going from the shoulder to the wrist. I finished the sweater in a month. The result was slightly lopsided — one sleeve was half an inch wider than the other around the elbow — but the arms looked more or less even once I put the sweater on. The small mistakes in a knitted garment disappear when the garment is on the body, where it belongs. That might have been the most important thing I learned from my first sweater.

In the twenty years since then, I've made sweaters, vests, hats, bedspreads, lap blankets, shawls, scarves, socks, and mittens. Like most people who knit, I have bags of yarn stashed in my closet for future projects. The bags are a record of the cities where I've wandered into yarn stores: Madison, Portland, Cambridge, New Orleans, Evanston, Washington, D.C. Like hair salons, yarn stores have slightly witty names: Woolgathering, Woolworks, Woolcotts, the Knitting Tree, the Quarter Stitch (New Orleans), Fiber Space. Inside each store, the walls are lined with plastic crates bursting with color. My friend Yenkuei took up knitting because she fell in love with the fuchsia sleeveless sweater in the window of Woolcotts in Harvard Square, floating, she thought, and beckoning to her. Another friend, who doesn't knit, comes along just to touch. She goes from shelf to shelf fingering the rayon chenilles, angoras, alpacas, and silk-cotton blends while I'm trying to figure out how much yarn I need. When I was five, in kindergarten, I was horrified to see other kids stick their fingers in the library paste, scoop up the pale glop, and put it in their mouths, but I tried to eat the raspberry-colored crayon on my teacher's desk because it looked so delicious. Knitting is about that same hunger for color. I never again picked up yellow yarn.

2

Knitting is a young craft. The oldest surviving examples — blue and white cotton socks and fabric fragments discovered in an Egyptian tomb — are dated around A.D. 1200. Knitting probably originated in Egypt or another Arabic country around that time and reached Europe through Spain. Two knitted cushions, found in the tomb of a thirteenth-century Castilian prince and princess, are the oldest known European artifacts of knitting. Once it reached Europe, the craft spread quickly. By the fourteenth century, Italian and German artists were painting the Virgin Mary knitting in a domestic setting.

Most of the early knitting in Europe was for socks and stockings. Elizabeth I preferred the knitted silk stockings from France to the woven-and-sewn foot coverings made in England. Mary, Queen of Scots, wore two pairs of French stockings — one plain white and the other patterned with gold stitches — on the day of her execution; the stockings were held up with green garters. By the end of the sixteenth century, cheap metal needles became widely available, enabling the rural families throughout England to knit socks and stockings during the winter months to supplement their income.

In the cities, guilds controlled the licensing of knitting workshops. An apprentice would spend three years working under one master and three more traveling as a "journeyman," to learn new techniques from various masters, before he could submit samples of his work for the guild's approval. In Vienna at the beginning of the seventeenth century, the samples had to include a six-colored tablecloth, a beret, a pair of silk stockings, and a pair of gloves.

Sweaters are not on this list because in Vienna at that time, as in most of Europe, upper-body garments such as shirts, tunics, vests, and jackets were cut and sewn from woven fabrics only. The first knitted upper-body garments were made in the fifteenth century, in the Channel Islands of Guernsey and Jersey, where fishermen and sailors needed thick tunics made of wool to repel water and protect against the cold. Although these garments spread slowly across the rest of Europe among laborers, they did not become popular as "sweaters" until the 1890s when American athletes wore heavy, dark blue pullovers before and after contests to ward off the chills.

Knitting is an activity that can be performed anywhere, while weaving requires a loom, a complicated piece of equipment that takes up space and is difficult to move. Still, the earliest proof of woven cloth predates knitting by more than eight thousand years. Clay balls found in Iraq and dated around 7000 B.C. have clear impressions of woven textiles on them. Numerous images of weavers are preserved on papyruses and tomb paintings from ancient Egypt. In the *Odyssey*, Penelope weaves and unweaves a funeral cloth to ward off the suitors; in Greek mythology, Aracne is turned into a spider when she challenges Athena to a weaving contest and loses. The knitting Madonnas of the fourteenth century represent some of the earliest depictions of women knitting, and no Greek hero's wife or foolish mortal ever won praise or punishment for this simple activity.

3

As with people, so with garments: the strengths and the weaknesses are often one and the same. A knitted garment, whose loose construction traps air next to the body, is warmer but more fragile than a woven one, and the stretching property of yarn makes knitting a less precise but more forgiving craft than sewing. On a knitted fabric, one broken loop can release all the loops, causing the fabric to "run." This same quality allows a knitter to unravel the yarn on purpose, undo a few inches of work, and correct a mistake she has discovered. Even after the garment is finished, a knitter can snip one of the stitches, carefully unravel one round of knitting, put the loops back on a needle, and redo the bottom of the sweater or the sleeve to make it smaller, larger, or a different shape. Sewing doesn't allow the same flexibility.

My first home ec sewing project was no better than the mittens: an Oxford shirt with cuffs, buttonholes, darts along the bust line, and square collars; a pleated skirt with a zipper closure. I'm sure there are much easier things to sew. Still, in sewing, you can't get away from cutting, assembling, and fitting. If you cut the pieces wrong, you'll have to buy more cloth and lay out the pattern again. If the finished shirt is half an inch too small, it's not going to stretch the way a sweater will.

Even the words "thread" (the stringlike material we sew with) and "yarn" (the stringlike material we knit with) convey different degrees of flexibility. Thread holds together and restricts, while yarn stretches and gives. Thread is the overall theme that gives meaning to our words and thoughts — to lose the thread is to be incoherent or inattentive. A yarn is a long, pointless, but usually amusing story whose facts have been exaggerated. It is infinitely more relaxing to listen to a yarn than to a lecture whose thread we must follow.

In my first ten years of knitting, I took full advantage of the forgiving quality of yarn and made hats and scarves from patterns that had only five- to ten-sentence directions. For sweaters, I made three tubes (one big tube for the body, two smaller tubes for the sleeves) and then knitted them together at the yoke and shoulders so I didn't have to sew the pieces together at the end. If, halfway through the body or the sleeve, I noticed the piece getting wider faster than I'd expected, I simply stopped increasing stitches; if the piece looked too small, I increased more. It was just as Sabina had told me: I could make things up as I went along.

My favorite project was a hat from a pattern I found in a yarn store on a visit to Portland, Oregon. I bought the thick mohair yarn and extra needles so I could start knitting the first one in my hotel room. The hat, which I finished on the flight home the next day, looked more like a lampshade; the brim came down to my shoulders. At home, I threw this enormous hat in the washer, set it on hot wash and cold rinse, and ran the cycle twice. Just as the pattern promised, the hat came out shrunk and "felted": the stitches had contracted till they were invisible, leaving a dense, fuzzy nap. I reshaped the hat on a mixing bowl about the size of my head, and by the time it dried, it looked like a professionally made bowler.

The washing-machine hat became a staple of my gift-giving. A few years later, I visited an antiques mall with a couple who had fallen in love with an oak dresser they thought was too expensive. Every weekend for two months, they brought a different friend to look at the dresser, to ooh and aah over it, and help them work up the nerve to spend the money. The antiques mall was a huge place out in the country, and we had to walk what felt like three city blocks crammed with furniture and knickknacks. When we finally got to the right section, I failed my friends completely by not notic-ing the dresser because to the right of it, on a small table, was a wooden hat form. To an untrained eye, the hat form looks like a wooden head, but I knew what it was. Tired of reshaping hats over a bowl, I had been trying to order one (except all the modern hat forms were made of Styrofoam and I didn't think I could stand the squeaky noise they would make). I grabbed the wooden head and walked around with it tightly clutched under my arm while my friends showed me all the other oak dressers, every one of them in-ferior to the one they wanted. At the counter, I paid $12 for my find.

This fall, I brought the wooden head with me to Wisconsin be-cause I still make those hats for gifts. But in the past five years, I've graduated to more complicated patterns. I had gotten tired of the rugged look of the make-it-as-you-go kind of sweater, but more than that, my reasons for knitting have changed. In my twenties and thirties, I wanted everything I did to express what I considered my essential nature: casual, relaxed, and intuitively creative, rather than formal, precise, and meticulous. That's why I chose knitting over sewing, running and cycling over tennis or golf. Now, in my mid-forties, I look instead for balance. If following step-by-step in-structions doesn't come naturally to me, that is all the more reason for me to try it. I would rather knit from a complicated pattern and make a few mistakes than execute an easier one flawlessly.

The folklore among knitters is that everything handmade should have at least one mistake so an evil spirit will not become trapped in the maze of perfect stitches. A missed increase or decrease, a crooked seam, a place where the tension is uneven — the mistake is a crack left open to let in the light. The evil spirit I want to usher out of my knitting and my life is at once a spirit of laziness and of overachieving. It's that little voice in my head that says, I won't even try this because it doesn't come naturally to me and I won't be very good at it.

4

A friend of mine fell in love with a young man at college because he was knitting a sweater between classes the first time she saw him. She concluded that he must be an extraordinarily sensitive and creative man, though eventually she found out he was neither. This man, whom I never met, is the only contemporary male knitter I know of, besides Kaffe Fasset, the British sweater designer.

Knitting wasn't always a feminine craft. The knitting masters and apprentices of the medieval guilds were all men, since women were not admitted into guilds. Before the Industrial Revolution, both men and women, of all ages, knitted socks in the countryside. The fishermen and the sailors from the English Channel Islands made their own sweaters during their long sea voyages. In the late nineteenth century, the Japanese samurai whose clans were faltering tried to supplement their income by knitting *tabi*, split-toed Japanese socks (essentially, mittens for feet). Even so, knitting — like sewing, spinning, weaving, and embroidery — has been historically associated with women's household skills and marriageability. One of the most remarkable examples involves the mitten.

In Latvia, until the early twentieth century, every girl learned to knit by the age of six so she could get an early start on her dowry chest. A full dowry chest would decrease the number of cattle her family would have to pay the groom's family when it came time for her to marry. The main contents of the dowry chest were mittens with multicolored, geometrical designs. On the day of the wedding, these mittens were distributed to all the participants from the carriage driver to the minister, as well as to the numerous relatives, in-laws, and neighbors. At the feast after the ceremony, the bride and the groom ate with mittened hands to invite good luck. At the end of the day, the bride walked around the inside and outside of her new home, laying mittens (to be collected later by her mother-in-law) on all the important locations: the hearth, the doors, the windows, the cow barn, the sheep shed, the beehives, and the garden. To properly complete these marriage rites, a bride needed one to two hundred pairs of mittens. The mittens were treasured as heirlooms, and the complicated knitting patterns were meant to show off a young woman's patience — her ability to perform meticulous and repetitive work — as well as her skill.

When my Japanese home ec teacher decided to teach us how to knit mittens, the assignment was, in a sense, grimly appropriate, since the not-so-hidden purpose of home ec was also to give us skills that showed off our patience and meticulousness. After the semester of knitting and sewing, we were required to take several semesters of cooking, in which we made elaborate casseroles and soufflés and desserts, food to impress people, food for parties, not the kind of food I would cook for myself when I moved out to live on my own.

In most schools in the United States and Japan now, home ec is an elective, open to both girls and boys. Young women in Latvia no longer make two hundred pairs of mittens in order to get married. Of course I'm happy for these changes, though a part of me worries whether anyone will preserve these centuries-old crafts. I have not met one man who has ever knitted, sewn, or embroidered clothes for his partner or children — or a woman knitter, quilter, garment maker, or embroiderer who has not made something for the men and the children among her family and friends. I don't know what to do with the weight of history and the way it affects our daily lives.

At least on a purely personal level, I've reconciled myself to the mitten. Last year in Cambridge, I tackled the ultimate mitten. The pattern, marked for "experienced knitters," called them "flip-flop mittens" because the top half could be made to flip back like a hinged lid, exposing the fingers in a fingerless glove. I thought of them as cat mittens: at the necessary moment, the sheath pulled back and out came the claws. It was a slow and complicated project. To achieve the gauge for the pattern, I had to use number zero needles, which were thinner than satay sticks. The fuzzy mohair yarn made the stitches difficult to see, and each finger had to be knitted separately. It took me two months to make myself a pair. Then I started another pair for my friend Junko, whose hands are smaller than the smallest measurement in the directions. I was proud of having managed to follow the directions and, at the same time, make a few adjustments on my own, until I finished the second mitten and realized that — only on that hand — I had made the top flip forward instead of back. After thirty years, I was back where I'd started: I had been blown back into the mitten purgatory of mismatched hands.

The next morning, I sat down and thought of the various tricks I'd learned. I looked at knitting books, went over the notes I'd made in the margins of some patterns. Finally I figured out how to unravel just a few rows of stitches and detach the flip at the front, make a new edging for it, and graft the stitches to the back of the hand so that the flip now faced the right way. The procedure left a small scar, hardly noticeable in the fuzzy mohair. When I gave the mittens to Junko, I showed her my mistake. Across the back of her left hand stretched a faint broken line, like a rural road on a map of the desert, a path across unknown terrain.

SUSAN ORLEAN

Lifelike

FROM THE NEW YORKER

As soon as the 2003 World Taxidermy Championships opened, the heads came rolling in the door. There were foxes and moose and freeze-dried wild turkeys; mallards and buffalo and chipmunks and wolves; weasels and buffleheads and bobcats and jackdaws; big fish and little fish and razor-backed boar. The deer came in herds, in carloads, and on pallets: dozens and dozens of whitetail and roe; half deer and whole deer and deer with deformities, sneezing and glowering and nuzzling and yawning; does chewing apples and bucks nibbling leaves. There were millions of eyes, boxes and bowls of them; some as small as a lentil and some as big as a poached egg. There were animal mannequins, blank-faced and brooding, earless and eyeless and utterly bald: ghostly gray duikers and spectral pine martens and black-bellied tree ducks from some other world. An entire exhibit hall was filled with equipment, all the gear required to bring something dead back to life: replacement noses for grizzlies, false teeth for beavers, fish-fin cream, casting clay, upholstery nails.

The championships were held in April at the Springfield, Illinois, Crowne Plaza hotel, the sort of nicely appointed place that seems more suited to regional sales conferences and rehearsal dinners than to having wolves in the corridors and people crossing the lobby shouting, "Heads up! Buffalo coming through!" A thousand taxidermists converged on Springfield to have their best pieces judged and to attend such seminars as "Mounting Flying Waterfowl," "Whitetail Deer — From a Master!," and "Using a Fleshing Machine." In the Crowne Plaza lobby, across from the concierge desk, a grooming area had been set up. The taxidermists were bent over their animals, holding flashlights to check problem areas like tear ducts and nostrils, and wielding toothbrushes to tidy flyaway fur. People milled around, greeting fellow taxidermists they hadn't seen since the last world championships, held in Springfield two years ago, and talking shop:

"Acetone rubbed on a squirrel tail will fluff it right back up."

"My feeling is that it's quite tough to do a good tongue."

"The toes on a real competitive piece are very important. I think Bondo works nicely, and so does Super Glue."

"I knew a fellow with cattle, and I told him, 'If you ever have one stillborn, I'd really like to have it.' I thought it would make a really nice mount."

That there is a taxidermy championship at all is something of an astonishment, not only to the people in the world who have no use for a Dan-D-Noser and Soft Touch Duck Degreaser but also to taxidermists themselves. For a long time, taxidermists kept their own counsel. Taxidermy, the three-dimensional representation of animals for permanent display, has been around since the eighteenth century, but it was first brought into popular regard by the Victorians, who thrilled to all tokens of exotic travel and especially to any domesticated representations of wilderness — the glassed-in miniature rain forest on the tea table, the mounted antelope by the front door. The original taxidermists were upholsterers who tanned the hides of hunting trophies and then plumped them up with rags and cotton, so that they reassumed their original shape and size; those early poses were stiff and simple, and the expressions fairly expressionless. The practice grew popular in this country, too: by 1882, there was a Society of American Taxidermists, which held annual meetings and published scholarly reports, especially on the matter of preparing animals for museum display. As long as taxidermy served to preserve wild animals and make them available for study, it was viewed as an honorable trade, but most people were still discomfited by it. How could you not be? It was the business of dealing with dead things, coupled with the questionable enterprise of making dead things look like live things. In spite of its scientific value, it was usually regarded as almost a black art, a wholly owned subsidiary of witchcraft and voodoo. By the early part of the twentieth century, taxidermists such as Carl E.

Akeley, William T. Horneday, and Leon Pray had refined techniques and begun emphasizing artistry. But the more the techniques of taxidermy improved, the more it discomfited: instead of the lumpy moose head that was so artless that it looked fake, there were mounts of pouncing bobcats so immaculately and exactly preserved they made you flinch.

For the next several decades, taxidermy existed in the margins — a few practitioners here and there, often self-taught, and usually known only by word of mouth. Then, in the late 1960s, a sort of transformation began: the business started to seem cleaner and less creepy — or maybe, in that messy, morbid time, popular culture started to again appreciate the messy, morbid business of mounting animals for display. An ironic reinterpretation of cluttered, bourgeois Victoriana and its strained juxtapositions of the natural and the man-made was in full revival — what hippie outpost didn't have a stuffed owl or a moose head draped with a silk shawl? — so, once again, taxidermy found a place in the public eye. Supply houses concocted new solvents and better tanning compounds, came out with lightweight mannequins, produced modern formulations of resins and clays. Taxidermy schools opened; previously, any aspiring taxidermist could only hope to learn the trade by apprenticing or by taking one of a few correspondence courses available. In 1971, the National Taxidermy Association was formed (the old society had moldered long before). In 1974, a trade magazine called *Taxidermy Review* began sponsoring national competitions. For the first time, most taxidermists had a chance to meet one another and share advice on how to glue tongues into jaw sets or accurately measure the carcass of a squirrel.

The competitions were also the first time that taxidermists could compare their skills and see who in the business could sculpt the best moose septum or could most perfectly capture the look on a prowling coyote's face. Taxidermic skill is a function of how deft you are at skinning an animal and then stretching its hide over a mannequin and sewing it into place. Top-of-the-line taxidermists sculpt their own mannequins; otherwise they will buy a ready-made polyurethane-foam form and tailor the skin to fit. Body parts that can't be preserved (ears, eyes, noses, lips, tongues) can be either store-bought or handmade. How good the mount looks — that is, how alive it looks — is a function of how assiduously the taxidermist has studied reference material (photographs, drawings, and actual live animals) so that he or she knows the particular creature literally and figuratively inside out.

To be good at taxidermy, you have to be good at sewing, sculpting, painting, and hairdressing, and mostly you have to be a little bit of a zoology nerd. You have to love animals — love looking at them, taking photographs of them, hunting them, measuring them, casting them in plaster of Paris when they're dead so that you have a reference when you're, say, attaching ears or lips and want to get the angle and shape exactly right. Some taxidermists raise the animals they most often mount, so they can just step out in the back yard when they're trying to remember exactly how a deer looks when it's licking its nose, especially because modern taxidermy emphasizes mounts with interesting expressions, rather than the stunned-looking creations of the past. Taxidermists seem to make little distinction between loving animals that are alive and loving ones that are not. "I love deer," one of the champions in the Whitetail division said to me. "They're my babies."

Taxidermy is now estimated to be a $570-million annual business, made up of small operators around the country who mount animals for museums, for decorators, and mostly for the thirteen million or so Americans who are recreational hunters and on occasion want to preserve and display something they killed and who are willing to shell out anywhere from $200 to mount a pheasant to several thousand for a kudu or a grizzly bear. There are state and regional taxidermy competitions throughout the year and the world championships, which are held every other year; two trade magazines; a score of taxidermy schools; and three thousand visits to Taxidermy.net every day, where taxidermists can trade information and goods with as little self-consciousness as you would find on a knitting Web site:

"I am in need of several pair of frozen goat feet!"

"Hi! I have up to 300 sets of goat feet and up to 1000 set of sheep feet per month. Drop me an email at frozencritters.com . . . or give me a call and we can discuss your needs."

"I have a very nice small raccoon that is frozen whole. I forgot he was in the freezer. Without taking exact measurements I would guess he is about twelve inches or so — very cute little one. Will make a very nice mount."

"Can I rinse a boar hide good and freeze it?"

"Bob, if it's salted, don't worry about it!"

"Can someone please tell me the proper way to preserve turkey legs and spurs? Thanks!"

"Brian, I inject the feet with Preservz-It . . . Enjoy!"

The word in the grooming area was that the piece to beat was Chris Krueger's happy-looking otters swimming in a perpetual circle around a leopard frog. A posting on Taxidermy.net earlier in the week declared, "EVERYTHING about this mount KICKS BUTT!!" Kicking butt, in this era of taxidermy, requires having a mount that is not just lifelike but also artistic. It used to be enough to do what taxidermists call "fish on a stick" displays; now a serious competitor worries about things like flow and negative space and originality. One of this year's contenders, for instance, Ken Walker's giant panda, had artistry and accuracy going for it, along with the element of surprise. The thing looked 100 percent pure panda, but you can't go out and shoot a panda, and you aren't likely to get hold of a panda that has met a natural end, so everyone was dying to know how he had done it. The day the show opened, Walker was in the grooming area, gluing bamboo into place behind the animal's back paws, and a crowd had gathered around him. Walker works as a staff taxidermist for the Smithsonian. He is a breezy, shaggy-haired guy whose hands are always busy. One day, I saw him holding a piece of clay while waiting for a seminar to begin, and within thirty seconds or so, without actually paying much attention to it, he had molded the clay into a little minklike creature.

"The panda was actually pretty easy," he was saying. "I just took two black bears and bleached one of them — I think I used Clairol Basic. Then I sewed the two skins together into a panda pattern." He took out a toothbrush and fluffed the fur on the panda's face. "At the world championship two years ago, a guy came in with an extinct Labrador duck. I was in awe. I thought, What could beat that — an extinct duck? And I came up with this idea." He said he thought that the panda would get points for creativity alone. "You can score a ninety-eight with a squirrel, but it's still a squirrel," he said. "So that means I'm going with a panda."

"What did you do for toenails, Ken?" someone asked.

"I left the black bear's toenails in," he said. "They looked pretty good."

Another passerby stopped to admire the panda. He was carrying a grooming kit, which appeared to contain Elmer's glue, brown and black paint, a small tool set, and a bottle of Suave mousse. "I killed a blond bear once," he said to Ken. "A two-hundred-pound sow. Whew, she made a beautiful mount."

"I'll bet," Ken said. He stepped back to admire the panda. "I like doing re-creations of these endangered animals and extinct animals, since that's the only way anyone's going to have one. Two years ago, I did a saber-toothed cat. I got an old lioness from a zoo and bleached her."

The panda was entered in the Re-Creation (Mammal) division, one of the dozens of divisions and subdivisions and sub-subcategories, ranging from the super-specific (Whitetail Deer Long Hair, Open Mouth division) to the sweepingly colossal (Best in World), that would share in $25,000 worth of prizes. (There is even a sub-sub-subspecialty known as "fish carving," which uses no natural fish parts at all; it is resin and wood sculpted into a fish form and then painted.) Nearly all the competitors are professionals, and they publicize their awards wherever possible. For instance, instead of ordering just any Boar Eye-Setting Reference Head out of a taxidermy catalogue, you can order the Noonkester's #NRB-ERH head sculpted by Bones Johnson, which was, as the catalogue notes, the 2000 National Taxidermy Association Champion Gamehead.

The taxidermists take the competition very seriously. During the time I was in Springfield, I heard conversations analyzing such arcane subjects as exactly how much a javelina's snout wrinkles when it snarls and which molars deer use to chew acorns as opposed to which ones they use to chew leaves. This is important because the ultimate goal of a taxidermist is to make the animal look as if it had never died, as if it were still in the middle of doing ordinary animal things like plucking berries off a bush or taking a nap. When I walked around with the judges one morning, I heard discussions that were practically Talmudic, about whether the eyelids on a bison mount were overdetailed, and whether the nostrils on a springbok were too wide, and whether the placement of whiskers on an otter appeared too deliberate. "You do get compulsive," a taxidermist in the exhibit hall explained to me one afternoon. At the time, he was running a feather duster over his entry — a bobcat hanging off an icicle-covered rock — in the last moments before the judging would begin. "When you're working on a piece, you forget to eat, you forget to drink, you even forget to sleep. You get up in the middle of the night and go into the shop so you can keep working. You get completely caught up in it. You want it to be perfect. You're trying to make something come back to life."

I said that his bobcat was beautiful, and that even the icicles on the piece looked completely real. "I made them myself," he said. "I used clear acrylic toilet-plunger handles. The good Lord sent the idea to me while I was in a hardware store. I just took the handles and put them in the oven at four hundred degrees." He tapped the icicles and then added, "My wife was pretty worried, but I did it on a nonstick cookie sheet."

So who wants to be a taxidermist? "I was a meat cutter for fifteen years," a taxidermist from Kentucky said to me. "That whole time, no one ever said to me, 'Boy, that was a wonderful steak you cut me.' Now I get told all the time what a great job I've done." Steve Faechner, who is the president and chairman of the Academy of Realistic Taxidermy, in Havre, Montana, started mounting animals in 1989, after years spent working on the railroad. "I had gotten hurt, and was looking for something to do," he said. "I was with a friend who did taxidermy and I thought to myself, I have got to get a life. And this was it." Larry Blomquist, who is the owner of the World Taxidermy Championships and of Breakthrough, the trade magazine that sponsors the competition, was a schoolteacher for three years before setting up his business. There are a number of women taxidermists (one was teaching this year's seminar on Problem Areas in Mammal Taxidermy), and there are budding junior taxidermists, who had their own competition division, for kids fourteen and younger, at the show.

The night the show opened, I went to dinner with three taxidermists who had driven in from Kentucky, Michigan, and Maryland. They were all married, and all had wives who complained when they found one too many antelope carcasses in the family freezer, and all worked full time mounting animals — mostly deer, for local hunters, but occasional safari work, for people who had shot something in Africa. When I mentioned that I had no idea that a person could make a living as a taxidermist, they burst out laughing, and the guy from Kentucky pointed out that he lived in a little town and there were two other full-time taxidermists in business right down the road.

"What's the big buzz this year?" the man from Michigan asked.

"I don't know. Probably something new with eyes," the guy from Maryland answered. "That's where you see the big advances. Remember at the last championship, those Russian eyes?" These were glass animal eyes that had a reflective paint embedded in them, so that if you shone a light they would shine back at you, sort of like the way real animals' eyes do. The men discussed those for a while, then talked about the new fish eyes being introduced this year, which have photographic transfers of actual fish eyes printed on plastic lenses. We happened to be in a restaurant with a sports theme, and there were about a hundred televisions on around the room, broadcasting dozens of different athletic events, but the men never glanced at them, and never stopped talking about their trade. We had all ordered barbecued ribs. When dinner was over, all three of them were fiddling around with the bones before the waitress came to clear our plates.

"Look at these," the man from Kentucky said, holding up a rib. "You could take these home and use them to make a skeleton."

In the seminars, the atmosphere was as sober and exacting as a tax-law colloquium. "Whiskers," one of the instructors said to the group, giving them a stern look. "I pull them out. I label them. There are left whiskers and there are right whiskers. If you want to get those top awards, you're going to have to think about whiskers." Everyone took notes. In the next room: "Folks, remember, your carcass is your key. The best thing you can do is to keep your carcass in the freezer. Freeze the head, cast it in plaster. It's going to really help if your head is perfect." During the breaks, the group made jokes about a T-shirt that had been seen at one of the regional competitions. The shirt said "PETA" in big letters, but when you got up close you saw that PETA didn't spell out People for the Ethical Treatment of Animals, the bane of all hunters and, by extension, all taxidermists; it spelled out People Eating Tasty Animals. Chuckles all around, then back to the solemn business of Mounting Flying Waterfowl: "People, follow what the bird is telling you. Study it, do your homework. When you've got it ready, fluff the head, shake it, and then get your eyes. There are a lot of good eyes out there on the market today. Do your legwork, and you can have a beautiful mount."

It was brisk and misty outside — the antler venders in the parking lot looked chilled and miserable — and the modest charms of Springfield, with its mall and the Oliver P. Parks Telephone Museum and Abraham Lincoln's tomb, couldn't compete with the strange and wondrous sights inside the hotel. The mere experience of waiting for the elevator — knowing that the doors would peel back to reveal maybe a man and a moose, or a bush pig, or a cougar — was much more exciting than the usual elevator wait in the usual Crowne Plaza hotel. The trade show was a sort of mad tea party of body parts and taxidermy supplies, things for pulling flesh off a carcass, for rinsing blood out of fur — a surreal carnality, but all conveyed with the usual trade-show earnestness and hucksterism, with no irony and no acknowledgment that having buckets of bear noses for sale was anything out of the ordinary. "Come take a look at our beautiful synthetic fur! We're the hair club for lions! If you happen to shoot a lion who is out of season or bald, we can provide you with a gorgeous replacement mane!" "Too many squirrels? Are they driving you nuts? Let us mount them for you!" "Divide and Conquer animal forms — an amazing advance in small-mammal mannequins, patent pending!"

The big winner at the show turned out to be a tiny thing — a mount of two tree sparrows, submitted by a strapping German named Uwe Bauch, who had grown up in the former East Germany dreaming of competing in an American taxidermy show. The piece was precise and lovely, almost haunting, since the more you looked at it the more certain you were that the birds would just stop building their nest, spread their wings, and fly away. Early one morning, before I left Springfield, I took a last walk around the competition hall. It was quiet and uncanny, with hundreds of mounts arranged on long tables throughout the room; the deer heads clustered together, each in a slightly different pose and angle, looked like a kind of animal Roman forum caught in mid-debate. A few of the mounts were a little gory — a deer with a mailbox impaled on an antler, another festooned with barbed wire, and one with an arrow stuck in its brisket — and one display, a coyote whose torso was split open to reveal a miniature scene of the destruction of the World Trade Center, complete with little firemen and rubble piles, was surpassingly weird. Otherwise, the room was biblically tranquil, the lion at last lying down with the Corsican lamb, the family of jackdaws in everlasting, unrequited pursuit of a big green beetle, and the stillborn Bengal tiger cub magically revived, its face in an eternal snarl, alive-looking although it had never lived.

ALEX ROSS

Rock 101

FROM THE NEW YORKER

DUKE ELLINGTON ONCE had to field a barrage of questions from an Icelandic music student who was determined to penetrate to the heart of the genius of jazz. At one point, Ellington was asked whether he ever felt an affinity for the music of Bach, and, before answering, he made a show of unwrapping a pork chop that he had stowed in his pocket. "Bach and myself," he said, taking a bite from the chop, "both write with individual performers in mind." Richard O. Boyer captured the moment in a Profile entitled "The Hot Bach," which appeared in *The New Yorker* in 1944. You can sense in that exquisitely timed pork-chop maneuver Ellington's bemused response to the European notions of genius that were constantly being foisted on him. He said on another occasion, "To attempt to elevate the status of the jazz musician by forcing the level of his best work into comparisons with classical music is to deny him his rightful share of originality." Jazz was a new language, and the critic would have to respond to it with a new poetry of praise.

Now Ellington is himself a classic, the subject of painstaking analytical studies. He occupies a Bachian position in an emergent popular pantheon, which is certain to look different from the marble-faced, bewigged classical pantheons that preceded it. The very idea of a canon of geniuses may be falling by the wayside; it makes more sense to talk about the flickering brilliance of a group, a place, or a people. In the future, it seems, everyone will be a genius for fifteen minutes. The past decade has seen the rise of pop-music studies, which is dedicated to the idea that Ellington, Hank Williams, and the Velvet Underground were created equal and deserve the same sort of scholarly scrutiny that used to be bestowed only on Bach and sons. Pop-music courses draw crowds of students on college campuses, and academic presses are putting out such portentous titles as *Instruments of Desire: The Electric Guitar and the Shaping of Musical Experience*, *Rock Over the Edge: Transformations in Popular Music Culture*, and *Running with the Devil: Power, Gender, and Madness in Heavy Metal Music*.

Pop-music professors, especially those who specialize in rock, are caught in an obvious paradox, which their students probably point out to them on the first day of class. Namely, it's not very rock-and-roll to intellectualize rock-and-roll. When Pink Floyd sang, "We don't need no education," they could not have foreseen the advent of research projects with titles like "Another Book in the Wall?: A Cultural History of Pink Floyd's Stage Performance and the Rise of Audiovisual *Gesamtkunstwerk*, 1965–1994." (That comes from Finland.) Ever since Ellington, Armstrong, and Jelly Roll Morton struck up the soundtrack to the bawdy, boozy twenties, popular music has been the high-speed vehicle for youth rebellion, sexual liberation, and chemical experimentation, none of which yield willingly to the academic mind. The pop scholar is forever doomed to sounding like the square kid at the cool kids' party, killing their buzz with sentences like this: "From the start, hip-hop's samples ran the gamut of genres, defying anyone who would delimit hip-hop's palette."

Then again, maybe it's not a problem that so much pop-music scholarship sounds conspicuously uncool. For decades, jazz rhapsodists and rock poets were so intent on projecting attitude that they never got around to saying much about the music itself. The pioneering rock critics of the sixties, such as Lester Bangs and Greil Marcus, wanted to mimic the music in their prose, and they had enough style to pull it off. Bangs, whose writings have been collected in a new anthology from Anchor Books, lived the life of a rock star, or at least died the death of one. But his writings are a better guide to the mentality of smart people who went to rock shows in the sixties and seventies than they are a reliable record of music and musicians. Discussing the Rolling Stones in 1974, Bangs wrote, "If you think I'm going to review the new 'It's Only Rock 'n' Roll' album right now, you are crazy. But I am going to swim in it." Between prose poetry and academic cant there has to be a middle ground, and pop-music studies is searching it out.

Interrogating Bruce's Butt

One weekend last spring, a few hundred scholars, journalists, musicians, and onlookers arrived in downtown Seattle for Pop Conference 2003, entitled "Skip a Beat: Rewriting the Story of Popular Music." The Pop Conference was created two years ago by Eric Weisbard, a former *Village Voice* rock critic, and Daniel Cavicchi, an assistant professor of American Studies at the Rhode Island School of Design. The decision to bring scholars and journalists together was unusual. It gave the critics an opportunity to drop arcane allusions instead of having to pretend to sound like teenagers, while the academics could loosen up a little. Weisbard and Cavicchi hope that the two worlds can cross-pollinate each other, breeding a sensibility that is scholarly but not stuffy, stylish but not frivolous.

The conference took place within the wavy-gravy walls of the Experience Music Project, a Frank Gehry culture palace, housing artifacts and bric-a-brac from a century of pop. The dress code was diverse to the point of incoherence: some of the older academics showed up in business attire, while younger ones wore T-shirts and jeans. (The divergence of styles became especially dissonant when sixties-generation scholars espoused radical political agendas while Gen X doctoral students sounded a neoformalist, let's-just-talk-about-the-music tone.) For three days, participants hawked their wares in a tight twenty-minute format, taking persnickety questions afterward. At any given time, there were three different panels running in the various rooms of the EMP, meaning that the curious onlooker had to choose among equally tempting offerings. In order to attend the Bob Dylan panel — entitled "The Dylan" — you had to skip panels on art music (one paper was "Changing the System: Brian Eno, Sonic Youth, and the Combination of Rock and Experimental Music") and contemporary R&B ("Supa Dupa Fly: Styles of Subversion in Black Women's Hip-Hop").

Some of the presentations, a few too many for comfort, lapsed into the familiar contortions of modern pedagogy. Likewise, in the many pop-music books now in circulation, post-structuralist, post-Marxist, post-colonialist, and post-grammatical buzzwords crop up on page after page. There is a whole lot of problematizing, interrogating, and appropriating goin' on. Walter Benjamin's name is dropped at least as often as the Notorious B.I.G.'s. The French

sociologist Pierre Bourdieu gets more props than Dr. Dre. At the
Pop Conference, I made it a rule to move to a different room the
minute I heard someone use the word "interrogate" in a non-
detective context or cite any of the theorists of the Frankfurt
school. Thus I ducked out of a talk on Grace Jones's *Slave to the
Rhythm* album when I heard a sentence that began with the phrase
"Invoking Walter Benjamin." And I bailed on a lecture entitled
"Bruce's Butt" — Bruce Springsteen's butt, as seen on the cover of
Born in the U.S.A. — when the speaker began to interrogate the image of the butt, which, under sharp questioning, wouldn't give anything away.

Scholars of this type always want to see pop music as the emana-
tion of an entity called popular culture, rather than as music that
happens to have become popular. As a result, songs and bands become fungible commodities in the intellectual marketplace. In the
anthology *Popular Music Studies,* the hip-hop scholar Ian Maxwell
asks the significant question "How can our analyses avoid reduc-
ing the objects of those analyses to desiccated cadavers on a slab?"
His solution — a "more rigorous understanding of what an ethno-
graphically informed approach might offer the study of popular
music, nuancing that approach through Bourdieu's reflexive criti-
cality" — gets us only so far.

Roger Beebe, one of the editors of the *Rock Over the Edge* anthology, even looks at music as purely a media phenomenon, inseparable from image and marketing. Analyzing Kurt Cobain's appearances on television, he says that Cobain mattered to his fans mainly
as a disembodied entity, not as an individual with a voice, and that
he exemplified something called "the postmodern *dispositif.*" Such
McLuhanesque musings have been rendered obsolete as MTV has
more or less stopped showing videos in favor of frat-house docu-
mentaries. Meanwhile, the Internet has become the main avenue
for the spread of music. The mania for downloading music may be
wreaking havoc with artists' careers, but it is interesting to see how
the ear trumps the eye when the computer takes over. Music is being consumed with no images attached — no videos, no TV appearances, not even album jackets. In the nineteenth century, the
Viennese critic Eduard Hanslick dreamed of a world "purely musical," beyond politics and personality. Such a world now exists in
the form of the MP3.

The Mathematics of "Superbad"

Despite minor infestations of Benjaminites, there was no shortage of up-close musical discussion at the Pop Conference. I often had the happy experience of being held hostage by an informed fanatic who convinced me that whatever he or she was discussing was the most important music on earth. The presenters tended to avoid obvious mainstream figures — there was nothing on Elvis, the Beatles, or the Rolling Stones — focusing, instead, on the margins and subtexts of pop history. There were papers on the lo-fi ideology of nineties indie rock, the Filipino DJ scene in San Francisco, and the trailblazing transsexual punk of Wayne/Jayne County, among a hundred others. You got a sense of music as a world of jostling subcultures, each with its resident inventors and masters, its purists and populists. The conference conjured up the everlasting complexity of how songs are made, heard, and remembered.

Rock-and-roll has generated more self-serving myths than any other genre, and scholars have been busy dismantling them. Too often, pop history has been written as a march forward to a handful of utopian moments in the late fifties and the sixties: Chuck Berry recording "Maybellene," Elvis appearing on *Ed Sullivan,* the Beatles appearing on *Ed Sullivan,* and Bob Dylan plugging in his guitar at the Newport Folk Festival. These events have acquired an exaggerated importance, mostly because they had sentimental value for the baby-boom generation that dominated early pop-music writing. Younger writers are especially impatient with the rock narrative — the "rockist paradigm," they call it — and delight in cataloguing its contradictions and omissions. Consider Dylan's famous rebellion against the folkies. At the Pop Conference, the historian Michael J. Kramer presented a paper in which he defended the folk music movement from the stereotype that prevails in Dylan studies — the image of humorless fanatics rejecting the visionary in their midst. Kramer pointed out that the singer took a great deal of his mocking, critical voice — "humorous impurity," he called it — from the very movement that he was supposed to have renounced. In a similar vein, Franklin Bruno, a doctoral student in philosophy who writes quirky, literate pop songs, noted that Dylan in his electric period relied heavily on the tricks of Tin Pan Alley songwriting, precisely the sort of mom-and-dad music that the singer was supposed to have left behind. *Blonde on Blonde,* Bruno said, was "a head-first dive into pop-song formalism." Everybody must get stoned, but not before the bridge and the modulation.

Again and again, popular music has been described as a story of youth rebellion, in which each generation breaks free of the oppressive mediocrity of its predecessor. When you place these rebellion narratives end to end, they cancel each other out. Whatever is considered edgy and liberating in one generation is dismissed as bland and confining for the next. An aging genre invariably becomes a straw man against which a new genre defines itself. Dylan "plugged in" and defied the folkies. Chuck Berry sang "Roll Over Beethoven" to get the original rock-and-roll revolution under way, using classical music as a foil. The Beatles were said to have swept aside the prefab pop of the early sixties, which happened to include some of the great early Motown songs. Punk sneered at disco. Why should the love of one kind of music necessitate the knocking down of another? Schopenhauer may have had the answer when he observed that the listener is always fighting battles in his head which he can never win in life. "We like to hear in its language the secret history of our will and of all its stirrings and strivings," the philosopher said. Music at its most potent creates the feeling that the world is about to undergo a vague but tremendous change, which is how political energies become attached to it. When the world fails to change as promised, however, the music becomes an object of ridicule.

The ultimate pop-music myth is the one that scholars file under the rubric "authenticity," according to which only the rudest, rawest music — the primal scream of the outcast — qualifies as "real." African-American music is usually expected to supply the perfume of the primitive. Since the 1920s, white teenagers have used black music as the Muzak of their pubescence. Some pop historians still perpetuate this mythology, but others make a point of celebrating all that is rigorous, complex, and exalted in the African-American tradition. One of my favorite passages in pop-music studies appears in *Instruments of Desire,* an erudite paean to the electric guitar, by Steve Waksman of Smith College. It describes how Bo Diddley came to invent his tremolando sound. "Tremolo involved an oscillation of the electronic signal," Waksman writes, "transmitted from the guitar to the amplifier so that the volume level would fluctuate at regular intervals between extreme loudness and virtual silence." I don't really know what this means, but it certainly puts Diddley's "bump-a-bump bump" in a new light. Likewise, David Brackett, the author of *Interpreting Popular Music,* lost me when he began to expound on James Brown's "Superbad" by way of the mathematical proportions of the Golden Section, positing that various parts of the song relate to each other by a ratio of 0.618 to 1. Bach has long been subject to this sort of arcane analysis, and there is no reason that the hardest-working man in show business shouldn't get the same treatment.

In a less pedantic vein, a paper by Portia K. Maultsby, who teaches in the Department of Folklore and Ethnomusicology at Indiana University, dismantled the clichés attached to Motown's "hit factory," which for a long time was accused of purveying what critics called a "diluted blackness." She stressed Motown's profound connections with the African-American tradition, especially jazz, gospel, and rhythm and blues: James Jamerson's restless, all-over bass lines are electric bebop. Maultsby's paper went hand in hand with an essay by John Sheinbaum in the *Rock Over the Edge* anthology — a devastating account of how white rockers are routinely celebrated as enigmatic artists while their African-American counterparts are made out to be simpleminded conduits of energy and fun. *The Rolling Stone Illustrated History of Rock and Roll* once described Motown as a "wholly mechanical style and sound." The Beatles, by contrast, were hailed as mop-top Beethovens immediately after releasing "I Want to Hold Your Hand." The Beatles were great, but they did not save music from oblivion when they arrived in America in 1964. In fact, as Keir Keightley notes in *The Cambridge Companion to Pop and Rock,* the blues-besotted British Invasion had the effect of putting a great many African-American session musicians out of work.

The Crucifixion Mambo

By common consent, the tour de force of the Pop Conference was a lecture by the Cuban music scholar and producer Ned Sublette, which took place at the not very funky hour of 9:30 A.M.

In the space of twenty minutes or so, Sublette conjured up the sweeping influence of Cuban music and Caribbean traditions on almost every popular form of the twentieth century. It was not so much a lecture as an all-out performance: Sublette, who also leads a Latin-country fusion band, sang, tapped, and danced the Cuban rhythms that have insinuated themselves into every breakthrough moment in American music, including ragtime (Scott Joplin's "The Entertainer" uses the *danzón* rhythm), New Orleans jazz, bebop, rock-and-roll (Bo Diddley's "hambone" beat is similar to the Cuban clave), and funk. Sublette called Cuban music "the elephant in the kitchen that pop-music historians have failed to see"; it was, he insisted, the site of the original marriage of African rhythm and European harmony.

By installing Cuban music as "the other great tradition," Sublette did the unthinkable: he questioned the primacy of African Americans in pop history. There were murmurs of unease when he announced that African-American music was not originally polyrhythmic. Robert Christgau, the fiercely informed critic of the *Village Voice*, said in the question-and-answer period that blues singers implied polyrhythm in the interplay of voice and guitar. In a way, though, Sublette's Cubacentric reading — the book version of which will be published next year — relieves African Americans of the burden of being the primitives of American music; they become the appropriators rather than the appropriated.

Sublette mentioned, in passing, the fascinating history of two old Spanish-American dances, the *zarabanda* and the *chacona,* which probably stemmed from the Afro-Caribbean melting pot. They spread to Europe in the sixteenth and seventeenth centuries and helped shape some of the masterpieces of the Baroque. In Seattle, I got to thinking about the tangled history of the *chacona,* or chaconne, which has appeared in so many diverse places in the past five hundred years that it could be considered one of the iconic images of the universal language. It is identifiable by its bass line: a constantly repeating, often downward-plunging figure, over which higher instruments and voices play variations. "A dance in the way of the mulatto's," Cervantes called it. The lyrics were bawdy and irreverent; the music was said to have been invented by the Devil. Once it reached Europe, it slowed down and took on more solemn connotations. In the hands of Monteverdi it led to the "Lamento" bass, which was well suited to the dying utterances of operatic heroines. In its most striking form, the "Lamento" proceeded down a grand, chilly staircase of semitones, or chromatic steps. You can hear this version of it in the heart-stopping final lament of Purcell's *Dido and Aeneas,* and in the "Crucifixus" from Bach's Mass in B Minor.

At the beginning of the twentieth century, a *chacona*-style figure reappeared in the hands of African-American musicians in New Orleans, Chicago, and, notably, the Mississippi Delta, where the Devil was again said to be active. It sounded obsessively in Skip James's "I'm So Glad," one of the greatest of the Delta blues, and can be heard rumbling beneath Ellington's "Reminiscing in Tempo." Descending chromatic basses gave a slow-marching power to some of the more ambitious rock songs of the sixties and seventies — Dylan's "Ballad of a Thin Man" and "Simple Twist of Fate," Led Zeppelin's "Dazed and Confused" and "Stairway to Heaven." Somehow, four centuries after the lamenting bass surfaced, its meaning remained the same. It summoned up the dark comfort of heartbreak and depression: the heart descending step by step to the bottom and going back up to repeat the journey.

Universal figures such as the *chacona* — "memes," as musicologists call them, borrowing from sociobiology — reveal the interconnectedness of all musical experience. If you could bring together a few seventeenth-century Afro-Cuban musicians, a continuo section led by the Master Bach, and players from Ellington's 1929 band, and then ask John Paul Jones to start them off with the bass line of "Dazed and Confused," they would, after a minute or two, find common ground. And very interesting music it would be, too. Purists of all genres can never stand the fact that the genealogy of music is one long string of miscegenations and mutations.

The Timberlake Perplex

When, in 1943, Ellington presented his symphonic masterpiece *Black, Brown, and Beige* at Carnegie Hall, he spoke of it in the first-person plural, including his band in the creative process. Scholars often point out that African-American genres, like their West African antecedents, resist the European cult of personality: they tend to take the form of a collective ritual, not of a declamation by a charismatic star to a passive crowd. The problem with the "genius" model is that it puts up a wall between performer and audience; this is surely why so many pop musicians reject it, even as they feed on the adulation that creates it. They look warily on the archivists and commentators who crowd around any long-lasting genre. If, as another old German dude said, the owl of Minerva flies at dusk, rock critics are Minerva's vultures: when enough of them take flight, it means that something is dying.

Still, we listeners want to talk about genius. We want a language that articulates and perpetuates our passions. What's bedeviling about pop music is that while we sense greatness in a song we have trouble saying where it comes from. It is often difficult to say who even wrote the thing in the first place. Some performers exert such a powerful presence — Billie Holiday, Sinatra, Elvis — that they seem to become the authors of songs that were actually the work of schlumpy men in the Brill Building. Then there are the rock songs that were written by committee, often in the middle of the night, and under the influence of something other than the muse Euterpe. Composers have the advantage of being shrouded in myth: we can project fantasies of omniscience upon them. Pop stars torment us with their inconvenient humanness — their tax problems, their noisome politics, their pornography collections, their unwanted comebacks. No wonder the greatest legends are the artists who die young.

Call this the Timberlake predicament. In the past year, rock critics found themselves in the faintly embarrassing position of having to hail Justin Timberlake's *Justified* as one of the better records of the year. Timberlake, for those who have let their subscription to *Teen People* lapse, is the blond, curly-haired twenty-two-year-old lead singer of 'N Sync. Encomiums from certifiably heterosexual male critics such as Christgau have demonstrated that Timberlake was not getting praised for his pretty face alone. Granted, cynics may see all this as a rationalization on the part of writers who can't admit that music keeps getting worse; they eat a Hostess Twinkie and call it a gourmet meal. But it shouldn't be forgotten that many of the most imposing achievements in pop history had their origins in ditsy teenybopper fads. The Beatles were once a boy band, too. What happened to them in the middle and late sixties was a mysterious transfer of energy, in which disposable fame was transmuted into artistic power. The band found fame first, then it found greatness. So it would be foolish to write Timberlake off too quickly.

In any case, the songs on *Justified* aren't really Timberlake's. A dozen names appear in the credits, and it's anyone's guess how much of a song like "Cry Me a River," the album's best track, actually came from Timberlake's pen, if he owns one. Every bit of the song shows the fingerprints of the hip-hop producer Tim Mosley, a.k.a. Timbaland, who is the éminence grise behind half of what is great in the Top Forty these days. He has sampled every genre under the sun, from world music to austere electronica. He likes to leave yawning gaps of silence between his speaker-puncturing beats, which inspire new kinds of vehemence on the dance floor. (As Virgil Thomson observed long ago, we dance to syncopated music because our bodies like to fill in the missing beats.) Modernist ideology accustoms us to think that experimentation can take place on the margins of a culture, but hip-hop production is the site of some of the weirdest, wittiest thinking in pop music today.

"Cry Me a River" has no apparent relation to the 1955 standard made famous by Julie London, although a future analysis of internal structural ratios may show otherwise. The vocals are plaintive to the point of whining, but the inner voices have a cool, contrapuntal flow, creating the sort of muscular melancholy so characteristic of postwar rhythm and blues. There are at least seven layers of simultaneous activity in the song — it's as if Timbaland wanted to see how much he could pile on without creating atonality. First there is an arpeggiated keyboard figure, followed by male voices singing a bit of Gregorian-style chant. Next comes a steady, somber pattern that sounds a little like the minor-key vamp in Ellington's "East St. Louis Toodle-Oo." Below it are four bass notes, recurring in *chacona* style. Now the angelic Timberlake enters, together with a more nasty-minded rhythm section, a vaguely Indian-sounding synthesized string orchestra, and, finally, sped-up versions of all the above.

In sum, "Cry Me a River" may be the most polyphonically complex teenybopper ballad in history. At the very least, it's not something that any idiot could have done. It has the inward delight of a song that is better than it needs to be. Popular music is full of this sort of mad tinkering; in the background of even the most ostentatiously numskulled acts may be a music geek who stays up all night trying to find a single chord. Pop-music scholars spend a lot of time describing the messages that become attached to songs, and this is a necessary part of the history of listening. Yet, when music passes from one generation to another, it leaves most of its social significance peeling off dorm room walls, and its persistence is best explained with reference to beats, chords, and raw emotion. Which is why pop writers have to find a new way to describe musical events, and not just by offering dopey imitations of classical musicology. No one would give much credence to a style of art criticism that alluded to paintings without mentioning their shapes and colors, or an architecture criticism that refused to say whether buildings were made of stone or metal.

It was disappointing to hear from attendees at the Pop Conference that they are still viewed with intense suspicion by their colleagues in classical musicology. Increasingly, leading colleges and universities have full-time pop specialists; the musicology department at UCLA is headed by Robert Walser, the author of books on jazz and heavy metal. Given the vast quantities of obscurantism that classical musicologists have churned out in the past fifty years — the impenetrable tautologies of Schenkerian analysis, the higher-math delirium of pitch-class set theory — classical scholars have no right to dismiss their pop counterparts as anything less than serious. They probably picture themselves fighting a last stand against the armies of ignorance, but any mode of teaching that promotes close, historically attuned listening can't be a bad thing. And those of us who write on classical music have a lot to learn from pop studies. It exposes the hard realities of how music is made, how it is paid for, and how it is consumed. To understand music only as art and not as entertainment, as classical scholars tend to do, is to dehumanize the past. For all we know, Bach may well have rolled his eyes and munched on a pork chop whenever someone asked him about his relationship with Palestrina.

Pop music is music stripped bare. It is like the haphazard funeral portrayed in Wallace Stevens's "Emperor of Ice Cream": a woman laid out with all her flaws intact, covered with a sheet from a chest of drawers that is missing three knobs, her horny feet protruding. Boys bring flowers in last month's newspapers, but she is noble to look upon. Twentieth-century music, the empire of ice cream, lies before us in all its damaged majesty.

OLIVER SACKS

The Mind's Eye

FROM THE NEW YORKER

IN HIS LAST LETTER, Goethe wrote, "The Ancients said that the animals are taught through their organs; let me add to this, so are men, but they have the advantage of teaching their organs in return." He wrote this in 1832, a time when phrenology was at its height, and the brain was seen as a mosaic of "little organs" subserving everything from language to drawing ability to shyness. Each individual, it was believed, was given a fixed measure of this faculty or that, according to the luck of his birth. Though we no longer pay attention, as the phrenologists did, to the "bumps" on the head (each of which, supposedly, indicated a brain-mind organ beneath), neurology and neuroscience have stayed close to the idea of brain fixity and localization — the notion, in particular, that the highest part of the brain, the cerebral cortex, is effectively programmed from birth: this part to vision and visual processing, that part to hearing, that to touch, and so on.

This would seem to allow individuals little power of choice, of self-determination, let alone of adaptation, in the event of a neurological or perceptual mishap.

But to what extent are we — our experiences, our reactions — shaped, predetermined, by our brains, and to what extent do we shape our own brains? Does the mind run the brain or the brain the mind — or, rather, to what extent does one run the other? To what extent are we the authors, the creators, of our own experiences? The effects of a profound perceptual deprivation such as blindness can cast an unexpected light on this. To become blind, especially later in life, presents one with a huge, potentially overwhelming challenge: to find a new way of living, of ordering one's world, when the old way has been destroyed.

A dozen years ago, I was sent an extraordinary book called *Touching the Rock: An Experience of Blindness*. The author, John Hull, was a professor of religious education who had grown up in Australia and then moved to England. Hull had developed cataracts at the age of thirteen, and became completely blind in his left eye four years later. Vision in his right eye remained reasonable until he was thirty-five or so, and then started to deteriorate. There followed a decade of steadily failing vision, in which Hull needed stronger and stronger magnifying glasses, and had to write with thicker and thicker pens, until, in 1983, at the age of forty-eight, he became completely blind.

Touching the Rock is the journal he dictated in the three years that followed. It is full of piercing insights relating to Hull's life as a blind person, but most striking for me is Hull's description of how, in the years after his loss of sight, he experienced a gradual attenuation of visual imagery and memory, and finally a virtual extinction of them (except in dreams) — a state that he calls "deep blindness."

By this, Hull meant not only the loss of visual images and memories but a loss of the very idea of seeing, so that concepts like "here," "there," and "facing" seemed to lose meaning for him, and even the sense of objects having "appearances," visible characteristics, vanished. At this point, for example, he could no longer imagine how the numeral 3 looked, unless he traced it in the air with his hand. He could construct a "motor" image of a 3, but not a visual one.

Hull, though at first greatly distressed about the fading of visual memories and images — the fact that he could no longer conjure up the faces of his wife or children, or of familiar and loved landscapes and places — then came to accept it with remarkable equanimity; indeed, to regard it as a natural response to a nonvisual world. He seemed to regard this loss of visual imagery as a prerequisite for the full development, the heightening, of his other senses.

Two years after becoming completely blind, Hull had apparently become so nonvisual as to resemble someone who had been blind from birth. Hull's loss of visuality also reminded me of the sort of "cortical blindness" that can happen if the primary visual cortex is damaged, through a stroke or traumatic brain damage — although in Hull's case there was no direct damage to the visual cortex but, rather, a cutting off from any visual stimulation or input.

In a profoundly religious way, and in language sometimes reminiscent of that of Saint John of the Cross, Hull enters into this state, surrenders himself, with a sort of acquiescence and joy. And such "deep" blindness he conceives as "an authentic and autonomous world, a place of its own . . . Being a whole-body seer is to be in one of the concentrated human conditions."

Being a "whole-body seer," for Hull, means shifting his attention, his center of gravity, to the other senses, and he writes again and again of how these have assumed a new richness and power. Thus he speaks of how the sound of rain, never before accorded much attention, can now delineate a whole landscape for him, for its sound on the garden path is different from its sound as it drums on the lawn, or on the bushes in his garden, or on the fence dividing it from the road. "Rain," he writes, "has a way of bringing out the contours of everything; it throws a coloured blanket over previously invisible things; instead of an intermittent and thus fragmented world, the steadily falling rain creates continuity of acoustic experience . . . presents the fullness of an entire situation all at once . . . gives a sense of perspective and of the actual relationships of one part of the world to another."

With his new intensity of auditory experience (or attention), along with the sharpening of his other senses, Hull comes to feel a sense of intimacy with nature, an intensity of being-in-the-world, beyond anything he knew when he was sighted. Blindness now becomes for him "a dark, paradoxical gift." This is not just "compensation," he emphasizes, but a whole new order, a new mode of human being. With this he extricates himself from visual nostalgia, from the strain, or falsity, of trying to pass as "normal," and finds a new focus, a new freedom. His teaching at the university expands, becomes more fluent, his writing becomes stronger and deeper; he becomes intellectually and spiritually bolder, more confident. He feels he is on solid ground at last.

What Hull described seemed to me an astounding example of how an individual deprived of one form of perception could totally reshape himself to a new center, a new identity.

It is said that those who see normally as infants but then become blind within the first two years of life retain no memories of seeing, have no visual imagery and no visual elements in their dreams (and, in this way, are comparable to those born blind). It is similar with those who lose hearing before the age of two: they have no sense of having "lost" the world of sound, nor any sense of "silence," as hearing people sometimes imagine. For those who lose sight so early, the very concepts of "sight" or "blindness" soon cease to have meaning, and there is no sense of losing the world of vision, only of living fully in a world constructed by the other senses.

But it seemed extraordinary to me that such an annihilation of visual memory as Hull describes could happen equally to an adult, with decades, an entire lifetime, of rich and richly categorized visual experience to call upon. And yet I could not doubt the authenticity of Hull's account, which he relates with the most scrupulous care and lucidity.

Important studies of adaptation in the brain were begun in the 1970s by, among others, Helen Neville, a cognitive neuroscientist now working in Oregon. She showed that in prelingually deaf people (that is, those who had been born deaf or become deaf before the age of two or so) the auditory parts of the brain had not degenerated or atrophied. These had remained active and functional, but with an activity and a function that were new: they had been transformed, "reallocated," in Neville's term, for processing visual language. Comparable studies in those born blind, or early blinded, show that the visual areas of the cortex, similarly, may be reallocated in function, and used to process sound and touch.

With the reallocation of the visual cortex to touch and other senses, these can take on a hyperacuity that perhaps no sighted person can imagine. Bernard Morin, the blind mathematician who in the 1960s had shown how a sphere could be turned inside out, felt that his achievement required a special sort of spatial perception and imagination. And a similar sort of spatial giftedness has been central to the work of Geerat Vermeij, a blind biologist who has been able to delineate many new species of mollusk, based on tiny variations in the shapes and contours of their shells.

Faced with such findings and reports, neurologists began to concede that there might be a certain flexibility or plasticity in the brain, at least in the early years of life. But when this critical period

was over, it was assumed, the brain became inflexible, and no further changes of a radical type could occur. The experiences that
Hull so carefully recounts give the lie to this. It is clear that his perceptions, his brain, did finally change, in a fundamental way. Indeed, Alvaro Pascual-Leone and his colleagues in Boston have recently shown that, even in adult sighted volunteers, as little as five
days of being blindfolded produces marked shifts to nonvisual
forms of behavior and cognition, and they have demonstrated the
physiological changes in the brain that go along with this. And
only last month, Italian researchers published a study showing that
sighted volunteers kept in the dark for as little as ninety minutes
may show a striking enhancement of tactile-spatial sensitivity.

The brain, clearly, is capable of changing even in adulthood,
and I assumed that Hull's experience was typical of acquired blindness — the response, sooner or later, of everyone who becomes
blind, even in adult life.

So when I came to publish an essay on Hull's book, in 1991, I
was taken aback to receive a number of letters from blind people,
letters that were often somewhat puzzled, and occasionally indig-
nant, in tone. Many of my correspondents, it seemed, could not
identify with Hull's experience, and said that they themselves, even
decades after losing their sight, had never lost their visual images
or memories. One correspondent, who had lost her sight at fifteen, wrote, "Even though I am totally blind . . . I consider myself a
very visual person. I still 'see' objects in front of me. As I am typing
now I can see my hands on the keyboard . . . I don't feel comfortable in a new environment until I have a mental picture of its appearance. I need a mental map for my independent moving, too."

Had I been wrong, or at least one-sided, in accepting Hull's experience as a typical response to blindness? Had I been guilty of
emphasizing one mode of response too strongly, oblivious to the
possibilities of radically different responses?

This feeling came to a head in 1996, when I received a letter from
an Australian psychologist named Zoltan Torey. Torey wrote to me
not about blindness but about a book he had written on the brain-
mind problem and the nature of consciousness. (The book was
published by Oxford University Press as *The Crucible of Consciousness,* in 1999.) In his letter Torey also spoke of how he had been

blinded in an accident at the age of twenty-one, while working at a chemical factory, and how, although "advised to switch from a visual to an auditory mode of adjustment," he had moved in the opposite direction, and resolved to develop instead his "inner eye," his powers of visual imagery, to their greatest possible extent.

In this, it seemed, he had been extremely successful, developing a remarkable power of generating, holding, and manipulating images in his mind, so much so that he had been able to construct an imagined visual world that seemed almost as real and intense to him as the perceptual one he had lost — and, indeed, sometimes more real, more intense, a sort of controlled dream or hallucination. This imagery, moreover, enabled him to do things that might have seemed scarcely possible for a blind man. "I replaced the entire roof guttering of my multi-gabled home single-handed," he wrote, "and solely on the strength of the accurate and well-focused manipulation of my now totally pliable and responsive mental space." (Torey later expanded on this episode, mentioning the great alarm of his neighbors at seeing a blind man, alone, on the roof of his house — and, even more terrifying to them, at night, in pitch darkness.)

And it enabled him to think in ways that had not been available to him before, to envisage solutions, models, designs, to project himself to the inside of machines and other systems, and, finally, to grasp by visual thought and simulation (complemented by all the data of neuroscience) the complexities of that ultimate system, the human brain-mind.

When I wrote back to Torey, I suggested that he consider writing another book, a more personal one, exploring how his life had been affected by blindness, and how he had responded to this, in the most improbable and seemingly paradoxical of ways. *Out of Darkness* is the memoir he has now written, and in it Torey describes his early memories with great visual intensity and humor. Scenes are remembered or reconstructed in brief, poetic glimpses of his childhood and youth in Hungary before the Second World War: the sky-blue buses of Budapest, the egg-yellow trams, the lighting of gas lamps, the funicular on the Buda side. He describes a carefree and privileged youth, roaming with his father in the wooded mountains above the Danube, playing games and pranks at school, growing up in a highly intellectual environment of writers, actors, professionals of every sort. Torey's father was the head of a large motion-picture studio and would often give his son scripts to read. "This," Torey writes, "gave me the opportunity to visualize stories, plots and characters, to work my imagination — a skill that was to become a lifeline and source of strength in the years ahead."

All of this came to a brutal end with the Nazi occupation, the siege of Buda, and then the Soviet occupation. Torey, now an adolescent, found himself passionately drawn to the big questions — the mystery of the universe, of life, and above all the mystery of consciousness, of the mind. In 1948, nineteen years old, and feeling that he needed to immerse himself in biology, engineering, neuroscience, and psychology, but knowing that there was no chance of study, of an intellectual life, in Soviet Hungary, Torey made his escape and eventually found his way to Australia, where, penniless and without connections, he did various manual jobs. In June of 1951, loosening the plug in a vat of acid at the chemical factory where he worked, he had the accident that bisected his life.

"The last thing I saw with complete clarity was a glint of light in the flood of acid that was to engulf my face and change my life. It was a nano-second of sparkle, framed by the black circle of the drumface, less than a foot away. This was the final scene, the slender thread that ties me to my visual past."

When it became clear that his corneas had been hopelessly damaged and that he would have to live his life as a blind man, he was advised to rebuild his representation of the world on the basis of hearing and touch and to "forget about sight and visualizing altogether." But this was something that Torey could not or would not do. He had emphasized, in his first letter to me, the importance of a most critical choice at this juncture: "I immediately resolved to find out how far a partially sense-deprived brain could go to rebuild a life." Put this way, it sounds abstract, like an experiment. But in his book one senses the tremendous feelings underlying his resolution — the horror of darkness, "the empty darkness," as Torey often calls it, "the grey fog that was engulfing me," and the passionate desire to hold on to light and sight, to maintain, if only in memory and imagination, a vivid and living visual world. The very title of his book says all this, and the note of defiance is sounded from the start.

Hull, who did not use his potential for imagery in a deliberate way, lost it in two or three years, and became unable to remember which way round a 3 went; Torey, on the other hand, soon became able to multiply four-figure numbers by each other, as on a blackboard, visualizing the whole operation in his mind, "painting" the suboperations in different colors.

Well aware that the imagination (or the brain), unrestrained by the usual perceptual input, may run away with itself in a wildly associative or self-serving way — as may happen in deliria, hallucinations, or dreams — Torey maintained a cautious and "scientific" attitude to his own visual imagery, taking pains to check the accuracy of his images by every means available. "I learned," he writes, "to hold the image in a tentative way, conferring credibility and status on it only when some information would tip the balance in its favor." Indeed, he soon gained enough confidence in the reliability of his visual imagery to stake his life upon it, as when he undertook roof repairs by himself. And this confidence extended to other, purely mental projects. He became able "to imagine, to visualize, for example, the inside of a differential gearbox in action as if from inside its casing. "I was able to watch the cogs bite, lock and revolve, distributing the spin as required. I began to play around with this internal view in connection with mechanical and technical problems, visualizing how subcomponents relate in the atom, or in the living cell." This power of imagery was crucial, Torey thought, in enabling him to arrive at a solution of the brain-mind problem by visualizing the brain "as a perpetual juggling act of interacting routines."

In a famous study of creativity, the French mathematician Jacques Hadamard asked many scientists and mathematicians, including Einstein, about their thought processes. Einstein replied, "The physical entities which seem to serve as elements in thought are . . . more or less clear images which can be 'voluntarily' reproduced and combined. [Some are] of visual and some of muscular type. Conventional words or other signs have to be sought for laboriously only in a secondary stage." Torey cites this, and adds, "Nor was Einstein unique in this respect. Hadamard found that almost all scientists work this way, and this was also the way my project evolved."

*

Soon after receiving Torey's manuscript, I received the proofs of yet another memoir by a blind person: Sabriye Tenberken's *My Path Leads to Tibet*. While Hull and Torey are thinkers, preoccupied in their different ways by inwardness, states of brain and mind, Tenberken is a doer; she has traveled, often alone, all over Tibet, where for centuries blind people have been treated as less than human and denied education, work, respect, or a role in the community. Virtually single-handed, Tenberken has transformed their situation over the past half-dozen years, devising a form of Tibetan Braille, establishing schools for the blind, and integrating the graduates of these schools into their communities.

Tenberken herself had impaired vision almost from birth but was able to make out faces and landscapes until she was twelve. As a child in Germany, she had a particular predilection for colors, and loved painting, and when she was no longer able to decipher shapes and forms she could still use colors to identify objects. Tenberken has, indeed, an intense synesthesia. "As far back as I can remember," she writes, "numbers and words have instantly triggered colors in me . . . The number 4, for example, [is] gold. Five is light green. Nine is vermillion . . . Days of the week as well as months have their colors, too. I have them arranged in geometrical formations, in circular sectors, a little like a pie. When I need to recall on which day a particular event happened, the first thing that pops up on my inner screen is the day's color, then its position in the pie." Her synesthesia has persisted and been intensified, it seems, by her blindness.

Though she has been totally blind for twenty years now, Tenberken continues to use all her other senses, along with verbal descriptions, visual memories, and a strong pictorial and synesthetic sensibility, to construct "pictures" of landscapes and rooms, of environments and scenes — pictures so lively and detailed as to astonish her listeners. These images may sometimes be wildly or comically different from reality, as she relates in one incident when she and a companion drove to Nam Co, the great salt lake in Tibet. Turning eagerly toward the lake, Tenberken saw, in her mind's eye, "a beach of crystallized salt shimmering like snow under an evening sun, at the edge of a vast body of turquoise water . . . And down below, on the deep green mountain flanks, a few nomads were watching their yaks grazing." But it then turns out that she has been facing in the wrong direction, not "looking" at the lake at all, and that she has been "staring" at rocks and a gray landscape. These disparities don't faze her in the least — she is happy to have so vivid a visual imagination. Hers is essentially an artistic imagination, which can be impressionistic, romantic, not veridical at all, where Torey's imagination is that of an engineer, and has to be factual, accurate down to the last detail.

I had now read three memoirs, strikingly different in their depictions of the visual experience of blinded people: Hull with his acquiescent descent into imageless "deep blindness," Torey with his "compulsive visualization" and meticulous construction of an internal visual world, and Tenberken with her impulsive, almost novelistic, visual freedom, along with her remarkable and specific gift of synesthesia. Was there any such thing, I now wondered, as a "typical" blind experience?

I recently met two other people blinded in adult life who shared their experiences with me.

Dennis Shulman, a clinical psychologist and psychoanalyst who lectures on biblical topics, is an affable, stocky, bearded man in his fifties who gradually lost his sight in his teens, becoming completely blind by the time he entered college. He immediately confirmed that his experience was unlike Hull's: "I still live in a visual world after thirty-five years of blindness. I have very vivid visual memories and images. My wife, whom I have never seen — I think of her visually. My kids, too. I see myself visually — but it is as I last saw myself, when I was thirteen, though I try hard to update the image. I often give public lectures, and my notes are in Braille; but when I go over them in my mind, I see the Braille notes visually — they are visual images, not tactile."

Arlene Gordon, a charming woman in her seventies, a former social worker, said that things were very similar for her: "If I move my arms back and forth in front of my eyes, I see them, even though I have been blind for more than thirty years." It seemed that moving her arms was immediately translated for her into a visual image. Listening to talking books, she added, made her eyes tire if she listened too long; she seemed to herself to be reading at such times, the sound of the spoken words being transformed to lines of print on a vividly visualized book in front of her. This involved a sort of cognitive exertion (similar perhaps to translating one language into another), and sooner or later this would give her an eye ache.

I was reminded of Amy, a colleague who had been deafened by scarlet fever at the age of nine but was so adept a lip reader that I often forgot she was deaf. Once, when I absent-mindedly turned away from her as I was speaking, she said sharply, "I can no longer hear you."

"You mean you can no longer see me," I said.

"*You* may call it seeing," she answered, "but I experience it as hearing."

Amy, though totally deaf, still constructed the sound of speech in her mind. Both Dennis and Arlene, similarly, spoke not only of a heightening of visual imagery and imagination since losing their eyesight but also of what seemed to be a much readier transference of information from verbal description — or from their own sense of touch, movement, hearing, or smell — into a visual form. On the whole, their experiences seemed quite similar to Torey's, even though they had not systematically exercised their powers of visual imagery in the way that he had, or consciously tried to make an entire virtual world of sight.

There is increasing evidence from neuroscience for the extraordinarily rich interconnectedness and interactions of the sensory areas of the brain, and the difficulty, therefore, of saying that anything is purely visual or purely auditory, or purely anything. This is evident in the very titles of some recent papers — Pascual-Leone and his colleagues at Harvard now write of "The Metamodal Organization of the Brain," and Shinsuke Shimojo and his group at Caltech, who are also exploring intersensory perceptual phenomena, recently published a paper called "What You See Is What You Hear," and stress that sensory modalities can never be considered in isolation. The world of the blind, of the blinded, it seems, can be especially rich in such in-between states — the intersensory, the metamodal — states for which we have no common language.

Arlene, like Dennis, still identifies herself in many ways as a visual person. "I have a very strong sense of color," she said. "I pick out my own clothes. I think, Oh, that will go with this or that, once I have been told the colors." Indeed, she was dressed very smartly, and took obvious pride in her appearance.

"I love traveling," she continued. "I 'saw' Venice when I was there." She explained how her traveling companions would describe places, and she would then construct a visual image from these details, her reading, and her own visual memories. "Sighted people enjoy traveling with me," she said. "I ask them questions, then they look, and see things they wouldn't otherwise. Too often people with sight don't see anything! It's a reciprocal process — we enrich each other's worlds."

If we are sighted, we build our own images, using our eyes, our visual information, so instantly and seamlessly that it seems to us we are experiencing "reality" itself. One may need to see people who are color-blind, or motion-blind, who have lost certain visual capacities from cerebral injury, to realize the enormous act of analysis and synthesis, the dozens of subsystems involved in the subjectively simple act of seeing. But can a visual image be built using nonvisual information — information conveyed by the other senses, by memory, or by verbal description?

There have, of course, been many blind poets and writers, from Homer on. Most of these were born with normal vision and lost their sight in boyhood or adulthood (like Milton). I loved reading Prescott's *Conquest of Mexico* and *Conquest of Peru* as a boy, and feel that I first saw these lands through his intensely visual, almost hallucinogenic descriptions, and I was amazed to discover, years later, that Prescott not only had never visited Mexico or Peru but had been virtually blind since the age of eighteen. Did he, like Torey, compensate for his blindness by developing such powers of visual imagery that he could experience a "virtual reality" of sight? Or were his brilliant visual descriptions in a sense simulated, made possible by the evocative and pictorial powers of language? To what extent can language, a picturing in words, provide a substitute for actual seeing, and for the visual, pictorial imagination? Blind children, it has often been noted, tend to be precocious verbally, and may develop such fluency in the verbal description of faces and places as to leave others (and perhaps themselves) uncertain as to whether they are actually blind. Helen Keller's writing, to give a famous example, startles one with its brilliantly visual quality.

When I asked Dennis and Arlene whether they had read John Hull's book, Arlene said, "I was stunned when I read it. His experiences are so unlike mine." Perhaps, she added, Hull had "renounced" his inner vision. Dennis agreed, but said, "We are only two individuals. You are going to have to talk to dozens of people . . . But in the meanwhile you should read Jacques Lusseyran's memoir."

Lusseyran was a French Resistance fighter whose memoir, *And There Was Light,* deals mostly with his experiences fighting the Nazis and later in Buchenwald but includes many beautiful descriptions of his early adaptations to blindness. He was blinded in an accident when he was not quite eight years old, an age that he came to feel was "ideal" for such an eventuality, for, while he already had a rich visual experience to call on, "the habits of a boy of eight are not yet formed, either in body or in mind. His body is infinitely supple." And suppleness, agility, indeed came to characterize his response to blindness.

Many of his initial responses were of loss, both of imagery and of interests:

> A very short time after I went blind I forgot the faces of my mother and father and the faces of most of the people I loved . . . I stopped caring whether people were dark or fair, with blue eyes or green. I felt that sighted people spent too much time observing these empty things . . . I no longer even thought about them. People no longer seemed to possess them. Sometimes in my mind men and women appeared without heads or fingers.

This is similar to Hull, who writes, "Increasingly, I am no longer even trying to imagine what people look like . . . I am finding it more and more difficult to realize that people look like anything, to put any meaning into the idea that they have an appearance."

But then, while relinquishing the actual visual world and many of its values and categories, Lusseyran starts to construct and to use an imaginary visual world more like Torey's.

This started as a sensation of light, a formless, flooding, streaming radiance. Neurological terms are bound to sound reductive in this almost mystical context. Yet one might venture to interpret this as a "release" phenomenon, a spontaneous, almost eruptive arousal of the visual cortex, now deprived of its normal visual input. This is a phenomenon analogous, perhaps, to tinnitus or phantom limbs, though endowed here, by a devout and precociously imaginative little boy, with some element of the supernal.

But then, it becomes clear, he does find himself in possession of great powers of visual imagery, and not just a formless luminosity.

The visual cortex, the inner eye, having now been activated, Lusseyran's mind constructed a "screen" upon which whatever he thought or desired was projected and, if need be, manipulated, as on a computer screen. "This screen was not like a blackboard, rectangular or square, which so quickly reaches the edge of its frame," he writes. "My screen was always as big as I needed it to be. Because it was nowhere in space it was everywhere at the same time . . . Names, figures and objects in general did not appear on my screen without shape, nor just in black and white, but in all the colors of the rainbow. Nothing entered my mind without being bathed in a certain amount of light . . . In a few months my personal world had turned into a painter's studio."

Great powers of visualization were crucial to the young Lusseyran, even in something as nonvisual (one would think) as learning Braille (he visualizes the Braille dots, as Dennis does), and in his brilliant successes at school. They were no less crucial in the real, outside world. He describes walks with his sighted friend Jean, and how, as they were climbing together up the side of a hill above the Seine Valley, he could say:

> "Just look! This time we're on top . . . You'll see the whole bend of the river, unless the sun gets in your eyes!" Jean was startled, opened his eyes wide and cried: "You're right." This little scene was often repeated between us, in a thousand forms.

"Every time someone mentioned an event," Lusseyran relates, "the event immediately projected itself in its place on the screen, which was a kind of inner canvas . . . Comparing my world with his, [Jean] found that his held fewer pictures and not nearly as many colors. This made him almost angry. 'When it comes to that,' he used to say, 'which one of us two is blind?'"

It was his supernormal powers of visualization and visual manipulation — visualizing people's position and movement, the topography of any space, visualizing strategies for defense and attack — coupled with his charismatic personality (and seemingly infallible "nose" or "ear" for detecting falsehood, possible traitors), which later made Lusseyran an icon in the French Resistance.

Dennis, earlier, had spoken of how the heightening of his other senses had increased his sensitivity to moods in other people, and to the most delicate nuances in their speech and self-presentation. He could now recognize many of his patients by smell, he said, and he could often pick up states of tension or anxiety which they might not even be aware of. He felt that he had become far more sensitive to others' emotional states since losing his sight, for he was no longer taken in by visual appearances, which most people learn to camouflage. Voices and smells, by contrast, he felt, could reveal people's depths. He had come to think of most sighted people, he joked, as "visually dependent."

In a subsequent essay, Lusseyran inveighs against the "despotism," the "idol worship" of sight, and sees the "task" of blindness as reminding us of our other, deeper modes of perception and their mutuality. "A blind person has a better sense of feeling, of taste, of touch," he writes, and speaks of these as "the gifts of the blind." And all of these, Lusseyran feels, blend into a single fundamental sense, a deep attentiveness, a slow, almost prehensile attention, a sensuous, intimate being at one with the world which sight, with its quick, flicking, facile quality, continually distracts us from. This is very close to Hull's concept of "deep blindness" as infinitely more than mere compensation but a unique form of perception, a precious and special mode of being.

What happens when the visual cortex is no longer limited, or constrained, by any visual input? The simple answer is that, isolated from the outside, the visual cortex becomes hypersensitive to internal stimuli of all sorts: its own autonomous activity; signals from other brain areas — auditory, tactile, and verbal areas; and the thoughts and emotions of the blinded individual. Sometimes, as sight deteriorates, hallucinations occur — of geometrical patterns, or occasionally of silent, moving figures or scenes that appear and disappear spontaneously, without any relation to the contents of consciousness, or intention, or context.

Something perhaps akin to this is described by Hull as occurring almost convulsively as he was losing the last of his sight. "About a year after I was registered blind," he writes, "I began to have such strong images of what people's faces looked like that they were almost like hallucinations."

These imperious images were so engrossing as to preempt consciousness: "Sometimes," Hull adds, "I would become so absorbed in gazing upon these images, which seemed to come and go without any intention on my part, that I would entirely lose the thread of what was being said to me. I would come back with a shock . . . and I would feel as if I had dropped off to sleep for a few minutes in front of the wireless." Though related to the context of speaking with people, these visions came and went in their own way, without any reference to his intentions, conjured up not by him but by his brain.

The fact that Hull is the only one of the four authors to describe this sort of release phenomenon is perhaps an indication that his visual cortex was starting to escape from his control. One has to wonder whether this signaled its impending demise, at least as an organ of useful visual imagery and memory. Why this should have occurred with him, and how common such a course is, is something one can only speculate on.

Torey, unlike Hull, clearly played a very active role in building up his visual imagery, took control of it the moment the bandages were taken off, and never apparently experienced, or allowed, the sort of involuntary imagery Hull describes. Perhaps this was because he was already very at home with visual imagery, and used to manipulating it in his own way. We know that Torey was very visually inclined before his accident, and skilled from boyhood in creating visual narratives based on the film scripts his father gave him. We have no such information about Hull, for his journal entries start only when he has become blind.

For Lusseyran and Tenberken, there is an added physiological factor: both were attracted to painting, in love with colors, and strongly synesthetic — prone to visualizing numbers, letters, words, music, etc., as shapes and colors — before becoming blind. They already had an overconnectedness, a "cross talk" between the visual cortex and other parts of the brain primarily concerned with language, sound, and music. Given such a neurological situation (synesthesia is congenital, often familial), the persistence of visual imagery and synesthesia, or its heightening, might be almost inevitable in the event of blindness.

Torey required months of intense cognitive discipline dedicated to improving his visual imagery, making it more tenacious, more stable, more malleable, whereas Lusseyran seemed to do this almost effortlessly from the start. Perhaps this was aided by the fact that Lusseyran was not yet eight when blinded (while Torey was twenty-one), and his brain was, accordingly, more plastic, more able to adapt to a new and drastic contingency.

But adaptability does not end with youth. It is clear that Arlene, becoming blind in her forties, was able to adapt in quite radical ways, too, developing not exactly synesthesia but something more flexible and useful: the ability to "see" her hands moving before her, to "see" the words of books read to her, to construct detailed visual images from verbal descriptions. Did she adapt, or did her brain do so? One has a sense that Torey's adaptation was largely shaped by conscious motive, will, and purpose; that Lusseyran's was shaped by overwhelming physiological disposition; and that Arlene's lies somewhere in between. Hull's, meanwhile, remains enigmatic.

There has been much recent work on the neural bases of visual imagery — this can be investigated by brain imaging of various types (PET scanning, functional MRIs, etc.) — and it is now generally accepted that visual imagery activates the cortex in a similar way, and with almost the same intensity, as visual perception itself. And yet studies on the effects of blindness on the human cortex have shown that functional changes may start to occur in a few days, and can become profound as the days stretch into months or years.

Torey, who is well aware of all this research, attributes Hull's loss of visual imagery and memory to the fact that he did not struggle to maintain it, to heighten and systematize and use it, as Torey himself did. (Indeed, Torey expresses horror at what he regards as Hull's passivity, at his letting himself slide into deep blindness.) Perhaps Torey was able to stave off an otherwise inevitable loss of neuronal function in the visual cortex; but perhaps, again, such neural degeneration is quite variable, irrespective of whether or not there is conscious visualization. And, of course, Hull had been losing vision gradually for many years, whereas for Torey blindness was instantaneous and total. It would be of great interest to know the results of brain imaging in the two men, and indeed to look at a large number of people with acquired blindness, to see what correlations, what predictions, could be made.

*

But what if their differences reflect an underlying predisposition independent of blindness? What of visual imagery in the sighted?

I first became conscious that there could be huge variations in visual imagery and visual memory when I was fourteen or so. My mother was a surgeon and comparative anatomist, and I had brought her a lizard's skeleton from school. She gazed at this intently for a minute, turning it round in her hands, then put it down and without looking at it again did a number of drawings of it, rotating it mentally by 30° each time, so that she produced a series, the last drawing exactly the same as the first. I could not imagine how she had done this, and when she said that she could "see" the skeleton in her mind just as clearly and vividly as if she were looking at it, and that she simply rotated the image through a twelfth of a circle each time, I felt bewildered, and very stupid. I could hardly see anything with my mind's eye — at most, faint, evanescent images over which I had no control.

I did have vivid images as I was falling asleep, and in dreams, and once when I had a high fever — but otherwise I saw nothing, or almost nothing, when I tried to visualize, and had great difficulty picturing anybody or anything. Coincidentally or not, I could not draw for toffee.

My mother had hoped I would follow in her footsteps and become a surgeon, but when she realized how lacking in visual powers I was (and how clumsy, lacking in mechanical skill, too) she resigned herself to the idea that I would have to specialize in something else.

I was, however, to get a vivid idea of what mental imagery could be like when, during the 1960s, I had a period of experimenting with large doses of amphetamines. These can produce striking perceptual changes, including dramatic enhancements of visual imagery and memory (as well as heightenings of the other senses, as I describe in "The Dog Beneath the Skin," a story in *The Man Who Mistook His Wife for a Hat*). For a period of two weeks or so, I found that I could do the most accurate anatomical drawings. I had only to look at a picture or an anatomical specimen, and its image would remain both vivid and stable, and I could easily hold it in my mind for hours. I could mentally project the image onto the paper before me — it was as clear and distinct as if projected by a camera lucida — and trace its outlines with a pencil. My drawings were not elegant, but they were, everyone agreed, very detailed and accurate, and could bear comparison with some of the drawings in our neuroanatomy textbook. This heightening of imagery attached to everything — I had only to think of a face, a place, a picture, a paragraph in a book to see it vividly in my mind. But when the amphetamine-induced state faded, after a couple of weeks, I could no longer visualize, no longer project images, no longer draw — nor have I been able to do so in the decades since.

A few months ago, at a medical conference in Boston, I spoke of Torey's and Hull's experiences of blindness, and of how "enabled" Torey seemed to be by the powers of visualization he had developed, and how "disabled" Hull was — in some ways, at least — by the loss of his powers of visual imagery and memory. After my talk, a man in the audience came up to me and asked how well, in my estimation, *sighted* people could function if they had no visual imagery. He went on to say that he had no visual imagery whatever, at least none that he could deliberately evoke, and that no one in his family had any, either. Indeed, he had assumed this was the case with everyone, until he came to participate in some psychological tests at Harvard and realized that he apparently lacked a mental power that all the other students, in varying degrees, had.

"And what do you do?" I asked him, wondering what this poor man *could* do.

"I am a surgeon," he replied. "A vascular surgeon. An anatomist, too. And I design solar panels."

But how, I asked him, did he recognize what he was seeing?

"It's not a problem," he answered. "I guess there must be representations or models in the brain that get matched up with what I am seeing and doing. But they are not conscious. I cannot evoke them."

This seemed to be at odds with my mother's experience — she, clearly, did have extremely vivid and readily manipulable visual imagery, though (it now seemed) this may have been a bonus, a luxury, and not a prerequisite for her career as a surgeon.

Is this also the case with Torey? Is his greatly developed visual imagery, though clearly a source of much pleasure, not as indispensable as he takes it to be? Might he, in fact, have done everything he did, from carpentry to roof repair to making a model of the mind, without any conscious imagery at all? He himself raises this question.

The role of mental imagery in thinking was explored by Francis Galton, Darwin's irrepressible cousin, who wrote on subjects as various as fingerprints, eugenics, dog whistles, criminality, twins, visionaries, psychometric measures, and hereditary genius. His inquiry into visual imagery took the form of a questionnaire, with such questions as "Can you recall with distinctness the features of all near relations and many other persons? Can you at will cause your mental image . . . to sit, stand, or turn slowly around? Can you . . . see it with enough distinctness to enable you to sketch it leisurely (supposing yourself able to draw)?" The vascular surgeon would have been hopeless on such tests — indeed, it was questions such as these which had floored him when he was a student at Harvard. And yet, finally, how much had it mattered?

As to the significance of such imagery, Galton is ambiguous and guarded. He suggests, in one breath, that "scientific men, as a class, have feeble powers of visual representation" and, in another, that "a vivid visualizing faculty is of much importance in connection with the higher processes of generalized thoughts." He feels that "it is undoubtedly the fact that mechanicians, engineers and architects usually possess the faculty of seeing mental images with remarkable clearness and precision," but goes on to say, "I am, however, bound to say, that the missing faculty seems to be replaced so serviceably by other modes of conception . . . that men who declare themselves entirely deficient in the power of seeing mental pictures can nevertheless give lifelike descriptions of what they have seen, and can otherwise express themselves as if they were gifted with a vivid visual imagination. They can also become painters of the rank of Royal Academicians." I have a cousin, a professional architect, who maintains that he cannot visualize anything whatever. "How do you think?" I once asked him. He shook his head and said, "I don't know." Do any of us, finally, know how we think?

When I talk to people, blind or sighted, or when I try to think of my own internal representations, I find myself uncertain whether words, symbols, and images of various types are the primary tools of thought or whether there are forms of thought antecedent to all of these, forms of thought essentially amodal. Psychologists have sometimes spoken of "interlingua" or "mentalese," which they conceive to be the brain's own language, and Lev Vygotsky, the great Russian psychologist, used to speak of "thinking in pure meanings." I cannot decide whether this is nonsense or profound truth — it is this sort of reef I end up on when I think about thinking.

Galton's seemingly contradictory statements about imagery — is it antithetical to abstract thinking, or integral to it? — may stem from his failure to distinguish between fundamentally different levels of imagery. Simple visual imagery such as he describes may suffice for the design of a screw, an engine, or a surgical operation, and it may be relatively easy to model these essentially reproductive forms of imagery or to simulate them by constructing video games or virtual realities of various sorts. Such powers may be invaluable, but there is something passive and mechanical and impersonal about them, which makes them utterly different from the higher and more personal powers of the imagination, where there is a continual struggle for concepts and form and meaning, a calling upon all the powers of the self. Imagination dissolves and transforms, unifies and creates, while drawing upon the "lower" powers of memory and association. It is by such imagination, such "vision," that we create or construct our individual worlds.

At this level, one can no longer say of one's mental landscapes what is visual, what is auditory, what is image, what is language, what is intellectual, what is emotional — they are all fused together and imbued with our own individual perspectives and values. Such a unified vision shines out from Hull's memoir no less than from Torey's, despite the fact that one has become "nonvisual" and the other "hypervisual." What seems at first to be so decisive a difference between the two men is not, finally, a radical one, so far as personal development and sensibility go. Even though the paths they have followed might seem irreconcilable, both men have "used" blindness (if one can employ such a term for processes which are deeply mysterious, and far below, or above, the level of consciousness and voluntary control) to release their own creative capacities and emotional selves, and both have achieved a rich and full realization of their own individual worlds.

LUC SANTE

My Lost City

FROM THE NEW YORK REVIEW OF BOOKS

THE IDEA OF WRITING a book about New York City first entered my head around 1980, when I was a writer more wishfully than in actual fact, spending my nights in clubs and bars and my days rather casually employed in the mailroom of this magazine. It was there that Rem Koolhaas's epochal *Delirious New York* fell into my hands. "New York is a city that will be replaced by another city" is the phrase that sticks in my mind. Koolhaas's book, published in 1978 as a paean to the unfinished project of New York the Wonder City, seemed like an archaeological reverie, an evocation of the hubris and ambition of a dead city. I gazed wonderingly at its illustrations, which showed sights as dazzling and remote as Nineveh and Tyre. The irony is that many of their subjects stood within walking distance: the Chrysler Building, the McGraw-Hill Building, Rockefeller Center. But they didn't convey the feeling they had when they were new. In Koolhaas's pages New York City was manifestly the location of the utopian and dystopian fantasies of the silent-film era. It was *Metropolis,* with elevated roadways, giant searchlights probing the heavens, flying machines navigating the skyscraper canyons. It was permanently set in the future.

The New York I lived in, on the other hand, was rapidly regressing. It was a ruin in the making, and my friends and I were camped out amid its potsherds and tumuli. This did not distress me — quite the contrary. I was enthralled by decay and eager for more: ailanthus trees growing through cracks in the asphalt, ponds and streams forming in leveled blocks and slowly making their way to the shoreline, wild animals returning from centuries of exile. Such a scenario did not seem so far-fetched then. Already in the mid-1970s, when I was a student at Columbia, my windows gave out onto the plaza of the School of International Affairs, where on winter nights troops of feral dogs would arrive to bed down on the heating grates. Since then the city had lapsed even further. On Canal Street stood a five-story building empty of human tenants that had been taken over from top to bottom by pigeons. If you walked east on Houston Street from the Bowery on a summer night, the jungle growth of vacant blocks gave a foretaste of the impending wilderness, when lianas would engird the skyscrapers and mushrooms would cover Times Square.

At that time much of Manhattan felt depopulated even in daylight. Aside from the high-intensity blocks of midtown and the financial district, the place seemed to be inhabited principally by slouchers and loungers, loose-joints vendors and teenage hustlers, panhandlers and site-specific drunks, persons whose fleabags put them out on the street at eight and only permitted reentry at six. Many businesses seemed to remain open solely to give their owners shelter from the elements. How often did a dollar cross the counter of the plastic-lettering concern, or the prosthetic-limb showroom, or the place that ostensibly traded in office furniture but displayed in its window a Chinese typewriter and a stuffed two-headed calf? Outside under an awning on a hot afternoon would be a card table, textured like an old suitcase with four metal corners, and around it four guys playing dominoes. Maybe they'd have a little TV set, up on a milk crate, plugged into the base of a streetlight, issuing baseball. On every corner was a storefront that advertised Optimo or Te-Amo or Romeo y Julieta, and besides cigars they sold smut and soda pop and rubbers and candy and glassine envelopes and sometimes police equipment. And there were Donuts Muffins Snack Bar and Chinas Comidas and Hand Laundry and Cold Beer Grocery and Barber College, all old friends. Those places weren't like commercial establishments, exactly, more like rooms in your house. They tended to advertise just their descriptions; their names, like those of deities, were kept hidden, could be discovered only by reading the license tacked up somewhere behind the cash register. At the bodega you could buy plantains and coffee and *malta* and lard, or a single cigarette — a loosie — or a sheet of paper, an envelope, and a stamp.

*

I drifted down from the Upper West Side to the Lower East Side in 1978. Most of my friends made the transition around the same time. You could have an apartment all to yourself for less than $150 a month. In addition, the place was happening. It was happening, that is, in two or at most three dingy bars that doubled as clubs, a bookstore or record store or two, and a bunch of individual apartments and individual imaginations. All of us were in that stage of youth when your star may not yet have risen, but your moment is the only one on the clock. We had the temerity to laugh at the hippies, shamefully backdated by half a decade. In our arrogance we were barely conscious of the much deeper past that lay all around. We didn't ask ourselves why the name carved above the door of the public library on Second Avenue was in German, or why busts of nineteenth-century composers could be seen on a second-story lintel on Fourth Street. Our neighborhood was so chockablock with ruins we didn't question the existence of vast bulks of shuttered theaters, or wonder when they had been new. Our apartments were furnished exclusively through scavenging, but we didn't find it notable that nearly all our living rooms featured sewing-machine tables with cast-iron bases.

When old people died without wills or heirs, the landlord would set the belongings of the deceased out on the sidewalk, since that was cheaper than hiring a removal van. We would go through the boxes and help ourselves, and come upon photographs and books and curiosities, evidence of lives and passions spent in the turmoil of 1910 and 1920, of the Mexican Border War and Emma Goldman's *Mother Earth* and vaudeville and labor unions and the shipping trade, and we might be briefly diverted, but we were much more interested in the boxes on the next stoop containing someone's considerably more recent record collection. One day something fell out of an old book, the business card of a beauty parlor that had stood on Avenue C near Third Street, probably in the 1920s. I marveled at it, unable to picture something as sedate as a beauty parlor anywhere near that corner, by then a heroin souk.

The neighborhood was desolate, so underpopulated that landlords would give you a month's free rent just for signing a lease, many buildings being less than half full, but it was far from tranquil. We might feel smug about being robbed on the street, since none of us had any money, and we looked it, and junkies — as distinct from the crackheads of a decade later — would generally not stab you for chump change. Nevertheless, if you did not have the wherewithal to install gates on your windows you would be burglarized repeatedly, and where would you be without your stereo? In the blocks east of Avenue A the situation was dramatically worse. In 1978 I got used to seeing large fires in that direction every night, usually set by arsonists hired by landlords of empty buildings who found it an easy choice to make, between paying property taxes and collecting insurance. By 1980 Avenue C was a lunar landscape of vacant blocks and hollow tenement shells. Over there, commerce — in food or clothing, say — was often conducted out of car trunks, but the most thriving industry was junk, and it alone made use of marginally viable specimens of the building stock. The charred stairwells, the gaping floorboards, the lack of lighting, the entryways consisting of holes torn in ground-floor walls — all served the psychological imperatives of the heroin trade.

Dealers knew that white middle-class junkies thrived on squalor, that it was a component of their masochism, and that their masochism, with an admixture of bourgeois guilt, was what had drawn them to the neighborhood. The dealers proved this thesis daily, at least to themselves, by requiring their customers to stand for an hour in pouring rain before allowing them inside, for example, and then shifting them up five flights with interstitial waits on the landings, and then possibly, whimsically, refusing to sell to them once they finally arrived in front of the slotted door. Of course, a junkie becomes a masochist by virtue of his habit, and any of those people would have done much worse to obtain a fix, but the dealers were correct to a degree. Some did indeed come to the neighborhood to revel in squalor, and junkiedom was part of the package, as surfing would be if they had moved to Hawaii instead. They were down with the romance of it, had read the books and gazed upon the pop stars. Junkiehood could happen to anyone, for a complex of reasons that included availability, boredom, anxiety, depression, and self-loathing, but many were tourists of scag, and if they wiped out as a consequence it was the inevitable effect of a natural law, like gravity. They had been culled.

For those of us who had been in the city for a while, squalor was not an issue. Most of the city was squalid. If this troubled you, you left, and if you were taken by the romance of it, a long regimen of squalor in everyday life would eventually scrub your illusions gray. At this remove I'm sometimes retrospectively amazed by what I took for granted. Large fires a few blocks away every night for a couple of years would seem conducive to a perpetually troubled state of mind, but they just became weather. I spent the summer of 1975 in a top-floor apartment on 107th Street, where at night the windows were lit by the glow of fires along Amsterdam Avenue. A sanitation strike was in progress, and mounds of refuse, reeking in the heat, decorated the curbs of every neighborhood, not excepting those whose houses were manned by doormen. Here, though, instead of being double-bagged in plastic, they were simply set on fire every night. The spectacle achieved the transition from apocalyptic to dully normal in a matter of days.

Two summers later I was living with two roommates in a tall building on Broadway at 101st Street. It had both a doorman and an elevator operator; most of the other tenants were elderly European Jews; our rent for five large rooms was $400 a month. I note these facts because the other buildings lining Broadway in that area were mainly "single-room-occupancy" hotels, tenanted by the luckless, the bereft, the unemployable, dipsomaniacs, junkies, released mental patients — exactly that portion of the population that would be turned out and left to conduct its existence in shelters or doorways or drainpipes or jails in the following decade. What those people had in common was that they could not blend into mainstream society; otherwise there was no stereotyping them. For example, a rather eerie daily entertainment in the warmer months was provided by a group of middle-aged transvestites who would lean against parked cars in their minidresses and bouffantes and issue forth perfect four-part doo-wop harmonies. You had to wonder in which volume of the Relic label's "Golden Groups" series they might figure, perhaps pictured on the sleeve in younger, thinner, pencil-mustached, tuxedo-clad incarnations. For them, as for most people on the street — including, we liked to think, us — New York City was the only imaginable home, the only place that posted no outer limit on appearance or behavior.

When the blackout happened, on the evening of July 13, 1977, it briefly seemed as though the hour of reckoning had arrived, when all those outsiders would seize control. Naturally, no such thing occurred. The outsiders seized televisions and toaster ovens and three-piece suits and standing rib roasts and quarts of Old Mr. Boston and cartons of Newports and perhaps sectional sofas, but few would have known what to do with the levers of society had they been presented in a velvet-lined box. But then, my friends and I wouldn't have known, either. For all the obvious differences between the SRO dwellers and ourselves, we were alike in our disconnection from any but the most parochial idea of community. In the end, the mob dissolved like a fist when you open your hand, and the benches on the Broadway traffic islands were repopulated by loungers occasionally pulling down a bottle hanging by a string from a leaf-enshrouded tree branch overhead.

The looters were exemplary Americans, whose immediate impulse in a crisis was to see to the acquisition of consumable goods. They had no interest in power. Neither did anyone I knew. We just wanted power to go away. Sometimes it seemed as though it already had. In those days the police, when not altogether invisible, were nearly benign, or at least showed no interest in the likes of us, being occupied with actual violent crime. Almost everybody had a story about walking down the street smoking a joint and suddenly realizing they had just passed a uniformed patrolman, who could not possibly have failed to detect the odor but resolutely looked the other way. Casual illegality was unremarkable and quotidian, a matter of drug use and theft of goods and services, petty things. We slid by in weasel jobs, in part because we were preoccupied with our avocations and in part because a certain lassitude had come over us, a brand of the era.

The revolution was deferred indefinitely, then, because we were too comfortable. Not, mind you, that we didn't live in dumps where the floors slanted and the walls were held together with duct tape and the window frames had last been caulked in 1912 and the heat regularly went off for a week at a time in the depths of winter. The landlords were the primary villains and the most visible manifestations of authority. Very few still went from door to door collecting rents, but most could be physically located, sitting at a secondhand metal desk on the telephone in some decrepit two-room office, and that included the ones who went home to mansions in Great Neck. Real estate was a buyer's market, and owners needed to hustle for every dollar, and were correspondingly reluctant to make expenditures that would be any greater than the anticipated legal costs of not making them. At the same time, you could let the rent go for a while and not face eviction, because the eviction process itself would cost the landlord some kale, besides which it might be hard to find anyone else to take up the lease, so that a tenant who only paid every other month was better than nothing. We were comfortable because we could live on very little, satisfying most requirements in a fiercely minimal style for which we had developed a defining and mitigating aesthetic. It was lucky if not entirely coincidental that the threadbare overcoat you could obtain for a reasonable three dollars just happened to be the height of fashion.

Suspicion in the hinterlands of New York City's moral fiber and quality of life, rampant since the early nineteenth century, reached new heights during the 1970s. Hadn't the president himself urged the city to drop dead? If you told people almost anywhere in the country then that you lived in New York, they tended to look at you as if you had boasted of dining on wormwood and gall. Images of the city on big or small screens, fictional or ostensibly journalistic, were a blur of violence, drugs, and squalor. A sort of apotheosis appeared in John Carpenter's *Escape from New York* (1981), in which the city has become a maximum-security prison by default. The last honest folk having abandoned the place, the authorities have merely locked it up, permitting the scum within to rule themselves, with the understanding that they will before long kill one another off. The story may have been a futuristic action-adventure, but for most Americans the premise was strict naturalism, with the sole exception of the locks, which ought by rights to have been in place. Aside from the matter of actual violence, drugs, and squalor, there was the fact that in the 1970s New York City was not a part of the United States at all. It was an offshore interzone with no shopping malls, few major chains, very few born-again Christians who had not been sent there on a mission, no golf courses, no subdivisions.

Downtown we were proud of this, naturally. We thought of the place as a free city, like one of those prewar nests of intrigue and licentiousness where exiles and lamsters and refugees found shelter in a tangle of improbable juxtapositions. I had never gotten around to changing my nationality from the one assigned me at birth, but I would have declared myself a citizen of New York City had such a stateless state existed, its flag a solid black. But what happened instead is that Reagan was elected and the musk of profit once again scented the air. It took all of us a while to realize that this might affect us in intimate ways — we were fixated on nuclear war. So while we were dozing money crept in, making its presence felt slowly, in oddly assorted and apparently peripheral ways. The first sign was the new phenomenon of street vendors. Before the early 1980s you never saw people selling old books or miscellaneous refuse from flattened boxes on the sidewalk. If you truly wanted to sell things you could rent a storefront for next to nothing, assuming you weren't choosy about location. But now, very quickly, Astor Place became a vast flea market, with vendors ranging from collectors of old comic books to optimists attempting to unload whatever they had skimmed from garbage cans the night before. Those effects of the deceased that had once been set out for the pickings of all were now the stock of whoever happened upon them first. The daily spectacle was delirious, uncanny, the range of goods boundless and utterly random. You had the feeling you would one day find there evidence of your missing twin, your grandfather's secret diary, a photograph of the first girl whose image kept you awake at night, and all the childhood toys you had loved and lost.

What it meant, though, was that people who had previously gotten by on charm and serendipity now needed ready cash. It also meant that there now existed consumers who would pay folding money for stuff that had once been available for nothing to anyone who read the sidewalks. Part of the reason the *Luftmenschen* had to have dollars was the vast increase in heroin traffic, caused by a steep plunge in prices. All of a sudden people who had been strictly holiday users were getting themselves strung out. While this was happening the neighborhood was filling up, rapidly. Every day the streets were visibly more congested than the day before. The vacancy rate fell to near zero. Speculators were buying up even gutted shells, even tenements so unsound they would require a fortune to fix. Was the fall in the price index of junk connected to the rise in that of real estate? Street-corner theorists were certain we were all marked for death. It was obvious, no? If you OD'd or went to jail your apartment would become vacant, and legally subject to a substantial rent increase. A folklore emerged, with tales of people paying rent to sleep on examination tables in medical offices, of landlords murdering rent-controlled tenants or simply locking them out and disposing of their chattel. Whether those tales were true or not, everyone spent increasing amounts of time in housing court, battling the fourth or fifth landlord in as many months, who all but treated the property as vacant. The neighborhood was subjected to lifestyle pieces in the glossies; a crowd of galleries sprang up. You could spot millionaires making the rounds in old sweaters.

The more I felt I was losing my city, the more preoccupied I became with it. I gradually became interested in its past, an interest that grew into an obsession. It was triggered by what seemed like chance — by things I spotted on the flattened cardboard boxes on the sidewalk. On Astor Place I acquired for a dollar a disintegrating copy of Junius Henry Browne's *The Great Metropolis* (1868) and, a week later, Joseph Mitchell's incomparable *McSorley's Wonderful Saloon,* a 1940s paperback with a ridiculous cover that almost dissuaded me from picking it up — I had never heard of it or him. In a heap of miscellanea on Seventh Street I found a pristine copy of Chuck Connors's very rare *Bowery Life,* and took it home for fifty cents. In a parking lot on Canal Street I bought a stereoscope card of the Second Avenue El; a table outside a junkshop on Thirtieth Street yielded lithographs pulled from nineteenth-century copies of *Valentine's Manual.* These things were mysterious, slices of a complex past of which I had little sense. I was already fascinated by the strange process whereby the glamorous city of the 1920s had become the entropic slum that was my home; now I was discovering that the slum had far deeper roots.

One day, probably early in 1980, a film crew commandeered Eleventh Street between Avenues A and B and, with minimal adjustments, returned the block to the way it had looked in 1910. All they did was to pull the plywood coverings off storefront windows, paint names in gold letters on those windows, and pile goods up behind them. They spread straw in the gutters and hung washlines across the street. They fitted selected residents with period clothes and called forth a parade of horse-drawn conveyances. They were shooting a few scenes of *Ragtime* (Milos Forman, 1981). After the production packed up a week later, the Dominican evangelical church on Avenue A held a sort of exorcism ceremony in the middle of the intersection. I hadn't paid much attention to the goings-on, but I had been struck by how little effort was needed to conjure up a seemingly unimaginable past. When I walked down that street at night, with all the trappings up but the crew absent, I felt like a ghost. The tenements were aspects of the natural landscape, like caves or rock ledges, across which all of us — inhabitants, landlords, dope dealers, beat cops, tourists — flitted for a few seasons, like the pigeons and the cockroaches and the rats, barely registering as individuals in the ceaseless churning of generations.

And now everything was up for grabs. The tenements were old and unstable; the speculators were undoubtedly buying them up for the value of their lots. One day in the near future they would be razed and housing units at least superficially more upscale would be built. Maybe the whole neighborhood would be reconfigured, the way Washington Market and the far Lower East Side were swept, to the point where whole streets had disappeared. Within a decade, all of us who had lived there in the last days of the tenement era might seem as distant and insubstantial as the first people to move in when the buildings were new. I told myself it was inevitable. I remembered Baudelaire's warning that the city changes faster than the human heart. I thought of my grandfather saying that progress was a zero-sum game in which every improvement carried with it an equivalent loss, and decided that the reverse was also true. I considered that at the very least nobody in the future would have to contend with a stiff wind sucking out an entire loose windowpane, as had once happened to me. Then I pictured the high-rises themselves falling inch by inch into ruin. I bore an old-timer's resentment toward the children of privilege who were moving into tastefully done-up flats and about to start calling themselves New Yorkers, even Lower East Siders, and go spend decades without once having spent a winter sitting in front of an open oven wearing an overcoat and hat, or having to move pots and pans and furniture by subway in the middle of the night, or having bottles thrown at them by crack dealers, or having to walk home from Brooklyn in the rain for want of carfare. But it was for more than personal reasons that I wanted to prevent amnesia from setting in.

Now, more than a decade after I finally finished my book *Low*

Life, the city has changed in ways I could not have pictured. The tenements are mostly still standing, but I could not afford to live in any of my former apartments, including the ones I found desperately shabby when I was much more inured to shabbiness. Downtown, even the places that used to seem permanently beyond the pale have been colonized by prosperity. Instead of disappearing, local history has been preserved as a seasoning, most visibly in names of bars. The economy has gone bad, but money shows no signs of loosening its grip. New York is neither the Wonder City nor a half-populated ruin but a vulnerable, overcrowded, anxious, half-deluded, all-too-human town, shaken by a cataclysm nobody could have foreseen. I don't live there anymore, and I have trouble going there and walking around because the streets are too haunted by the ghosts of my own history. I wasn't born in New York, and I may never live there again, and just thinking about it makes me melancholy, but I was changed forever by it, and my imagination is manacled to it, and I wear its mark the way you wear a scar. Whatever happens, whether I like it or not, New York City is fated always to remain my home.

MARK SLOUKA

Arrow and Wound

FROM HARPER'S MAGAZINE

FIVE YEARS BEFORE his death in 1986, Jaroslav Seifert, the unofficial poet laureate of Prague (and official Nobel laureate of
Stockholm), published *Všecky krásy světa* (*All the Beauties of the
Earth*), a book that was neither autobiography nor history nor
fiction, precisely, but all of these and more: a gallery of small, precise portraits, each characteristically anchored in the mind's eye by
a single, telling anecdote: a peddler's cart, picturesque with eight
decades' worth of well-turned stories and three o'clock in the
morning, second-bottle speculations; a collection of madeleines
(or, rather, small Bohemian pastries), summoning a past both personal and, inevitably, cultural. In short, a celebration and a leave-
taking: tender, spendthrift, large. A visitor to Tolstoy's Yasnaya
Polyana recalled seeing the count, then in his last years, scoop a
double handful of violets from the wet earth, breathe in their
aroma with a kind of ecstasy, then let them fall carelessly at his feet.
That gesture, captured on paper, is Seifert's book.

But this is not about *Všecky krásy světa*, exactly, nor is it about Tolstoy. It is about a curious little section near the book's center, in
which Seifert — no decadent after all, no Baudelaire — admits to
having once been jealous of another writer's near-death experience. That other writer was Fyodor Mikhailovich Dostoevsky.

The incident at Semenovsky Square that winter morning of December 22, 1849, when Dostoevsky and his fellow subversives were
led before the firing squad in a mock execution, then pardoned at
the last moment in order to impress upon them the full magnitude
of the czar's mercy, is well known; like Byron's incestuous relation-

ship with his half-sister, say, or Wilde's self-aided lynching, it has passed out of literary biography and joined that select company of events the generally literate misremember with confidence. Still, the narrative of those hours, progressing like a medieval passion play from suffering to near death to something like resurrection, remains compelling. Reconstituted in the willing imagination, it can stab us, suddenly, unexpectedly, with the quickening thought of our own extinction — a nectar not to be indulged in too often, lest it become a self-indulgence, an obscenity.

Imagine it, then. The sounds of voices and carriages in the prison courtyard that morning. The church bells, uncharacteristically diminished by the sound of cell doors opening down the corridor — the sudden, irrepressible, dizzying thought of freedom. You are given your clothes — the ones you were arrested in eight months ago — and told to remember to put on your socks, for the morning is cold. You must hurry. No one answers your questions.

Dawn. You are led into the snowy yard. A line of carriages stands waiting, flanked by mounted police. Your comrades are there; you see Speshnev, peering out of a shaggy mat of tangled hair and matted beard, and then you are in the carriage. The windows are covered with frost. Perhaps you scratch at the pane with a fingernail. Perhaps the guard sitting next to you lets you. You want to see the world. God in heaven, you say to yourself, it's over. A day, a week, a month, whatever it takes for the process to run its course, and it will be over. You'll see your brother again. You'll be able to release the stories burgeoning in your mind, threatening to burst your skull. You'll be free.

The line of carriages comes to a stop. Semenovsky Square lies under a foot of snow. The sun appears and disappears behind the mist. Soldiers stand around the perimeter of the square. A small crowd has gathered on the far end. You wait around in the snow, talking excitedly with your old comrades. No one knows what is happening. A four-sided wooden scaffolding, draped in black crepe, stands in the center of the square. Probably you will be sentenced to some time of penal servitude, lectured on your presumption and ingratitude. There are worse things.

It is then, maybe, that you first notice the row of head-high stakes, like great, fat nails holding down the field of snow.

Or do you? In the sudden shock of knowing (which instantly reshapes the minutes remaining into a strange, circumscribed eternity, an ocean disappearing down a drain), can a person think at all, much less in metaphor? What really happens in those final few moments? Does the world, under the pressure of extinction, blossom into tropes as never before, madly, ferociously, birthing stakes like Christic nails, or crosses symbolically shorn of the horizontal, or huge, ironic exclamation points? Does it, instead, taper down to some small perfection — the godhead glimpsed in a drop of sweat, freezing to a pearl? Or does the world simply bend its head and grow mute, and you with it? And if it does, isn't it possible that, should you be miraculously delivered out of that silence by the czar's pardon, you would emerge with a voice that could speak the truths of this world with a clarity unavailable to others? That you would be repaid for your suffering — as is sometimes the case, after all — in the coin of wisdom?

It would be nice to think so. Which brings us back to Seifert, who did. "Though fully aware of the impossibility of drawing a comparison between us," he writes, self-effacingly, "I envied Dostoevsky . . . that singular experience: to be sentenced to death, to know the moment when you must, of necessity, say goodbye to life, accept that unappeasable fact, and then taste again the certainty and sweetness of life, and save yourself." The notion compelled him, fascinated him. "To experience those few, horrifying minutes when time is quickly dragging you to your erasure," he continues, "and then to look again upon the broad expanse of time that stretches out before you like a gorgeous landscape. What a drama it must be, which plays itself out in a man during those few instants! What does an experience like that mean, for anyone, but particularly for a writer, who has the ability to articulate it?"

Seifert had been able to answer that question for himself. Saturday, May 5, 1945, found him, then forty-four years old, in the Lidové building on Hybernská Street in Prague, laboring, along with a small crew of fellow journalists, to bring out the next edition of the newly decriminalized newspaper *Rudé právo*. Outside their windows, the stylus of history had begun to move, inscribing another bloody paragraph. After six years of occupation, the fingers of the Reich had begun suddenly to loosen. In a frenzy of rage and joy, Czechs of all ages began demolishing German businesses, lighting fires, erecting barricades. The Prague uprising had begun.

It would take its measure of lives before it was done. The Germans, as Seifert and his companions soon learned, had taken a stand in the Anglobank building just down the way. The concussion of cannon and the staccato pattering of small-arms fire filled the streets; windows shattered; the Masaryk train station was in flames. Seeking safety from the crossfire, the entire staff, along with a group of citizens who had taken shelter with them, moved down to the basement, then lower still, into the paper-storage rooms, and continued writing. Days passed. They barely ate. Somehow, incredibly, the presses continued to roll.

And then, as Seifert tells it, things turned. Quickly. The Germans retook the train station. From there, they captured the building on the corner of Hybernská and Havlíčková streets and entered the system of passageways connecting the buildings' cellars. And suddenly Seifert and his comrades were being marched to the train station, where, they were informed, they would be executed. Just like that. In the station, their shoes sticky with blood, they stood by a heap of dead Czechs while the Germans worked to dispatch a train filled with tier upon tier of their own wounded. They waited. A young boy, found with an antique bayonet under his coat, was shot in the back of the neck.

When the train didn't leave, they were led back out, two by two. Buildings were burning. The heat was immense. They were lined up against a wall, presently, and told they would be shot in the courtyard behind them as soon as it was empty of German families preparing to flee. And again they waited.

So what did Seifert do, those ostensibly last few minutes of his life? What did he think? This was it, after all — the experience he had envied Dostoevsky. This was consciousness in the crucible, distilled to its essence. Did the heat of those minutes crystallize his understanding into some new, unbreakable alloy? Reorder his life?

Apparently not. Standing against the wall next to his friend Píša, waiting to be shot, Seifert discovered a piece of bread and some cheese, no longer quite fresh, in his pocket. The two ate it hungrily. For a few moments, he tells us, he thought about his family. He knew they were relatively safe. The thought that he might never see them again did not occur to him. He looked at the buildings across the street. All the windows were closed. Now and then a corner of a curtain lifted slightly and a face appeared. Then, far off,

he spotted the public toilet by the Karlín viaduct and suddenly recalled how, when he was a boy, someone had drawn a wonderfully
obscene picture of a woman on one of its walls, and how he and his
friends would walk kilometers just to look at it. How it had aroused
and disturbed them. Then he looked again at the buildings across
the street. Smoke rose languidly out of the chimneys. He found
himself wondering what the people inside, who didn't have to
stand with their backs against a wall, were making for lunch.

Then, after twenty minutes or half an hour had passed, he and
the others were informed that they could go.

And that was that, claims Seifert. The condemned scattered in
all directions. And when, soon afterward, the city's radios announced that Nazi Germany had officially capitulated and that the
war in Europe was effectively over, they forgot all about what had
just passed. Seifert himself never thought of it. Decades later, finding himself in that same district of the city, he actually passed by
the very wall he had stood against that fateful day, and never even
realized it until after he'd arrived home and was sitting down to
dinner.

So much for Semenovsky Square. So much for the romance of almost dying. Pushed to the wall, given ample time to consider his
situation, to breathe, to weep, Seifert had eaten lunch. No epiphany. No prophetic voice rising out of the silence. Nothing.

Compare and contrast. Standing in the snow in Semenovsky
Square, Dostoevsky experienced a kind of "mystic terror," a strange
and fearful exaltation. *"Nous serons avec le Christ"* (We shall be with
Christ), he supposedly whispered to Speshnev, quoting Victor
Hugo's *Le dernier jour d'un condamné*. Seifert just looked at the ugly
buildings across the street. From the moment the roll of the drums
signaled to him that his life would be spared, Dostoevsky's life had
shifted course, surging, like a river around an insurmountable ob-
stacle, toward the kind of tortured religiosity we now associate with
his greatest work. Seifert? Seifert was untouched. Life went on.
Thirty-five years later, writing about the hour he had expected to
be his last, he recalled (not without some small, remembered pleasure) a picture of a spread-eagled woman drawn with a piece of
coal on the side of a public toilet.

Whose version do we believe? I suspect that the romantics

among us (as well as the more conventionally and narrowly devout) side with Dostoevsky. And perhaps the rest of us do as well.
How could a person not be touched, altered, by such an experience? We don't want to be like an old horse led to the slaughter.
We want awareness, insight. We want to believe that our consciousness, like putty, will take the imprint of great events. Suffer, and
ye shall be rewarded with, if nothing else, the memory of your suffering. No, when it comes to the art of almost dying, Dostoevsky is
our man.

Literature backs us up. "And anything that happened to me afterwards, I never felt the same about again," concludes the narrator of Frank O'Connor's great short story "Guests of the Nation,"
looking back on the day when the exigencies of war forced him to
kill two men who had become his friends. "They are not to lose it,"
intones Faulkner, referring to the witnesses of Joe Christmas's murder in *Light in August,* "in whatever peaceful valleys, beside whatever placid and reassuring streams of old age, in the mirroring
faces of whatever children they will contemplate old disasters and
newer hopes." Yes, indeed, we say. Just so. And although we recognize the fact that O'Connor's and Faulkner's narrators, unlike
Dostoevsky, contemplated their own extinction only by proxy, as it
were, they still flatter our sense of the gravity of the thing, our notion of what it *ought* to be like. Death is a big deal, after all. If it
frightens us, it *ought* to be large.

What of Seifert, then? Do we write off his amnesia as denial, de-
bunk him with a pinch of Freud? Do we see his parable of the
bread and the public toilet for what it is: a re-presentation of
events, an attempt to impose a shape, nearly thirty-six years afterward, on a harrowing, unmanageable experience — in sum, a
fiction? Do we classify it, perhaps, as an absurdist and in many
ways classically Czech response to trauma? Do we pat the author on
the head and leave him to carve his figures in the tranquillity of
old age?

I think not. To do so, it seems to me, would be to assume that
consciousness can be teased apart from its retelling, which it cannot. To see Dostoevsky's experience as essentially truthful, and
Seifert's as some form of artifice, is to limit the dominion of
fiction, which, from the moment we wake to the power of language, rules our lives with czarist authority and reach. It is also to
forget a more intriguing and complicated truth: that we in some

measure shape the events that befall us just as surely as we are shaped by them.

There is no point in being coy; I am indulging in these kinds of end-time speculations because I, too, was once given the "singular experience" of believing that I had arrived at the terminus of my life, of seeing myself dragged to the brink of my own erasure, only to be pardoned at the last minute by some combination of arrangement and accident. Like Seifert and Dostoevsky (in this way if in no other), I was given the opportunity to know my last minutes on earth. I didn't care for it.

My case was different, of course. Apolitical, ahistorical — set, above all, in the New World wilderness rather than in a European square — it lacked both the cruelty of Dostoevsky's mock execution and the context of routine and unimaginable suffering that backlights Seifert's ordeal. My experience, in short, was smaller. No one's life was at stake besides my own and that of the woman who was to become my wife. I suppose that in the spirit of charity I might add the life of the man who seemed to have decided to take our lives along with his own. That makes three. That morning, it seemed enough.

Quickly, then. The year was 1985. My wife and I (to see her as anything but my wife now seems like an affectation) had just crossed the spine of the Sierras. We were in our late twenties. That July morning, we were hitchhiking back to the San Joaquin Valley. I knew the area, a harsh and perpendicular landscape of considerable beauty, from some years earlier, when I had worked with a crew doing trail maintenance in the backcountry. I knew, therefore, that there were two roads to the western side of the Sierra Nevada: a highway looping around the foot of the range, and a rarely taken shortcut through the town of Lake Isabella.

We started out at first light, eager to avoid as much of the desert heat as possible, joking in the coolness. Our first three rides were uneventful. We saw the fourth from far off, a large white car, approaching the highway at an oblique angle on a ruler-straight road, raising a wall of dust. It was coming very quickly. Perhaps a quarter mile behind us, the car came to a stop, then gunned out onto the highway. It never crossed my mind that it would stop for us. I would have bet everything I had against it.

I remember him getting out of his car — thick, steak-fed body, sun-red face, not unkind — and asking us if we wanted to put our things in his trunk. "Give you kids some room," he said. He called us kids. I remember him arranging and rearranging our battered packs, closing the trunk carefully to avoid damaging something. I remember the blue jacket on the passenger seat with its "Kern County Fire Department" insignia; he drove casually, a thick right arm around the seat next to him as though around an invisible companion. We made small talk — hitchhiking etiquette. He asked where we were headed. We told him. He was going to Bakersfield, too, he said. We were in luck. We asked if he lived there. No, he lived in the Owens Valley. My wife asked politely what took him to Bakersfield. He laughed. "Well, it's like this," he said. "My mother had a massive heart attack at ten-fifteen this morning. They're trying to keep her alive until I get there."

Somewhere inside, an alarm went off. A small herd of questions, like panicked horses, stampeded across the landscape. Why would a man racing to his mother's deathbed stop to pick up two hitchhikers? Why would he take five minutes to arrange their packs in his trunk? Why would he be so calm, so level, so apparently undisturbed?

And yet, on the surface, everything seemed fine. He was driving well enough — a bit casually, perhaps, a bit faster than necessary, but well within the normal range. When we expressed our condolences, he thanked us politely. The minutes passed. No further warnings came. For a few moments, I considered asking him to let us out in the town of Lake Isabella on some pretext, but, stymied by my inability to think of a good excuse as well as, more damnably, by my own sense of politeness (the man was doing us a favor, after all), I said nothing.

In retrospect, my own inertia staggers me. I knew what lay ahead: a twenty-mile stretch of unimproved canyon road running, at times, a full 150 feet above the Kern River. A road so narrow that the few cars that did take it would invariably stop at every turn and honk to make sure no one was approaching from the other direction. A road without walls or guardrails of any kind. I had taken it twice, years before, to save the four hours, and driven it, each time, at barely over walking speed.

He stopped at the cattle guard where the canyon road began and turned half around over his right shoulder. He was smiling, but he looked as though he were about to cry. "Don't forget those seat belts, kids," he said, like a television announcer on the verge of a nervous breakdown. That same instant he stomped on the gas.

Let me dispense with the rational right off: this was not, for example, a superb if reckless driver testing his skill, or some variety of local daredevil, intimately familiar with the landscape, out to terrify the college kids. This was something entirely different. This was a man in such pain that he no longer cared to live; a man calmly holding a revolver to his temple and, with four chambers empty, two to go, pulling the trigger. This was a man making a bet with God — or lunging at him. It's quite possible that he himself had no idea why he had picked us up. In some essential way, we were beside the point.

What followed was madness. We skidded blindly into turn after turn, fishtailed wildly down the straights. Again and again we sideswiped the wall, with a sickening screech of metal, and bounced toward the edge. Once, twice, three times, I felt the right rear wheel actually begin to drop, felt the car begin to lighten, sickeningly, sensed the pull of the canyon air below us.

So what did I think of, those thirty minutes or so? Nothing very original, I'm afraid. I remember realizing, dimly, with a mixture of rage and disbelief, that this was it. That my life, our life, was somehow, impossibly, over. I remember my mind racing madly, searching for options. Hit the crazy bastard? Unthinkable. There was no margin. We were over the margin already. Try to say something, calm him somehow? Impossible. He was elsewhere now. And I knew, as surely as I've ever known anything, that if I said even one word, he would turn around to look at me and simply turn the wheel into the empty air.

I'll confess that I did not believe we would live. I knew the road we were on. We had nearly gone over a half-dozen times already, and there were sixteen or seventeen miles of curves still ahead. My wife, a genuinely brave woman, had buried her face in my shirt.

But here's the thing: although I knew we weren't going to make it, my mind, divided against itself, stupidly refused to accept that fact. And so, never a religious man, I did the only thing I could: I willed that car to stay on the road. Irrational? Absurd? Of course. And yet that is what I did. As though it were possible. As though, like those sad individuals forever trying to bend forks with their minds, I could simply force the physical world's attention. As though reality were that malleable. And the mind that crude a weapon. I willed that car not to go over, to hold. I fought for every inch. Rigid with fear, I drove those twenty miles like a ghost inside his body, wrestling for the wheel, turning the skid, forcing us, again and again, back to the wall.

But enough of that. We lived. When we emerged from the canyon, he slowed, and when I asked him, as soon as I was able to speak, to please let us out, he pulled over on the shoulder. I could barely get out of the car. I was soaked in sweat, clenched tight as a fist. He pulled away, leaving us standing by our packs in the desert heat.

For a minute, as though embarrassed by something, we didn't speak. Then we slipped on our packs and walked across the road to a store of some kind, where we treated ourselves to a cold soda. It was over.

It's not the *experience* that interests me here. The event itself, after all, was almost banal: two kids catch the proverbial bad ride, and don't die. So what? What interests me is the aftermath, the effect.

For almost twenty years, you see, I didn't know there was an effect. We went on. We finished our soda, married, had children. Along the way, I began to write. We didn't forget, à la Seifert, what had happened to us — far from it. We told the tale again and again. For twenty years we regaled new friends with it, tricked it up like a pet poodle and made it dance about, bored each other silly with it. In time, it came to have nothing to do with us. Although all the essential details were still there (altered just enough to spare ourselves the pain of an identical retelling), it had become a pose, a self-dramatizing tic, an amusing story recounted over dinner ("And that's when he turned to me — by the way, what do you think of this wine? — and said . . .").

What I didn't realize was that the thing itself had gone underground. And although it surfaced periodically, sometimes in ways almost laughably obvious, I remained oblivious to it. In a recurrent nightmare that visited me perhaps once a year — to take just one, particularly humiliating, example — I would be behind the wheel of a car, my wife beside me, when it plunged over the side of some impossible height: wind whistling against the steel, and a realization that there was nothing to be done, no way to live. And yet, through all those years, I swear I did not make the connection. I assumed, for some reason, that I had always had this particular dream. My blindness, at times, was comical. When the melodramatic ending of *Thelma & Louise* made me almost physically ill, I wrote it off as a token neurosis — my little burden — and thought nothing more of it.

The lid did not come off the pot for seventeen years — until the day I found myself, so to speak, walking past the wall where I had expected to die. Unlike Seifert, however, I knew precisely where I was and what I was there for. Turning up the road from Lake Isabella, my wife beside me and our children in the back seat, I stopped at the cattle guard, then drove the road again. Slowly. By the time we emerged from the shadow of the canyon walls, I understood (no blare of trumpets here, no flash of revelation) the genesis of all those years of dreams, and knew, as well, that I was shut of them forever.

Time makes liars of us all. The moment passes; our words alone are left us. An obvious truth. That our character can prefigure an event as well as be shaped by one, that reality and consciousness are mutually dependent, is, perhaps, less obvious. Did the twenty-eight-year-old Dostoevsky really quote Hugo while waiting to be tied to a stake and shot, as his comrade F. N. Lvov remembered a decade later? Did Jaroslav Seifert really remember a picture on a public toilet, then wonder idly what the people across the way were making for lunch? Should we see the letter Dostoevsky wrote to his brother immediately after the ordeal as an accurate representation of his thoughts those last few minutes in Semenovsky Square, or read the famous mock-execution scene in *The Idiot,* written some twenty years later, as the truest depiction of what he endured that December morning? Should you, finally, believe my retelling of the ride we caught that summer day in 1985, or accept my recollections of what went through my mind those few minutes? Should I?

Yes and no. Every retelling is inevitably a distortion, but that does not mean it is without value. We can't help but tell the truth. Although we will never know what Dostoevsky experienced that December morning in Semenovsky Square, we can, from his retelling, with its particular fingerprint of stresses and omissions, learn a great deal about him. Although we will never know what Jaroslav Seifert really thought or felt standing against that wall (although he himself may no longer know — indeed, may never have known), we can see, with perfect clarity, what he wants us to believe he thought or felt. Nothing reveals us as clearly as our attempt to shape the past. Retrospection is, by definition, reflexive.

What our inadvertent self-portrait reveals, if we study it closely enough, is that our consciousness, rather than being shaped by a particular event, predated it. That we were, in a sense, anticipating it. That, to recall Kafka's haunting insight, "the arrows fit exactly in the wounds" for which they were intended. Dostoevsky experienced what he did in Semenovsky Square because he was Dostoevsky. Because he already carried inside him, like a patient wound, the "cursed questions" he would seek to answer the rest of his life. Seifert, the poet of the quotidian and the small, thought about the things he did because he was Jaroslav Seifert, the man who, thirty-five years later, would write a book called *All the Beauties of the Earth*. Because, like Tolstoy at Yasnaya Polyana, he gathered the things of this life, and let them fall at his feet. The experience, in other words, was already prepared for him by the time he got there. As it is, to some extent, for all of us.

As for me, I had been driving that canyon road all my life. In all my work, in all my deepest imaginings, tragedy had always been invited, played with, then sent on its way. How appropriate, then, how predictable, that it would do the same for me.

There's the event, waiting for us. And we fit it as perfectly as the arrow fits its wound.

JANNA MALAMUD SMITH

My Father Is a Book

FROM THE THREEPENNY REVIEW

WHEN I WAS SEVENTEEN or so, I read William Faulkner's novel *As I Lay Dying*, about a poor Southern family. As you might recall, the youngest boy, Vardamon, has caught a large fish the same day his mother dies, and in the density of emotion he becomes confused, merging her with the dead creature that the assembled mourners eventually cook and eat. "My mother is a fish," he observes, and then intones the expression to himself, a wacko mantra that — in the midst of the grievous chaos and staggering adult incompetence — becomes his guidepost, the queer story he tells himself.

As soon as I read the sentence, it was mine. "My father is a book." The parallel was obvious . . . and yet pleasing. I knew there was something more serious within, but I didn't consider exactly what it might be. And while, in the intervening thirty years, whole continents of knowledge — for example, almost every other detail of Faulkner's novel — have disappeared from my brain, this sentence stayed.

My real father, Bernard Malamud, not the book, died in 1986. One odd part of a writing parent is that they don't die in the same fashion as everyone else. Certainly there is the obvious correspondence with any lost love, the way that the grief gores and tosses you, and then you slowly recover. But unlike other people, deceased writers are dead and not-dead. The flesh rots and leaves behind the words. You read a page, and it is as if you have found some still animate piece of them broken off from the rest and in motion. It is disconcerting — at its worst lacking in propriety, like a voice of someone deceased kept too long on the answering machine; at its best providing a kind of eerie companionship. Mostly, it is what you imagined they always wanted. The inessential has evaporated; the mind's glory remains.

By which I also mean that my father was frequently uncomfortable with the messy, fleshbound reality of his life. He rather preferred himself as a book — at least sometimes. I know during his childhood he felt humiliated by the on-and-off bizarre behavior of his schizophrenic mother, Bertha Fidelman. And for that reason, among others, he was often a little formal or cautious. While he was funny and enjoyed sociability, he was rarely casual; one had a sense that he was uncertain if a spontaneous remark would show something unacceptable — or foreign, or even mad. Not only were his parents poor Jewish shtetl immigrants from Russia who misspoke American, and couldn't guide him, but his mother was insane. When I asked him, he described feeling loved by her, and yet on the street, her misdressed, lopsided carriage, hat skewed upon her head, mortified and terrified him. I imagine that her condition was part of what kindled his urgency to tell stories. He wanted to cover them both; he wanted, if you will, to create a cover story.

Dad's maternal grandfather was the chief *shochet* in their village. His great-grandfather may have been a rabbi, though no one is certain. And while Yiddish was the primary language spoken in the home, the transmission of religious practice was disrupted both by Bertha's illness and by Dad's father Max's adherence to a more secular, agnostic socialism. Furthermore, my grandfather's little grocery store (where they also lived) was in Flatbush, a neighborhood of Brooklyn in which Jews were a minority. Max was uncomfortable. He was a kindly man, carrying poor customers on credit. Sometimes he appeared ineffectual to his older son.

I don't know how Dad felt as a little boy about being Jewish. As he got into adolescence, he made friends in school with Jewish kids from better-off families. He spent time at their homes but did not bring them to his. When he was about fourteen, he demanded to know why he had not been bar mitzvahed, and his father performed the ceremony for him himself. Some years later, after the Second World War, he read books about Judaism and Jewish history.

My father disliked the label "Jewish writer." My mother recalls how, when they visited Mexico in the early 1980s, a taxi driver identified him as Jewish and he answered stiffly, "I am an American professor." I suspect that the source of his pedantic correction was not simply his resistance to being boxed, nor the immigrant son's renouncing of Old World categories, but also the reinforcing of a deeper bulwark: I am not my mother. I am a writer. I am a teacher. I am a book.

Dad was fourteen or fifteen when his mother died in a mental asylum, possibly from pneumonia, possibly suicide. His father re-married — Liza, a woman whom Dad did not much like. Soon af-ter, though he lived at home, he left home — first to the free City College, then for a year of graduate school at Columbia University, where he wrote his master's thesis on Thomas Hardy. Later, he worked in Washington, and moved, after World War II, to Oregon — for a New York Jew, truly the frontier edge of the continent. When he and my mother and brother arrived there in 1949, the bread was white, the cheese a local orange cheddar, and smoked salmon meant not lox but pungent chunks of native Pacific fish. During the Oregon years, Dad occasionally returned east for visits; mostly he wrote letters. After his father died in 1954, first Liza and then a cousin looked after Dad's one brother, Eugene, who had be-come psychotic — later diagnosed as schizophrenic — while serv-ing in the Pacific in World War II. I think I met Liza once and Eu-gene twice.

While he openly claimed the identity among intimates and friends, Dad addressed his Jewishness and his past almost exclu-sively in his writing. I believe that my great-great-grandfather was a rabbi because I still have a note I wrote on a yellowing piece of pa-per one of the few times Dad and I talked about family history. On one or two occasions I asked my father specifics about his family, and learned a few names of relatives and a few stories from him. For a man who loved narrative, he was markedly silent with me about both his personal and religious past. He told us lots of stories when we were kids, but they were whimsical, funny ones about rac-coons and brave knights. The little I now know about Passover or Yom Kippur I have mostly gleaned from friends. The only direct teaching I remember him giving me about being Jewish occurred when I was eight and we still lived in Oregon. One night, as he was tucking me in, we got to talking about Hitler. He used the occasion to offer what I experienced as a rather pointed lesson: "If we lived in Nazi Germany, you would likely be dead," he said. "The Nazis would kill you because you are my daughter and half Jewish." The larger Jewish patrimony he embodied and expressed was richer and less dire. My father passed on to us — in truth, both parents did, though in somewhat different terms — a humane code about how one ought to try to live: decency and an effort at honesty were two of its tenets, together with a great valuing of art and books.

Dad was a slow reader, which continually distressed him; but he read steadily. Most nights after dinner, he would sit down with a book. He underlined words or phrases and occasionally made notes in margins. He envied his Bennington College colleague, the literary critic Stanley Edgar Hyman, because Stanley could read a book a day, though — as Dad noted — the feat often required at least a fifth of bourbon. I believe it was Stanley with whom, in the mid-1960s, he had the argument about whether, forced to choose, you would save one baby or the only copy of a play by Shakespeare. It seems that any wag's first question would be, "Which play?" But Dad hung in tenaciously for the baby — and then proudly dined out on the story. What strikes me as remarkable now about their conversation is that they had it. Two things were most precious, each human life and each great work of art. If the baby won, it was by a hair's breadth. I suspect that part of Dad's delight was that Stanley gave him the opportunity to argue the side of himself he liked better. He was torn about how to divide his energies. He always supported the family by teaching. How much of the rest of his time should go to writing, how much to the people around him?

All in all, I think any rabbi would have found deep resonances in the debate about the baby, would have recognized it for what it was — a Talmudic discourse rooted in Solomon, a Jewish moral legacy partially stripped of its context. And although my lapsed-Catholic mother, herself the child of Italian immigrants, tried to instill a bit of formal religion by briefly sending my brother and me to Unitarian Sunday school, it was books — or at least the ideas and artistry they contained — that were held with reverence, and a large part of the patrimony I inherited. In fact, although we never had any money until after *The Fixer* was published in 1966, when I was fourteen, from early on Dad made a point of buying me books. Every so often he would sit me down with the children's book reviews in the Sunday *Times* and have me circle those I wanted. His rule was that you had to read fifty pages before you decided that you didn't want to finish it. On occasion, he would time how many words my brother and I could read in a minute.

For six years or so starting in 1962, we lived in college housing in Bennington, Vermont, where Dad had his first study. He also had the hi-fi. And when he was not home, I would sit in a chair or lie on the guest bed, listening to records and staring at his floor-to-ceiling bookshelves, reading the iconic titles. *Crime and Punishment, War and Peace,* a two-volume biography of Dickens, groups of novels by Faulkner, Hemingway, Fitzgerald, Joyce, Virginia Woolf. His shelves were serious. I remember that *And Quiet Flows the Don* and *The Don Flows Home to the Sea* by Mikhail Sholokhov sat at eye level. Their somber brown and black paper covers were worn, yet steadfast. Many books came into our house, but only some stayed. The rest were boxed and carried by him or my mother to college and town libraries. The ones he kept became a second family tree.

I experienced my father's study as a kind of sanctuary. I liked the quiet of it when he wasn't there, and I liked the way we talked when I would knock on the door and briefly join him. He could be curt about interruptions, yet I knew that I had privilege — and was often welcomed with a smile, especially if I came to speak about a book or idea, or a notion that amused him. At the same time, I found his book collection imposing, an iron gate that both invited and intimidated. As well as reaching toward the past, it marked something beyond — some place that I might or might not eventually enter. Books, writing, writers, became confused; all were magnified.

At the same time, I feared my mind would always be in the thrall of their and his authority. In my mid-twenties, I wrote a poem about Ariel's feelings at the moment in *The Tempest* when Prospero sets him free. In my version, Ariel is uncertain, aware that liberation entails loss. The poem ends, "Without him, I am the playwright's fantasies untethered from the pen, bounding too fast for human eyes to see. No servitude, no art. No way to enter time." My parents had taken us to see *The Tempest* at the Shakespearean Festival in Ashland, Oregon, when I was seven. It made a big impression. On the most personal level, it became a story about the ambivalence of being held in or released not only from the spell of a father's love but, in a broader sense, from the overwhelming larger-than-life quality of his unattainable talent, his standards about art: how good something had to be before you could like it and, indirectly, how good you had to be at something before you had permission to esteem yourself a bit as its producer . . . even as its admirer.

Just out of college, I taught in a summer school program at Phillips Academy, Andover. I was assisting a senior teacher in a course called "Growing Up in America." We had the teenage students read a three-page short story published in the *Atlantic Monthly* called "The Day No Pigs Would Die." About a father who could not bring himself to force the slaughter of a pig his son had raised, the tale moved me. In fact, I loved it, and I brought it home. My first teaching experience had been exhilarating; I felt I had something to offer. One morning I gave Dad the story to read, and then asked him about it later over lunch. "Second-rate," he announced with quiet irritation. "Let me show you how it ought to be done." He got up from the table, disappeared into his study, and returned a few minutes later with a copy of *Jude the Obscure*. He opened up to the scene in which Jude's wife, Arabella, sets him to butchering their pig, and where he fails to do it correctly — so the blood can drain slowly — because he can't stand to see the creature suffer. Dad read the page aloud. "This," he announced, "is how a first-rate artist talks about killing a pig."

When, in the process of writing this piece, I returned after twenty-five years to that page in *Jude the Obscure*, I found I had remembered it exactly. His pedagogy was effective. In truth, I am still almost incapable of knowingly reading a bad book. You can imagine how foolhardy, almost kamikaze-esque I felt as I gradually realized how much I wanted to write. Flying out of a blinding sun, I would surely augur in and self-destruct . . . upon a pig.

Needless to say, at the time I felt put down — and, in fact, spent much of my twenties trying to use the anger from such exchanges to free myself from the knotted golden rope of his overbearing influence. But the question that interests me now is why he felt the need to teach that lesson at that moment. When I recall the scene, I include my husband, then my new boyfriend, in it. Certainly, a rival male presence might explain the outburst — on one level a kind of simian chest-thump asserting dominance. But Da-

vid, whose recall tends to be keen on these matters, does not remember such a lunch. So there must have been other forces at
play. Perhaps I disappointed him. How could his almost grown
daughter in whom he had invested so much not be able to distinguish sentimentality from high art? Maybe he took it as an insult,
felt that his own labor and sacrifice were being slighted. How could
someone he loved reveal that she missed the whole point of his
life? Or perhaps he simply felt bad about the page he had written
that morning, and I was handy.

Yet there is another dimension to the exchange. At the time, I
experienced his comments as ruthless, at least in miniature. By
which I mean that at that moment he was completely indifferent to
any feelings but his own; he didn't care if he humiliated. And,
more than coincidentally, it is Jude's inadequate ruthlessness — as
manifest when he ineptly knifes the pig — that symbolically mud-
dles his chance to realize himself, and renders him obscure. As
with the quandary between the Shakespeare play and the baby, I
think Dad struggled mightily with this dilemma of ruthlessness.
How much should you allow yourself to pain, or harm, or simply
not take care of the people around you in the service of art-mak-
ing? Jude's cry to Arabella, "have a little pity on the creature,"
could have been my father's central moral tenet. In truth, it comes
as close as possible, for a one-line summary, to capturing the moral
essence of how he tried to live — and to raise me, day in and day
out. At the same time, he had mostly left family and Brooklyn behind in order to write.

Once, when I was twelve or so, we were visiting New York City.
Dad was to give a reading. With time on our hands, we went to grab
dinner at a small diner. Eating nearby was an older woman — lay-
ered in filthy clothes, muttering over her plate of fried eggs, clearly
poor and crazy. When we went to pay our check, Dad asked to pay
for the woman's meal, too. He caused a bit of a scene. I think the
cook was insulted. I suspect the ill diner was a regular whom they
looked after themselves and they thought the stranger was intrud-
ing. I felt embarrassed, convinced at the time that he had made
the gesture for my benefit — another lesson. Retrospectively, I
don't know. Certainly adolescents are too quick to jump to such
conclusions. But the question captures the slight paranoia that his
growing fame brought into our relationship. What was still genu-

ine, and simply between us? After one day when he read me excerpts from F. Scott Fitzgerald's letters to his daughter, Scottie, I started experiencing his occasional missives to me differently. I became suspicious that they were written with an eye on posterity — seemingly private, but really for a larger audience. Who knows. It has taken me way too long to grow up enough to see him with fair perspective; and in truth, though I was thirty-four when he died, it was still a work in progress.

My father's cremated remains are buried in the arboretum-like Mount Auburn Cemetery in Cambridge, Massachusetts, not far from where I live. Every year or so, I drop by. His stone lies flat on the grass under an old tree overlooking a small pond. When I was struggling very hard to write my first book, oppressed by the weight of his ghost, I visited and sat next to the grave. "Did you talk to him?" a friend asked later. I hemmed and hawed. The question seemed quite personal. She repeated it. "Did you talk to him?"

"Yeah," I grudgingly acknowledged.

"Well, what did you say?" she pushed.

I paused, and then confessed. "I told him . . . I told him to drop dead!"

We both laughed hard. Several years later I returned for another visit. I had finished one book and was on to a second. Not intending anything, I found myself teary. I touched his stone, on which I had already placed a lilac. "Thank you," I said.

GERALD STERN

Bullet in My Neck

FROM THE GEORGIA REVIEW

I AM SO USED TO having a bullet in my neck that I never think of it, only when the subject comes up and someone — full of doubt or amazement — gingerly reaches a hand out to feel it. It is a memento of the shooting on an empty road on the edge of Newark, New Jersey, when Rosalind Pace and I got lost on the way from Newark airport to a conference of poets in Bethlehem, Pennsylvania. We made the mistake of stopping at a red light and were cornered immediately by two boys, sixteen or so, dressed in starched jeans and jackets and sporting zip guns. Before we could reason with them, or submit, or try to escape, they began shooting through the open windows. The boy on Rosalind's side pointed his gun, a .22, directly in her face, a foot away, but it misfired. The boy on my side emptied his gun, hitting the steering wheel, the window, and the dashboard. One bullet grazed my right shoulder, and one hit my chin then buried itself in the left side of my neck, less than a half inch from the carotid artery.

Everything in such a situation takes on a life of its own, and the few seconds it took me to realize I wasn't going to die seemed like a much longer stretch of time, and though my neck swelled up and blood was pouring out, my only thought was to get out of there as quickly as possible. My memory was that I fell to the floor, pushed the gas pedal down with one hand, and with the other put the gear into drive till Rosalind took over and drove us out of there. All the time I was screaming at her not to lose control, that she had to save our lives. It was Friday night and we were someplace in downtown Newark, and it was 1986 or 1987. No one would give us directions to the hospital; it seemed as if everyone was drunk or high. I kept jumping out of the car to stop cabs, but when they saw the blood they rushed off. Then, by some fluke, we found ourselves driving up a lawn to the back entrance of Beth Israel where, after a crazy altercation with a ten-dollar-a-day rent-a-cop with a noisy beeper, we drove over another lawn to the emergency entrance where, thanks to the fake cop, two doctors were waiting to rip my clothes off and save my life. I'd told the fake cop that if there wasn't some- one waiting I would crawl back and kill him, even if it was the last thing I did in this life — I think I said "with my bare hands" for, af- ter all, I was in the midst of a great drama — and that may have awakened him.

The one thing the doctors, the nurses, and the police lieuten- ant, who came later, said over and over was that it was a mistake to stop at the red light. "Why did you stop at the red light?" I was asked. "No one stops at that light!" I felt guilty, as if I myself were the perpetrator. It was as if Newark lived by a different set of rules. Certainly it was a battle zone and probably more intensely so in the mid-eighties than it is now in the twenty-first century, at least at this point. There is rebuilding and there is talk about rebirth. But the burning and the racial wars and the final flight may have been too much, and New Jersey may have lost its only true city.

Rosalind has written an essay about the event. Some of the dif- ferences in our memory are striking, particularly in details, but what interests me is the emotional difference, what we make — or made — of the shooting. She remembered the boys as eleven or twelve years old — I thought they were a little older; she remem- bers the one on her side as wearing a sweatshirt — I remember them both in freshly ironed matching jacket and jeans, almost like uniforms; she remembers us going up a drive, at the hospital, into an entrance — I remember us driving across the lawn. We could ei- ther be right, or neither, and it makes little difference — it is how we received the event in our lives, how we absorbed it and located it. For her the initial emotional response was a mixture of shock, disbelief, and fear. Later, it was more anger, mixed with guilt, sad- ness, and frustration. My initial response was also disbelief and fear, though later it was mostly grief — and almost no anger. I don't mean to make an odious comparison; if anything, I am per- plexed at my lack of anger, and if I comment on my own feelings it

is not by way of either denigrating or elevating Rosalind's. I may
have been only concealing or converting my anger; furthermore it
is a quite decent and quite useful emotion — anger — one which I
make use of all the time, and I get furious at soft-spoken cheek-
turners who smile lovingly at the slaps, however their eyes are wet
with pain, rage, and disappointment. It just didn't happen for me
here. Also, Rosalind's experience was different from mine in two
ways: she was driving and therefore felt responsible, and she wasn't
shot, and I was. It was more than guilt, her pain; it was agony.

I know that I was more "accepting" of the event than she was. I
never argued with the circumstances or raged against the gods.
Nor, for a second, did I blame her. We did make a wrong turn off
the highway, we did stop at the red light, we didn't leave ten minutes earlier — or later. That's that! If anything, I felt lucky. The
bullet didn't kill me, the gun on her side misfired. There were angels watching over us and they had a hell of a time leaping from
side to side of the car, deflecting and stopping the shots as well as
they could, keeping enough blood in my body, helping us out of
there, guiding us to the hospital. If anything, I am grateful, and I
love and kiss everyone and everything involved. I regret Rosalind
had to go through this. I'm sorry for her suffering. But I don't hate
the boys and I'm not angry with them and I don't hold it against
Newark. In a way, once it happened I was glad it did, which doesn't
mean I wouldn't prefer that it didn't. I suffered a few months from
a stiff jaw and swollen neck, but there's no permanent damage except for the bullet that lodged in my neck and was never removed
and, as I say, I forget it's there unless I'm telling the story to someone and press his or her amazed finger to the center of my neck, a
little to the left of the windpipe.

When I describe my "state" after I was shot, I say I was totally alert
and responding in a manner to save both of our lives. I'm certain I
argued a little, but after the bullets started coming I had the usual
rush of adrenaline and reverted to the fight-or-flight pattern, however it's described medically or physiologically. I didn't go into
shock, in spite of the loss of blood and the trauma, though when
we got to the hospital a certain "forgetfulness" set in, maybe when I
was released of responsibility and was under care and protection.

I do remember the doctors waiting for me at the entrance, that they cut my shirt off, laid me down, stopped the bleeding, and examined the wound. I remember there was a long consultation, a discussion, and I was a part of it. The question was whether to remove the bullet or not, given how close it was to the artery, since there was always the danger of the instrument slipping. I don't know whether we took a vote or what, but the choice was against operating. Apparently, there had been some problems in Vietnam. My dear friend Alex Greenberg, a head surgeon and poet, told me he would not have hesitated to remove the bullet, but all ER doctors are not like him. A surgeon was called and he agreed with the others.

In the emergency room I was attached to a half-dozen machines and instruments, and my face — which I saw in a mirror — was covered with blood and my neck — black, yellow, purple — was swollen grotesquely. I asked Rosalind about my poems, in an old leather briefcase, which she set down beside me. For the next two hours, while I was undergoing tests, I was busy orchestrating the immediate future. I directed Rosalind to telephone the conference leader — it was the middle of the night — to explain what happened, and to reschedule my appearance for Sunday, but the shithead said he couldn't change the schedule until Rosalind, under my direction, battered him into submission. I told Rosalind that it was extremely important for me to attend a part of the conference and to read and talk. I didn't care, as such, for the conference itself, nor for the measly bucks they were probably giving me; what I cared about was being there, going back to my life, not letting the shooting defeat me. And Rosalind drove me there — Sunday afternoon, a day and a half after I'd been shot. I gave a talk on Gil Orlovitz — one of the lost poets — and read some of my own poems. I must have been a pretty sight, on whatever stage they were using, neck of three colors, rotten clothes, wild eyes. Rosalind, dear supporter, says I was "clear, spontaneous, coherent, witty, profound, and brilliant as usual." I don't remember who the other writers were. Friends, I know, but they were — some of them — resentful and embarrassed when I appeared. They had learned I was shot, I'm not sure when, and had a reading of my poems in absentia: a memorial service. Then I appeared, a blood-swollen ghost, to interrupt the order of things. I wanted to apologize to them, but I had to quickly demythologize and locate the shooting, to put a skin around it just as my body eventually put a skin around the bullet, so I could go on with my life's work.

Orlovitz, a native of Philadelphia, died on the sidewalk in front of his apartment building on the Upper West Side. He was a poet, novelist, and playwright, who had published over a hundred poems — most of them sonnets — in major and minor periodicals, but never had a serious book publication. At his best, he was a powerful and original writer, but he is virtually unknown today. He is probably remembered by writers in their seventies and beyond, but younger than that only by severe scholars and devouring readers. He popped pills and drank unmercifully and died at fifty-four in 1973. He was incredibly well read, passionate, and generous. I lent him money, read his poems, and got him a couple of readings. I'll never forget him descending from the bus for his reading at Rutgers. He wore a stylish suit, a black tie, and an overcoat. He was modest and self-assured, a beautiful reader. He drank gin straight, with a bit of chaser from time to time.

As for Rosalind, it was crazy not to do something for her in the hospital. They should have given her a sedative, talked to her, maybe offered her a bed, let her undress and take a shower, see if she could or could not drive home. I remember her washing the blood out of her coat and my jacket in a tiny sink. She describes how her hands were plunged in red water and the padding came out of the shoulder of my jacket where a bullet had lodged. She was more or less ignored and had the fear and pain — and boredom — of waiting, and going over and over again the events of the evening. She describes herself trying to sleep on a couch somewhere in the hospital, of a nurse giving her a blanket, of waking up to the cold morning with the sudden knowledge of what happened, of confronting the car, blood on the windshield, rearview mirror, door handle, seats, and windows, bullets embedded in the steering wheel and the dashboard, and a two-hour ride home, alone in the car, weeping, screaming, pounding her head, pounding the steering wheel. She said she screamed for two hours.

Me they treated well — almost like a guest rather than a patient. They seemed to have a collective guilt, as if I were mistreated on their watch. I was mistreated, but it was surprising to me that they assumed anything like responsibility. I had to reassure them, tell them how conscientious they were, even kind. They were ashamed of their city. It may be that they were acknowledging class. I was educated, a college professor; they were professionals. In a city that had exploded fifteen or so years before over race, poverty, redlining, corruption, brutality, injustice, I got the treatment that doctors give to each other or to the privileged. Moreover, the hospital never charged me, and I don't feel it was an accident. I don't mean my Blue Cross (from Iowa) covered the whole thing. There was no paperwork, no processing, no bills, no ER charges, no statement that said at the bottom "this is not a bill," no surgeon's fees, no giant profit on Band-Aids and tap water. It was as if the hospital itself was ashamed.

When I was being wheeled into the intensive care unit, I joked with the doctors, reciting the names of famous people in history who had been shot — presidents, kings, and the like. For some reason, I couldn't remember the name of Emma Goldman's lover, whom she sent off to Pittsburgh to shoot Henry Frick. He arrived at Frick's office in the early evening while he was still at his desk and shot him with a little revolver that barely wounded the bastard. Frick stayed at his desk till the accustomed time and Berkman — his name was Berkman — was thrown in jail for a couple of decades, then deported to Russland, home of the pink and the brave. Berkman was a good anarchist, but a poor marksman. Red Emma didn't want anything to do with him when he finally came home; I think he disappointed her.

Later, when I got to my room and finally lay down on the coarse sheets, I alternated between pure joy and grief. Joy at being alive; at having escaped the way I did; at having such amazing luck — and grief that there was such malice, such willful indifference to life in the world. I kept saying to the nurses, to Rosalind, to my callers, "I can't believe one person would do that to another." And I wept over it uncontrollably.

I thought of two things. I know that because I have kept track. One was the 1942 shooting of Bruno Schulz by the German officer he encountered on the street in front of his house, after he had brilliantly and devotedly painted the officer's nursery for his children. The other was the malicious destruction of a small animal, a frog, by a friend of mine when we were both about twelve. He had stuffed a bullfrog into a number 2 Mason jar, screwed the lid on, and threw him from the third floor onto the sidewalk in front of our apartment house. A bullfrog is not a Jewish slave, let alone a gifted and famous one, but the state of mind — of heart — may have been the same in those two murderers. I thought about the frog for years. I rushed downstairs and he was still alive, with large pieces of glass embedded in his body. I had to kill him before I went back upstairs to beat the shit out of my friend. As for the murder of Schulz, that beautiful writer — and painter — it has become for me, as I know it has for others, a symbol of capricious and perverse human behavior. And it is the method of killing, a casual shot to the head, almost as an afterthought, or a preprandial bit of exercise, that horrifies me. I understand that in Byelorussia, during the war, German pilots shot Jews in the same way when they came back from their bombings and dogfights. As a sort of celebratory act.

I have taken up the trade of poet in part because of the difficulty in understanding — and the need to "explain" — just that willful, capricious, perverse behavior. It's as if there's no other way. Auden says that "wild Ireland" drove Yeats into poetry. Easily — if beautifully — said. I was driven into it by nearsightedness and unforgivable innocence. What I learned I learned with a vengeance even if it came late. And quickly enough I got used to my learning. When the two boys stood at the two sides of our car, whether engaged in an initiation rite or a robbery or just to see what it felt like to kill someone, I wasn't at all surprised, even if later I was grief-stricken.

There was one other book that came to my mind as I lay there — Thomas Mann's *Doctor Faustus*. And it was only when I reread it that I realized how direct the connection was. The pact with the Devil itself occurs during a small afternoon nap of the "hero," Adrian Leverkühn. The narrator, one Serenus Zeitblom, a high school Latin teacher, is nominally writing a biography of Leverkühn, a boyhood chum and a musical prodigy who studied theology and then went back to music, but it may as well have been a critical history — a kind of allegory — of Germany in the first half of the twentieth century. Leverkühn became a great, little known, deeply experimental composer, a cult figure and a recluse. His last composition was a symphonic cantata titled — naturally — *The Lamentation of Dr. Faustus;* brutal, pure, formal, expressive, "the most frightful lament ever set up on this earth." Leverkühn made

the pact with the Destroyer, and so did Germany and even Zeitblom, with his flabby middle-class piety and his righteous scholarship, though he was both witness and spokesman, even if seen
through Mann's irony and scorn. The year was 1944 when *The
Lamentation* was released, just before the landing at Normandy. It is
an ode to sorrow, the reverse, the opposite, the negative to Beethoven's "Ode to Joy"; in a way it is the revocation and there is a chorus of grief to match Beethoven's chorus. The whole book — very
German in this — is based on opposites, the daemonic, the dark,
the uncanny, versus the humane, the enlightened, the civilized;
the irrationalism of the "folk" versus reason, dignity, culture, science; the Nazi state versus the democratic. It's not a simple matter.
It's not as if Zeitblom represents one side and Leverkühn the
other. There is a hopeless mixture, and there is the limitation of
language and of knowledge.

The most moving scene in the novel is the one where the di-
vinely beautiful little Echo, Leverkühn's five-year-old nephew, first
enchants the household in Leverkühn's country retreat with his
goodness and innocence and then is suddenly struck down by
cerebrospinal meningitis and suffers days of unmitigated agony.
The child, whose name is Nepomuck, shortened to Nepo, calls
himself Echo, quaintly skipping the first consonant, and speaks of
himself in the third person. Overcome with convulsions, vomiting,
and skull-splitting headaches, his neck rigid, his eye muscles para-
lyzed, he pleads with the powers. "Echo will be good, Echo will be
good." I first read the novel — I remember — in Scotland, so the
year would be 1953. Echo, and his cry, I never could forget. It compares to Lear, and there is the additional fact that my own sister, my
only sibling, twelve months older than I, was struck down by the
same disease when she was nine years old. I sometimes imagine her
hydrocephalic shrieks, her heartrending moans, dear Sylvia.

It took me two, three months to recover from the wound. The
physical pain was greater than I thought it would be. I couldn't lift
my chin up so I didn't shave. My neck was so swollen that I couldn't
turn it. I slept ten hours a night — five, six more hours than I normally do. I was exhausted all the time. But emotionally I recovered
quickly, which surprised me. Growing up in a brutal time, in a brutal city, I was always alert to vicious, unexpected, and insane behav-

ior. I learned early not to be astonished at the undeserved and out-
rageous. I was a warrior, alas, and my one task was to preserve
dignity and honor the human, though I didn't know such words
yet. It was a sad way to be nudged out of one world into another
and to achieve thereby not only a small kinship with the brutalized
but an understanding of brutality itself.

It's ironic about the two worlds, isn't it? Sometimes the brutalized is brutal, the oppressed is oppressor. It's an agony to think of
it, though sometimes it's a comedy. We can be both at once; we can
even split the difference. Maybe only Diogenes was not oppressive.
But who knows what his wife would say? And wasn't his dour, puri-
tanical, and fearless message itself oppressive? Ah lamb! Ah, your
slit throat and the blood flowing on your white chest! Why are you
here? Are you sheep or shepherd? Apocalypse would have it that
the slaughtered lamb, albeit with seven horns and seven eyes, was
the one who took up the book, and the one who sat on the throne.
He was slaughtered, and yes he was a judge. Or was he a butcher,
this lamb?

> all those who worship the beast
> and his image and receive a mark on his forehead
> even those humans will drink
> the wine of the wrath of God, which is poured
> undiluted into the cup of anger
> of their God, and they will be tormented
> in fire and in sulfur before the holy angels
> and *before the lamb*. The smoke of their torment
> will rise forevermore, and there's no rest
> day and night for any who worship the beast
> and his image or wear the mark of his name.
> Such is the endurance of the saints, who keep
> the commandments of God and faith in Yeshua.

It's not that I imagine a world without butchers and it's not that I
ever forget the horrors of the century we have just gone through.
My friend Jerry Ostriker, an astronomer and spokesman for the
universe, says that it is entirely indifferent to this minute speck of
dust we call earth. In the dining room of his house in Princeton he
has a "map" of that universe which we can study as we sit there eating. I tell him that, after all, we have invented the universe, and the
dust is supremely important. We both make light of our dilemma.

A little gallows humor in both of us. The height of stubbornness, and loyalty.

I hope the two boys are all right. If they survived the life in Newark, if they aren't dead yet, they would be in their thirties. They could be in prison, or they could have made a breakthrough. Maybe one of them went to college, is in computers, selling cars, studying law. I want to apologize for turning them into symbols, or vehicles. They weren't pernicious, though what they did was unjust and stupid. And I want to remember how small was my brief "suffering" compared to thousands of others', what cruelty, absurdity, insanity, maliciousness they were forced to experience, how the lamb itself was twisted and pulled in a thousand ways, how it wept for itself at last, just as it wept for others — and continues to do so.

TENNESSEE WILLIAMS

Amor Perdida

Or, How It Feels to Become
a Professional Playwright

FROM MICHIGAN QUARTERLY REVIEW

Editor's Note: Tennessee Williams presumably wrote "Amor Perdida" in the early 1940s. It shows the anxious, novice playwright in Mexico at "a time in between" the "old life" and the "new." This previously unpublished essay was edited and annotated by Nicholas Moschovakis and David Roessel from a typescript in the Williams Collection at the University of Texas. Their full introduction to the essay can be found in the Summer 2003 issue of *Michigan Quarterly Review.* (R.A.)

IT IS ABOUT a month ago today. I am seated in an open *cantina* facing the square in Acapulco, Gro., Mexico, and in accordance with one of my oldest and most respected traditions, I have just finished spending my last silver coin on a drink. I am seated with two favorite companions. At my left elbow is a juke-box which is playing what I seriously believe to be the most beautiful of all musical compositions, a bolero called *Amor Perdida*. At my right elbow is Mr. Orrin Beebe who is a confessed cousin of Lucius[1] and has just opened a rival *cantina* on the other side of the square.

We are drinking rum-cocos which is a drink made by knocking one end off a cocoanut and pouring in a couple of jiggers of rum, a dash of lemon and a little cracked ice and sugar.

We are blinking and squinting into the strong yellow sunlight of the square and the dark natives are drifting meaninglessly about us like figures in a dream. Not far from our table is a wretched old dog, slowly dying. I have noticed him before, slinking among the tables with quiet, pleading eyes. Careful not to approach too closely, his large yellow eyes expressing wisdom and sadness and complete acquiescence. I have given him scraps of *tortillas* and *tacos* and he has gulped them down with the frenzied haste of starvation. But now the old dog is dying. The pleading look has gone out of his eyes, he has finally given up his mendicant career. He lies on his side in the sun, breathing in spasms, and his eyes have a look of dark and patient endurance. Nobody seems to notice his condition. The death of dogs in the street is a Mexican commonplace and the natives of Acapulco, a gentle and kindly people, pay no attention to it. I look at the dog and I feel a sympathy for him. I pull his desiccated body into the shade of the cantina and pour a little water on the concrete in reach of his tongue. He ignores the water but glances up at me for an instant of recognition. His brief look is apologetic. Then he stares back into space and I return to my table.

A small boy is selling newspapers, *Excelsior* and *El Universel*. In great black type are such words as *Londres* and *Bombas* and *Destructiones*.

It seems less immediate, less important than the mongrel's death.

A dusty old *camione*, beach-taxi, is taking on passengers for Los Hornos, which is the afternoon beach. A stout American woman in one of those huge, gaudy sombreros which only Americans wear is bawling out the driver for his delay in starting.

But drinking is a process of insulation against such things and in a few moments my interest has returned to its usual center, inside my own skull.

After a while I turn to Mr. Beebe.

"Well, Beebe, it looks like I am back on the beach."

"How do you mean?"

"I sold a play in New York a few months ago. Ever since then I've been in a fool's Paradise, living on ninety dollars a month with nothing to do but write and lie around here. Now that's all over."

"They dropped your play?"

"Uh-huh. I knew they would sooner or later but hoped it would be a little later than this. The checque for this month's advance royalties was due about five days ago and it hasn't come yet. So I feel pretty goddam sure they've already dropped it."

"What are you going to do?"

"I'm going back to my old profession."

"What's that?"

"Waiting tables."

"You got a job lined up?"

"Yes."

"Where?"

"In your *cantina.*"

"Huh! — How much experience have you had?"

"Quite a good deal," I tell him. "I've waited tables in New Orleans, Iowa City, St. Louis, Memphis, Chicago, Los Angeles, San Francisco and Laguna Beach."

"Can you sing?"

"Sing? Like a nightingale!"

"Okay," he says finally. "You'll need a clean white shirt and a black bow tie."

Beebe rises from the table and wanders across the square. But I remain at the table. The juke-box has started again. That amazingly over-dressed woman known as the Princess Olga appears on the square. Three men follow about one step behind her. She talks very loudly, the three men listen and smile. I think she is explaining the mysteries of the universe to them. That's the nice thing [about] a language you don't understand — it is possible to believe the conversation is so much more elevated than it probably is.

After a while I get up. I think I will go over to Wells-Fargo on the opposite corner and see if any mail has come in for me. I am no longer concerned about it — but go anyway.

My name is printed at the top of the telegraph list. Mr. Tennessee Williams.

I receive the yellow envelope and seat myself in a wicker chair beneath the mildly-agitated punkas.

I tear the envelope open and read this message.

BETTER RETURN AT ONCE. WE ARE CASTING YOUR PLAY FOR IMMEDIATE PRODUCTION.

Signed: Theresa Helburn, Theatre Guild, New York.

When people are facing imminent destruction their lives are supposed to pass before them in lightning review. What I faced at the moment was something quite different from imminent destruction, and yet that same phenomenon occurred.

As I sat in the wicker chair beneath the languid punkas I thumbed my way back through twenty-six years of living.

Various periods in the past were revived before me. I remembered particularly the *Vieux Carré* of New Orleans where I first learned how a poor artist lives. I remembered the Quarter Rats, as we were called. The prostitute Irene who painted the marvelous pictures and disappeared, Helen who entered my life through a search for a lost black cat, the jobless merchant seaman, Joe, who wrote sea-stories more exciting than Conrad's which were destroyed when the house he lived in burned. I remembered The Quarter Eat Shop, Meals for a Quarter in the Quarter, and passing out pink, yellow, and blue cards on Royal, Bourbon, and Canal. The sunlight rich as egg-yolk in the narrow streets, great, flat banana leaves, and the slow, slow rain. The fog coming up from the river, swallowing Andrew Jackson on his big iron horse. Tamale vendors at midnight, their haunting voices. Mother O'Neill pouring kettles of boiling water through the floor to break up a studio party. The big fight, the riot call, the Black Maria, Night Court and the House of Detention. The big bare room and the filthy, desperate prisoners. Words scrawled on the dirty white walls. Life getting bigger and plainer and uglier and more beautiful all the time.

I remembered thumbing a ride from Santa Monica to San Francisco to see William Saroyan and the Golden Gate Exposition. Saroyan wasn't there but the fair was marvelous. Sunset from Telegraph Hill and a room that I slept in half way down it and curious scraps of conversation heard through a very thin wall. I remembered days of slightly glorified beachcombing in Southern California. Picking squabs and dropping one feather for each bird in a bottle and collecting afterwards two cents for each feather. Selling shoes across from the M.G.M. lot in Culver City and spending lunch hour watching for Greta Garbo. Never with any success. Taking care of a small ranch up Canyon Road in Laguna Beach. And the sound of dogs barking a long way off at night when the moon started rising. A thirty-year-old schoolteacher from Oklahoma having her last fling before marriage on the California beaches. Waking up at two or three in the morning to find her at the foot of my bunk with a middle-aged man in a crumpled white linen suit, saying, Tenn, this is Jack, Jack's come here to bring me home, we're getting married tomorrow! Sitting up all night, drinking, playing the guitar, singing *El Rancho Grande* — celebrating sadly. And Jacobs who used to conk the "queers" in back of Mona's place with an ice-cleaver wrapped in a towel and roll them for their money, and yet was the most good-natured person I've known. And Jim who played juvenile leads in Miami University productions and was going to crash Hollywood — and worked with me as a pin-boy in a Hollywood bowling alley. Trying to get on the W.P.A. Writers' Project once in Chicago. My negro friends there who had so much more charm than white intellectuals have. Joe Jones' free art-class in the old Court-house in St. Louis, the Artists and Writers League there being evicted by the Police because they were Communistic. Screaming and bloody noses and hours in the bull-pen.[2]

School-days in Mississippi. Walking along aimless country roads through a delicate spring rain with the fields, flat, and wide, and dark, ending at the levee and at the cypress brakes, and the buzzards wheeling leisurely a long way up. Dark life. Confused, tormented, uncomprehendable [*sic*] and fabulously rich and beautiful . . .[3]

When finally I got up from the wicker chair, the brilliant yellow sunlight outside the Wells-Fargo office had faded. Beebe had gone home and had come forth again in a crisp white linen suit. He was seated once more by the juke-box in the rival cantina.

I went over where he was sitting and sat down by him.

"Have you got a white shirt?" he asked me.

"No," I told him.

"What size collar do you wear? Fifteen?"

"Fourteen and half," I told him.

"Okay. I'll lend you one of mine that's shrunk a little."

"No, thanks," I told him.

I handed him the yellow piece of paper.

It was getting so dark he had to bend way over to read it.

When he had made it out, he gravely extended his hand.

"Congratulations, Tenn. How do you feel?"

"Old," I told him.

"Huh?"

"Yes. Old. The irresponsible days of my youth are over."

There was a silence.

After a while Beebe smiled. "Has it occurred to you," he said, "that the play might be a failure?"

"No," I answered honestly. "I hadn't thought of that."

"You'd better think of it, Son."

Another brief silence.

"Beebe," I said. "Will you keep that job open for me?"

"Sure," said Beebe. "I'll save the shirt for you, too."

After a while we both got up and crossed the plaza and entered Beebe's cantina.

Things were festive and bright. It was going to rain. A cool, damp wind was blowing off the Pacific.

I dropped a nickel in the juke-box and wandered out into the patio which was still unlighted. I had a curious sense of isolation. The old life seemed to be over. The new one had not begun yet. This was a time in between. Somehow it made me think of the time when I tore a hole in my one pair of pants and had to spend a motionless half hour behind a screen in a Jewish tailor's shop while the pants were mended. It was an interlude, a period of suspended animation.

Then all at once the Mexican girl started singing *Amor Perdida,* the Japanese lanterns among the dark mango trees bloomed into pastel color. I caught my breath, for it seemed as though I were standing with empty pockets and greedy hands in Aladdin's orchard of jewels.

Notes

1. Lucius Morris Beebe (1902–1966) published a column called "The New York," about New York café society, in the *New York Herald* during the thirties and forties. In 1950 he moved to Virginia City, Nevada, with his companion Charles Clegg and bought a newspaper there.

2. Joe Jones (1909–1963) was an artist and Communist activist in St. Louis who in 1934 set up art classes in the city's old courthouse with the permission of the St. Louis Art League, which owned the building at the time. The league soon had second thoughts as it became aware of the art that was being produced, including a large mural entitled *Social Unrest in St. Louis.* When Jones and his group were evicted from the building, he proceeded to hold classes on the sidewalk in front of it, "causing a near riot when police interceded" (Douglas Wixson, *Worker-Writer in America: Jack Conroy and the Tradition of Midwestern Literary Radicalism, 1898–1990* [Urbana: University of Illinois Press, 1994], 369).

3. Many of the reminiscences in the preceding three paragraphs are corroborated in passages in Williams's other autobiographical writings, especially his *Memoirs.*

CYNTHIA ZARIN

An Enlarged Heart

FROM THE NEW YORKER

IT BEGAN WITH A COUGH. Her brother had a cough. And, after all, what was a cough? They had all had them. In winter, they passed them around like sweets. Enough coughing meant no school. Although sometimes we sent them off anyway — risking a call from the school nurse, who only half the time would be convinced by our pleading that it was nothing — so that a few more hours might elapse before the apartment filled with their books and the paper wrappers from their snacks.

But now it was August, and we were at the beach. All winter we dreamed of the house, with its blue floors, the tiny periscope hole in the roof, the red chairs, the rickety porch with its view of the bay. The children turned brown. It was hot. The sea was flat. At low tide, a little pool appeared, and a sandbar, and she, the youngest at three, stood on tiptoe in the water, screeching when an inch-high wave hit. "I think the water's actually cold," she ran to tell us. "No, I think it's actually warm." We sat by the edge in our low beach chairs, the same chairs that used to embarrass us when our parents brought them to the beach. Why do we have so much stuff? we would ask them, eager to be free of it all, of the towels and swimsuits and bottles of juice and fruit, imagining ourselves alone on an empty stretch of beach, naked, with a rucksack. Now we're the ones who unload the car and carry the heaviest bags.

She's so little we let her run naked, even though we have learned that turning brown is bad. We are careless, self-indulgent, to let her do it. By late afternoon, the sun has slipped behind the enormous high dunes, and blue shadows lap at the water. When she comes up from the edge, she is shivering. Her older sisters and brother and their friends are far out in the waves, on their boogie boards and surfboards, unidentifiable in their black wetsuits. We keep track by counting. One, two, three, four, five, six. Is that Anna? we ask each other. Do you see Nick? There's Rose. "Come in now! Come in!" we scream at them, our arms making huge pinwheels so they will pay attention. It is easy for them to pretend they don't see us.

During the night, she coughs on and off, and wakes once. The wind on the bluff pounds the house. In the morning, it is hot and blue again. We get to the beach after lunch, but the sun is still high. From the top of the dune, shielding our eyes, we look for the cluster of bright umbrellas that mark the colony of our friends. They hail us. The older children jump like seals into the waves and swim out to their pals. She stays by the edge. Today, there is another child her age, but she's cranky and won't play. It's too much sun, she didn't sleep, we explain to the other child's parents, chagrined. Secretly, we're annoyed: Why won't she just play nicely? The younger children are fooling around with the surfboard, and she wants to try. A wave rears up suddenly, a dragon, foaming at the mouth, she's hurled underwater and onto the sand. Everyone races to help. How can we have allowed this to happen? This is appalling! She is young, much too young for these high jinks. She comes up sputtering. What kind of parents are we? Until someone else makes a mistake, our reputation is shaken.

That night, she wakes up every hour coughing. The cough catches her throat, grips it, then lets go. We give her some children's medicine to make her sleep. At some point, I lie down beside her in her bed, and when I wake up it is morning.

The day is blustery and cool. On and off, we feel her forehead. Tonight is a friend's birthday, and we will be nine people for dinner. The middle children go next door to babysit for the younger ones. She sleeps upstairs through the noise. When everyone has left, she wakes up, coughing. When I put my arms around her, she begins to vomit. Get a bucket, I say to the nearest child. They know the drill. We've been through this countless times, with one or the other of them. We have been awakened by children standing by the side of the bed with bloodied noses, by a decade of earaches. But now — and we don't know why — we are frightened. She vomits again and again into the bucket, taking rasping breaths. Her forehead is warm but not hot. Her arms flail, and she isn't focusing.

We do not have a telephone. The cell phone works only if you walk a quarter mile down Corn Hill to the public-beach parking lot. There are no all-night drugstores. This is why we come here. We like it. We are against the plans for the new Stop & Shop in this small Cape Cod village.

Get Anne, I say. One of the children, white-faced, returns from next door with Anne, who left the table only twenty minutes ago. While we are nonchalant about our children, Anne's father was a doctor in rural South Africa, and knowing more — knowing what can happen — she is careful. When she peers into the bed, she agrees right away that something is wrong: the child looks odd. Her breathing is coming in shudders. Someone remembers that Giulia's grandmother, down the way, has a telephone. No doctor at the Health Services, in Provincetown, is on call for summer residents; we must call the Rescue Squad. We worry that we are being ridiculous, but we call. "What's the worst thing that could happen?" Anne asks. "That you don't need them?" Her father goes out into the dark to wait for the Rescue Squad.

The van comes in five minutes, red lights flashing. Her temperature is 100.1; her vital signs are normal. If we are worried, we can take her to the hospital in Hyannis, an hour away.

We decide to wait until morning. In the kitchen, she sits on my lap in one of the red chairs. Because we have run out of medicine and not replaced it during the day — another sign of our foolhardiness, our nonchalance — even though it is too late, we call our friends up the road, Luke and Emily, the parents of our children's friends, and they arrive by car in what seems like an instant, bottle in hand. I take off my vomit-covered sweater. She throws up, just a little, on my shirt. But she is smiling, at Emily, who is looking at her with great tenderness, saying, Poor baby.

The next morning, while the other children sleep, we take her in the station wagon to the health clinic in Provincetown. The waiting room, streaming with light, is almost empty. Two emaciated men sit next to each other on the wall facing the parking lot. There are no appointments until later in the day, but the nurse, after looking at me, comes out to the parking lot to have a look at

her. Immediately, there is an appointment. The nurses are beautiful and tall. This is Provincetown, and I wonder briefly if they are
transvestites. The doctor's lovely mild face is perplexed. It looks
like a virus. Her fever is 101.2. We are to alternate Tylenol and
Motrin every three hours. Her skin is dry to the touch.

At home, she is hungry and wants lunch. She eats ramen noo-
dles, and throws up. The older children wake up, eat breakfast,
and are taken to the beach with the surfboards and boogie boards,
their horrible pink juice, their box of Goldfish. Her fever disappears.

She wants to play Wiffle ball on the strip of sand on top of our
dune. After playing for ten minutes, she goes inside and sleeps
with her blanket on the couch. That night, she vomits twice. In the
morning, she gets into our bed and, turning her head, vomits directly into my hair. She is hot again. On her back there are a few
scattered red marks, as if a bird had walked along the short length
of her spine. We call her doctor in New York. He is away, taking his
child to college. We speak to another doctor, his partner. He says,
Take her back to Provincetown.

Now at the clinic we are treated like old friends. "Hello, hello,"
they say.

One of the tall and beautiful nurses takes her blood pressure.
The doctor arrives. Her temperature is 102.4. When she coughs,
she takes a moment to catch her breath. Her breathing is shallow,
and she is whimpering. The doctor decides to take a blood count:
Maybe there is an infection we can't see?

The blood test shows nothing. Her white-blood-cell count is normal. The doctor examines her again. The rash on her back has
spread to her stomach: small red dots just under her skin, from
sternum to groin. But by now she has an infection in her left ear.
This is good: there is something to do. New York is called, and
agrees with the doctor's recommendation: a massive shot of antibiotics, called Ceftriaxone. It may also attack any bacterial infection
that may be lurking. That day's notes say, "Case assumed by Dr.
Lazarus in New York," followed by the phone number of the pediatrician's West End Avenue office. The antibiotics will be injected
into the muscle of her thigh. Her father leaves the room. Hold her
legs down, I'm told. I hold her small legs. Are her eyes red? It's
hard to tell. She is crying. When we leave the clinic, we are both
given get-well stickers. One for Mommy, the nurse says.

In the car back to Truro, past the long sweep of dunes where the Pilgrims first found fresh water, I think: Scarlet fever. Malaria. Diphtheria. Smallpox. Scurvy. Leeches. Flu? My aunt and my father had polio when they were children. My grandparents closed up their house in Brooklyn and moved to a hotel near the hospital. When we get home, she lies on the couch with her blanket. It's a rainy day, and the hill is full of children. Anna, Lev, and Joseph take turns reading to her. The Wolf eats Grandma; the Troll bellows from under the bridge. She smiles, on and off, eats a few Goldfish crackers. Her four-year-old friend Adam goes in and out of the house cheerily, checking in. I count up in my head. Taking our children together, we have 38 years of child-rearing experience. If you include our friends who drop by and stand over the couch like figures in a nineteenth-century print, *The Invalid,* the number lurches up to 133. The consensus is: something's wrong with this child. And our friends are not keeping their own children away: the unspoken feeling is that, whatever this is, it isn't contagious. Later I will think, How did we know?

For supper, we have corn from the farm stand, cherrystones and grilled tuna for the grownups, and hamburgers for the children. She eats nothing. Asleep in our bed at the back of the house, she wakes every half hour and throws up. She asks for water, but it comes right back up. In the morning, she begins vomiting long streaks of bright-green bile. When I change her soiled pajamas, which should be soaked because her skin is hot but are not, the rash has melted together into an angry range of welts across her trunk and back.

It is raining again. In the parking lot down the hill, I am on the cell phone to New York. For the first time, I lose my temper when talking to a doctor's office. Told "The doctor will call you back," I begin to scream into the phone that, no, he will not call me back, you will get him, now. I know this is a bad idea. After a long time, the receptionist comes back to the phone. All the doctors are with patients. By now, I am crying. I tell her that we have been patients in this practice for a decade, that I've never made such a phone call before, that I know exactly what is going on in the office — there are two kids with ear infections and five kids waiting for school checkups — and she is to get someone right now. Dr. Lazarus comes to the phone.

*

We return to Provincetown. It sounds to New York that she's lost so much fluid she may need to be hydrated. How will Provincetown know? They'll look at her, they'll know. When we get there, they call an ambulance.

Inside the ambulance, it's our old friends from the Rescue Squad. Should we have taken her to the hospital on Tuesday? They check her vital signs. This includes pressing her finger until the flesh under the nail turns white, and counting how long it takes for it to flush pink again. It takes too long. She's not getting enough oxygen. Or maybe just enough. Just enough isn't okay. I'm given a choice: either she can hold — or I can hold — a green bear that will breathe pure oxygen into her face or an oxygen mask will be put on over her face. I choose the green bear.

I'm crouched next to the car seat, on the floor of the ambulance. The green bear starts to work. The technician has a last name — Silva — that's common in Provincetown. Is she a local girl? "You bet I am," she says. "When I was in high school, I couldn't date — everyone was my cousin." She has two kids. Last weekend, the two town ambulances made fourteen trips, a record. Looking down at my own child on the stretcher, I notice two things: the whites of her eyes are bright red, and the fingers on both hands look scorched, as if somewhere along the way she's burned herself.

In the emergency room, the technicians slide her onto a bed. Goodbye, goodbye. I am alone. Her father has followed the ambulance in the station wagon. When he explained in Provincetown that he wanted to do this, it became immediately clear that he meant that literally: behind the ambulance, at ambulance speed. He was dissuaded. So he has driven, at a moderately reasonable pace, on the highway, but he's not here yet. A covey of nurses has gathered around her, and they insert an IV into her left hand. She is screaming. Then the ER doctor comes in. He is a man my own age called Nate Rudman — a familiar name. Do I know him? I knew a Seth Rudman in high school, I know a poet called Mark Rudman. Nate comes up blank. No. She is calming down on the bed. By now I am quite sure I know what is wrong: the little boy next door in New York had been exposed to Coxsackie disease, a minor, irritating childhood malady. Before we left, it was going around the neighborhood. I am very busy being sure. I am relieved: the proof is her inflamed hands. I inform the doctor, Nate Rudman, that she has Coxsackie disease, but he pays no attention to me.

He is gone from the room. The nurses flutter like pigeons. He returns. I tell him again about the boy next door with Coxsackie. No, he says. She does not have Coxsackie. His exact words are: She doesn't have Coxsackie disease. She has Kawasaki disease. It will take two weeks before I can say this properly. Excuse me? This disease, he says, is the primary cause of acquired, potentially fatal, coronary aneurysms in young children.

The blue room turns green. I am standing by the side of the bed. The bed has a bar. I hold on to it. A chair materializes. I sit down on it. Once, when I was a girl, I dove down from a high bank covered with damp moss into a deep lake and my mind went blank in the black cold water. I surface now into the brightly lit room. Before she was born, before we decided to have a child together — she is the first child of our marriage, and the only one — I thought of this. I thought, We are too happy, we are asking the evil eye to come among us. Kenaharah, my grandmother would say if we were too much praised. Don't shine too much light or the Devil will see. The Devil is like a moth — he is attracted to light. When the children are admired, I instinctively deflect it. Pretty is as pretty does, I say. Stop reading twigs in the forest, you idiot Russian, my oldest friend laughs at me. But now it has come to pass.

The doctor, my new friend, my enemy, the bringer of bad news, says, You need to go to Boston, immediately. He has called Children's Hospital in Boston; we can wait if we like for a confirmation of the diagnosis, but he is sure. Can you stick out your tongue for me, baby, he says to her, tiny in the bed. Her tongue is the bright red color of blood. See, he says to me. See?

I lie down next to her. A nurse puts the bar up behind me, so I don't fall out. Now we are both patients. The doctor is speaking to me, and I listen carefully, because I know this is a test. It is the first of a score of explanations we will be given over the next days and weeks, but I don't know that yet. As I listen, I think, This is what growing old is. We think we will learn Sanskrit, learn Greek. Instead, what we learn is more than we ever wanted to know about things we wish we'd never heard of. I think only, You cannot fall apart.

"Kawasaki disease," Dr. Rudman, a total stranger, says, "was discovered by a Japanese doctor. No one knows what causes it; it may be an autoimmune disease that reacts to staphylococcus bacteria. If it is not treated early, within the first ten days, 20 percent of patients, primarily children between the ages of six months and five years old, will suffer heart damage. The aneurysm can be fatal. It can be easy to miss, because the symptoms often do not present themselves at once: the red eyes, the swollen hands, the fever, the rash. The symptoms can come and go."

I lie on the bed holding her hand and think, How dare he talk to me like this? Later, I will realize that he had no choice, that he had to tell me right away so that I would not argue with him, so that I would pay attention, but now I am angry. He tells me what we are going to do: Children's Hospital in Boston is the best place in the world to go; that is where we are going. Arrangements have been made. The treatment is a massive dose of intravenous immunoglobulin. She has had a fever for five days. It is the earliest that Kawasaki disease can be diagnosed. Already, the rash on her hands is fading: once it had disappeared, diagnosis would have been more difficult. In a moment, we have gone from being ravaged to being lucky. I realize it is Nate Rudman who has caught it early.

Her father arrives. When she sees him, she throws up. I wipe her face. It's the first time he has seen her on an IV. I am an old hand now, having been here for half an hour. There are four nurses in the room. I ask them if it would be possible for them to leave us alone for a minute. I ask him to sit down, and then I tell him.

We sit in the room together for a little while, and then he goes out to make phone calls. Our other children are scattered about; we must have someone collect them. Their grandparents live nearby. They go to our house on the hill and wait for our children to be dropped off by friends. Where are their surfboards, where are their wetsuits?

While he makes calls, I lie on the bed. She is hot but not sweating. I tell her we are going to Boston in another ambulance. Wait until you tell your brother Jack you rode in an ambulance! I say. I tell her the doctors are going to help her get better. They're hurting me, she says. When the nurse looms over us to fix the IV, I tell her about our house, how I am a terrible housekeeper, how I am careless when I cook. I am maniacal. I tell her that I never clean properly, that I feed the children chocolate mousse made with raw eggs. She says it is not my fault, ten thousand children could be exposed to some weird thing, and only one will react with Kawasaki. Anyway, no one knows what causes it.

Of course it is my fault.

It will take an hour and fifteen minutes to get to Boston by ambulance. Behind us, cars clot the side of the road. This time the technician is young, overweight, and sweating in his uniform. He is twenty-four years old. I am told to strap myself in on the bench next to the stretcher. Instead, I crouch on the floor, beside her head. She does not let go of my hand. I remind her how when we drove up to the Cape a few weeks ago our car started to rattle, and we took it to a garage. Remember how it went up in the air, and the little man came to fix it? It was the gasket, she says, nodding solemnly. Her huge blue eyes stand out like anemones against the reddened whites. And then he fixed it and we went to Corn Hill? That's what this is like, I tell her. In the next days, we will talk about the car, and the little man, again and again. And it cost thirty-five dollars! she says with a whisper of glee.

Her hand is hot, her fingers like burning twigs. I hold on to it. I think, If this child dies, I will go mad. I think of a woman who wishes me ill, and I think, If something happens to this child, I will kill her. The technician asks me if I am all right, because I am crying. "If you act upset, you know, it can upset her," he says.

I give him a look of pure malevolence. He is right. He says, "I know how you feel."

Do you have children? I ask him.

"No, not yet."

I tell him he is wrong.

He has a girlfriend. She works in Sandwich. He was in a car accident last year and she came every Sunday to see him. The problem is she's always tired.

Drop her, I think. She's twenty-three and she's tired?

It's dark in Boston. In the busy emergency room, the walls are yellow. The nurse is called Mike. The television set is on in the little room. She takes three bites of a turkey sandwich, and immediately vomits. Sheets are brought. I change them myself. Once, then twice. So what's going on here? Mike asks. For the fourth time in as many hours, I recite our recent history: the fever, the rash. He nods. He pulls up her hospital gown to look at the rash, which completely covers her trunk. The rash has colonized the scrapes on her knee and on her elbow. (She fell, I think, defensively. She's three, it happens!)

We are waiting for "the Kawasaki team," doctors who are pediatric rheumatologists. No decisions can be made until the Kawasaki team arrives. We are lucky to be here, lucky, lucky, where there is a Kawasaki team. I call Dr. Lazarus in New York. They'll know, he says, they'll know. Her father comes in. He is too big to lie on the bed, so he pulls up a chair next to it. I go out to call the children. I ask each one what they would like to be doing if we were home. Rose wants to go back to Corn Hill to see her Italian friend, Giulia, who is leaving on Sunday. Jack wants to go to the flea market, Anna wants to go to the movies, to see *Blue Crush*. The phone is passed around, these things will be accomplished. Anna, the eldest, gets back on the phone. She's talked to my sister, who is a pediatrician, who has told her the truth. She'll be okay, won't she? Of course she'll be okay, I say.

At eleven-thirty, four hours after we arrived in the emergency room in Boston, the Kawasaki team arrives. They are friendly and handsome, a matched pair. There is no doubt, they say after examining her, that she has Kawasaki disease, but every indication is that she will be fine. I gather myself up from the bed. You can't tell me that with absolute certainty, can you? I ask. No, they say.

Her father and I are in new territory. I need to go to the very end, to the worst possible outcome, and see where I am. He thinks this is a waste of time.

We are moved upstairs, to a room on the eighth floor. It's an all-purpose floor. Some children breathe on their own, some don't. In the room, we try to sleep but she keeps waking up. She is covered with wires. It hurts when they pull. She was a colicky baby and for three months stopped crying only when I held her. I held her. When can we go home? she asks. I am ashamed of myself even as I think it that I am angry we are missing our time at the beach. It is Friday. We can leave once she has had no fever for twenty-four hours. Before she leaves, she'll have an echocardiogram, to establish the extent of the damage. The nurse comes in every hour. Right now her temperature is 103.5.

Kawasaki disease is about time and space: it's about measurement. If the coronary arteries expand too far — the difference is in millimeters — the damage is irreversible. There are only 3,500 cases a year in the United States, but it is suspected that more are undiagnosed. It's apparently not contagious. Occasionally there are geographic clusters, three or four children from the same area, but there's no real evidence. The dose of immunoglobulin retards the expansion of the arteries, and it matters how quickly the child receives the dose. The product has to be mixed. The components are frozen, and they have to be defrosted. Her dose is ordered by the Kawasaki team at midnight, but it doesn't appear on the eighth floor until 5 A.M., because for two hours the order sat on someone's desk.

We are so exhausted that, even as wretched as we are, we could probably manage to sleep, but at 3 A.M. the room is rocked with noise. It's a double room, and three feet away, beyond the curtain, someone heavy is hurling himself (herself?) against the walls of a crib. Bang, bang, bang. Then a high-pitched keening, with no words. Yelping. In the din, a woman's voice says, "Oh dear, you got up too early, didn't you, didn't you." She croons this. The banging and growling continue. Holding hands, we hide in the white bed. In this long night, we have plunged, hapless, into a fairy tale. A nurse comes in on the hour to check her vital signs. What is that noise? I ask the nurse. She shakes her head at me, censoriously. The roar continues. A nurse comes in, finally, with the immunoglobulin, which replaces the hydration IV pack. The countdown starts. Gray light creeps into the room. At 8 A.M. a head peeks around the curtain. It belongs to the night crooner: a pale, dumpy woman with short, dyed red hair. She is wearing a Red Sox sweatshirt and navy-blue sweatpants. She could be forty, or sixty.

"Did she keep you up?" she asks. There is no word for her tone but consoling. "She's deaf and blind, you know, so she can't hear herself. I'm sorry if she kept you up."

She vanishes into the bathroom.

We look at each other. We have known from the beginning that things could be worse. Here is worse. Sunny, composed, the woman emerges from the bathroom. She says, "I'm going to brush her hair. She loves to have her hair brushed." We listen, and from the other side of the curtain comes the sound of crooning, and what we can just make out as laughter.

A few minutes later, she rounds the curtain again. She is pushing a wheelchair. In the chair is a little girl with gleaming hair. She is wearing a pinafore, pink socks, and white sneakers. Her arms hit out at nothing, and her legs are oddly flaccid. Her ears are too big for her face, and the lobes are pointed. How terrible, I am thinking, to bear such a child.

Her mother looks at her. "She's four. She's adopted," she says to us matter-of-factly. "When she was ten weeks old. Her parents couldn't take it — you know, the problems. They're wealthy, in California." She pauses, stroking her hair. "Sometimes he sends me money. I send him pictures, but I have to mail them to his office. The mother — she can't stand to look at them." She looks at us fiercely. "Their own flesh and blood."

Then she's benign again. "We live in New Hampshire, but we're here a lot. Cyclical vomiting. But I think we're going home today." She unbuckles her from the wheelchair and takes her by two hands, like a toddler.

"Look who's walking," cries a nurse in the reception area. There's a muffled sound of applause. Our own child, in bed but awake, looks after her. "That girl is like me," she says. We look at her aghast. She points to the IV in her hand. "She has a mitten, too."

A moment later, the same nurse — the nurse who would not speak to me in the early dawn — comes in again. She is all of twenty-five, twenty-eight. Boston Irish. She shakes her head. "There are three more of them at home. She takes care of them with her sister." She pauses, checking the monitor. "I think she's very religious." Later, we will tell our friend Storm, a priest, about the little girl, and we will accuse Storm of sending her to us. For now, we are stunned.

The days blur. Her father goes back to the Cape to take care of the other children, to round up their socks and flip-flops and towels from the houses of friends where they've left them. He drives back to the hospital the next day. We make telephone calls. No one's ever heard of this. Everyone goes on the Net: the phone rings with facts. Her grandmother flies up from New York and takes up residence in a hotel across the street from the hospital. I become an old hand; I know where the Jell-O is kept down the hall. I do not leave the hospital. The immunoglobulin drips into her arm.

Her temperature drops, and for a few hours she responds. The fog lifts, and in those minutes we can see her, we get our child back. She wants blue Jell-O, she wants red. She wants ice cream. "I think my soup is actually warm," she says. "No, it's actually cold." But three hours after the IV drip stops, her fever almost immediately shoots back up again and she is gone. We have to do it again, says the Kawasaki team, which has become one person, a doctor from Nebraska in a violet sweater who has been in the hospital two days. In one or two percent of the cases we see, she says, this happens. What she actually said, first, was: I don't want to tell you this.

Because I am an idiot — even now! — a person (still!) who would send her children to school with a cough, I point out that it's early evening, the witching hour: everyone's fever goes up at night. She's cranky and tired. I have four children, I know this. No, the doctor, whose name is Dr. Woodward, says. Her pale face is rigid with sleeplessness. I am sitting on a hard wooden chair, a rocking chair, next to the monitor. By now I am so far, far away from anywhere I have ever been that I barely recognize my own voice asking a question. I know the thing to do is to turn and look directly at the doctor, and I do this. "What happens," I ask, "if the fever doesn't go down this time? What will we do?"

The answer is nothing. There will be nothing to do.

They had left the IV tube in her hand after the first dose of immunoglobulin in case they had to do it again. I didn't know that; now I do. Her father is on the way back to the Cape. I wait to call him until he's off the road, but he calls from the car. We decide he will stay with the other children. This time, Dr. Woodward takes the request for the immunoglobulin down to the lab herself. It is mixed quickly: the new dose starts three hours later.

By now, she has had Kawasaki disease for seven days, during which she's been feverish for all but three hours. At night, she and I sleep in the same bed. In the middle of the third night, she sits bolt upright in bed and screams, "Where's my mommy?" The immunoglobulin drips into her arm through the clear tube. Wires cover her chest. Despite the tube, she tries to get out of bed. "I'm looking for my mommy!" she screams. Her body is covered with wires. The fluids leach from the IV into her bandaged hand.

"Don't look at the monitor," the nurses say. "It doesn't mean anything." When it flashes, they run in to check. Four aspirins a day
keep her blood from clotting, and I grind them up and put them
in her blueberry yogurt. "Just a spoonful of sugar helps the medicine go down," sings Julie Andrews, on the video screen. Everyone
passing by looks in and says, "I love Mary Poppins."

She has two echocardiograms. Her heart is like a pulsing flower.
She lies on her side while I tell her the story of "The Nutcracker
Prince." She is coated like a jujube with blue jelly. We go further
and further into the forest. We learn the first findings. The function of her left ventricle is slightly depressed; there is a small
pericardial effusion, which means she has fluid around her heart;
her aortic root is at the upper limits of what's considered normal,
as is her left coronary artery. This is what they would expect to find
with acute Kawasaki disease. When I was a little girl, I played every
summer on the same beach where my children play now, with the
children of my parents' friends. When the phone next rings, it is
one of these friends. Now he is a pediatric cardiologist. Listen to
me, he says. He sets up appointments — here, there — for when
we return to New York. I call Dr. Lazarus in New York. Good, he
says. Good. These are the people to see.

The second treatment works. She eats a dish of rice and peas.
The nurse comes in every hour and checks her temperature. I become more superstitious than ever. I cross my fingers. Her fever
stays down.

We have not been outside the hospital for five days. The night
before we leave, another child, a little boy, is admitted with Kawasaki
disease. His mother is a nurse. "I called my friend on the way
here," she says, "and I said, 'Look it up.' My friend called me right
back, and started reading." The mother pauses. She is in tears. "I
thought, How can he have something I've never heard of? I had to
pull off the road."

I decide to make the homecoming festive, and take the ferry
across Cape Cod Bay to Provincetown. Her grandmother accompa-
nies us. The day is warm and windy, and the bay glistens. If her fever goes up even half of one degree, we are to return to the hospital immediately. Over the next days, I will put my hand on her
forehead so often she swats me away; back in New York, she'll see
four doctors in three weeks, and the one they all lead to, a large,

kind man, the wizard at the very center of the maze, who listens to her heart intently for a full five minutes while she sits absolutely still, as she has learned to do, will say to me, in early October, She's fine. Her left aortic root may be slightly enlarged, but she's fine. Two weeks later, she'll cough while she's eating breakfast and I'll start to shake and have to leave the room.

When the ferry pulls in, the wind stops. Her father brings the other children to meet us at the dock. She has slept on my lap during the ride, and the button on my jacket has made a red mark on her face. The children are horrified: all their anxiety is centered on that one splotch. What did they do to her face? they cry.

There is news right away. The waves are good, the waves are bad. They ate marshmallows. The biggest news is the mouse. They have found an infant mouse, in the grass at Lev and Joseph's house, and Daddy said they could keep it.

"No mice," I say.

I am instantly a pariah.

"You can't tell them they can't have this mouse," their father says.

"What?" I say. We have been down this route before. We have two turtles, two cats, a fish, and four children, and we are not going to have a mouse.

"Wait," he says.

When we arrive on the top of the hill, the door to the cottage is plastered with homemade welcome-home signs. The mouse is in a matchbox. Hairless, pink, it is only a little bigger than a fingernail. They found it the night we went to the hospital, and have kept it alive by loading a grass stalk with milk and waiting while he sucks it. They have taken it in turn to do this.

Biographical Notes

Notable Essays of 2003

Biographical Notes

JAMES AGEE was born in Knoxville, Tennessee, in 1909. After attending Phillips Exeter Academy and Harvard, he joined *Fortune* magazine and was sent with the photographer Walker Evans to Alabama to cover Southern sharecropping. Agee's lyrical and textured prose was too experimental for the magazine's editors, but he developed his material and methods further and in 1941 published the documentary classic *Let Us Now Praise Famous Men*. Agee also served as a film reviewer for *Time* and *The Nation* and is credited with such well-known screenplays as *The African Queen* (1952) and *Night of the Hunter* (1955). His only novel, *A Death in the Family* (1957), was published two years after the forty-six-year-old author died of a massive heart attack.

KATHRYN CHETKOVICH is the author of *Friendly Fire*, a collection of short stories. She lives in Boulder Creek, California, and New York City.

JARED DIAMOND is a professor of geography and of environmental health sciences at UCLA. He is the author of the best-selling and award-winning *The Third Chimpanzee* (1992), *Why Is Sex Fun?: The Evolution of Human Sexuality* (1997), and *Guns, Germs, and Steel: The Fates of Human Societies* (1997), which won a Pulitzer Prize. He is the recipient of a MacArthur Foundation fellowship and the 1999 National Medal of Science, awarded at the White House. He lives in Los Angeles with his wife and two sons.

ANNE FADIMAN is the author of *The Spirit Catches You and You Fall Down*, which won the National Book Critics Award for general nonfiction, and *Ex Libris*, a collection of essays on reading and language. A winner of National Magazine Awards for her reporting and her essays, she has contributed articles and essays to *Civilization, The New Yorker, Harper's Magazine,* and the *New York Times,* among other publications. Fadiman was the editor of *The Best American Essays 2003,* and for seven years the editor of *The American Scholar.* She was recently appointed the first Francis Writer in Residence at Yale.

JONATHAN FRANZEN's third novel, *The Corrections,* won the National Book Award for fiction in 2001. He is the author of two other novels, *Strong Motion* and *The Twenty-Seventh City,* and a collection of essays, *How to Be Alone.* He lives in New York City and has been a contributor to *The New Yorker* since 1994.

ADAM GOPNIK is a staff writer for *The New Yorker* and the author of *Paris to the Moon.* He has also written a long adventure story for children, *The King in the Window,* which will appear in 2005.

LAURA HILLENBRAND was born in 1967. She is the author of *Seabiscuit: An American Legend,* winner of the Book Sense Book of the Year Award and the William Hill Sports Book of the Year Award, and a finalist for the National Book Critics Circle Award and the Los Angeles Times Book Prize. Her subject essay, "A Sudden Illness," won the National Magazine Award. She lives in Washington, D.C.

TIM JUDAH was born in 1962. From 1991 to 1995 he lived in Belgrade and covered the Croatian and Bosnian wars for *The Economist* and the *Times* of London. He then returned home to London and wrote *The Serbs: History, Myth, and the Destruction of Yugoslavia.* After the war in Kosovo he wrote *Kosovo: War and Revenge.* After 9/11 he covered the fall of the Taliban for *The New York Review of Books* and *The Economist,* and in 2003 he went to Saddam's Baghdad to cover the Iraq War. He lives in London with his wife and five children.

WAYNE KOESTENBAUM, writer, professor of English at the City University of New York's Graduate Center, and winner of a Whiting Writers' Award, is the author of three books of poetry and several volumes of criticism, including *The Queen's Throat: Opera, Homosexuality, and the Mystery of Desire* (1993), a National Book Critics Circle nominee; and *Jackie Under My Skin: Interpreting an Icon* (1995). *Cleavage: Essays on Sex, Stars, and Aesthetics* (2000) includes six pieces originally published in *Artforum.* His brief biography of Andy Warhol for the Penguin Lives series appeared in 2001. A new novel, *Moira Orfei in Aigues-Mortes,* and a book-length poem, *Model Homes,* will be published in fall 2004.

LEONARD MICHAELS was born to Polish-Jewish immigrant parents in New York City in 1933. After receiving his B.A. in English from New

York University in 1953, he earned his M.A. and Ph.D. at the University of Michigan. For over thirty years he taught at the University of California, Berkeley. He was the recipient of a Guggenheim fellowship, awards from the American Academy and Institute of Arts and Letters and the National Endowment for the Arts, and a Pushcart Prize. His fiction includes *Going Places* (1969), *I Would Have Saved Them If I Could* (1975), *The Men's Club* (1981), for which he also wrote the screenplay, *Shuffle* (1990), *Sylvia* (1992), and *A Girl with a Monkey* (2000). He was also the author of several nonfiction books, including *To Feel These Things* (1993) and *Time Out of Mind: Diaries, 1961–1995* (1999). Michaels died in May 2003. "He was one of the most important prose writers of twentieth-century America — a writer whose sentences were composed with the care of poetry, and whose voice came through clearly in both fiction and nonfiction," said Wendy Lesser, editor of *The Threepenny Review,* where Michaels served as an adviser and contributor for more than twenty years.

BEN MILLER was born in Davenport, Iowa. His prose and poetry have appeared in *The North American Review, New Letters, Seneca Review, Chicago Review, One Story, Quick Fiction, Raritan, Fourth Genre, American Letters & Commentary,* and many other literary journals. His nonfiction is regularly featured in *The Common Review,* a publication of the Great Books Foundation. The recipient of a creative writing fellowship from the National Endowment for the Arts, he lives in New York City with his wife.

RICK MOODY has published three novels, *Garden State, The Ice Storm,* and *Purple America;* two short story collections, *The Ring of the Brightest Angels Around Heaven* and *Demonology;* and a book of nonfiction, *The Black Veil.* His awards include the Pushcart Prize Editor's Choice Award, the Addison Metcalf Award from the American Academy of Arts and Letters, and a Guggenheim fellowship.

KYOKO MORI is the author of two nonfiction books — *The Dream of Water: A Memoir* and *Polite Lies: On Being a Woman Caught Between Cultures* — as well as three novels, the most recent of which is *Stone Field, True Arrow.* Born in Kobe, Japan, Mori has lived in the American Midwest for most of her adult life. She currently teaches creative writing at Harvard University.

SUSAN ORLEAN has been a staff writer for *The New Yorker* since 1992. In addition, she has contributed to *Vogue, Outside, Rolling Stone,* and *The New York Times Magazine.* Her books include *The Orchid Thief, The Bullfighter Checks Her Makeup, Saturday Night,* and *Homewrecker.* In 2004 she was a fellow at the Nieman Foundation for Journalism at Harvard University. She is currently at work on a biography of Rin Tin Tin.

ALEX ROSS has been the music critic of *The New Yorker* since 1996. His writing has also appeared in *The New Republic, The London Review of Books, Lingua Franca,* and *Transition.* From 1992 to 1996 he was a critic at the *New York Times.* He has received an ASCAP–Deems Taylor Award for outstanding writing in the field of music and a Holtzbrinck fellowship at the American Academy in Berlin. He is finishing his first book, *The Rest Is Noise: Listening to the Twentieth Century,* a cultural history of music since 1900.

OLIVER SACKS, M.D., was born in London in 1933 and educated in London, Oxford, and California. A clinical professor of neurology at the Albert Einstein College of Medicine, he has received numerous honors for his writings, which include *Awakenings, The Man Who Mistook His Wife for a Hat,* and *An Anthropologist on Mars.* His most recent books are *Uncle Tungsten: Memories of a Chemical Boyhood* (2001) and *Oaxaca Journal* (2002). Dr. Sacks practices neurology in New York City, and he is a fellow of both the American Academy of Arts and Letters and the American Academy of Arts and Sciences.

LUC SANTE's books include *Low Life* and *The Factory of Facts.* He has received a Whiting, a Guggenheim, an Award in Literature from the American Academy of Arts and Letters, and a Grammy, for album notes. He is general editor of the Library of Larceny series, and he teaches writing and the history of photography at Bard College.

MARK SLOUKA is the author of the novel *God's Fool* (2002), a collection of stories, *Lost Lake* (1998), and *War of the Worlds* (1995), a cultural critique of the digital revolution. His essays and fiction have appeared in *Harper's Magazine, Story, Epoch, Agni, The Georgia Review,* and *The Best American Essays 1999* and *2000,* and his fiction has won a National Magazine Award. A contributing editor for *Harper's,* he divides his time between Prague, a cabin with an outhouse, and a cave in New York City, where he teaches at Columbia University.

JANNA MALAMUD SMITH is a writer and a clinical social worker who practices and teaches psychotherapy. She first wrote "My Father Is a Book" as a talk for a 2001 conference, Jewish Identities and American Writing, organized by Hermione Lee and Ron Bush under the auspices of the Rothermere American Institute at Oxford University. She is the author of two books, *Private Matters* (2003) and *A Potent Spell* (2004), each of which was chosen as a New York Times Notable Book. She has published in many magazines and newspapers, including the *New York*

Times and *The Threepenny Review.* She is currently at work on a full-length memoir about her father.

GERALD STERN is the author of fourteen books of poetry, a play, and a collection of personal essays entitled *What I Can't Bear Losing* (2003). He won a National Book Award in 1998 for *This Time: New and Selected Poems* and taught for fourteen years at the Iowa Writers' Workshop, before his retirement in 1996. He lives on the Delaware River in Lambertville, New Jersey.

TENNESSEE WILLIAMS was one of the nation's leading dramatists. Born in Mississippi in 1911, the son of a traveling salesman, Williams discovered early on that writing could offer "an escape from a world of reality in which I felt acutely uncomfortable." In 1938, after graduating from the University of Iowa with a major in playwriting, he traveled widely, and while taking numerous odd jobs and searching for a new identity, he changed his name from Thomas Lanier Williams to Tennessee Williams, hoping to infuse himself with the pioneer spirit of his ancestors. His first play, *Battle of Angels,* was a failure, but he achieved astonishing success with *The Glass Menagerie* (1944), which won the New York Drama Critics' Circle Award, an award he also received, along with a Pulitzer Prize, for *A Streetcar Named Desire* (1947). Williams won both awards again for *Cat on a Hot Tin Roof* (1955). He wrote many more successful plays and film scripts, and published his *Memoirs* in 1975, but he was unable to duplicate the success of his major trio of plays. He died in 1983.

CYNTHIA ZARIN is a staff writer for *The New Yorker* and an artist in residence at the Cathedral of St. John the Divine in New York City. She also writes a monthly column for *Gourmet* magazine. She is the author of three books of poems — *The Swordfish Tooth, Fire Lyric,* and *The Watercourse,* which won the Los Angeles Times Book Award for poetry in 2002 — as well as several books for children.

Notable Essays of 2003

SELECTED BY ROBERT ATWAN

GERALD WILLIAMS
French . . . So to Speak. *Callaloo,*
Winter.

ELEANOR WILNER
Comedy, Self and Otter. *American
Letters & Commentary,* no. 15.

JASON WILSON
House of Cards. *The Washington Post
Magazine,* February 9.

MARK YATES
When He Spoke. *Notre Dame
Magazine,* Autumn.

PAUL ZIMMER
Real Words. *New Letters,* vol. 69, nos.
2 and 3.

Notable Special Issues of 2003

American Letters & Commentary, "Senses
of Humor: Survival, Subversion,
Going for the Jocular," ed. Anna
Rabinowitz, no. 15.

Crab Orchard Review, "Taste the World:
Writers on Food," ed. Allison
Joseph, Spring/Summer.

The Kenyon Review, "Culture and Place,"
ed. David H. Lynn, Summer/Fall.

The Literary Review, "Expat Writing,"
guest ed. David Applefield, Fall.

Michigan Quarterly Review, "Mainly on
the 1950s," ed. Laurence Goldstein,
Spring.

River Styx, "The Route 66 Issue," ed.
Richard Newman, no. 66.

Sport Literate, "Father's Issue," ed.
William Meiners, vol. 4, no. 3.

Witness, "Ethnic America," ed. Peter
Stine, vol. 17, no. 2.

THE BEST AMERICAN SHORT STORIES® 2004

Lorrie Moore, guest editor, Katrina Kenison, series editor. "Story for story, readers can't beat *The Best American Short Stories* series" (*Chicago Tribune*). This year's most beloved short fiction anthology is edited by the critically acclaimed author Lorrie Moore and includes stories by Annie Proulx, Sherman Alexie, Paula Fox, Thomas McGuane, and Alice Munro, among others.

0-618-19735-4 PA $14.00 / 0-618-19734-6 CL $27.50
0-618-30046-5 CASS $26.00 / 0-618-29965-3 CD $30.00

THE BEST AMERICAN ESSAYS® 2004

Louis Menand, guest editor, Robert Atwan, series editor. Since 1986, *The Best American Essays* series has gathered the best nonfiction writing of the year and established itself as the best anthology of its kind. Edited by Louis Menand, author of *The Metaphysical Club* and staff writer for *The New Yorker,* this year's volume features writing by Kathryn Chetkovich, Jonathan Franzen, Kyoko Mori, Cynthia Zarin, and others.

0-618-35709-2 PA $14.00 / 0-618-35706-8 CL $27.50

THE BEST AMERICAN MYSTERY STORIES™ 2004

Nelson DeMille, guest editor, Otto Penzler, series editor. This perennially popular anthology is a favorite of mystery buffs and general readers alike. This year's volume is edited by the best-selling suspense author Nelson DeMille and offers pieces by Stephen King, Joyce Carol Oates, Jonathon King, Jeff Abbott, Scott Wolven, and others.

0-618-32967-6 PA $14.00 / 0-618-32968-4 CL $27.50 / 0-618-49742-0 CD $30.00

THE BEST AMERICAN SPORTS WRITING™ 2004

Richard Ben Cramer, guest editor, Glenn Stout, series editor. This series has garnered wide acclaim for its stellar sports writing and topnotch editors. Now Richard Ben Cramer, the Pulitzer Prize–winning journalist and author of the best-selling *Joe DiMaggio,* continues that tradition with pieces by Ira Berkow, Susan Orlean, William Nack, Charles P. Pierce, Rick Telander, and others.

0-618-25139-1 PA $14.00 / 0-618-25134-0 CL $27.50

THE BEST AMERICAN TRAVEL WRITING 2004

Pico Iyer, guest editor, Jason Wilson, series editor. *The Best American Travel Writing 2004* is edited by Pico Iyer, the author of *Video Night in Kathmandu* and *Sun After*

Dark. Giving new life to armchair travel this year are Roger Angell, Joan Didion, John McPhee, Adam Gopnik, and many others.

0-618-34126-9 PA $14.00 / 0-618-34125-0 CL $27.50

THE BEST AMERICAN SCIENCE AND NATURE WRITING 2004

Steven Pinker, guest editor, Tim Folger, series editor. This year's edition promises to be another "eclectic, provocative collection" (*Entertainment Weekly*). Edited by Steven Pinker, author of *The Blank Slate* and *The Language Instinct*, it features work by Gregg Easterbrook, Atul Gawande, Peggy Orenstein, Jonathan Rauch, Chet Raymo, Nicholas Wade, and others.

0-618-24698-3 PA $14.00 / 0-618-24697-5 CL $27.50

THE BEST AMERICAN RECIPES 2004–2005

Edited by Fran McCullough and Molly Stevens. "Give this book to any cook who is looking for the newest, latest recipes and the stories behind them" (*Chicago Tribune*). Offering the very best of what America is cooking, as well as the latest trends, timesaving tips, and techniques, this year's edition includes a foreword by the renowned chef Bobby Flay.

0-618-45506-X CL $26.00

THE BEST AMERICAN NONREQUIRED READING 2004

Edited by Dave Eggers, Introduction by Viggo Mortensen. Edited by the best-selling author Dave Eggers, this genre-busting volume draws the finest, most interesting, and least expected fiction, nonfiction, humor, alternative comics, and more from publications large, small, and on-line. This year's collection features writing by David Sedaris, Daniel Alarcón, David Mamet, Thom Jones, and others.

0-618-34123-4 PA $14.00 / 0-618-34122-6 CL $27.50 / 0-618-49743-9 CD $26.00

THE BEST AMERICAN SPIRITUAL WRITING 2004

Edited by Philip Zaleski, Introduction by Jack Miles. The latest addition to the acclaimed Best American series, *The Best American Spiritual Writing 2004* brings the year's finest writing about faith and spirituality to all readers. With an introduction by the best-selling author Jack Miles, this year's volume represents a wide range of perspectives and features pieces by Robert Coles, Bill McKibben, Oliver Sacks, Pico Iyer, and many others.

0-618-44303-7 PA $14.00 / 0-618-44302-9 CL $27.50

HOUGHTON MIFFLIN COMPANY www.houghtonmifflinbooks.com